# Tax Reform and the
# Cost of Capital

# Tax Reform and the Cost of Capital

## An International Comparison

**DALE W. JORGENSON**
**RALPH LANDAU**
*editors*

**THE BROOKINGS INSTITUTION**
**WASHINGTON, D.C.**

## About Brookings

The Brookings Institution is a private nonprofit organization devoted to research, education and publication on important issues of domestic and foreign policy. Its principal purpose is to bring knowledge to bear on current and emerging policy problems.

The Institution was founded on December 8, 1927, to merge the activities of the Institute for Government Research, founded in 1916, the Institute of Economics, founded in 1922, and the Robert Brookings Graduate School of Economics, founded in 1924.

The Institution maintains a position of neutrality on issues of public policy. Interpretations or conclusions in Brookings publications should be understood to be solely those of the authors.

Copyright © 1993
THE BROOKINGS INSTITUTION
1775 Massachusetts Avenue, N.W., Washington, D.C. 20036

*Library of Congress Cataloging-in-Publication data:*

Tax reform and the cost of capital : an international comparison /
   Dale W. Jorgenson, Ralph Landau [editors].
      p.  cm.
   Includes bibliographical references and index.
   ISBN 0–8157–4716–0—ISBN 0–8157–4715–2(pbk.)
   1. Capital levy.  2. Income tax.  3. Capital gains tax.
I. Jorgenson, Dale Weldeau, 1993– . II. Landau, Ralph.
HJ4132.T39  1993
336.2'05—dc20                 93-18812
                                  CIP

9 8 7 6 5 4 3 2 1

The paper used in this publication meets the minimum requirements of the American National Standard for Information Sciences—Permanence of paper for Printed Library Materials, ANSI Z39.48-1984

# Contents

## 5.  Germany                                                    166
### *Willi Leibfritz*

## 6.  Italy                                                      191
### *Julian S. Alworth and Laura Castellucci*

## 7.  Japan                                                      244
### *Toshiaki Tachibanaki and Tatsuya Kikutani*

## 8.  Sweden                                                     270
### *Jan Södersten*

## 9.  United Kingdom                                             300
### *Mervyn A. King and Mark H. Robson*

Tables

## Figures

## Appendix Tables

# Preface

THIS BOOK originated with the International Conference on the Cost of Capital, held at the Kennedy School of Government, Harvard University, on November 19–21, 1987. The conference was sponsored by the Program on Technology and Economic Policy at the Kennedy School, directed by the editors of this volume. The purpose of the conference was to review research on the taxation of income from capital, with a focus on the tax systems of industrialized countries. The conference attracted tax economists, business leaders, and tax policymakers from sixteen countries and several international organizations.

The most notable development in tax policy at the time of the conference was the adoption of the Tax Reform Act of 1986 in the United States. The act had been signed into law by President Ronald Reagan on October 22, 1986, and its main provisions had gone into effect on January 1, 1987. This landmark legislation abruptly reversed the course of U.S. tax policy. Repeated liberalizations of capital income taxes beginning in 1954 had substantially enhanced incentives for investment through the corporate income tax and saving through the personal income tax. In the process, however, the United States had moved steadily away from the economic concept of income as a basis for taxation.

The ultimate liberalization of capital income taxation was embodied in the Economic Recovery Tax Act of 1981. This legislation effectively divorced tax liabilities from economic measurements of income by greatly broadening saving and investment incentives. But the capricious distribution of these incentives led to widespread violations of the fundamental principle of horizontal equity, which holds that taxpayers in the same circumstances should have the same tax liabilities. In view of wide disparities among different taxpayers, the only way to achieve horizontal equity in practice is to apply this principle to all transactions within a given tax jurisdiction.

The appeal of the principle of horizontal equity is threefold. First, it achieves fairness in the sense of equitable treatment of citizens before the law — in this case the tax law. Second, under the rubric of "tax neutrality"

it expunges possibilities for increasing economic efficiency by redistribut-
ing the tax burden. Finally, it leads to simplicity by eliminating detailed
specifications of transactions subject to special tax provisions. Such provisions create knotty problems for tax administrators and, or course, important business opportunities for tax advisers and lobbyists and their clients.

Publicity surrounding particularly egregious examples of horizontal inequities under the 1981 tax act led President Reagan to call for a renewal
of tax reform in his State of the Union address of January 1984. The fact
that 1984 was a presidential election year may have entered into the considerations leading to this dramatic announcement. The U.S. Department
of the Treasury responded by presenting a comprehensive proposal for tax
reform in November 1984, immediately after the election. The so-called
Treasury Proposal was set out in a three-volume treatise, presenting the
Treasury's view and comparing it with alternatives.

As mentioned, piecemeal tax reforms over more than a quarter century,
eventuating in the 1981 tax act, had led to substantial departures from tax
policies based on income. By the end of the 1970s a powerful movement
had developed among public finance economists, tax accountants, and tax
lawyers to complete this series of reforms by adopting consumption, rather
than income, as the tax base. This movement, which had an important
international dimension, led to proposals for reform along these lines
in Sweden and the United Kingdom as well as in the United States. The
Treasury rejected this approach and proposed that income be reestablished
as the basis for taxation by reducing or eliminating many well-established
saving and investment incentives.

By broadening the tax base to include a wider spectrum of different
types of capital income, the Treasury Proposal produced sharply lower
statutory tax rates. That the proposal radically deemphasized tax progressivity greatly strengthened its appeal. It successfully linked "base broadening" with "rate reduction," thereby reasserting the primacy of horizontal
equity in tax policy. It thus resolved a perennial dilemma in the formulation of tax policy: that the beneficiaries of special tax provisions have a
well-focused and intense interest in retaining these provisions, while the
interest of all taxpayers in fairness, efficiency, and simplicity is often too
diffuse to be mobilized politically.

Base broadening in the Tax Reform Act of 1986 was facilitated by an
important addition to the tax economist's tool kit, forged in the debate
that preceded the 1981 tax legislation. This new analytical tool had the
somewhat esoteric-sounding name of the *marginal effective tax rate* and
had been derived from the familiar idea of the *cost of capital* by two

Harvard economists, Alan Auerbach and Dale Jorgenson, in 1979. They described this concept in the September–October 1980 issue of the *Harvard Business Review*. Although the cost-of-capital approach had no effect on the 1981 legislation, it began to germinate among tax economists and policy analysts and ultimately provided the key to "leveling the playing field" by equalizing marginal effective tax rates among different assets in the 1986 tax act.

An exposition of the cost-of-capital approach to tax policy analysis was given by Jorgenson and Kun-Young Yun in their book, *Tax Reform and the Cost of Capital*, summarizing Jorgenson's Lindahl Lectures at Uppsala University in September 1987. This volume presented a comprehensive history of tax provisions for capital income in the United States during the postwar period and an extensive analysis of the proposals that led to the 1986 tax act, including the Treasury Proposal of 1984. The cost-of-capital approach makes the complex tax provisions for capital income far more transparent by summarizing them in terms of marginal effective tax rates. A large part of the appeal of this approach is its ability to absorb an almost unlimited amount of descriptive detail on alternative tax policies.

These momentous developments in tax policy and analysis provided the background for the International Conference. Contributors to the conference documented the rapid international diffusion of the cost-of-capital approach to tax policy analysis. Jorgenson and Yun presented marginal effective tax rates for the United States, and other contributors presented them for more than a dozen countries. The predominant methodology was based on the book by Mervyn King and Don Fullerton, *The Taxation of Income from Capital*, published in 1984. This pioneering contribution offered an international comparison of marginal effective tax rates among four countries—Sweden, the United Kingdom, the United States, and West Germany—for the year 1980. These marginal effective tax rates quantified striking departures from horizontal equity in all four countries.

By 1987 the King-Fullerton approach had been implemented for most industrialized countries, and an effort was under way at the World Bank to extend the approach to developing countries. Tax experts at the International Conference discovered that reform efforts aimed at "leveling the playing field" along the lines of the U.S. Tax Reform Act of 1986 had already started in many of these countries. In the following years these tax reforms have been implemented around the world. The Program on Technology and Economic Policy at Harvard decided to assemble a volume describing these historic developments, rather than summarizing the proceedings of the conference.

The initial design of the volume called for international comparisons along King-Fullerton lines for nine countries, including the four countries of the original study (with West Germany now a reunified Germany). Fortunately, all the authors of the country chapters of the King-Fullerton volume agreed to participate. The study added Australia, Canada, France, Italy, and Japan, completing coverage of the so-called G-7 countries, along with Australia and Sweden. The plan was to include results for 1990 as well as 1980, the year covered by King and Fullerton, and 1985, the focus of the International Conference. The decade 1980–90 witnessed major tax reforms in most of the countries included in the study.

The basic conceptual framework was to be the same as that used by King and Fullerton. The implementation of this framework was greatly facilitated by the distribution of King's computer program TURBO PTAX to all contributors. We are greatly indebted to King for making his program available. We augmented this conceptual framework by taking advantage of Fullerton's insightful separation of marginal effective tax rates for corporate income between components due to corporate and personal income taxes and his extensions to noncorporate business and owner-occupied housing. These extensions were developed at the U.S. Treasury while Fullerton was Deputy Assistant Secretary for Tax Policy and are indispensable in analyzing the full consequences of tax policy changes.

International comparisons are presented for all nine countries for the three years—1980, 1985, and 1990—in the introductory chapter to this volume, except for Sweden, where a major reform went into effect in 1991. More detailed information for individual countries is given in chapters 2 through 10. These chapters have been written by leading experts on tax policy for each country. Marginal effective tax rates for the international comparisons were prepared by the authors of the country chapters, and we are greatly indebted to them for their assistance. Documentation for the international comparisons is presented in a series of appendix tables, following the King-Fullerton format. These data were also generously provided by authors of the country chapters. Special thanks are due to Michael Daly for his detailed comments on the original draft of the introductory chapter.

During the lengthy gestation period for this volume, the Program for Technology and Economic Policy at Harvard has held a series of workshops on economic policy in collaboration with the Center for Economic Policy Research at Stanford University. Many of these workshops have focused on tax reform and the cost of capital. The most recent took place in Washington, D.C., on July 28, 1992, in the midst of the presidential campaign. Ralph Landau has summarized the results of the workshops in his paper "From Analysis to Action," prepared for the Conference on Capital Allocation and Investment Performance. This conference was sponsored by the Board on Science, Technology, and Economic Policy of the National Research Council and held in Washington, D.C., on September 10–11, 1992. The paper will appear in the conference proceedings to be published by the National Academy Press.

In January 1993 the administration of U.S. President Bill Clinton announced a series of tax proposals that reflected a significant erosion in support for the Tax Reform Act of 1986. These proposals subordinated the principle of horizontal equity to the objective of providing "short-term stimulus" through tax incentives financed by increases in marginal tax rates. Congress, however, rejected the stimulus proposals. The Omnibus Budget Reconciliation Act of 1993, signed into law by President Clinton on August 10, 1993, incorporated only modest departures from horizontal equity, but raised the statutory corporate tax rate from 34 to 35 percent and increased marginal personal income tax rates for high-income taxpayers substantially. The goal of tax reformers whose efforts are documented in this volume is to make the allocation of capital within a market economy more efficient. This goal is obviously under serious attack, and the debate that is now unfolding will be closely monitored by tax economists and policy analysts around the world.

We would like to thank June Wynn of Harvard for her excellent assistance in organizing the International Conference and assembling the manuscripts for this volume. She produced the tables for the introductory chapter and the appendix. Warren Hrung, a senior at Harvard College, assembled the data for these tables and carefully checked successive versions for consistency with the original King-Fullerton format. The staff of the Publications Department of Brookings, especially Nancy Davidson, Robert Faherty, and Caroline Lalire, has been helpful at every stage of the project. We are also grateful to Vincent Ercolano for editing the manuscript, and William Richardson and his associates for providing the index. As always, the editors retain responsibility for any remaining deficiencies in the volume.

D.W.J.

R.L.

# Contributors

Julian S. Alworth
*Mediolanum Consulenza*

François Bourguignon
*Département et Laboratoire
d' Economie Théorique
et Appliquée*

Laura Castellucci
*Università di Roma*

Michael J. Daly
*Organization for Economic
Cooperation and Development*

Don Fullerton
*Carnegie-Mellon University*

Robert Jones
*Industry Commission, Australia*

Dale W. Jorgenson
*Harvard University*

Marios Karayannis
*Price Waterhouse*

Tatsuya Kikutani
*Kyoto Sangyo University*

Mervyn A. King
*Bank of England*

Ralph Landau
*Stanford University*

Willi Leibfritz
*Institut für Wirtschafts-
forschung*

Pierre Mercier
*Statistics Canada*

Mark H. Robson
*Organization for Economic
Cooperation and Development*

Thomas Schweitzer
*Statistics Canada*

Jan Södersten
*Uppsala University*

Toshiaki Tachibanaki
*Kyoto University*

# Tax Reform and the Cost of Capital

# CHAPTER ONE

# Introduction and Summary

*Dale W. Jorgenson*

SINCE THE EARLY 1980s, the taxation of income from capital in industrialized countries has undergone a surprising series of reversals. The 1980s
began with a gradual shift from income to expenditure as the basis for
taxation of capital income. At the corporate level the objective was to
provide investment incentives, while at the personal level the goal was to
stimulate saving. Earlier, three landmark reports in Sweden, the United
Kingdom, and the United States had proposed taking these developments
to their logical conclusion by substituting expenditure for income as a
basis for taxation at both corporate and personal levels.[1]

The initial step in providing tax incentives for investment was to accelerate capital consumption allowances by permitting taxpayers to write off
investment outlays against income more quickly. The ultimate manifestation of this approach was to treat investment expenditures symmetrically
with outlays on current account by allowing immediate expensing of investment. An alternative approach was to offset tax liabilities by subsidies
or grants for investment. In the United States this took the form of an
investment tax credit, that is, a credit against tax liabilities in proportion
to investment expenditures.

In order to stimulate saving through tax policy, taxpayers were permitted to establish tax-favored or tax-free accounts. These were usually for
specific purposes, such as the accumulation of funds to finance a period
of retirement. By allowing contributions to these accounts as deductions
from income for tax purposes and postponing taxation until funds are
withdrawn, the base for the personal income tax was shifted from income

---

1. See Lodin (1978), Meade and others (1978), and U.S. Department of the Treasury (1977).
Hall and Rabushka (1983) and Bradford (1986) have presented proposals for implementation of an
expenditure-based tax system in the United States. The income-based approach incorporated into the
Tax Reform Act of 1986 was proposed by the U.S. Department of the Treasury (1984).

1

toward expenditure. In the United States these accounts took the form of pension funds for corporate and noncorporate businesses and individual retirement accounts (IRAs).

The reversal in tax policies for capital income during the 1980s is best illustrated by the experience of the United States. When the administration of President Ronald Reagan took office in January 1981, there was widespread concern about the slowdown of U.S. economic growth. Tax reform proposals by the Reagan administration received overwhelming support from Congress with the enactment of the Economic Recovery Tax Act of 1981. The 1981 tax act combined substantial reductions in statutory tax rates for persons and corporations with sizable enhancements of investment incentives.[2]

Beginning with the introduction of accelerated depreciation in 1954 and the investment tax credit in 1962, U.S. tax policy had incorporated a series of progressively more elaborate tax preferences for specific forms on capital income. The tax act of 1981 brought this development to its highest point with adoption of the accelerated cost recovery system and the introduction of a 10 percent investment tax credit. With these provisions the 1981 tax act totally severed the connection between the economic concept of depreciation and capital cost recovery for tax purposes.

The tax reforms of the early 1980s substantially reduced the burden of taxation on capital income. However, these policy changes also heightened the discrepancies among tax burdens borne by different types of capital. These discrepancies gave rise to concerns in Congress about the impact of tax-induced distortions on the efficiency of capital allocation. In his State of the Union address in January 1984 President Reagan announced that he had requested a plan for further reform from the Department of the Treasury, setting off a lengthy debate that eventuated in the Tax Reform Act of 1986.[3]

The 1986 tax act represented an abrupt change in the direction of U.S. policy for taxation of income from capital. Statutory tax rates were low-

---

2. A detailed description of the Economic Recovery Tax Act of 1981 is given by the Joint Committee on Taxation (1981). Changes in tax policy have been discussed by Gravelle (1982) and Hulten and O'Neill (1982). The impact of the 1981 tax act on U.S. economic growth is analyzed by Jorgenson and Yun (1986b, especially pp. 365–70).

3. An illuminating account of the tax reform debate that preceded the 1986 tax act is provided by Birnbaum and Murray (1987). A detailed description of the legislation is given by the Joint Committee on Taxation (1986). The changes in tax policy have been analyzed by Steuerle (1991), in symposiums edited by Aaron (1987) and Slemrod (1991), and the symposium by Bosworth and others (1992). Henderson (1991) has surveyed studies of the economic impact of these tax policy changes.

ered as in 1981, but the tax base was broadened by wholesale elimination of tax preferences for both persons and corporations. This included sharp cutbacks in tax incentives for investment. The 1986 tax act repealed the 10 percent investment tax credit for property placed in service after December 31, 1985. In addition, accelerated capital consumption allowances were substantially scaled back.

During the 1980s the taxation of income from capital in the United Kingdom underwent a similar reversal. In 1981 immediate expensing of 75 percent of investment in industrial buildings and structures was introduced, bringing the tax treatment of these investments more closely into line with 100 percent expensing of manufacturing plant and machinery, previously incorporated into U.K. tax law. In 1983 the corporate tax rate was lowered from 52 to 50 percent. Mervyn A. King and Don Fullerton have described these developments as a continuation of a gradual movement toward a tax system based on expenditure rather than income.[4]

The U.K. budget of 1984 phased out 100 percent expensing of plant and machinery and 75 percent expensing of industrial buildings and structures in the United Kingdom over a three-year period. This significantly broadened the base for income taxes, especially at the corporate level. The corporate tax rate was reduced to 45 percent in 1984, 40 percent in 1985, and, finally, 35 percent in 1986. In 1988 the top personal tax rate was abruptly reduced from 60 to 40 percent. As in the United States, the U.K. reforms employed the revenues generated by base broadening to reduce corporate and personal tax rates.

The U.K. budget for 1984 and the U.S. Tax Reform Act of 1986 arrested the erosion of the income tax base in the two countries by curtailing investment incentives and broadening the base for income taxes. Capital consumption allowances were brought back into line with economic depreciation, thereby leveling the playing field for income from different assets. The additional revenues generated by base-broadening were used to reduce statutory tax rates at the corporate and personal levels. These rate reductions were intended to reduce distortions in resource allocation.[5]

The provisions for capital cost recovery in the U.K. budget of 1984 and the U.S. Tax Reform Act of 1986 reflected a new conceptual framework for the analysis of capital income taxation. This framework had its origins in two concepts introduced in the 1960s—the effective tax rate, pioneered

4. King and Fullerton (1984).

5. King (1985) provides a detailed comparison between the 1984 tax reform in the United Kingdom and tax reform proposals in the United States.

by Arnold C. Harberger, and the cost of capital, originated by Dale W. Jorgenson.[6] The cost of capital and the effective tax rate were combined in the marginal effective tax rate introduced by Alan J. Auerbach and Jorgenson.[7]

Widespread applications of the cost of capital and the closely related concept of the marginal effective tax rate are due to the fact that these concepts facilitate the representation of the economically relevant features of highly complex tax statutes in a very succinct form. This has greatly enhanced the transparency of tax rules related to investment incentives. The cost of capital summarizes the information about the future consequences of investment decisions that is essential for current decisions about capital allocation. The marginal effective tax rate characterizes the tax consequences of investment decisions in a way that is particularly suitable for comparisons among alternative tax policies.

Auerbach and Jorgenson used marginal effective tax rates to expose differences in the tax treatment of income from different types of capital in the 1981 tax act. Marginal effective tax rates under the 1981 act were presented for all types of assets and all industries by Jorgenson and Martin A. Sullivan.[8] Subsequently, these effective tax rates helped frame the debate over alternative proposals that led to the Tax Reform Act of 1986. An important objective of tax reform was to level the playing field by equalizing marginal effective tax rates on different forms of capital income.[9]

In this book we present an international comparison of tax reforms for capital income over the period 1980–90. Comparisons are provided among the "Group of Seven" (or "G-7") countries—Canada, France, Germany, Italy, Japan, the United Kingdom, and the United States—together with Australia and Sweden, nine countries in all.[10] The empirical framework for these comparisons is provided by marginal effective tax rates for

6. Harberger (1962, 1966); Jorgenson (1963, 1965).

7. Auerbach and Jorgenson (1980). A discussion of alternative notions of the effective tax rate is presented by Fullerton (1984). A summary of the literature on empirical implementation of the cost of capital is given by Harper, Berndt, and Wood (1989).

8. Jorgenson and Sullivan (1981).

9. The objectives of the 1986 tax reform are discussed by McLure and Zodrow (1987).

10. Pechman (1988) provides comparisons among tax reform efforts in eleven industrialized countries, as of the end of 1987, including the nine countries covered by this study, Denmark, and The Netherlands. Boskin and McLure (1990) have provided similar comparisons for industrialized and developing countries through the end of 1988.

different types of capital income in all nine countries for the years 1980, 1985, and 1990. The measurements of marginal effective tax rates are based on the methodology developed by King and Fullerton.[11]

Previous international comparisons of marginal effective tax rates have been focused on a single point in time. For example, King and Fullerton have given marginal effective tax rates for four countries—Sweden, the United Kingdom, the United States, and West Germany—for 1980. They present separate measurements of effective tax rates for eighty-one different types of projects within each of the four countries. These projects are classified by type of asset, industry, source of finance, and owner; three categories are distinguished within each of these classifications. However, comparisons are limited to capital income generated within the corporate sector of each country.[12]

More extensive sets of international comparisons of marginal effective tax rates have been given by the Organization for Economic Cooperation and Development for twenty-four OECD member countries and by the Commission of the European Communities (CEC) for the European Community member states as of January 1, 1991.[13] The OECD study is limited to the manufacturing sector of each country and classifies investment projects only by type of asset and source of finance. However, this study also provides a very important extension of the conceptual framework of King and Fullerton by incorporating complex provisions for taxation of capital income of nonresidents and taxation of foreign-source income of residents.[14] The study develops effective tax rates for savers in each OECD country with investments in the manufacturing industry of each other OECD country. The CEC report adopts the same methodology used in the OECD study.

We extend the international comparisons of effective tax rates for four countries for 1980 given by King and Fullerton to all nine countries included in our study for all three years—1980, 1985, and 1990. Comparisons among the time periods for each country provide the information

11. King and Fullerton (1984).
12. King and Fullerton (1984) also provide estimates for 1960 and 1970 and Bernheim and Shoven (1987) have updated the King-Fullerton study through 1985, replacing Sweden with Japan.
13. Organization for Economic Cooperation and Development (1991); Commission of the European Communities (1992).
14. This extension of the King-Fullerton framework is presented by the Organization for Cooperation and Development (1991), pp. 207–18. International aspects of taxation are discussed by Alworth (1988), Frenkel, Razin, and Sadka (1991), and in the volume edited by Razin and Slemrod (1990).

needed to analyze successive reforms of tax policy for capital income. For capital income originating in the corporate sector, we divide the tax burden between components attributable to corporate and personal income taxes. This important extension of the King-Fullerton framework makes it possible to identify sources of differences in effective tax rates.

For example, the tax base for the corporate income tax depends on provisions for capital cost recovery, while the tax base for the personal income tax depends on the tax treatment of corporate distributions of capital income in the form of dividends, interest, and capital gains or losses. To analyze the impact of changing tax incentives for investment, the corporate income tax is the appropriate focus. To study the effects of alterations in incentives to save, attention must be concentrated on the personal income tax. Of course, consideration of both levels of the tax structure is required to provide an appropriate basis for assessing the economic impact of the corporate income tax.

Whereas King and Fullerton and the OECD study limit international comparisons of effective tax rates to income generated in the corporate sector, in this book we also present effective tax rates for the noncorporate sector and owner-occupied housing. This information is essential for comparisons of the taxation of income originating in the corporate sector with taxation of noncorporate enterprises and income generated from owner-occupied housing. Since the corporate tax is not levied on noncorporate income or income from owner-occupied housing, this tax leads to underallocation of capital to the corporate sector.

In the appendix to this chapter I review the King-Fullerton framework and its extensions. I define a tax wedge as the difference between the remuneration of capital before taxes, which corresponds to the marginal product of capital, and the compensation after taxes available to holders of financial claims on the firm. The effective tax rate is the ratio of the tax wedge to the marginal product. The cost of capital is the key to measuring the tax wedge. For income originating in the corporate sector this wedge depends on provisions of both corporate and personal income taxes. The cost of capital incorporates statutory tax rates and definitions of the tax bases at both levels of taxation.

I extend the King-Fullerton framework by expressing the tax wedge as the sum of corporate and personal tax wedges. I define a marginal effective corporate tax rate as the ratio of the corporate tax wedge to the marginal product of capital. Similarly, I define a marginal effective personal tax rate as the ratio of the personal tax wedge to the rate of return to capital after the corporate tax. The corporate tax rate reflects differences between rates of remuneration to capital before and after corporate taxes, while the personal tax rate on corporate source income is based on rates of compensation before and after personal taxes.

I also extend the King-Fullerton framework to encompass the taxation of capital income in the noncorporate sector and owner-occupied housing.[15] Capital income of noncorporate enterprises is subject to taxation at the personal level, but not at the corporate level. Except in Italy, income from owner-occupied housing is not included in the tax base for either personal or corporate income taxes. However, these two types of income, as well as corporate income, are subject to taxation through property and wealth taxes. Further extensions of the King-Fullerton framework relevant to the individual countries included in our international comparisons are given in chapters 2 through 10.

In the section that follows I present a detailed international comparison of marginal effective tax rates for 1980, 1985, and 1990 for all nine countries studied in this volume. I find that changes in tax policy for capital income in many countries took similar directions to those outlined above for the United Kingdom and the United States. Base broadening through elimination of investment incentives and rate reductions is nearly universal. This has resulted in a leveling of the playing field for different forms of assets. However, wide gaps among tax rates remain in all countries included in our study, so that many important opportunities remain for further tax reform.

The King-Fullerton approach has been the subject of an extensive critical literature dealing with the empirical implications of specific assumptions incorporated into the cost of capital. The most important of these assumptions is the adoption of the "new" view of taxation and corporate finance introduced by King.[16] This can be contrasted with the "traditional" view employed in the literature on corporate finance. The international comparisons presented in this section, like those of King and Fullerton, present results only for the new view of the corporate tax.

I then compare alternative approaches to measurement of the cost of capital and marginal effective tax rates. I first review the empirical evidence on the validity of new and traditional views of the corporate income tax. Jorgenson and Kun-Young Yun have provided a detailed alternative to

---

15. This extension follows Fullerton (1987) and Fullerton, Gillette, and Mackie (1987).
16. King (1974a, 1974b, 1977).

the King-Fullerton framework, based on the traditional view.[17] They have used this framework in analyzing tax reforms in the United States since 1947 by compiling marginal effective tax rates on an annual basis. They have also presented a comparison of marginal effective tax rates under alternative tax reform proposals considered in the debate that preceded the Tax Reform Act of 1986.[18]

Statutory tax rates and definitions of capital income for tax purposes provide only part of the information needed to measure the cost of capital. In addition, estimates of economic depreciation are needed to incorporate the impact of tax provisions on capital cost recovery. This requires extensive empirical research on the relationship of asset prices to the age of assets. Since income tax bases are not insulated from the effects of inflation, the rate of inflation must also be taken into account in measuring the cost of capital. In the discussion of alternative approaches I summarize the empirical literature on the effects of depreciation and inflation on the cost of capital.

In my summary and conclusion I evaluate the cost of capital approach to tax policy analysis. This approach has amply proved its usefulness as a guide to tax reform. For example, while the U.S. tax policy changes of the early 1980s introduced additional obstacles to efficient capital allocation, the Tax Reform Act of 1986 reduced these obstacles substantially. However, significant discrepancies remain between effective tax rates on income generated by owner-occupied housing and income from corporate and noncorporate enterprises. These discrepancies present the most important opportunities for increasing the efficiency of capital allocation.[19]

The cost of capital has also become an indispensable analytical tool for studies of the economic impact of changes in tax policies for the taxation of capital income. These studies have taken two forms. First, the cost of capital has been incorporated into the investment functions used in standard macroeconometric models. These models are useful in modeling the short-run dynamics of an economy's response to changes in tax policy. More recently, the cost of capital has been incorporated into applied general equilibrium models that focus on the impact of tax policy on the allocation of capital. These models are essential for capturing the long-run effects of tax reforms.

17. Jorgenson and Yun (1991b).
18. Fullerton (1987) and Fullerton, Gillette and Mackie (1987) have analyzed the Tax Reform Act of 1986 and alternative proposals within the King-Fullerton framework.
19. Jorgenson and Yun (1990, 1991a) provide quantitative estimates of the potential gains in efficiency for the United States.

## International Comparisons

In this section I present a detailed international comparison of marginal effective tax rates for 1980, 1985, and 1990 for the nine countries studied in this volume—Australia, Canada, France, Germany, Italy, Japan, Sweden, the United Kingdom, and the United States. These effective tax rates are based on the elaborations of the King-Fullerton methodology outlined in the preceding section. Differences among the nine countries in overall effective tax rates at corporate and personal levels for income originating in the corporate sector are considered. Changes in these tax rates over the period 1980–90 are also considered as a means of analyzing the consequences of tax reform in each country.

King and Fullerton have shown that effective tax rates for the four countries—Sweden, the United Kingdom, the United States, and West Germany—included in their study for 1980 were very sensitive to rates of inflation.[20] The tax bases for corporate and personal income taxes in these four countries were not fully indexed for inflation in 1980. None of the nine countries included in our study for 1980, 1985, and 1990 has adopted complete indexation of corporate and personal income tax bases for inflation. To reduce the complexity of international comparisons and the analysis of tax policy changes for individual countries for 1980–90, our estimates of marginal effective tax rates are based on a rate of inflation of 5 percent. Assessments of the sensitivity of effective tax rates for each country to variations in the rate of inflation are presented in chapters 2 through 10.

Marginal effective corporate tax rates provide the information required for a comparison of incentives to invest in different types of assets and different industries. Differences among these tax rates indicate barriers to efficient allocation of capital among assets and industries, since corporations equalize rates of return *after* corporate taxes. However, efficient allocation of corporate capital requires equal rates of return *before* corporate taxes. Similarly, marginal effective personal tax rates on income originating in the corporate sector are needed to compare incentives for saving through different financial instruments and different forms of ownership. Differences among these tax rates indicate barriers to efficient allocation of capital among financial instruments and different forms of ownership.

20. King and Fullerton (1984, especially pp. 268–302).

The next step is to compare marginal effective tax rates for income originating in the corporate sector with tax rates for noncorporate enterprises and owner-occupied housing. These comparisons are essential for assessing the economic impact of the corporate income tax. Savers equalize rates of return *after* both corporate and personal taxes, but efficient allocation of capital among corporate enterprises, noncorporate enterprises, and owner-occupied housing requires that rates of return *before* taxes must be equalized among the three sectors.

The final step is to compare marginal effective tax rates by type of asset, industry, source of finance, and form of ownership. I provide these comparisons for effective corporate and personal tax rates on income originating in the corporate sector. For comparisons among tax rates on noncorporate income, only the type of asset, industry, and debt-versus-equity sources of finance are relevant, since noncorporate enterprises are owned by households. Similarly, only debt and equity finance are relevant for comparisons among tax rates for owner-occupied housing.

Table 1-1 gives marginal effective corporate tax rates for 1980, 1985, and 1990 for all nine countries included in our study. In 1980 these tax rates were negative for four of the nine countries—France, Italy, Sweden, and the United Kingdom. Effective corporate tax rates were substantially below statutory rates for all nine countries. For example, the statutory corporate tax rate for the United States was 46.0 percent, while the effective rate was only 14.4 percent. This reflects investment incentives included in provisions for capital recovery under the corporate income tax. Australia had the highest corporate tax rate at 41.8 percent, while Italy had the lowest at a negative 91.6 percent, so that the gap between tax rates for the two countries was a stunning 133.4 percent.

In 1985 marginal effective corporate tax rates were negative for France, Italy, and Sweden. The most significant change in the taxation of corporate income between 1980 and 1985 was for the United Kingdom, which underwent a sharp reversal in tax policy with the budget of 1984, described by Mervyn A. King and Mark Robson in chapter 9. The U.K. corporate tax rate jumped from a negative 31.4 percent in 1980, lower than for any other country except Italy, to a positive 21.4 percent in 1985, the highest among all nine countries. The gap between the United Kingdom and Italy, the countries with the highest and lowest tax rates in 1985, was 116.8 percent, a modest decrease from 1980. Sweden and Canada instituted increases in corporate tax rates between 1980 and 1985, while tax rates declined for the remaining six countries. The largest decline was from 41.8 percent in 1980 to 17.0 percent in 1985 for Australia. This reflected the substantial enhancement of investment incentives, described by Robert Jones in chapter 2.

In 1990 only France and Italy retained negative marginal effective corporate tax rates. The corporate tax rate for Italy rose from a negative 95.4 percent in 1985 to a negative 72.8 percent in 1990, still the lowest level among the nine countries included in our study. Canada, Japan, Sweden, the United Kingdom, and the United States also raised corporate tax rates. As in 1985, the United Kingdom had the highest rate at 28.0 percent. The 1990 gap between Italy and the United Kingdom was 100.8 percent, a further modest decrease from 1980 and 1985. From 1980 to 1990, increases in corporate tax rates predominated slightly over declines.

The reduction of the corporate tax rate in the 1981 tax act in the United States was reversed by a substantial increase in the Tax Reform Act of 1986. This was the consequence of cutbacks in investment incentives described by Don Fullerton and Marios Karayannis in chapter 10. Parallel reductions in investment incentives in Canada, described by Michael J. Daly, Pierre Mercier, and Thomas Schweitzer in chapter 3, were partly offset by a reduction in the statutory corporate tax rate. Effective corporate tax rates in the United States and Canada rose from 9.2 to 24.0 and 19.0 to 25.9 percent, respectively, between 1985 and 1990.

Table 1-2 gives marginal effective personal tax rates on corporate source income for all nine countries included in our study. In 1980 France had the highest personal tax rate at 74.1 percent, while Japan had the lowest at 15.6 percent. The gap between the two was 58.5 percent. In 1985 personal tax rates were the highest for the three countries with negative corporate tax rates—France, Italy, and Sweden. Australia lowered the personal tax rate from 23.4 to 18.7 percent, while the United States lowered this rate from 22.5 to 18.7 percent. France retained the highest personal tax rate, raising it slightly, from 74.1 to 75.2 percent. The gap between France and Japan, the country with the lowest rate at 16.3 percent, was 58.9 percent, almost the same as in 1980.

In 1990 marginal effective personal tax rates were, once again, highest for France and Italy, the only remaining countries with negative effective corporate tax rates. France lowered this rate from 75.2 to 65.4 percent, again retaining the highest rate. Between 1985 and 1990 Sweden reduced the personal tax rate substantially from 37.0 to 27.8 percent, while the

Table 1-1. *Marginal Effective Corporate Tax Rates, Nine Countries, 1980, 1985, 1990*

Percent

| Item | Australia | Canada | France | Germany | Italy | Japan | Sweden | United Kingdom | United States |
|---|---|---|---|---|---|---|---|---|---|
| | | | | | *1980* | | | | |
| **Asset** | | | | | | | | | |
| Machinery | 28.1 | 4.3 | -42.1 | 15.2 | -101.1 | 2.6 | -54.4 | -67.0 | -12.0 |
| Buildings | 46.4 | 30.3 | -42.2 | 9.3 | -90.5 | 0.5 | -9.3 | 20.4 | 19.1 |
| Inventories | 55.7 | 20.6 | -5.2 | 23.9 | -79.4 | 5.7 | -5.6 | -34.2 | 28.5 |
| **Industry** | | | | | | | | | |
| Manufacturing | 41.4 | 10.3 | -30.3 | 16.2 | -94.4 | 7.6 | -19.7 | -53.3 | 33.8 |
| Other industry | 33.3 | 25.6 | -23.1 | 28.1 | -87.8 | -8.8 | -28.6 | -24.2 | -13.7 |
| Commerce | 44.1 | 19.2 | -36.6 | 7.6 | -88.4 | 7.0 | -25.9 | 12.7 | 15.5 |
| **Source of finance** | | | | | | | | | |
| Debt | -22.2 | -25.0 | -46.9 | -46.0 | -104.5 | -70.6 | -59.5 | -157.8 | -49.2 |
| New share issues | 57.0 | 44.7 | -29.6 | 52.4 | -13.9 | 54.5 | -6.5 | -61.2 | 47.1 |
| Retained earnings | 57.1 | 44.7 | -13.7 | 83.0 | -82.4 | 57.0 | 19.0 | 2.3 | 45.6 |
| **Owner** | | | | | | | | | |
| Households | 37.0 | 19.2 | -30.3 | 16.0 | -91.5 | 0.7 | -14.1 | -45.5 | 15.8 |
| Tax-exempt institutions | 49.4 | 10.7 | -21.9 | 14.3 | 0.0 | 16.0 | -34.8 | -12.9 | 9.1 |
| Insurance companies | 52.9 | -6.9 | -17.0 | 9.7 | -104.5 | 17.0 | -15.2 | -29.5 | 26.3 |
| Overall tax rate | 41.8 | 16.9 | -28.8 | 15.2 | -91.6 | 3.1 | -22.5 | -31.4 | 14.4 |
| | | | | | *1985* | | | | |
| **Asset** | | | | | | | | | |
| Machinery | -9.2 | 8.2 | -58.3 | 11.5 | -109.7 | 1.7 | -14.2 | -5.4 | -18.6 |
| Buildings | 26.7 | 31.6 | -37.9 | -1.4 | -92.1 | -2.4 | -1.5 | 43.9 | 12.2 |
| Inventories | 50.3 | 20.4 | -3.1 | 23.9 | -79.2 | 2.7 | 0.3 | 46.8 | 28.7 |
| **Industry** | | | | | | | | | |
| Manufacturing | 13.6 | 11.2 | -35.3 | 11.1 | -100.3 | 1.0 | -0.9 | 14.7 | 27.5 |
| Other industry | 0.5 | 28.3 | -26.6 | 21.9 | -91.3 | 0.2 | 14.7 | 14.5 | -16.7 |
| Commerce | 24.8 | 22.8 | -40.1 | 1.3 | -89.4 | -0.5 | -9.0 | 38.9 | 9.2 |

| | | | | | | | | | |
|---|---|---|---|---|---|---|---|---|---|
| **Source of finance** | | | | | | | | | |
| Debt | -50.1 | -20.5 | -54.3 | -53.6 | -130.4 | -82.5 | -37.7 | -36.8 | -55.5 |
| New share issues | 41.9 | 45.2 | 12.5 | 48.2 | -25.1 | 58.3 | 9.5 | -10.1 | 43.0 |
| Retained earnings | 41.9 | 45.3 | -17.8 | 80.1 | -75.8 | 62.0 | 31.7 | 38.0 | 42.1 |
| **Owner** | | | | | | | | | |
| Households | 4.4 | 21.2 | -34.8 | 10.6 | -96.8 | -6.9 | 1.7 | 14.9 | 9.5 |
| Tax-exempt institutions | 32.6 | 13.2 | -21.8 | 8.8 | -82.0 | 10.4 | -15.1 | 30.1 | 2.4 |
| Insurance companies | 36.8 | -3.4 | -20.1 | 4.1 | -85.8 | 27.3 | 1.7 | 22.2 | 25.1 |
| Overall tax rate | 17.0 | 19.0 | -33.0 | 9.9 | -95.4 | 0.5 | -5.0 | 21.4 | 9.2 |

*1990*

| | | | | | | | | | |
|---|---|---|---|---|---|---|---|---|---|
| **Asset** | | | | | | | | | |
| Machinery | 9.0 | 15.5 | -48.1 | 11.5 | -86.3 | 8.8 | -11.3 | 8.0 | 18.5 |
| Buildings | 11.7 | 35.9 | -45.8 | 1.6 | -57.2 | 2.5 | 1.3 | 49.7 | 25.3 |
| Inventories | 27.5 | 30.7 | -18.1 | -0.3 | -72.9 | 7.0 | 12.5 | 39.8 | 26.3 |
| **Industry** | | | | | | | | | |
| Manufacturing | 15.0 | 24.5 | -37.3 | 5.2 | -78.4 | 6.7 | n.a. | 24.8 | 34.0 |
| Other industry | 10.2 | 29.1 | -33.5 | 19.7 | -76.1 | 5.9 | n.a. | 21.2 | 11.7 |
| Commerce | 15.1 | 25.0 | -28.7 | -2.7 | -64.8 | 5.2 | n.a. | 37.8 | 21.8 |
| **Source of finance** | | | | | | | | | |
| Debt | -15.9 | -6.3 | -40.9 | -55.0 | -111.3 | -74.6 | -19.0 | -15.9 | -14.7 |
| New share issues | -15.9 | 47.2 | 9.1 | 46.7 | -14.2 | 70.9 | 5.8 | 4.1 | 44.1 |
| Retained earnings | 48.8 | 47.3 | -30.0 | 69.4 | -51.1 | 62.8 | 23.2 | 40.5 | 43.7 |
| **Owner** | | | | | | | | | |
| Households | 3.3 | 26.9 | -33.9 | 5.3 | -74.3 | -1.2 | 4.8 | 23.1 | 23.6 |
| Tax-exempt institutions | 25.0 | 20.2 | -29.8 | 3.7 | -59.2 | 14.3 | -4.8 | 34.5 | 19.3 |
| Insurance companies | 27.4 | 31.1 | -29.1 | -0.8 | -69.5 | 30.7 | 5.0 | 28.7 | 40.9 |
| Overall tax rate | 14.6 | 25.9 | -33.4 | 4.6 | -72.8 | 6.1 | 1.0 | 28.0 | 24.0 |

Source: Data drawn from the chapters in this volume.
n.a. Not available.

Table 1-2. Marginal Effective Personal Tax Rates on Corporate Source Income, Nine Countries, 1980, 1985, 1990

Percent

| Item | Australia | Canada | France | Germany | Italy | Japan | Sweden | United Kingdom | United States |
|---|---|---|---|---|---|---|---|---|---|
| | | | | | *1980* | | | | |
| **Asset** | | | | | | | | | |
| Machinery | 20.4 | 21.4 | 70.4 | 32.8 | 57.3 | 15.7 | 34.5 | 35.9 | 22.6 |
| Buildings | 23.9 | 18.1 | 70.4 | 32.9 | 58.3 | 15.8 | 38.0 | 23.1 | 22.6 |
| Inventories | 26.9 | 20.1 | 82.7 | 33.0 | 60.2 | 15.3 | 40.9 | 31.3 | 22.3 |
| **Industry** | | | | | | | | | |
| Manufacturing | 23.4 | 20.0 | 73.6 | 33.0 | 58.0 | 15.0 | 31.8 | 33.9 | 21.8 |
| Other industry | 21.5 | 18.4 | 75.8 | 29.3 | 59.2 | 16.9 | 56.9 | 29.8 | 23.3 |
| Commerce | 23.8 | 21.4 | 71.9 | 33.4 | 59.2 | 15.2 | 39.1 | 24.2 | 23.8 |
| **Source of finance** | | | | | | | | | |
| Debt | 29.3 | 37.1 | 61.7 | 40.1 | 43.0 | 22.7 | 37.5 | 105.7 | 26.0 |
| New share issues | 51.4 | 10.4 | 81.4 | 19.8 | 87.5 | 25.0 | 70.8 | 50.7 | 53.0 |
| Retained earnings | 6.1 | 8.4 | 86.8 | 25.4 | 71.0 | 8.1 | 38.2 | 10.6 | 18.2 |
| **Owner** | | | | | | | | | |
| Households | 30.5 | 26.1 | 76.4 | 43.4 | 59.1 | 17.8 | 64.2 | 52.5 | 44.4 |
| Tax-exempt institutions | 0.0 | 0.0 | 72.7 | 7.4 | 0.0 | 0.9 | 0.0 | 0.0 | −31.9 |
| Insurance companies | 33.9 | −22.9 | 48.7 | −9.9 | −19.1 | 7.3 | 22.9 | 32.3 | −17.2 |
| Overall tax rate | 23.4 | 20.0 | 74.1 | 32.9 | 58.5 | 15.6 | 37.9 | 30.7 | 22.5 |
| | | | | | *1985* | | | | |
| **Asset** | | | | | | | | | |
| Machinery | 15.9 | 22.2 | 68.6 | 31.5 | 57.9 | 16.2 | 34.2 | 21.1 | 18.9 |
| Buildings | 18.8 | 19.1 | 73.8 | 31.5 | 60.1 | 16.5 | 37.1 | 13.9 | 18.8 |
| Inventories | 23.4 | 21.4 | 87.3 | 31.7 | 61.9 | 16.1 | 39.5 | 13.5 | 18.4 |
| **Industry** | | | | | | | | | |
| Manufacturing | 18.5 | 21.1 | 74.5 | 31.6 | 58.8 | 16.2 | 31.9 | 18.2 | 17.7 |
| Other industry | 16.9 | 19.3 | 77.4 | 28.4 | 60.4 | 16.4 | 53.2 | 18.3 | 19.8 |
| Commerce | 19.4 | 22.3 | 73.1 | 32.0 | 60.7 | 16.4 | 37.6 | 14.6 | 19.2 |

| | | | | | | | | | |
|---|---|---|---|---|---|---|---|---|---|
| **Source of finance** | | | | | | | | | |
| Debt | 29.3 | 39.5 | 61.2 | 37.9 | 43.5 | 23.6 | 34.6 | 62.8 | 23.6 |
| New share issues | 38.5 | 10.4 | 105.5 | 16.3 | 83.1 | 22.6 | 68.6 | 32.3 | 44.2 |
| Retained earnings | 6.3 | 8.3 | 89.3 | 24.9 | 71.6 | 9.3 | 39.5 | 4.8 | 14.0 |
| **Owner** | | | | | | | | | |
| Households | 26.1 | 27.3 | 77.6 | 41.0 | 62.5 | 19.3 | 62.5 | 28.4 | 36.5 |
| Tax-exempt institutions | 0.0 | 0.0 | 76.8 | 8.8 | 66.1 | 1.1 | 0.3 | 0.0 | −25.3 |
| Insurance companies | 32.2 | −22.9 | 39.0 | −7.9 | 18.9 | 5.6 | 23.8 | 21.4 | −13.6 |
| Overall tax rate | 18.7 | 20.9 | 75.2 | 31.5 | 59.7 | 16.3 | 37.0 | 17.2 | 18.7 |
| *1990* | | | | | | | | | |
| **Asset** | | | | | | | | | |
| Machinery | 27.4 | 20.6 | 61.5 | 28.5 | 56.1 | 22.6 | 27.6 | 16.3 | 19.1 |
| Buildings | 27.6 | 17.7 | 62.1 | 28.6 | 61.1 | 23.4 | 27.8 | 11.0 | 19.1 |
| Inventories | 30.0 | 19.2 | 70.5 | 28.6 | 58.1 | 22.9 | 28.0 | 12.3 | 19.0 |
| **Industry** | | | | | | | | | |
| Manufacturing | 28.2 | 18.5 | 64.3 | 28.6 | 57.0 | 22.6 | n.a. | 14.2 | 18.8 |
| Other industry | 27.5 | 18.4 | 65.5 | 26.4 | 57.8 | 23.7 | n.a. | 14.6 | 19.4 |
| Commerce | 28.2 | 21.5 | 66.8 | 29.0 | 59.9 | 23.3 | n.a. | 12.5 | 19.2 |
| **Source of finance** | | | | | | | | | |
| Debt | 32.4 | 37.6 | 53.4 | 34.6 | 39.4 | 38.0 | 29.4 | 44.0 | 20.5 |
| New share issues | 40.6 | 24.9 | 92.4 | 7.4 | 83.7 | 20.0 | 42.9 | 22.3 | 35.7 |
| Retained earnings | 20.0 | 4.4 | 75.0 | 22.4 | 73.0 | 9.2 | 26.2 | 5.6 | 17.0 |
| **Owner** | | | | | | | | | |
| Households | 32.4 | 24.5 | 67.6 | 36.1 | 61.0 | 27.8 | 44.8 | 23.5 | 32.8 |
| Tax-exempt institutions | 12.7 | 0.0 | 67.4 | 11.5 | 69.2 | 1.0 | 10.0 | 0.0 | −14.6 |
| Insurance companies | 47.7 | −6.4 | 27.0 | −5.2 | 23.5 | 5.4 | 24.4 | 14.5 | −7.9 |
| Overall tax rate | 28.1 | 19.3 | 65.4 | 28.6 | 58.2 | 23.0 | 27.8 | 13.8 | 19.1 |

Source: Data drawn from the chapters in this volume.
n.a. Not available.

United Kingdom became the country with the lowest rate by reducing this rate from 17.2 to 13.8 percent. The gap between the highest and lowest rates was 51.6 percent, a decline from 1985. Canada, Germany, and Italy slightly reduced the personal tax rate, while Australia, Japan, and the United States increased this rate. Tax reductions predominated over increases from 1985 to 1990.

The next step is to compare marginal effective tax rates for corporate source income with effective tax rates for the noncorporate sector and owner-occupied housing. For this purpose I first combine corporate and personal tax rates into a tax rate on corporate source income in table 1-3. In 1980 Australia and France had the highest tax rates for corporate source income at 55.4 and 66.6 percent, respectively, while the United Kingdom had the lowest rate at 8.9 percent. The result was a difference between the highest and lowest rates of 57.7 percent.

Between 1980 and 1985 France slightly raised the marginal effective tax rate on corporate source income from 66.6 to 67.0 percent, while Australia cut this rate sharply from 55.4 to 32.5 percent. The United Kingdom raised the tax rate on corporate source income from 8.9 to 34.9 percent, whereas Japan reduced this rate from 18.2 to 16.7 percent, in the process replacing the United Kingdom as the country with the lowest tax rate. The gap between the highest and lowest tax rates narrowed modestly from 57.7 to 50.3 percent. Germany and the United States also lowered the tax rate on corporate source income, whereas Canada, Italy, and Sweden raised it. Overall, no trend in tax rates on corporate source income is discernible from the results presented in table 1-3 for 1980 and 1985.

Changes in marginal effective tax rates on corporate source income between 1985 and 1990 also revealed no trend. Despite the adoption of a full imputation scheme for corporate income taxation by Australia, the tax rate actually rose from 32.5 to 38.6 percent. Integration of the corporate and personal income tax was offset by the elimination of investment incentives described by Jones in chapter 2. Canada, Italy, Japan, the United Kingdom, and the United States also raised these rates, while France, Germany, and Sweden lowered them. Australia, Japan, and the United States lowered the rates between 1980 and 1985 and raised them between 1985 and 1990. France and Sweden raised rates between 1980 and 1985 and lowered them between 1985 and 1990. Canada, Italy, and the United Kingdom increased rates in both periods, while Germany lowered rates in both periods. I conclude that reversals of direction predominated over rate increases or decreases.

Table 1-4 gives marginal effective personal tax rates on income from noncorporate enterprises for all nine countries included in our study. In 1980 Germany and Italy had full imputation systems for corporate source income and gaps between effective tax rates on corporate source income and noncorporate income of 3.9 and 13.2 percent, respectively. Canada, France, Japan, Sweden, and the United Kingdom had partial imputation systems for corporate source income. Only Canada had a higher tax rate for noncorporate income (36.3 percent) than for corporate income (33.5 percent). The gaps for France, Japan, Sweden, and the United Kingdom were 8.7, 3.0, 25.9, and 2.4 percent, respectively. Australia and the United States had classical systems for corporate source income and gaps of 13.4 and 16.3 percent, respectively. Surprisingly, the integration of corporate and personal taxes for corporate source income was not closely correlated with differences between effective tax rates on corporate and noncorporate income. These differences indicate obstacles to efficient allocation of capital between corporate and noncorporate sectors.

Australia reduced the marginal effective tax rate for noncorporate income from 42.0 to 28.2 percent between 1980 and 1985, and Sweden increased this rate from a negative 2.0 percent to 17.8 percent. More modest declines took place in France, Germany, Italy, Japan, and the United States, while smaller increases occurred in Canada and the United Kingdom. Marginal effective tax rates on noncorporate income rose for seven of the nine countries between 1985 and 1990, with the greatest increase—from 28.2 to 41.0 percent—occurring in Australia.

During the period 1985–90 Australia adopted the full imputation system for corporate source income described by Robert Jones in chapter 2, but sharply reduced investment incentives, raising the effective corporate tax rate from 32.5 to 38.6 percent, below the tax rate of 41.0 percent on noncorporate income. As pointed out by Toshiaki Tachibanaki and Tatsuya Kikutani in chapter 7, Japan modified its split-rate system for corporate source income with a reduced corporate tax rate for distributed profits and abolished tax-free savings accounts. This increased the effective tax rate from 16.7 to 27.7 percent, still the lowest among the nine countries. Gaps between effective tax rates on corporate source income and noncorporate income narrowed for a substantial number of countries, primarily as a consequence of the elimination of investment incentives from provisions for capital recovery for noncorporate enterprises.

Table 1-3.  Marginal Effective Tax Rates on Corporate Source Income, Nine Countries, 1980, 1985, 1990

Percent

| Item | Australia | Canada | France | Germany | Italy | Japan | Sweden | United Kingdom | United States |
|---|---|---|---|---|---|---|---|---|---|
| | | | | | 1980 | | | | |
| **Asset** | | | | | | | | | |
| Machinery | 42.8 | 24.8 | 57.9 | 43.0 | 14.1 | 17.9 | -1.1 | -7.0 | 13.3 |
| Buildings | 59.2 | 42.9 | 57.9 | 39.1 | 20.6 | 16.2 | 32.2 | 38.8 | 37.4 |
| Inventories | 67.6 | 36.6 | 81.8 | 49.0 | 28.6 | 20.1 | 37.6 | 7.8 | 44.4 |
| **Industry** | | | | | | | | | |
| Manufacturing | 55.1 | 28.2 | 65.6 | 43.9 | 18.4 | 21.5 | 18.4 | -1.3 | 48.2 |
| Other industry | 47.6 | 39.3 | 70.2 | 49.2 | 23.4 | 9.6 | 44.6 | 12.8 | 12.8 |
| Commerce | 57.4 | 36.5 | 61.6 | 38.5 | 23.1 | 21.1 | 23.3 | 33.8 | 35.6 |
| **Source of finance** | | | | | | | | | |
| Debt | 13.6 | 21.4 | 43.7 | 12.5 | -16.6 | -31.9 | 0.3 | 114.7 | -10.4 |
| New share issues | 79.1 | 50.5 | 75.9 | 61.8 | 85.8 | 65.9 | 68.9 | 20.5 | 75.1 |
| Retained earnings | 59.7 | 49.3 | 85.0 | 87.3 | 47.1 | 60.5 | 49.9 | 12.7 | 55.5 |
| **Owner** | | | | | | | | | |
| Households | 56.2 | 40.3 | 69.2 | 52.5 | 21.7 | 18.4 | 59.2 | 30.9 | 53.2 |
| Tax-exempt institutions | 49.4 | 10.7 | 66.7 | 20.6 | 0.0 | 16.8 | -34.8 | -12.9 | -19.9 |
| Insurance companies | 68.9 | -31.4 | 40.0 | 0.8 | -143.6 | 23.1 | 11.2 | 12.3 | 13.6 |
| Overall tax rate | 55.4 | 33.5 | 66.6 | 43.1 | 20.5 | 18.2 | 23.9 | 8.9 | 33.7 |
| | | | | | 1985 | | | | |
| **Asset** | | | | | | | | | |
| Machinery | 8.2 | 28.6 | 50.3 | 39.4 | 11.7 | 17.6 | 24.9 | 16.8 | 3.8 |
| Buildings | 40.5 | 44.7 | 63.9 | 30.5 | 23.4 | 14.5 | 36.2 | 51.7 | 28.7 |
| Inventories | 61.9 | 37.4 | 86.9 | 48.0 | 31.7 | 18.4 | 39.7 | 54.0 | 41.8 |
| **Industry** | | | | | | | | | |
| Manufacturing | 29.6 | 29.9 | 65.5 | 39.2 | 17.5 | 17.0 | 31.3 | 30.2 | 40.3 |
| Other industry | 17.3 | 42.1 | 71.4 | 44.1 | 24.2 | 16.6 | 60.1 | 30.1 | 6.4 |
| Commerce | 39.4 | 40.0 | 62.3 | 32.9 | 25.6 | 16.0 | 32.0 | 47.8 | 26.6 |

**Source of finance**

| | | | | | | | | | |
|---|---|---|---|---|---|---|---|---|---|
| Debt | −6.1 | 27.1 | 40.1 | 4.6 | −30.2 | −39.4 | 9.9 | 49.1 | −18.8 |
| New share issues | 64.3 | 50.9 | 104.8 | 56.6 | 78.9 | 67.7 | 71.6 | 25.5 | 68.2 |
| Retained earnings | 45.6 | 49.8 | 87.4 | 85.1 | 50.1 | 65.5 | 58.7 | 41.0 | 50.2 |

**Owner**

| | | | | | | | | | |
|---|---|---|---|---|---|---|---|---|---|
| Households | 29.4 | 42.7 | 69.8 | 47.3 | 26.2 | 13.7 | 63.1 | 39.1 | 42.5 |
| Tax-exempt institutions | 32.6 | 13.2 | 71.7 | 16.8 | 38.3 | 11.4 | −14.8 | 30.1 | −22.3 |
| Insurance companies | 57.2 | −27.1 | 26.7 | −3.5 | −50.7 | 31.4 | 25.1 | 38.8 | 14.9 |
| Overall tax rate | 32.5 | 35.9 | 67.0 | 38.3 | 21.3 | 16.7 | 33.9 | 34.9 | 26.2 |

*1990*

**Asset**

| | | | | | | | | | |
|---|---|---|---|---|---|---|---|---|---|
| Machinery | 33.9 | 32.9 | 43.0 | 36.7 | 18.2 | 29.4 | 19.4 | 23.0 | 34.1 |
| Buildings | 36.1 | 47.2 | 44.7 | 29.7 | 38.8 | 25.3 | 28.7 | 55.2 | 39.6 |
| Inventories | 49.3 | 44.0 | 65.2 | 28.4 | 27.6 | 28.3 | 37.0 | 47.2 | 40.3 |

**Industry**

| | | | | | | | | | |
|---|---|---|---|---|---|---|---|---|---|
| Manufacturing | 39.0 | 38.5 | 51.0 | 32.3 | 23.3 | 27.8 | n.a. | 35.5 | 46.4 |
| Other industry | 34.9 | 42.1 | 53.9 | 40.9 | 25.7 | 28.2 | n.a. | 32.7 | 28.8 |
| Commerce | 39.0 | 41.1 | 57.3 | 27.1 | 33.9 | 27.3 | n.a. | 45.6 | 36.8 |

**Source of finance**

| | | | | | | | | | |
|---|---|---|---|---|---|---|---|---|---|
| Debt | 21.7 | 33.7 | 34.3 | −1.4 | −28.0 | −8.3 | 16.0 | 35.1 | 8.8 |
| New share issues | 31.2 | 60.3 | 93.1 | 50.6 | 81.4 | 76.7 | 46.2 | 25.5 | 64.1 |
| Retained earnings | 59.0 | 49.6 | 67.5 | 76.3 | 59.2 | 66.2 | 43.3 | 43.8 | 53.3 |

**Owner**

| | | | | | | | | | |
|---|---|---|---|---|---|---|---|---|---|
| Households | 34.6 | 44.8 | 56.6 | 39.5 | 32.0 | 26.9 | 47.4 | 41.2 | 48.7 |
| Tax-exempt institutions | 34.5 | 20.2 | 57.7 | 14.8 | 51.0 | 15.2 | 5.7 | 34.5 | 7.5 |
| Insurance companies | 62.0 | 26.7 | 5.8 | −6.0 | −29.7 | 34.4 | 28.2 | 39.0 | 36.2 |
| Overall tax rate | 38.6 | 40.2 | 53.8 | 31.9 | 27.8 | 27.7 | 28.5 | 37.9 | 38.5 |

Source: See table 1-1.
n.a. Not available.

Table 1-4. Marginal Effective Noncorporate Tax Rates, Nine Countries, 1980, 1985, 1990

| Item | Australia | Canada | France | Germany | Italy | Japan | Sweden | United Kingdom | United States |
|---|---|---|---|---|---|---|---|---|---|
| | | | | | *1980* | | | | |
| Asset | | | | | | | | | |
| Machinery | 31.1 | 25.8 | 47.5 | 36.2 | -1.2 | 15.1 | -55.7 | 0.0 | -3.1 |
| Buildings | 46.1 | 47.0 | 47.7 | 37.4 | 8.5 | 14.6 | 14.9 | 19.5 | 22.6 |
| Inventories | 52.7 | 40.2 | 75.8 | 45.7 | 17.8 | 15.9 | 32.5 | 0.0 | 25.0 |
| Industry | | | | | | | | | |
| Manufacturing | 41.7 | 29.4 | 56.8 | 39.5 | 5.2 | 15.8 | -8.8 | n.a. | 19.8 |
| Other industry | 35.1 | 41.5 | 61.9 | 45.5 | 10.2 | 13.6 | 19.1 | n.a. | 9.2 |
| Commerce | 43.8 | 42.6 | 52.3 | 36.2 | 9.8 | 16.0 | -0.6 | n.a. | 23.3 |
| Source of finance | | | | | | | | | |
| Debt | 21.9 | 29.2 | 42.5 | 9.7 | -25.6 | 1.6 | -60.8 | 6.3 | 24.6 |
| Equity | 46.8 | 41.1 | 70.0 | 69.5 | 25.8 | 26.9 | 62.2 | 6.7 | 13.7 |
| Overall tax rate | 42.0 | 36.3 | 57.9 | 39.2 | 7.3 | 15.2 | -2.0 | 6.5 | 17.4 |
| | | | | | *1985* | | | | |
| Asset | | | | | | | | | |
| Machinery | 7.4 | 30.3 | 37.0 | 36.4 | -4.4 | 15.6 | -5.5 | 19.0 | -8.8 |
| Buildings | 36.1 | 48.4 | 52.3 | 32.1 | 9.3 | 14.2 | 18.1 | 17.6 | 17.2 |
| Inventories | 54.6 | 42.5 | 78.6 | 48.3 | 18.8 | 15.7 | 40.0 | 60.4 | 22.8 |
| Industry | | | | | | | | | |
| Manufacturing | 26.4 | 31.8 | 54.0 | 38.4 | 2.7 | 14.9 | 15.7 | n.a. | 14.6 |
| Other industry | 13.7 | 44.5 | 61.6 | 43.4 | 9.7 | 16.1 | 25.7 | n.a. | 5.9 |
| Commerce | 33.7 | 46.2 | 49.9 | 34.2 | 11.4 | 14.9 | 17.2 | n.a. | 17.7 |

| | | | | | 1990 | | | | |
|---|---|---|---|---|---|---|---|---|---|
| **Source of finance** | | | | | | | | | |
| Debt | 4.8 | 34.9 | 40.6 | 7.3 | −33.8 | 1.1 | −42.3 | 31.4 | 20.7 |
| Equity | 37.0 | 42.1 | 68.2 | 69.4 | 29.4 | 27.4 | 83.6 | 33.2 | 8.6 |
| Overall tax rate | 28.2 | 39.2 | 56.1 | 37.9 | 6.6 | 15.1 | 17.8 | 32.3 | 12.7 |
| **Asset** | | | | | | | | | |
| Machinery | 36.4 | 36.2 | 36.6 | 30.4 | 5.2 | 26.4 | 9.5 | 20.2 | 18.3 |
| Buildings | 38.3 | 51.9 | 40.1 | 26.1 | 27.7 | 23.7 | 27.2 | 29.8 | 23.7 |
| Inventories | 51.7 | 51.3 | 66.9 | 26.6 | 15.6 | 24.7 | 45.5 | 49.0 | 20.5 |
| **Industry** | | | | | | | | | |
| Manufacturing | 41.4 | 42.4 | 47.4 | 28.0 | 11.1 | 24.5 | n.a. | n.a. | 21.0 |
| Other industry | 37.4 | 45.7 | 52.9 | 35.2 | 13.2 | 26.9 | n.a. | n.a. | 21.6 |
| Commerce | 41.3 | 48.3 | 42.2 | 24.4 | 22.0 | 25.1 | n.a. | n.a. | 23.1 |
| **Source of finance** | | | | | | | | | |
| Debt | 21.9 | 43.1 | 26.7 | −0.5 | −25.7 | 18.4 | 3.9 | 32.1 | 29.6 |
| Equity | 50.2 | 46.1 | 65.6 | 56.8 | 39.0 | 31.0 | 53.3 | 33.7 | 17.7 |
| Overall tax rate | 41.0 | 44.9 | 48.5 | 27.7 | 15.6 | 25.1 | 27.6 | 32.9 | 21.7 |

Source: See table 1-1.
n.a. Not available.

Table 1-5 gives marginal effective tax rates on owner-occupied housing. In 1980 all nine countries had substantial gaps between tax rates on corporate source income and owner-occupied housing. Japan had a negative effective tax rate of 29.9 percent on owner-occupied housing and a positive tax rate on corporate source income of 18.2 percent, resulting in a gap of 48.1 percent. This reflects the highly favorable tax treatment of owner-occupied housing in Japan described by Tachibanaki and Kikutani in chapter 7. However, the largest gaps were for Australia at 53.0 percent and France at 64.0 percent, reflecting high tax rates on corporate source income for these countries. Only Italy and Sweden had tax rates for owner-occupied housing that exceeded the tax rates for noncorporate income.

Marginal effective tax rates for owner-occupied housing in Sweden rose from 15.0 percent in 1985 to 31.0 percent in 1991, higher than effective rates on corporate and noncorporate income. This reflects the radical revamping of tax provisions for owner-occupied housing in the Swedish tax reform of 1991 described in detail by Jan Södersten in chapter 8. Smaller increases occurred in Australia, Canada, and Italy, while decreases took place in France, Germany, Japan, and the United States. Large differences remained between effective tax rates on corporate source income and income from owner-occupied housing in all countries except Sweden. These differences present much more formidable obstacles to efficient capital allocation than differences between effective tax rates on corporate and noncorporate income.

Despite the reversals in tax policy for corporate source income that characterized the period 1980–90, many countries succeeded in narrowing the gap between marginal effective tax rates on corporate and noncorporate income. An effective strategy for equalizing these tax rates, successfully employed by Australia, was to eliminate investment incentives in both sectors while introducing partial or full imputation of corporate tax payments and income to corporate stockholders through the personal income tax. By itself, integration of corporate and personal income taxes was largely ineffective in eliminating differences between tax rates for corporate and noncorporate income. This is an implication of the "new" view of corporate taxation discussed in more detail later in this chapter under "Alternative Approaches."

Sweden was the only country that succeeded in eliminating the differences between marginal effective tax rates on corporate source income and owner-occupied housing. The most straightforward approach to this problem is to include an imputation for income from owner-occupied

Table 1-5. *Marginal Effective Housing Tax Rates, Nine Countries, 1980, 1985, 1990*

| Item | Australia | Canada | France | Germany | Italy | Japan | Sweden | United Kingdom | United States |
|------|-----------|--------|--------|---------|-------|-------|--------|----------------|---------------|
| | | | | | *1980* | | | | |
| Method of finance | | | | | | | | | |
| Debt | 31.5 | 51.2 | 0.3 | 29.0 | .7 | −0.8 | −96.1 | 0.0 | 8.5 |
| Equity | 0.0 | 10.7 | 6.0 | −6.0 | 8.8 | −16.2 | 36.4 | 0.0 | 15.0 |
| Overall tax rate | 2.4 | 15.4 | 2.6 | 11.5 | 8.4 | −29.9 | 3.3 | 0.0 | 12.8 |
| | | | | | *1985* | | | | |
| Method of finance | | | | | | | | | |
| Debt | 34.8 | 56.1 | 0.5 | 32.0 | .7 | −0.8 | −39.2 | 0.0 | 6.4 |
| Equity | 4.6 | 12.3 | 5.0 | −3.0 | 7.0 | −16.2 | 44.2 | 0.0 | 14.5 |
| Overall tax rate | 7.0 | 17.4 | 2.3 | 14.5 | 6.6 | −29.9 | 15.0 | 0.0 | 11.8 |
| | | | | | *1990* | | | | |
| Method of finance | | | | | | | | | |
| Debt | 35.5 | 61.0 | 0.6 | 27.0 | .5 | 0.1 | 7.0 | 0.0 | 5.2 |
| Equity | 8.8 | 18.0 | 4.5 | −8.0 | 9.2 | −29.5 | 43.9 | 0.0 | 14.1 |
| Overall tax rate | 11.0 | 23.0 | 2.2 | 9.5 | 8.4 | −34.4 | 31.0 | 0.0 | 11.2 |

housing in the personal income tax base. In practice such an imputation is vulnerable to political pressures from homeowners and is usually reduced far below the value of income generated by housing. As Julian Alworth and Laura Castellucci point out in chapter 6, only Italy has retained this approach. The Swedish tax reform of 1991 described by Södersten in chapter 8 replaced the imputation of housing income by a nondeductible property tax on housing. In addition, the Swedish value-added tax (VAT) was broadened to include investment expenditures on housing. The reduction in statutory corporate and personal tax rates also helped to eliminate the gap between the respective tax rates on corporate income and housing.

Differences among marginal effective tax rates on corporate source income, noncorporate income, and owner-occupied housing constituted substantial barriers to efficient allocation of capital for the countries included in our study, except for Sweden. Despite the predominance of reversals of changes in tax rates over the period 1980–90, modest progress was made in reducing these barriers. However, an important limitation of our study is the omission from consideration of special tax treatment of investments in favored regions. Although many of these special provisions were reduced or eliminated during the period 1980–90, Germany is an important exception. A new system of special tax incentives, described in detail by Willi Leibfritz in chapter 5, was instituted in 1990 for investment in former East Germany.

The third and final step is to compare marginal effective tax rates for different types of investments. We focus on corporate tax rates for different assets and industries, since provisions for capital recovery under the corporate income tax are the most important source of differences in tax rates by type of asset and industry. The tax treatment of corporate distributions under both corporate and personal income taxes is important in analyzing differences among financial instruments and ownership forms. For example, tax deductibility of interest at the corporate level must be weighed against personal taxation of interest payments.

Table 1-1 gives marginal effective corporate tax rates for 1980, 1985, and 1990 by type of asset and industry. In 1980 machinery was the most favorably treated type of asset for Australia, Canada, Italy, Sweden, the United Kingdom, and the United States, while inventories were the least favorably treated for Australia, France, Germany, Italy, Japan, Sweden, and the United States. Five countries—France, Italy, Sweden, the United Kingdom, and the United States—had negative tax rates for machinery. Except for the United States, these countries had negative but higher tax rates for inventories. Effective tax rates for machinery and inventories reflected the predominance of investment incentives for machinery in provisions for capital recovery under the corporate tax and the taxation of inflationary gains on inventories at corporate income tax rates.

To compare barriers to efficient allocation of capital among countries and trace the course of tax reforms, it is useful to consider the difference between marginal effective tax rates for the most and least favorably treated assets. In 1980 the largest gap was that for the United Kingdom, at 87.4 percent, while the smallest was that for Japan, at 5.2 percent. For the United States the gap was near the midpoint of this range, at 40.5 percent. Modest tax reforms in the United Kingdom described by King and Robson in chapter 9 cut the gap to 52.2 percent in 1985, while adoption of tax incentives for investment in Australia outlined by Jones in chapter 2 more than doubled this gap, from 27.6 to 59.5 percent. In addition, France, Germany, Italy, and the United States increased the difference in tax rates between 1980 and 1985 through enhancement of investment incentives, while Canada, Japan, and Sweden reduced this difference. Japan retained its position as the country with the smallest gap, at only 5.1 percent. Australia, France, Italy, Sweden, the United Kingdom, and the United States had negative tax rates for machinery in 1985.

Australia reversed course and reduced the difference between marginal effective tax rates to only 18.5 percent in 1990, a 41 percentage point decline from 1985. This slightly exceeded the U.S. decline from 47.3 to only 7.8 percent. Canada, France, Germany, Italy, and the United Kingdom also narrowed this gap. For France this reversed the enhancements of incentives between 1980 and 1985 described by Alworth and François Bourguignon in chapter 4. From 1980 to 1990 only France, Italy, and Japan failed to make substantial progress in narrowing the difference between the most and least favorably treated types of assets. In 1990, as in 1980, the United Kingdom had the largest gap at 41.7 percent, less than half that in 1980, and Japan had the smallest gap at only 6.3 percent, essentially unchanged from 1980 and 1985. Only France, Italy, and Sweden retained negative tax rates for machinery in 1990.

The predominant direction of tax policy changes in 1980–85 was to increase differences in effective tax rates among types of assets. This tendency was reversed, however, between 1985 and 1990, when tax incentives for investment in machinery were reduced. Machinery was given the most favorable tax treatment in all countries except Germany and Japan in

1990. France, Italy, and Sweden continued to tax machinery at negative rates. Tax reform efforts from 1980 to 1990 resulted in a definite trend toward leveling the playing field by equalizing tax rates among assets. These efforts were especially successful in the United States, where the difference between effective tax rates on machinery and inventories fell to 7.8 percent in 1990. In Japan no reforms were required to maintain the lowest differences in effective tax rates among assets for all nine countries for the years 1980, 1985, and 1990.

In 1980 the largest differences in marginal effective corporate tax rates between industries were 66.0 percent between manufacturing and commerce in the United Kingdom and 47.5 percent between manufacturing and other industry in the United States. The smallest differences were 6.6 and 8.9 percent between manufacturing and other industry for Italy and Sweden, respectively. Tax rates were negative for all industries for France, Italy, and Sweden, for manufacturing and other industry in the United Kingdom, and for other industry in the United States. Tax reform narrowed the difference in the United Kingdom to 24.2 percent in 1985. This difference was also reduced in Germany, Japan, and the United States, although the change in Germany was negligible. Tax policy changes increased gaps between the most and least favored industries in Australia, Canada, France, Italy, and Sweden.

Tax reforms between 1985 and 1990 reduced differences among industries in corporate tax rates for Australia, Canada, France, the United Kingdom, and the United States, and increased the differences for Germany, Italy, and Japan. (No information on these differences is available for Sweden.) The changes for Germany and Japan were very small, so that tax policy changes predominantly narrowed the gaps. This represented a substantial reversal from tax policy changes for 1980–85 for Australia, Canada, and France. From 1980 to 1990 only Germany and Italy failed to reduce differences in tax rates between most and least favored industries. Germany's tax rates for 1980, 1985, and 1990 were essentially unchanged, whereas Italy widened the gap from 6.6 percent in 1980 to 10.9 percent in 1985 and, finally, to 13.6 percent in 1990.

The overall trend in tax policy changes from 1980 to 1990 was to reduce differences in marginal effective corporate tax rates between the most and least favored industries. These efforts achieved the greatest success in the United Kingdom and the United States, where the gaps were reduced by almost 50 percentage points and more than 25 percentage points, respectively. Australia, Canada, France, and Japan succeeded in narrowing the gaps to less than 10 percent. Italy was an exception to this trend, with steadily widening gaps among industries throughout the period.

Differences among marginal effective tax rates by type of asset and industry for noncorporate enterprises presented in table 1-4 largely reflect the differences among these tax rates for corporations given in table 1-1. Tax incentives included in provisions for capital recovery favor investment in machinery for all countries except Japan in 1980, all countries except Japan, Germany, and the United Kingdom in 1985, and all countries except Germany and Japan in 1990. In 1980 and 1985, Italy, Sweden, and the United States had negative tax rates for machinery, but these were eliminated in 1990 for all three countries. Differences in tax rates among industries exceeded 10 percent in 1990 only for France and Italy. The most important remaining opportunities for gains in the efficiency of capital allocation within the noncorporate sector are through equalizing tax rates for different types of assets. Tax reforms similar to those I have suggested for corporations would be the most effective to achieve these gains.

Marginal effective corporate tax rates for debt finance presented in table 1-1 were negative for 1980, 1985, and 1990 for every country included in our study. These tax rates were also well below the corresponding rates for equity finance for every country except Australia in 1990, where the rates on debt and new share issues were the same. Combining provisions of corporate and personal taxes in table 1-3, one finds that marginal effective tax rates on corporate source income were negative for debt finance only for Italy, Japan, and the United States for 1980. These three countries, together with Australia, had negative tax rates for debt in 1985, but Australia and the United States eliminated negative rates while Germany adopted a negative rate in 1990. With the important exception of the United Kingdom, tax rates for debt finance were below those for equity in all three years.

Differences among marginal effective corporate tax rates by form of ownership presented in table 1-1 were relatively unimportant by comparison with differences by source of finance. Marginal effective tax rates on corporate source income given in table 1-3 reveal that with few exceptions households had higher tax rates than tax-exempt institutions and insurance companies. Insurance companies in Australia and Japan had higher rates for 1980, 1985, and 1990. Tax-exempt institutions had higher rates in Australia, France, and Italy in 1985 and France and Italy in 1990. In 1990 substantial gaps among tax rates remained for all countries except

Japan and the United Kingdom. These gaps indicate important opportunities for further gains in efficiency of capital allocation through tax reform.

Marginal effective tax rates by source of finance for noncorporate enterprises largely reflect the differences for corporations given in table 1-3. Tax deductibility of interest under the personal income tax results in lower tax rates for debt than for equity for all countries except the United States in 1980, 1985, and 1990. In 1980 the difference between tax rates on debt and equity is greatest for Sweden, 123.0 percent, and least for the United Kingdom, 0.4 percent. In 1985 this gap was also largest for Sweden, 125.9 percent, and smallest for the United Kingdom, 1.8 percent. Finally, in 1990 the gap was largest for Italy, 64.7 percent, and smallest for the United Kingdom, 1.6 percent.

Marginal effective tax rates for debt were higher than those for equity finance for owner-occupied housing in 1980, 1985, and 1990 for Australia, Canada, Germany, and Japan, and higher for equity than debt for France, Italy, Sweden, and the United States. Tax rates for debt were negative for Japan and Sweden in 1980 and 1985 and negative for equity for Japan in 1980, 1985, and 1990. I conclude that debt was favored relative to equity for corporate and noncorporate sectors in almost all countries included in our study. Elimination of tax deductibility of interest in corporate and personal income taxes would provide an obvious remedy. For housing the elimination of tax deductibility of mortgage interest presents a similar opportunity for tax reform in many countries, including the United States.

In conclusion, very significant progress in reducing differences in tax rates among assets, industries, or both has been made by every country except Italy. However, opportunities remain for further gains in efficiency of capital allocation through reducing these differences. This can be done by eliminating the remaining investment incentives from provisions for capital recovery, especially accelerated capital consumption allowances for machinery, and reducing taxation of inflationary gains on inventories by permitting taxpayers to substitute LIFO (last in, first out) for FIFO (first in, first out) inventory accounting. Except for Sweden, important opportunities also exist to improve efficiency through the elimination of the tax-favored status of owner-occupied housing.

Another important goal for tax reform in all countries is to reduce the special tax treatment of debt finance and the tax-favored status of tax-exempt institutions and insurance companies. High priority should also be given to the elimination of tax deductibility of mortgage interest for owner-occupied housing. This is an important source of the tax advantages given to investment in housing in many countries, including the United States. Obviously, much remains to be accomplished before the goal of equalizing marginal effective tax rates on all forms of income from capital is achieved.

## Alternative Approaches

Many of the most important issues in the implementation of marginal effective tax rates have been debated for nearly three decades, following the introduction of the cost of capital by Jorgenson.[21] The first of these issues is the incorporation of inflation in asset prices. This was the focus of a detailed empirical comparison of the effects of alternative measures of the cost of capital on investment expenditures by Jorgenson and Calvin D. Siebert.[22] The assumption of perfect foresight or rational expectations of inflation emerged as the most appropriate formulation and has been used in almost all measures of marginal effective tax rates, including those in the preceding section of this chapter.

The second empirical issue in the implementation of the cost of capital is the measurement of economic depreciation. Charles R. Hulten and Frank C. Wykoff developed the econometric methodology appropriate for this purpose.[23] This methodology is based on modeling the acquisition prices of assets as a function of age. The important innovation by Hulten and Wykoff was to take account of the fact that the sample of used-asset prices is "censored" by retirements of assets from service. Hulten and Wykoff have shown that censoring must be taken into account in estimating the rate of depreciation. They have also demonstrated that geometric decline in efficiency of assets provides a satisfactory approximation of the actual decline in efficiency of durable goods.[24]

The empirical research of Hulten and Wykoff rekindled the debate over the decline in efficiency of assets with age.[25] The stability of patterns of decline in efficiency in the face of changes in tax policy and shocks such as the sharp rise in energy prices during the 1970s was carefully

---

21. Jorgenson (1963, 1965).
22. Jorgenson and Siebert (1968a, 1968b, 1972).
23. Hulten and Wykoff (1981b).
24. See, especially, Hulten and Wykoff (1981b, p. 387).
25. This debate is summarized by Biorn (1989) and Jorgenson (1989).

documented by Hulten, James W. Robertson, and Wykoff. They concluded that "the use of a single number to characterize the process of
economic depreciation (of a given type of capital asset) seems justified in
light of the results of this chapter."[26] Measures of economic depreciation
based on those of Hulten and Wykoff[27] have been used in constructing
estimates of marginal effective tax rates by Hulten and Wykoff, Jorgenson
and Sullivan, King and Fullerton, Jorgenson and Yun, and the OECD,[28]
and in the preceding section of this chapter.

The third empirical issue in the measurement of the cost of capital is
the description of complex tax provisions for capital-cost recovery. The
cost-of-capital formula originally used by Jorgenson allowed for differences between tax and economic depreciation.[29] The modeling of provisions for capital-cost recovery as the present value of reductions in tax
liabilities was the crucial innovation in the papers of Robert E. Hall and
Jorgenson.[30] This important reformulation of the cost of capital has been
adopted in almost all subsequent studies, including those in the preceding
section of this chapter.

Initially, the modeling of tax provisions for capital-cost recovery was
based on the assumption that taxpayers choose among alternative for-
mulas so as to minimize their tax liabilities. This assumption was used,
for example, by Hall and Jorgenson and by Laurits R. Christensen and
Jorgenson.[31] A detailed study of actual practices for calculating capital consumption allowances and the investment tax credit for the United
States was carried out by Jorgenson and Sullivan.[32] The resulting description has been used in many subsequent studies, including those of King
and Fullerton and Jorgenson and Yun.[33]

The introduction of the marginal effective tax rate by Alan J. Auerbach and Jorgenson was limited to the effective corporate tax rate.[34] The
resolution of major issues concerning the appropriate representation of
inflation in asset prices, depreciation in the value of assets with age, and
tax incentives for investment—such as capital consumption allowances

26. Hulten, Robertson, and Wykoff (1989, p. 255).

27. Hulten and Wykoff (1981b).

28. Hulten and Wykoff (1981a); Jorgenson and Sullivan (1981); King and Fullerton (1984); Jorgenson and Yun (1991b); OECD (1991).

29. Jorgenson (1963, 1965).

30. Hall and Jorgenson (1967, 1969, 1971).

31. Christensen and Jorgenson (1969, 1973).

32. Jorgenson and Sullivan (1981).

33. King and Fullerton (1984); Jorgenson and Yun (1986b, 1991b).

34. Auerbach and Jorgenson (1980).

and the investment tax credit—cleared the way for detailed measurement of marginal effective corporate tax rates for the United States by Jorgenson and Sullivan, Hulten and Wykoff, and many others.[35]

The integration of corporate and personal income tax provisions into the marginal effective tax rate for corporate-source income was initiated by Robert E. Hall.[36] This tax rate, including both corporate and personal taxes, provided the basis for the detailed studies of taxation of the corporate sector in Canada by Robin Boadway, Neil Bruce, and Jack M. Mintz, and Germany, Sweden, the United Kingdom, and the United States by King and Fullerton.[37] Fullerton, as well as Fullerton, Robert Gillette, and James Mackie, gave comparisons among tax rates for corporate, noncorporate, and housing sectors for the United States.[38]

The marginal effective tax rates presented in the preceding section must be carefully distinguished from the average effective tax rates introduced by Harberger.[39] Marginal and average tax rates differ substantially, since changes in tax laws usually apply only to new assets. Since new and existing assets are perfect substitutes in production in the model of capital as a factor of production, it is marginal rather than average rates that are relevant to measurements of distortions in the allocation of capital. Leonard G. Rosenberg presented a set of average effective tax rates for the United States for the period 1953–59 that includes a breakdown by forty-five industry groups.[40] The average effective tax rates given by Harberger[41] and Rosenberg include corporate income taxes and property taxes, but do not incorporate individual taxes on distributions from corporate and noncorporate business. Harberger included taxes on dividends paid by the corporate sector as well as taxes on capital gains realized by holders of corporate equity.[42]

Martin S. Feldstein and Lawrence H. Summers have presented average effective tax rates for the U.S. corporate sector that incorporate individual as well as corporate income tax liabilities.[43] The estimates of Feldstein

---

35. Jorgenson and Sullivan (1981), Hulten and Wykoff (1981a). Effective corporate tax rates are also presented by Bradford and Fullerton (1981) and Hall (1981), and, subsequently, by Gravelle (1982), Auerbach (1983a, 1987), and Hulten and Robertson (1984).

36. Hall (1981); alternative marginal effective tax rate concepts are compared and analyzed by Bradford and Fullerton (1981).

37. Boadway, Bruce, and Mintz (1984); King and Fullerton (1984).

38. Fullerton (1987); Fullerton, Gillette, and Mackie (1987).

39. Harberger (1962, 1966).

40. Rosenberg (1969).

41. Harberger (1962).

42. Harberger's estimates (1966) were revised and corrected by Shoven (1976).

43. Feldstein and Summers (1979).

and Summers cover 1954–77 and are given separately for twenty two-digit industries within manufacturing. The estimates for the corporate sector as a whole have been updated and revised to cover 1953–78 by Feldstein, 1953–79 by Feldstein, Louis Dicks-Mireaux, and James Poterba, and 1953–84 by Feldstein and Joosung Jun.[44]

Since the effect of the personal income tax on the corporate cost of capital depends on the determinants of corporate financial policy, the incorporation of personal taxes into the corporate cost of capital has raised a host of new issues. A number of alternative approaches to taxation and corporate finance have been discussed in the literature.[45] In the new view proposed by King, the corporation retains earnings sufficient to finance the equity portion of investment and dividends are determined by the residual cash flow.[46] The marginal source of equity funds is retained earnings, so the rate of return on corporate source income does not depend on the taxation of dividends at the personal level. The tax rate on dividends does not affect the rental price of capital services or the effective tax rate on corporate source income.

Under the new view of corporate finance and taxation, the most attractive investment opportunity available to the corporation is to liquidate its assets and repurchase its outstanding shares. Each dollar of assets liquidated reduces the value of the firm's outstanding shares. However, if repurchasing the firm's outstanding shares is ruled out by assumption, equity is "trapped" in the firm and it makes sense for the firm to continue holding assets. Accordingly, this view of corporate taxation has been characterized as the "trapped-equity" approach.[47]

Jorgenson and Yun have presented an alternative model of the cost of capital in the corporate sector based on a fixed ratio of dividends to corporate income.[48] This is the "traditional" view of corporate finance and

44. Feldstein (1982); Feldstein, Dicks-Mireaux, and Poterba (1983); Feldstein and Jun (1987). Fullerton (1984) has discussed the distinction between average and marginal effective tax rates and concludes that empirical measures of effective tax rates based on these two different concepts are not closely related. King and Fullerton (1984, table 6.34, p. 265) provide an estimate of the average effective tax rate for the United States in 1978–80, and the accompanying text provides comparisons with the results of Feldstein, Dicks-Mireaux, and Poterba and the earlier work of Rosenberg.

45. Summaries of the alternative views of taxation and corporate finance are given by Atkinson and Stiglitz (1980, especially pp. 128–59), Auerbach (1983b), and Sinn (1991a).

46. King (1974a, 1974b, 1977); this view is discussed by Auerbach (1979), Bradford (1981), and Sinn (1987).

47. An important issue for the trapped-equity approach is how equity initially enters the firm. A resolution of this issue based on the life cycle of the firm has been proposed by King (1989) and Sinn (1991b).

48. Jorgenson and Yun (1986b, 1991b).

taxation employed, for example, by Harberger, Feldstein and Summers, Charles E. McLure, Jr., and Poterba and Summers.[49] In this view the marginal source of funds for the equity portion of the firm's investments is new share issues, since dividends are fixed. An important implication of the traditional view is that an additional dollar of new issues adds precisely one dollar to the value of the firm's assets, so that the value of outstanding financial liabilities of the firm is equal to the value of the firm's assets.

It is important to emphasize the critical role of the assumption that dividends are a fixed proportion of corporate income in the traditional view of taxation and corporate finance. If the firm were to reduce dividend payments by one dollar and retain the earnings in order to finance investment, stockholders would avoid personal taxes on dividend payments. The addition to retained earnings would result in a capital gain taxed at a lower rate, so that shareholders would experience an increase in wealth. Following this line of reasoning, it would always be in the interest of the shareholders for the firm to finance investment from retained earnings rather than new issues of equity, as in the new view.

As Hans-Werner Sinn has emphasized, both the traditional and the new views of corporate taxation depend critically on assumptions about financial policy of the firm.[50] The traditional view depends on the assumption that dividends are a fixed proportion of corporate income, so that the marginal source of funds for financing investment is new issues of equity. The new view depends on the assumption that new issues of equity (or repurchases) are fixed, so that the marginal source of funds is retained earnings.[51] In fact, firms use both sources of equity finance, sometimes simultaneously. The King-Fullerton framework outlined in the appendix to this chapter is based on the actual distribution of new equity finance from new issues and retained earnings. Since retained earnings greatly predominate over new issues as a source of equity finance, this approach turns out to be empirically equivalent to adopting the new view.[52]

49. Harberger (1966); Feldstein and Summers (1979); McLure (1979); Poterba and Summers (1983, 1985).

50. Sinn (1991a).

51. The third view of taxation and corporate finance presented by Stiglitz (1973) drops the assumption that the debt-equity ratio is fixed, so that the cheapest source of finance is debt, which is tax deductible at the corporate level. This provides an interesting rationale for the Modigliani-Miller (1958, 1961) theory of corporate finance in which dividend policy and the financial structure of the firm are independent of tax policy.

52. Sinn (1991a) has suggested choosing new issues and retained earnings so as to minimize the cost of equity finance. The results presented in table 1-3 show that this is also empirically equivalent to the new view for most countries.

A satisfactory resolution of issues that have been raised in taxation and corporate finance would require the formulation of a theory of corporate finance with endogenous determination of financial structure and dividend policy.[53] A possible avenue for development of such a theory might be to require explicit incorporation of uncertainty about the returns from capital. The incorporation of uncertainty into the cost of capital by means of risk-adjusted rates of return has been discussed by Auerbach, Jeremy I. Bulow and Summers, and John B. Shoven.[54]

An important implication of the new view of taxation and corporate finance is that investment expenditures of the firm are independent of the rate of taxation of dividends at the individual level. Poterba and Summers have presented the results of tests of this hypothesis that support the traditional view, while Auerbach has presented evidence that the cost of capital for new issues is higher than that for retained earnings.[55] These findings support the new view.[56]

The second set of issues raised by the introduction of personal taxes into the corporate cost of capital relates to the treatment of debt and equity in the corporate tax structure. Jorgenson and Yun, and King and Fullerton, have assumed that debt-capital ratios are the same for all assets within the corporate sector. Barry Bosworth, and Gordon, Hines, and Summers, have argued that different types of assets should be associated with different debt-equity ratios.[57] Empirical evidence supporting the view that debt-equity ratios are independent of the composition of assets has been provided by Auerbach and Jane C. Gravelle.[58]

The inclusion of personal taxes on corporate distributions to holders of equity also raises more specific issues concerning the impact of inflation on asset prices. A comprehensive treatment of these issues is provided by Feldstein.[59] Since nominal interest expenses are deductible at the corporate level while nominal interest payments are taxable at the individual level, an important issue is the impact of inflation on nominal interest rates. Feldstein and Summers have assumed that Fisher's Law holds; namely, that a change in inflation is reflected point for point in changes

---

53. This has been suggested,for example, by Scott (1987).

54. Auerbach (1983a), Bulow and Summers (1984), Shoven (1990).

55. Poterba and Summers (1983, 1985), Auerbach (1984).

56. Jorgenson and Yun (1986b, 1991b); King and Fullerton (1984).

57. Bosworth (1985); Gordon, Hines, and Summers (1987). Sunley (1987) has disputed this assertion. Ballentine (1987) has suggested resolving this issue by making the debt-equity ratio endogenous.

58. Auerbach (1983a); Gravelle (1987).

59. Feldstein (1983).

in nominal interest rates.[60] This assumption is used by Jorgenson and Yun.[61] King and Fullerton have used a modified version of Fisher's Law in which nominal rates of return after tax increase point for point with the rate of inflation.[62] Empirical support for Fisher's Law is provided by Summers.[63]

The second issue in the impact of inflation on the cost of capital is the relationship between accrual and realization of capital gains. As pointed out earlier in this section, capital gains are taxed when they are realized and not when they are accrued. However, capital consumption allowances for used assets reflect the price at which an asset is acquired. This presents opportunities for "churning"; that is, selling assets, realizing capital gains, and acquiring a higher basis for capital consumption allowances. Optimal strategies for churning are analyzed by Robert H. Gordon, James R. Hines, Jr., and Summers, and by Gravelle.[64] Emil M. Sunley argues that churning is negligible empirically, a view Gravelle supports with empirical evidence.[65]

The final set of issues in corporate finance relates to more detailed descriptions of the tax structure for capital income. These issues revolve around multiperiod tax rules. For example, firms experiencing losses may be unable to avail themselves of the tax benefits of deductions for interest, depreciation, and other expenses. However, some of these benefits may be carried forward to periods in which the firms make profits. A general approach to this problem has been developed by Auerbach and implemented empirically for data on individual firms by Auerbach and Poterba.[66] J. Gregory Ballentine has argued for the incorporation of these and other tax provisions for specific assets into marginal effective tax-rate calculations.[67] Fullerton, Gillette, and Mackie have examined the importance of these provisions and have concluded that the impact on marginal effective tax rates for industry groups is relatively modest.[68] Obviously, the importance of this issue is much greater at the level of the individual firm.

60. Feldstein and Summers (1979).
61. Jorgenson and Yun (1986b, 1991b).
62. King and Fullerton (1984).
63. Summers (1983). However, see the exchange between McCallum (1984, 1986) and Summers (1986).
64. Gordon, Hines, and Summers (1987); Gravelle (1987).
65. Sunley (1987); Gravelle (1987).
66. Auerbach (1986); Auerbach and Poterba (1987).
67. Ballentine (1987).
68. Fullerton, Gillette, and Mackie (1987).

An important objective of further research in taxation and corporate finance will be to endogenize the responses of debt-capital and dividend-payout ratios to changes in tax policy at both corporate and personal levels. In addition, more detailed features of the tax structure, such as opportunities for "churning" and, more generally, optimal realization of capital gains, must be encompassed by the theory. Finally, a more finely grained description of tax statutes, including the complexities introduced by provisions for multiperiod treatment of corporate income, tax deductions, and tax credits, must be utilized.[69]

## Summary and Conclusion

The purpose of this section is to evaluate the usefulness of the cost of capital as a practical guide to tax reform. The primary focus is U.S. tax reform, since the cost of capital has been used much more extensively in the United States than in the other countries analyzed in this chapter. Auerbach and Jorgenson introduced the key concept, the *marginal effective tax rate*, early in the debate over the U.S. Economic Recovery Tax Act of 1981.[70] They used this concept as a means of comparing the tax burdens among different types of assets under the provisions for capital-cost recovery ultimately incorporated into the 1981 tax act.

The initial results of applying the cost-of-capital approach to the 1981 tax act had no effect on the final legislation. However, this approach spread very rapidly among the community of tax policy analysts, both inside and outside the U.S. government. The initial impetus for the diffusion of the cost-of-capital approach was testimony by Jorgenson before the Senate Committee on Finance on October 22, 1979, and the House Committee on Ways and Means on November 14, 1979.[71] This testimony included the first presentation of marginal effective tax rates, based on the work of Auerbach and Jorgenson.

A milestone in the diffusion of the cost-of-capital approach was provided by the Conference on Depreciation, Inflation, and the Taxation of Income from Capital, held at the Urban Institute in Washington, D.C., on December 1, 1980. The participants in this conference included tax analysts from universities, research institutions, the U.S. Department of

69. An important reformulation of the theory of taxation and corporate finance dealing with many of these issues has been presented by Scholes and Wolfson (1992).

70. Auerbach and Jorgenson (1980).

71. Jorgenson (1979a, 1979b). These committees have responsibility for all tax legislation emanating from the U.S. Congress.

the Treasury, and the staff of Congress. Key papers on the implementation of the-cost-of-capital approach by Bradford and Fullerton, Hall, Hulten and Wykoff, and Jorgenson and Sullivan were presented at the conference. The publication of the conference proceedings in 1981 was followed shortly by presentation of the first official estimates of marginal effective tax rates by the President's Council of Economic Advisers.[72]

The literature on the cost-of-capital approach developed at an explosive pace during the early 1980s, leading up to the presentation of the Treasury proposal, requested by President Reagan, in November 1984.[73] The proposal was accompanied by marginal effective corporate tax rates for different types of assets. A primary objective of the proposal was to "level the playing field" by equalizing marginal effective tax rates on business assets. A second objective was to insulate the definition of capital income from the impact of inflation. However, leveling the playing field between the household and business sectors was not included among the objectives of the Treasury proposal.[74]

The initial application of the cost-of-capital approach to tax policy analysis was based on the inclusion of investment functions incorporating the cost of capital in macroeconometric forecasting models. Investment functions of this type were first proposed for the Brookings quarterly econometric model of the United States by Jorgenson.[75] By the beginning of the debate over the Economic Recovery Tax Act of 1981, the investment equations for all major forecasting models for the U.S. economy had incorporated the cost of capital.[76] Simulations of alternative tax policies by means of these models had become the staple fare of debate over the economic impact of specific tax proposals.[77]

An important issue in this type of application, emphasized by Robert E. Lucas, Jr., in his critique of econometric methods for policy evaluation, is the modeling of expectations of future prices of investment goods.[78] This is required in measuring the cost of capital and simulating the impact of

72. President's Council of Economic Advisers (1982).

73. This proposal is described by the U.S. Department of the Treasury (1984).

74. The political reasons for this crucial omission are discussed by McLure (1986).

75. Jorgenson (1965). A much more detailed version of this model was constructed by Jorgenson and Stephenson (1967a, 1967b, 1969) and Jorgenson and Handel (1971). A detailed review of the initial studies of investment behavior incorporating the cost of capital is given by Jorgenson (1971a).

76. See, for example, Chirinko and Eisner (1983) and Gravelle (1984).

77. Illustrations of this type of simulation study are provided by Jorgenson (1971b) and Gordon and Jorgenson (1976), using modifications of the DRI quarterly econometric model of the United States.

78. Lucas (1976).

changes in tax policy on investment expenditures. The resolution of this issue can be found in the model of capital as a factor of production. The key dynamic relationships are an accumulation equation, which expresses capital stock as a weighted sum of past investments, and a capital asset pricing equation, which expresses the price of acquisition of investment goods as the sum of future rental prices of capital services. Both these relationships must be incorporated into the simulation of the effects of changes in tax policy. Macroeconometric models have incorporated the backward-looking equation for capital stock but have omitted the forward-looking equation for the price of investment goods.

The reason for the omission of the capital-asset pricing equation from macroeconometric models is that such an equation would have required simulation techniques appropriate for perfect foresight or rational expectations. These techniques were introduced by David Lipton and others, and Ray C. Fair and John B. Taylor, long after the methodology for constructing and simulating macroeconometric forecasting models had crystallized.[79] To evaluate the economic impact of the 1981 tax reforms, Jorgenson and Yun constructed a dynamic general-equilibrium model that incorporates both the backward-looking equation for capital stock in terms of past investment and the forward-looking equation for the price of acquisition of investment goods in terms of future prices of capital services.[80]

Shortly after the passage of the Tax Reform Act of 1986, the Office of Tax Analysis of the U.S. Treasury published a detailed study of the impact of the new legislation on marginal effective tax rates.[81] The results were incorporated into an applied general equilibrium model of the U.S. economy by Fullerton, Yolanda K. Henderson, and Mackie and used to estimate the economic impact of the 1986 tax act.[82] Fullerton presented a closely related study of marginal effective tax rates; Fullerton and Henderson incorporated the results into an applied general equilibrium model of the U.S. economy and analyzed the impact of the legislation and directions for future tax reform.[83] However, these applied general equilibrium models did not include the capital asset pricing equation and are subject to the "Lucas critique."

79. Lipton and others (1982); Fair and Taylor (1983).
80. Jorgenson and Yun (1986a). As suggested by Lucas (1976), this model also includes expectations about future changes in tax policy.
81. Fullerton, Gillette, and Mackie (1987).
82. Fullerton, Henderson, and Mackie (1987).
83. Fullerton (1987); Fullerton and Henderson (1989).

Jorgenson and Yun have evaluated the economic impact of the 1986 tax reform, using a new version of their dynamic general equilibrium model of the U.S. economy.[84] In this model, equilibrium is characterized by an intertemporal price system that clears the markets for all four commodity groups included in the model—labor services, capital services, consumption goods, and investment goods. Equilibrium at each point of time links the past and the future through markets for investment goods and capital services. Assets are accumulated as a result of past investments, while the prices of assets must be equal to the present values of future capital services. The time path of consumption must satisfy the conditions for intertemporal optimality of the household sector under perfect foresight. Similarly, the time path of investment must satisfy requirements for the accumulation of assets by both business and household sectors.

Jorgenson and Yun have summarized the 1986 tax reform in terms of changes in tax rates, the treatment of deductions from income for tax purposes, the availability of tax credits, and provisions for indexing taxable income for inflation.[85] They have also summarized proposals for tax reform that figured prominently in the debate leading up to the 1986 tax act. For this purpose they used the concepts of marginal effective tax rates and tax wedges, defined in terms of differences in tax burdens imposed on different forms of income. These gaps are indicators of the likely impact of substitutions among different kinds of capital induced by changes in tax policy.

In other studies Jorgenson and Yun have analyzed the impact of each of the alternative tax policies on U.S. economic growth.[86] They have also evaluated the effects of changes in tax policy on economic efficiency by measuring the corresponding changes in potential economic welfare. The reference level of welfare, which serves as the basis of comparison among alternative tax policies, is the level attainable by the U.S. economy under the tax law in effect prior to the 1986 tax reform. Finally, they have analyzed losses in efficiency associated with tax wedges among different kinds of capital income.

Jorgenson and Yun found that much of the potential gain in welfare from the 1986 tax reform was dissipated through failure to index the income tax base for inflation. At rates of inflation near zero the loss is not

---

84. Jorgenson and Yun (1990, 1991a). Henderson (1991) surveys six studies of the economic impact of the 1986 tax act by means of applied general-equilibrium models.

85. Jorgenson and Yun (1991b).

86. Jorgenson and Yun (1990, 1991a).

substantial. However, at moderate rates of inflation, like those prevailing since the early 1980s, the loss is highly significant. Second, the greatest welfare gains would have resulted from incorporating the income from household assets into the tax base, while reducing tax rates on income from business assets. The potential welfare gains from an income-based tax system, reconstructed along these lines, would have exceeded those from an expenditure-based system.

My conclusion is that the cost-of-capital approach to tax policy analysis has proved its value as a guide to the formulation of proposals to improve the taxation of income from capital in the United States. The initial focus of the cost-of-capital approach originated by Auerbach and Jorgenson was on the allocation of capital within the corporate sector. This focus also characterized the extensions of the cost-of-capital approach by others.[87] More recent work has also encompassed allocation between business and household sectors. The tax policy changes of the early 1980s, especially the 1981 tax act, increased barriers to efficient allocation of capital. By contrast, the 1986 tax act reduced these barriers substantially.

It must be emphasized that effective tax rates or tax wedges do not provide a complete analysis of the distortionary effects of capital-income taxation. The distortion of resource allocation depends on substitutability between assets as well as the tax wedges. As an example, consider the allocation of capital between short-lived and long-lived depreciable assets in the corporate sector. Even if the interasset difference in tax treatment is large, the distortion of capital allocation can be small if the services of the two types of assets are not substitutable. Similarly, the distortion in the allocation of resources for consumption over time can be small if intertemporal substitutability in consumption is small.

The analysis of the economic impact of tax policy requires the integration of the cost of capital into macroeconometric models and applied general equilibrium models. The impact of the Tax Reform Act of 1986 has been analyzed by means of models of both types. The Jorgenson-Yun model incorporates long-run dynamics based on the backward-looking accumulation equation for capital stock and the forward-looking asset-pricing equation for the acquisition price of investment goods. Each tax policy is associated with an intertemporal equilibrium based on optimization by producers and consumers. This equilibrium includes markets for different types of capital, including corporate, noncorporate, and house-

---

87. See Boadway, Bruce, and Mintz (1984); King and Fullerton (1984).

hold capital, broken down by short-lived and long-lived assets. The detailed disaggregation exposes all the margins for substitution affected by changes in tax policy.

The cost-of-capital approach to tax policy analysis will continue to be a useful guide to tax reform within the framework of the corporate and individual income tax. Income taxation remains the primary basis for taxation in the United States and all the other countries analyzed in this book. The shift toward expenditure and away from income as a basis for taxation in the 1970s was reversed during the 1980s. The erosion of the income tax base to provide tax incentives for investment and saving has been arrested through vigorous and far-reaching tax-reform efforts in many of the countries included in our study. Investment incentives have been curtailed and efforts have been made to equalize marginal effective tax rates among corporate, noncorporate, and household sectors.

The intellectual impetus for recent tax-reform efforts has been provided by the cost of capital and the closely related concept of the marginal effective tax rate. Effective tax rates at both corporate and personal levels are now available for many countries around the world. In this book our objective is to use the results for an international comparison of tax reforms for income from capital. This comparison provides extensive illustrations of the work on the cost of capital that has been accomplished, using data sources of the type that are readily available for most industrialized countries. Our hope is that these illustrations will serve as an inspiration for policymakers who share our goal of making the allocation of capital within a market economy more efficient.

## Appendix: King-Fullerton Framework

The starting point for presentation of the King-Fullerton framework is the concept of a tax wedge.[88] Presentation of this concept requires the following notation: $p$ is the before-tax rate of return, and $s$ is the after-tax rate of return.

The tax wedge, $w$, is defined as the difference between before-tax and after-tax rates of return:

$$(1A-1) \qquad w = p - s.$$

---

88. A more detailed presentation is given by King and Fullerton (1984, pp. 7–30).

Given the tax wedge one can define the effective tax rate, $t$, as the ratio of the tax wedge to the before-tax rate of return $p$:

(1A-2)
$$t = \frac{w}{p} = \frac{p - s}{p}.$$

To express the tax wedge as the sum of components associated with provisions of corporate and personal taxes I introduce the notation $q$— after-corporate, before-personal tax rate of return.

The corporate tax wedge, $w_c$, is defined as the difference between the before-tax rate of return and the after-corporate, before-personal tax rate of return:

(1A-3)
$$w_c = p - q.$$

Similarly, the personal tax wedge, $w_p$, is defined as the difference between the after-corporate, before-personal tax rate of return and the after-tax rate of return:

(1A-4)
$$w_p = q - s.$$

The tax wedge equation (1A-1) is the sum of corporate and personal tax wedges (equations 1A-3 and 1A-4),

$$w = w_c + w_p,$$

since

$$p - s = (p - q) + (q - s).$$

Given the corporate tax wedge equation (1A-3), one can define the effective corporate tax rate $t_c$, as the ratio of corporate tax wedge to the before-tax rate of return:

(1A-5)
$$t_c = \frac{w_c}{p} = \frac{p - q}{p}.$$

Similarly, given the personal tax wedge (equation 1A-4), one can define the effective personal tax rate, $t_p$, as the ratio of the personal tax wedge to the after-corporate, before-personal tax rate of return:

(1A-6)
$$t_p = \frac{w_p}{q} = \frac{q - s}{q}.$$

The effective tax rates (equations 1A-2, 1A-5, and 1A-6) satisfy the identity

$$1 - t = (1 - t_c)(1 - t_p),$$

so that

$$t = t_c + t_p - t_c t_p,$$

since

$$\frac{s}{p} = \frac{q}{p} \cdot \frac{s}{q}.$$

The measurement of effective tax rates depends on statutory tax rates and the definition of taxable income at both corporate and personal levels. This information is summarized by means of the cost of capital. The simplest form of the cost of capital arises in a model of capital as a factor of production.[89] The rental price of capital services is the unit cost of using a capital good for a specified period of time. For example, a building can be leased for a number of months or years, an automobile can be rented for a number of days or weeks, and computer time can be purchased by the second or the minute. The cost of capital transforms the acquisition price of an asset into an appropriate rental price.

The distinguishing feature of capital as a factor of production is that durable goods contribute services to production at different points in time. The technology of this model is described in terms of *relative efficiencies* of capital goods of different ages. The relative efficiency of a capital good depends on the age of the good and not on the time it is acquired. When a capital good is retired, its relative efficiency drops to zero. For simplicity I assume that the relative efficiencies of durable goods of different ages decline geometrically.[90] The rate of decline in efficiency, $\delta$, is constant, so that the relative efficiencies take the form

$$1, 1 - \delta, (1 - \delta)^2 \ldots,$$

where I normalize the relative efficiency of a new durable good at unity.

In the durable-goods model of production, the rental prices of capital goods of different ages are proportional to the rental price of a new capital good. The constants of proportionality are the relative efficiencies $(1 - \delta)^\tau$. The acquisition price of investment goods is the present value of future rental prices of capital services, weighted by the relative efficiencies of

89. Capital as a factor of production has been discussed by Jorgenson (1967), Diewert (1980), and Hulten (1990).

90. While the assumption of geometric decline in relative efficiency of capital goods is a convenient simplification, this assumption is inessential to modeling capital as a factor of production. For a more general treatment, see Jorgenson (1973, 1989) and Biorn (1989).

capital goods in each future period. The future rental prices are discounted in order to express prices for different time periods in terms of present values. Depreciation is the decline in the acquisition price of a durable good with age. The acquisition price declines geometrically with age, so that the rate of depreciation is constant, where $\delta$ is the rate of depreciation.

The before-tax rate of return $p$ can be expressed in terms of the cost of capital, net of depreciation, $c(q)$:

$$(1A-7) \qquad p = c(q) = \frac{1 - A}{1 - \tau}(q + \delta) - \delta,$$

where $q$ is the after-corporate, before-personal tax rate of return, $\delta$ is the rate of depreciation, $A$ is the present value of allowances for capital recovery, and $\tau$ is the corporate tax rate.

Provisions for recovery of investment expenditures under the corporate income tax can be summarized by means of the present value of allowances for capital recovery.[91]

$$(1A-8) \qquad A = f_1 A_d + f_2 \tau + f_3 g,$$

where $f_1, f_2, f_3$ are proportions of an asset subject to "standard" capital-consumption allowances, immediate expensing, and grants or subsidies, respectively; $A_d$ is the present value of capital consumption allowances; and $g$ is the rate of grant or subsidy.

To integrate provisions of the personal income tax into the cost of capital, I consider the tax treatment of corporate distributions in the form of interest, dividends, and capital gains. Under debt finance these distributions take the form of interest payments, so that the rate of return after corporate and personal taxes, $s$, is

$$(1A-9) \qquad s = (1 - m)i - \pi,$$

where $\pi$ is the inflation rate, $i$ is the interest rate, not corrected for inflation, and $m$ is the marginal personal tax rate on interest income.

If interest is deductible from corporate income for tax purposes, the rate of return after corporate tax but before personal tax $q$ is

$$(1A-10) \qquad q = (1 - \tau)i - \pi,$$

where $\tau$ is the corporate tax rate.

---

91. This approach to modeling provisions for capital recovery was introduced by Hall and Jorgenson (1967, 1969, 1971).

The tax treatment of dividends and capital gains depends on whether the corporate and personal income taxes are integrated. Under a *classical* corporate income tax like that in the United States, no additional tax is collected or refunded when dividends are paid out.[92] Under a *partial imputation* system, like that in France and the United Kingdom, a personal tax credit is attached to dividends paid out or dividends are subject to lower tax rates at the personal level. Under a *full imputation* system, like that in Australia, Germany, and Italy, dividends are fully deductible from income under the corporate tax in the same way that interest is, so that dividends are taxed at personal rather than corporate tax rates. Various other forms of partial tax relief of shareholders are used in Canada, Japan, and Sweden.

To represent alternative corporate income tax systems, King and Fullerton introduce a variable $\theta$ that reflects the degree of discrimination between retentions and distributions in the tax system.[93] This variable is defined as the additional dividends stockholders would receive if an additional unit of earnings after corporate taxes were distributed. For a classical system the variable $\theta$ is equal to unity, since the distribution of dividends does not affect corporate tax liabilities. For a partial imputation system the variable is

$$\theta = \frac{1}{1 - c},$$

where $c$ is the rate of imputation of corporate income tax to stockholders. For a full imputation system the parameter is

$$\theta = \frac{1}{1 - \tau},$$

where $\tau$ is the corporate tax rate, since dividends are fully deductible at the corporate level.

I have defined tax wedges for projects that are debt financed. Now these wedges can be considered for projects financed by new share issues and retained earnings. For new share issues the dividend yield after corporate taxes, net of tax credits at the personal level, must be equal to the stockholder's opportunity cost of funds, both after personal taxes. The

92. The U.S. Department of the Treasury (1984, 1992) has recommended replacing the classical system with a partial imputation system. Integration of corporate and personal taxes in the United States has been discussed in detail by McLure (1979).

93. King and Fullerton (1984).

dividend yield is $(1 - m)\theta(q + \pi)$ and the opportunity cost is $(1 - m)i$, where $m$ is the marginal personal tax rate on dividends. The rate of return after corporate taxes, but before personal taxes, $q$, is

$$(1A\text{-}11) \qquad\qquad q = \frac{i}{\theta} - \pi.$$

Projects financed through retained earnings enable stockholders to be taxed at the personal level at capital gains rates rather than income tax rates. Since capital gains are taxed upon realization, not as they are accrued, the rate of return after corporate taxes, but before personal taxes, $q$, is

$$(1A\text{-}12) \qquad\qquad q = i\frac{(1 - m)}{(1 - z)} - \pi,$$

where $z$ is the proportion of accrued capital gains subject to taxation.

To complete the King-Fullerton framework for income from depreciable assets originating in the corporate sector it is necessary to incorporate property or wealth taxes. If these taxes are not deductible from corporate income for tax purposes, they are subtracted from the rate of return after corporate taxes in determining the after-corporate, before-personal rate of return. If these taxes are deductible, they must be subtracted from the tax base before one calculates the corporate tax liability. For nondepreciable assets, such as inventories, the rate of depreciation $\delta$ is equal to zero. The corporate income tax base may be defined in terms of inventories at historical cost, so that inflationary gains on inventories are taxed at the corporate rate. This requires further modification of the corporate rate of return.[94]

King and Fullerton consider different types of investment projects by corporate enterprises. For each project they consider a fixed rate of return $p$ before corporate and personal income taxes, which they take to be 10 percent. They then calculate an appropriate rate of return $s$ after corporate and personal income taxes. The difference between the two rates of return is the tax wedge equation (1A-1) used in calculating the marginal effective tax rate equation (1A-2). The international comparisons given in this book also include the rate of return after corporate taxes, but before personal

---

94. Details are given by King and Fullerton (1984, pp. 20–21). Additional modifications required for specific tax provisions of the nine countries included in our study are given in chapters 2 through 10.

taxes, $q$, for each project. The corporate tax wedge and the personal tax wedge (equations 1A-3 and 1A-4) are then determined and used in calculating the marginal effective corporate tax rate and the marginal effective personal tax rate (equations 1A-5 and 1A-6).[95]

The King-Fullerton framework has been extended by defining effective tax rates for projects undertaken by noncorporate enterprises and owner-occupied housing.[96] For this purpose the noncorporate tax wedge is defined as the difference between noncorporate rates of return before and after personal taxes. This tax wedge is strictly analogous to the corporate tax wedge defined above, but with the marginal personal tax rate on noncorporate income $m$ in place of the corporate tax rate $\tau$. All the tax provisions described here for corporate enterprises—capital recovery allowances for depreciable assets, property and wealth taxes, and the treatment of inflationary gains on inventories—must be incorporated into the cost of capital for noncorporate enterprises. For income generated from owner-occupied housing the tax-deductibility of mortgage interest and the tax treatment of wealth and property taxes at the personal level must be taken into account.

King and Fullerton have implemented their framework for hypothetical investment projects in the corporate sector classified into the following categories:

— Classes of assets: machinery, buildings, and inventories.
— Industries: manufacturing, other industry, and commerce.
— Sources of finance: debt, new share issues, and retained earnings.
— Forms of ownership: households, tax-exempt institutions, and insurance companies.[97]

To aggregate rates of return for the eighty-one different types of projects resulting from all the possible combinations of assets, industries, sources

95. King and Fullerton (1984) refer to the approach outlined here as the "fixed-$p$" approach. They also consider a "fixed-$r$" approach, based on a fixed real rate of return $r = i - \pi$ of 5 percent. Under the "fixed-$p$" approach, international comparisons are limited to differences in provisions for taxation of capital income. Poterba (1991) has surveyed a parallel literature on international comparisons of the cost of capital, focusing on differences in the costs of debt and equity finance.

96. Fullerton (1987); Fullerton, Gillette, and Mackie (1987).

97. King and Fullerton (1984). The OECD (1991) study includes only manufacturing industries and considers ownership by stockholders with different marginal tax rates ranging from zero to the top marginal rate in each OECD country. This study is based on the "fixed-$r$" approach rather than the "fixed-$p$" approach employed here.

of finance, and forms of ownership, King and Fullerton define the average rate of return before taxes, $\bar{p}$, as a weighted average of rates of return before taxes for the individual projects:

$$\bar{p} = \sum_{k=1}^{81} p_k \alpha_k,$$

where $p_k$ is the before-tax rate of return on the $k$th project and $\alpha_k$ is the share of the $k$th type of project in total capital stock. Similarly, the average rate of return after taxes, $\bar{s}$, is defined as

$$\bar{s} = \sum_{k=1}^{81} s_k \alpha_k,$$

where $s_k$ is the after-tax rate of return on the $k$th project.

The average tax wedge, $\bar{w}$, is defined as the difference between average before- and after-tax rates of return:

(1A-13)                         $$\bar{w} = \bar{p} - \bar{s}.$$

This average tax wedge is a weighted average of tax wedges for the individual projects:

$$\bar{w} = \sum_{k=1}^{81} (p_k - s_k)\alpha_k,$$

$$= \sum_{k=1}^{81} w_k \alpha_k,$$

where $w_k$ is the tax wedge on the $k$th project.

The average marginal effective tax rate, $\bar{t}$, is defined as the ratio of the average tax wedge $\bar{w}$ to the average rate of return before taxes $\bar{p}$:

$$\bar{t} = \frac{\bar{w}}{\bar{p}},$$

(1A-14)                         $$= \frac{\displaystyle\sum_{k=1}^{81} (p_k - s_k)\alpha_k}{\displaystyle\sum_{k=1}^{81} p_k \alpha_k}.$$

If the rate of return before taxes $p$ is the same for all projects,

$$\bar{t} = \sum_{k=1}^{81} t_k \alpha_k,$$

so that the average effective tax rate is a weighted average of effective tax rates for individual projects.

One can define the average after corporate, before personal tax rate of return, $\bar{q}$, as a weighted average of these rates of return for individual projects:

$$\bar{q} = \sum_{k=1}^{81} q_k \alpha_k.$$

The average corporate tax wedge, $w_c$, can be defined as a weighted average of corporate tax wedges for individual projects:

(1A-15) $$\bar{w}_c = \sum_{k=1}^{81} (s_k - q_k)\alpha_k.$$

Similarly, the average personal tax wedge, $w_p$, can be defined as a weighted average of personal tax wedges for these projects:

(1A-16) $$\bar{w}_p = \sum_{k=1}^{81} (p_k - q_k)\alpha_k.$$

Finally, the average marginal effective corporate and personal tax rates, $\bar{t}_c$ and $\bar{t}_p$, can be defined in terms of the tax wedges (equations 1A-15 and 1A-16), as

(1A-17) $$\bar{t}_c = \frac{\bar{w}_c}{\bar{p}}, \bar{t}_p = \frac{\bar{w}_p}{\bar{q}}.$$

## References

Aaron, Henry J. 1987. "Symposium on Tax Reform." *Journal of Economic Perspectives* 1 (Summer): 7–10.

Alworth, Julian S. 1988. *The Finance, Investment, and Taxation Decisions of Multinationals*. Oxford: Basil Blackwell.

Atkinson, Anthony B., and Joseph E. Stiglitz. 1980. *Lectures on Public Economics*. MIT Press.

Auerbach, Alan J. 1983a. "Corporate Taxation in the U.S." *Brookings Papers on Economic Activity* 2: 451–505.

———. 1983b. "Taxation, Corporate Financial Policy, and the Cost of Capital." *Journal of Economic Literature* 21 (September): 905–40.

———. 1984. "Taxes, Firm Financial Policy and the Cost of Capital: An Empirical Analysis." *Journal of Public Economics* 23 (February–March): 27–57.

———. 1986. "The Dynamic Effects of Tax Law Asymmetries." *Review of Economic Studies* 53 (April): 205–25.

———. 1987. "The Tax Reform Act of 1986 and the Cost of Capital." *Journal of Economic Perspectives* 1 (Summer): 73–86.

Auerbach, Alan J., and Dale W. Jorgenson. 1980. "Inflation-Proof Depreciation of Assets." *Harvard Business Review* 58 (September–October): 113–18.

Auerbach, Alan J., and James M. Poterba. 1987. "Tax Loss Carryforwards and Corporate Tax Incentives." In Feldstein, ed., *Effects of Taxation*, 305–38.

Ballentine, J. Gregory. 1987. "Comment." In Feldstein, ed., *Effects of Taxation*, 437–43.

Bernheim, B. Douglas, and John B. Shoven. 1987. "Taxation and the Cost of Capital: An International Comparison." In *The Consumption Tax: A Better Alternative?* edited by Charls E. Walker and Mark A. Bloomfield, 61–86. Cambridge: Ballinger.

Biorn, Erik. 1989. *Taxation, Technology, and the User Cost of Capital*. Amsterdam: North-Holland.

Birnbaum, Jeffrey H., and Alan S. Murray. 1987. *Showdown at Gucci Gulch: Lawmakers, Lobbyists and the Unlikely Triumph of Tax Reform*. Random House.

Boadway, Robin, Neil Bruce, and Jack M. Mintz. 1984. "Taxation, Inflation, and the Effective Marginal Tax Rate on Capital in Canada." *Canadian Journal of Economics* 17 (February): 62–79.

Boskin, Michael J., and Charles E. McLure, Jr., eds. 1990. *World Tax Reform: Case Studies of Developed and Developing Countries*. San Francisco: ICS Press.

Bosworth, Barry P. 1985. "Taxes and the Investment Recovery." *Brookings Papers on Economic Activity* 1: 1–38.

Bosworth, Barry P., and Gary Burtless. 1992. "Effects of Tax Reform on Labor Supply, Investment, and Saving." *Journal of Economic Perspectives* 6 (Winter): 3–25.

Bradford, David F. 1981. "The Incidence and Allocation Effects of a Tax on Corporate Distributions." *Journal of Public Economics* 15 (February): 1–22.

———. 1986. *Untangling the Income Tax*. Harvard University Press.

Bradford, David F., and Don Fullerton. 1981. "Pitfalls in the Construction and Use of Effective Tax Rates." In Hulten, ed., *Depreciation, Inflation*, 251–78.

Bulow, Jeremy I., and Lawrence H. Summers. 1984. "The Taxation of Risky Assets." *Journal of Political Economy* 92 (February): 20–39.

Chirinko, Robert S., and Robert Eisner. 1983. "Tax Policy and Investment in Major U.S. Macroeconometric Models." *Journal of Public Economics* 20 (March): 139–66.

Christensen, Laurits R., and Dale W. Jorgenson. 1969. "The Measurement of U.S. Real Capital Input, 1929-1967." *Review of Income and Wealth,* series 15 (December): 293–320.

Commission of the European Communities. 1992. *Report of the Committee of Independent Experts on Company Taxation.* Luxembourg.

Council of Economic Advisers. 1982. *Economic Report of the President, February.* Government Printing Office.

Diewert, W. Erwin. 1980. "Aggregation Problems in the Measurement of Capital." In *The Measurement of Capital,* edited by Dan Usher, 433–528. University of Chicago Press.

Fair, Ray C., and John B. Taylor. 1983. "Solution and Maximum Likelihood Estimation of Dynamic Nonlinear Rational Expectations Models." *Econometrica* 51 (July): 1169–85.

Feldstein, Martin S. 1982. "Inflation, Tax Rules and Investment: Some Econometric Evidence." *Econometrica* 50 (July): 825–62.

——. 1983. *Inflation, Tax Rules, and Capital Formation.* University of Chicago Press.

——, ed. 1987. *The Effects of Taxation on Capital Accumulation.* University of Chicago Press.

Feldstein, Martin S., Louis Dicks-Mireaux, and James Poterba. 1983. "The Effective Tax Rate and the Pretax Rate of Return." *Journal of Public Economics* 21 (July): 129–58.

Feldstein, Martin S., and Joosung Jun. 1987. "The Effects of Tax Rules on Nonresidential Fixed Investment: Some Preliminary Evidence from the 1980s. In Feldstein, ed., *Effects of Taxation,* 101–56.

Feldstein, Martin S., and Lawrence H. Summers. 1979. "Inflation and the Taxation of Capital Income in the Corporate Sector." *National Tax Journal* 32 (December): 445–70.

Frenkel, Jacob A., Assaf Razin, and Efraim Sadka. 1991. *International Taxation in an Integrated World.* MIT Press.

Fullerton, Don. 1984. "Which Effective Tax Rate?" *National Tax Journal* 37 (March): 23–41.

——. 1987. "The Indexation of Interest, Depreciation, and Capital Gains and Tax Reform in the United States." *Journal of Public Economics* 32 (February): 25–51.

Fullerton, Don, and Yolanda K. Henderson. 1989a. "A Disaggregate Equilibrium Model of Distortions among Assets, Sectors, and Industries." *International Economic Review* 30 (May): 391–413.

——. 1989b. "The Marginal Excess Burden of Different Capital Instruments." *Review of Economics and Statistics* 71 (August): 435–42.

Fullerton, Don, Robert Gillette, and James Mackie. 1987. "Investment Incentives under the Tax Reform Act of 1986." In Office of Tax Analysis, *Compendium of Tax Research, 1987,* 131–72. U.S. Department of the Treasury.

Gordon, Roger H., James R. Hines, Jr., and Lawrence H. Summers. 1987. "Notes on the Tax Treatment of Structures." In Feldstein, ed., *Effects of Taxation,* 223–54.

Gordon, Roger H., and Dale W. Jorgenson. 1976. "The Investment Tax Credit and Counter-Cyclical Policy." In *Parameters and Policies in the U.S. Economy,* edited by Otto Eckstein, 275–314. Amsterdam: North-Holland.

Gravelle, Jane G. 1982. "Effects of the 1981 Depreciation Revisions on the Taxation of Income from Business Capital." *National Tax Journal* 35 (March): 1–20.

——. 1984. "Assessing Structural Tax Revision with Macroeconomic Models: The Treasury Tax Proposals and the Allocation of Investment." Report 85-645E. Congressional Research Service.

——. 1987. "Tax Policy and Rental Housing: An Economic Analysis." Report 87-536E. Congressional Research Service.

Hall, Robert E. 1981. "Tax Treatment of Depreciation, Capital Gains, and Interest in an Inflationary Economy." In Hulten, ed., *Depreciation, Inflation,* 149–67.

Hall, Robert E., and Dale W. Jorgenson. 1967. "Tax Policy and Investment Behavior." *American Economic Review* 57 (June): 391–414.

——. 1969. "Tax Policy and Investment Behavior: Reply and Further Results." *American Economic Review* 59 (June): 388–401.

——. 1971. "Application of the Theory of Optimal Capital Accumulation." In *Tax Incentives and Capital Spending,* edited by Gary Fromm, 9–60. Brookings.

Hall, Robert E., and Alvin Rabushka. 1983. *Low Tax, Simple Tax, Fair Tax.* McGraw-Hill.

Harberger, Arnold C. 1962. "The Incidence of the Corporate Income Tax." *Journal of Political Economy* 70 (June): 215–40.

——. 1966. "Efficiency Effects of Taxes on Income from Capital." In *Effects of the Corporation Income Tax,* edited by Marian Krzyzaniak, 107–117. Wayne State University Press.

Harper, Michael J., Ernst R. Berndt, and David O. Wood. 1989. "Rates of Return and Capital Aggregation Using Alternative Rental Prices." In Jorgenson and Landau, eds., *Technology and Capital Formation,* 331–72.

Henderson, Yolanda K. 1991. "Applications of General Equilibrium Models to the 1986 Tax Reform Act in the United States." *De Economist* 139 (Spring): 147–68.

Hulten, Charles R. (1990). "The Measurement of Capital." In *Fifty Years of Measurement in Economics,* edited by Ernst R. Berndt and Jack Triplett, 119–52. University of Chicago Press.

——, ed. 1981. *Depreciation, Inflation, and the Taxation of Income from Capital.* Washington: Urban Institute Press.

Hulten, Charles R., and June A. O'Neill. 1982. "Tax Policy." In *The Reagan Experiment: An Examination of Economic and Social Policies under the Reagan Administration,* edited by John L. Palmer and Isabel V. Sawhill, 97–128. Washington: Urban Institute Press.

Hulten, Charles R., and James W. Robertson. 1984. "The Taxation of High Technology Industries." *National Tax Journal* 37 (September): 327–45.

Hulten, Charles R., James W. Robertson, and Frank C. Wykoff. 1989. "Energy, Obsolescence, and the Productivity Slowdown." In Jorgenson and Landau, eds., *Technology and Capital Formation,* 225–58.

Hulten, Charles R., and Frank C. Wykoff. 1981a. "Economic Depreciation and Accelerated Depreciation: An Evaluation of the Conable-Jones 10-5-3 Proposal." *National Tax Journal* 34 (March): 45–60.

———. 1981b. "The Estimation of Economic Depreciation Using Vintage Asset Prices: An Application of the Box-Cox Power Transformation." *Journal of Econometrics* 15 (April): 367–96.

———. 1981c. "The Measurement of Economic Depreciation." In Hulten, ed., *Depreciation, Inflation,* 81–125.

Joint Committee on Taxation. 1981. *General Explanation of the Economic Recovery Tax Act of 1981.* 97 Cong. 1 sess. Government Printing Office.

———. 1986. *Summary of Conference Agreement on H.R. 3838 (Tax Reform Act of 1986).* 99 Cong. 2 sess. Government Printing Office.

Jorgenson, Dale W. 1963. "Capital Theory and Investment Behavior." *American Economic Review* 53 (May): 366–78.

———. 1965. "Anticipations and Investment Behavior." In *The Brookings Quarterly Econometric Model of the United States,* edited by James S. Duesenberry and others, 35–92. Chicago: Rand-McNally.

———. 1967. "The Theory of Investment Behavior." In *The Determinants of Investment Behavior,* edited by Robert Ferber, 129–56. Columbia University Press.

———. 1971a. "Econometric Studies of Investment Behavior: A Survey." *Journal of Economic Literature* 9 (December): 1111–47.

———. 1971b. "The Economic Impact of Investment Incentives." In Joint Economic Committee, *Long-Term Implications of Current Tax and Spending Proposals,* 176–92. 92 Cong. 1 sess. Government Printing Office.

———. 1974. "The Economic Theory of Replacement and Depreciation." In *Econometrics and Economic Theory: Essays in Honor of Jan Tinbergen,* edited by Willy Sellekaerts, 189–221. Macmillan.

———. 1979. "Statement." In House Committee on Ways and Means, *Tax Restructuring Act of 1979,* 62–76. 96 Cong., 1 sess., Government Printing Office.

———. 1980. "Statement." In Senate Committee on Finance, *Tax Cut Proposals,* pt. 2, 349–78. 96 Cong. 1 sess. Government Printing Office.

———. 1989. "Capital as a Factor of Production." In Jorgenson and Landau, eds. *Technology and Capital Formation,* 1–35.

Jorgenson, Dale W., and Sidney S. Handel. 1971. "Investment Behavior in U.S. Regulated Industries." *Bell Journal of Economics and Management Science* 2 (Spring): 213–64.

Jorgenson, Dale W., and Ralph Landau, eds. 1989. *Technology and Capital Formation.* MIT Press.

Jorgenson, Dale W., and Calvin D. Siebert. 1968a. "A Comparison of Alternative Theories of Corporate Investment Behavior." *American Economic Review* 58 (September): 681-712.

———. 1968b. "Optimal Capital Accumulation and Corporate Investment Behavior." *Journal of Political Economy* 76 (November–December): 1123–51.

———. 1972. "An Empirical Evaluation of Alternative Theories of Corporate Investment." In *Problems and Issues in Current Econometric Practice,* edited by Karl Brunner, 155–218. Ohio State University Press.

Jorgenson, Dale W., and James A. Stephenson. 1967a. "Investment Behavior in U.S. Manufacturing, 1947–1960." *Econometrica* 35 (April): 169–220.
———. 1967b. "The Time Structure of Investment Behavior in U.S. Manufacturing, 1947–1960." *Review of Economics and Statistics* 49 (February): 16–27.
———. 1969. "Anticipations and Investment Behavior in U.S. Manufacturing, 1947–1960." *Journal of the American Statistical Association* 64 (March): 67–89.
Jorgenson, Dale W., and Martin A. Sullivan. 1981. "Inflation and Corporate Capital Recovery." In Hulten, ed., *Depreciation, Inflation*, 171–238, 311–13.
Jorgenson, Dale W., and Kun-Young Yun. 1986a. "The Efficiency of Capital Allocation." *Scandinavian Journal of Economics* 88 (1): 85–107.
———. 1986b. "Tax Policy and Capital Allocation." *Scandinavian Journal of Economics* 88 (1): 355–77.
———. 1990. "Tax Reform and U. S. Economic Growth." *Journal of Political Economy* 98 (October): S151-93.
———. 1991a. "The Excess Burden of U.S. Taxation." *Journal of Accounting, Auditing, and Finance* 6 (Fall): 487–509.
———. 1991b. *Tax Reform and the Cost of Capital*. Oxford University Press.
King, Mervyn A. 1974a. "Dividend Behavior and the Theory of the Firm." *Economica* 41 (February): 25–34.
———. 1974b. "Taxation and the Cost of Capital." *Review of Economic Studies* 41 (January): 21–35.
———. 1977. *Public Policy and the Corporation*. London: Chapman and Hall.
———. 1985. "Capital Tax Reform." *Economic Policy* 1 (July): 220–38.
———. 1989. "Economic Growth and the Life-Cycle of Firms." *European Economic Review* 33 (March): 325–34.
King, Mervyn A., and Don Fullerton. 1984. *The Taxation of Income from Capital*. University of Chicago Press.
Lipton, David, and others. 1982. "Multiple Shooting in Rational Expectations Models." *Econometrica* 50 (September): 1329–33.
Lodin, Sven-Olof. 1978. "Progressive Expenditure Tax—An Alternative?" *A Report of the 1972 Government Commission on Taxation*. Stockholm: LiberForlag.
Lucas, Robert E., Jr. 1976. "Econometric Policy Evaluation: A Critique." In *The Phillips Curve and Labor Markets*, edited by Karl Brunner and Allan H. Meltzer, 19–46. Amsterdam: North-Holland.
McCallum, Bennett T. 1984. "On Low-Frequency Estimates of Long-Run Relationships in Macroeconomics." *Journal of Monetary Economics* 14 (July): 3–14.
———. 1986. "Estimating the Long-Run Relationship between Interest Rates and Inflation." *Journal of Monetary Economics* 18 (July): 87–90.
McLure, Charles E., Jr. 1979. *Must Corporate Income Be Taxed Twice?* Brookings.
———. 1986. "The Tax Treatment of Owner-Occupied Housing: The Achilles' Heel of Tax Reform?" In *Tax Reform and Real Estate*, edited by James R. Follain, 219–32. Washington: Urban Institute Press.

McLure, Charles E., Jr., and George R. Zodrow. 1987. "Treasury I and the Tax Reform Act of 1986: The Economics and Politics of Tax Reform." *Journal of Economic Perspectives* 1 (Summer): 37–58.

Meade, James E., and others. 1978. *The Structure and Reform of Direct Taxation: Report.* London: Allen and Unwin.

Modigliani, Franco, and Merton H. Miller. 1958. "The Cost of Capital, Corporation Finance, and the Theory of Investment." *American Economic Review* 48 (June): 261–97.

———. 1961. "Dividend Policy, Growth, and the Valuation of the Firm." *Journal of Business* 34 (October): 411–33.

Organization for Economic Cooperation and Development. 1991. *Taxing Profits in a Global Economy: Domestic and International Issues.* Paris.

Pechman, Joseph A., ed. 1988. *World Tax Reform: A Progress Report.* Brookings.

Poterba, James M., and Lawrence H. Summers. 1983. "Dividend Taxes, Investment, and 'Q'." *Journal of Public Economics* 22 (November): 135–67.

———. 1985. "The Economic Effects of Dividend Taxation." In *Recent Advances in Corporate Finance,* edited by Edward I. Altman and Marti G. Subrahmanyam, 227–84. Homewood, Ill.: Richard D. Irwin.

Razin, Assaf, and Joel Slemrod, eds. 1990. *Taxation in the Global Economy.* University of Chicago Press.

Rosenberg, Leonard G. 1969. "Taxation of Income from Capital, by Industry Group." In *The Taxation of Income from Capital,* edited by Arnold C. Harberger and Martin J. Bailey, 123–84. Brookings.

Scholes, Myron S., and Mark A. Wolfson. 1992. *Taxes and Business Strategy: A Planning Approach.* Prentice-Hall.

Scott, Maurice F. G. 1987. "A Note on King and Fullerton's Formulae to Estimate the Taxation of Income from Capital." *Journal of Public Economics* 34 (November): 253–64.

Shoven, John B. 1976. "The Incidence and Efficiency Effects of Taxes on Income from Capital." *Journal of Political Economy* 84 (December): 1261–83.

———. 1990. "Alternative Tax Policies to Lower the U.S. Cost of Capital." In Center for Policy Research, *Business Taxes, Capital Costs, and Competitiveness,* 1–24. Washington: American Council for Capital Formation.

Sinn, Hans-Werner. 1987. *Capital Income Taxation and Resource Allocation.* Amsterdam: North-Holland.

———. 1991a. "Taxation and the Cost of Capital: The 'Old' View, the 'New' View, and Another View." In *Tax Policy and the Economy,* edited by David Bradford, 25-54. MIT Press.

———. 1991b. "The Vanishing Harberger Triangle." *Journal of Public Economics* 45 (August): 271–300.

Slemrod, Joel, ed. 1990. *Do Taxes Matter? The Impact of the Tax Reform Act of 1986.* MIT Press.

Steuerle, C. Eugene. 1992. *The Tax Decade: How Taxes Came to Dominate the Public Agenda.* Washington: Urban Institute Press.

Stiglitz, Joseph E. 1973. "Taxation, Corporate Financial Policy, and the Cost of Capital." *Journal of Public Economics* 2 (February): 1–34.

Summers, Lawrence H. 1983. "The Nonadjustment of Nominal Interest Rates: A Study of the Fisher Effect." In *Macroeconomics, Prices and Quantities: Essays in Memory of Arthur M. Okun,* edited by James Tobin, 204–41. Brookings.

——. 1986. "Estimating the Long-Run Relationship between Interest Rates and Inflation: A Response. *Journal of Monetary Economics* 18 (July): 77–86.

Sunley, Emil M. 1987. "Comment." In Feldstein, ed., *Effects of Taxation,* 254–57.

U.S. Department of the Treasury. 1977. *Blueprints for Basic Tax Reform.*

——. 1984. *Tax Reform for Fairness, Simplicity, and Economic Growth,* 3 vols.

——. 1992. *Report of the Department of the Treasury on Integration of the Individual and Corporate Tax Systems: Taxing Business Income Once.*

CHAPTER TWO

# Australia

*Robert Jones*

THE TAXATION of income from capital in Australia has seen some radical changes in the postwar period. Many of these have related to alterations to company taxation itself, including changes in tax rates and incentives. Other changes have been to the personal taxation of income from capital, in terms of both the structure of personal rates and arrangements for investment through institutions.

It can be argued, however, that the most rapid period of reform of all has occurred since 1985. Most significant has been the introduction of a system of full imputation of company income to final shareholders. This replaced the classical system of taxation that had prevailed since the end of World War II. Under the form of imputation adopted, the degree of integration between personal and company taxation achieved is now virtually as high as is possible without fully attributing to shareholders all company income as it is earned.

Other reforms of the latter part of the 1980s included the base-broadening rate-lowering changes also occurring in other countries, which were a consequence of the desire to achieve a more level playing field. In some cases these measures evened out undulations that had themselves been put into place only in the early 1980s. In addition, Australians began paying capital gains taxes on a comprehensive basis for the first time.

In this chapter I attempt to quantify some of those changes in terms of effective tax rates using the Mervyn A. King and Don Fullerton procedure.[1] The measurements concentrate on the developments of the 1980s with special attention paid to the status of the tax system at the end of

The views expressed are those of the author and not necessarily those of the Bureau of Industry Economics. I am grateful to Paul Drake for assistance with this research.

1. King and Fullerton (1984).

the decade. In addition, a longer perspective is gained by examining the tax system at two earlier points: 1970 and 1960. Besides the taxation of income originating in companies, I also consider the taxation of owner-occupied housing and income earned in the unincorporated sector.

The structure of this chapter is as follows. The first section, "Features of the Australian Tax System," contains a description of the main Australian tax system as it affects the taxation of income from capital over the 1980s. The results for 1990, 1985, and 1980 are examined in the three subsequent sections. The distortions over time, by category, are then compared in the section "An Overview of Effective Tax Rates, 1960–90," which includes results for 1960 and 1970. Noncorporate investment and owner-occupied housing are considered in the next section, "Unincorporated Investment and Housing." The effect of inflation on the taxation of corporate source income is considered in the section "Inflation and Taxation—the Income Tax Issue of the 1990s," followed by concluding comments. In the appendix I explain differences between some of my assumptions and those of King-Fullerton.

## Features of the Australian Tax System

As a preliminary to the discussion of effective tax rates, the features of the Australian tax system in the 1980s are described in this section. In the interests of brevity, the tax systems in 1960 and 1970 are not discussed, but the salient features of those tax systems are included as part of the discussion of results later in the chapter under "An Overview of Effective Tax Rates, 1960 to 1970."

At the beginning of the 1980s, Australia's structure for the taxation of income from capital included full taxation of company income, personal taxation of some receipts of income such as interest and dividends, concessional taxation of income in the form of superannuation, and exemption of the taxation of imputed rent from durables and housing.[2] The taxation of income from the corporate sector was classical.

With the exception of the introduction of accelerated depreciation for plant and equipment in the early part of the decade, the story of the 1980s was one of steady progression toward a more comprehensive tax

2. At the same time, interest payments on mortgages were not deductible. Taxation of income from investments in human capital (forgone earnings) was then, as now, also untaxed.

system based on the income of individuals. Not only was full imputation introduced as a way of attributing more closely the income of companies to individual shareholders, but the base itself was broadened to include capital gains. As well, concessions for some types of physical investment were removed.

Throughout the decade inflation remained relatively high. Its impact was compounded on a taxation system based predominantly on nominal income with historical cost depreciation. (Please note: because no wealth taxes are levied in Australia, that form of taxation is not discussed in this chapter.)

### The Personal Income Tax

During the 1980s Australia's personal income taxation was based on the application of a progressive rate scale to nominal income, with a tax-free threshold for all taxpayers. For most of the time there was, as there is now, a levy for medical care which in 1990 was set at a rate of 1.25 percent of taxable income. For most taxpayers this operates as an addition to the marginal tax rate.

The rate scale was frequently altered. While there was a broad tendency toward lower marginal rates over the period, the effect of inflation was to push more and more income into higher rate classes. One indication of the net effect of these two factors over time is given by the calculation of the average marginal income tax rate, using total taxable income as a weight. This rose from a rate of 0.37 at the beginning of the decade, to 0.43 in 1986–87, subsequently falling to an estimated 0.40 in 1989–90.

Until 1985 income earned as a capital gain had been generally exempt for individual shareholders in Australia, except for property sold within twelve months of purchase. As part of the major tax reform package of September 1985,[3] however, a tax on capital gains was announced which applies to real gains on realization. Gains on principal residence are excluded.

### The Corporate Tax System

Australia fundamentally altered the way in which corporate source income was taxed when, in September 1985, the treasurer announced the replacement of the previous classical tax arrangements with a system of

---

3. Commonwealth of Australia (1985); Evans (1987).

full imputation. Under this system, which began operation in 1987–88, credit is given against personal taxation liabilities for taxes actually paid at the corporate level on income distributed as a dividend. Individuals are required to gross up dividends in their assessable income but are able to use the credit against their total tax liability (not just their liability on dividends). The credit is given at the full statutory corporate tax rate, but the value of franking credits may not exceed the amount of corporate tax paid.

Companies that have paid little tax but have profits to distribute may pay part of the dividend unfranked. Unfranked dividends are taxed under personal taxation without gross-up in the hands of shareholders. A consequence of these taxation arrangements for franked and unfranked dividends is that income paid as a dividend will bear the personal rate of taxation whatever the rate of taxation in the company.

One highly important feature of the Australian imputation arrangements is the ability of companies to retain income but allow shareholders immediate credit for company tax paid on the income. This is done by means of the issue of franked bonus shares. These are taxed as dividends and increase the basis for capital-gains-tax purposes. In effect, these shares' issue allows shareholders to be taxed only once, at their personal tax rate, on company earnings which have borne company tax and which are retained.

Initially, imputation was to apply only to household shareholders. This was altered in 1988 when superannuation funds and insurance companies were given access to imputation credits. This change was associated with some further alterations to their taxation. In the case of insurance companies, the intercorporate dividend rebate which had previously freed dividends received by them from taxation was repealed. In the case of superannuation funds, a new tax on fund earnings was introduced with the intention of its being set at a level which soaked up imputation credits. The denial of refunds of imputation credits in Australia remains.

The company tax rate in Australia now stands at 39 percent. This was reduced from 49 percent in 1988 as part of the broader tax reform which included, among other things, the abolition of accelerated (5/3) depreciation. The 49 percent rate had itself been introduced at the time of the introduction of imputation (1985) with the aim of aligning the company tax rate and the top marginal personal rate. Before that time the rate had been 46 percent. The company tax rate of 39 percent is now well below the top marginal personal tax rate of 47 percent (plus medicare levy).

## Tax Allowances for Depreciation and Inventories

The basic depreciation schedule for plant and equipment in Australia is based on economic lives of assets. Standard depreciation rates are then set as straight-line proportions of the historical cost of the asset, or 1.5 times the straight-line figure on the diminishing balance.[4] Although this schedule remained in force throughout the 1980s, and formed the basis for allowed depreciation, it was subject to significant variation in its actual application.

In 1980 a 20 percent loading applied to the rates prescribed in the schedule. (Depreciation rates were 1.2 times those otherwise allowable.) The loading was reduced to 18 percent in 1981. The year 1982 saw the announcement of the introduction of accelerated depreciation, which provided for a linear rate of 20 percent where the ordinary straight-line rate plus loading was 20 percent or less, and a rate of 33.33 percent if the standard rate exceeded 20 percent. Taxpayers could elect not to adopt the accelerated rate, in which case the standard rate (plus the 18 percent loading) would apply. This was known as *5/3 depreciation*. Abolished in 1988, 5/3 depreciation was replaced by the original schedule, with a loading of 20 percent. Buildings have been subject to quite different arrangements. Before 1982 most factory and commercial buildings did not qualify for depreciation. In 1982, however, a straight-line rate of 2.5 percent was permitted. This was raised to 4 percent in 1984, but dropped back to 2.5 percent in 1987.

In the late 1970s, following the work of the Mathews committee,[5] there had been some experimentation with trading stock valuation adjustment to attempt to mitigate the effects of inflation on taxation burdens on capital required for inventory. By 1980 this had been abandoned, and the system returned to one which taxed changes in values due to inflation. This arrangement still applies.

## Estimates of Economic Depreciation

Preferred estimates of economic depreciation are taken from Robert Walters and Robert J. Dippelsman.[6] Plant and equipment is assumed to

4. The aggregate-allowed lives used in this work are based on estimates by category and sector in Walters and Dippelsman (1985).

5. Commonwealth of Australia (1975). Inventory valuations can, under current rules, be based on either FIFO (first in, first out) or the average-costing method. In determining replacement values either internal costing or external market prices may be used. The LIFO (last in, first out) valuation method may not be used.

6. Walters and Dippelsman (1985).

last nineteen years in manufacturing and fourteen years elsewhere, and buildings forty-five years in manufacturing, forty-seven years in other industry, and sixty years in commerce. These are converted to exponential decay rates $\delta$ using the formula $\delta = 2/L$, where $L$ is asset life.

### Investment Grants and Incentives

An investment allowance at various rates was a common feature of taxation arrangements in the 1970s in Australia. This continued into the early 1980s with a lump-sum deduction from taxable income of 20 percent applicable until 1981, and a similar deduction of 18 percent allowed from then until June 1985. These deductions did not reduce the amount of depreciation that could be claimed.

Eligibility for the allowance was, however, somewhat restricted, not least because individual items costing less than $1,000 were partly or wholly excluded. Quite large investment packages could thus be excluded to the extent that they contained small components. To determine the portion of equipment eligible for the allowance for the purposes of this work, the amount of allowance claimed in each sector is grossed up by the rate of allowance and expressed as a proportion of total equipment investment. The value of the allowance is then entered into the model as an immediate expensing equivalent equal to the proportion of investment eligible multiplied by the rate of allowance. The results are presented in table 2-1.

### Local Taxes

Taxes at the local government level in Australia are restricted to rates. Rates are sometimes levied on land and buildings together, and sometimes on land alone. The calculation here of average rates borne on buildings is based on the ratio of total revenue from rates on land and buildings expressed as a proportion of the total value of land and buildings.

Taxes on land and buildings are levied in four states, and it is estimated that, even in these states, 30 percent of revenue is raised from sources other than land and buildings together.[7] Table 2-2 shows the derivation of an average rate on buildings of 0.0018, which is the value for $w_c$ used throughout this work.

7. See Prest (1983).

Table 2-1. *Expensing Equivalent of Investment Allowance, Australia, 1980–81, 1984–85*

| Item | Investment allowance (millions of dollars)[a] (1) | Eligible investment (col. 1/r)[b] (2) | Total investment (millions of dollars)[c] (3) | Proportion eligible (col. 2/col. 3) (4) | Expensing equivalent (col. 4 · r)[b,d] (5) |
|---|---|---|---|---|---|
| | *1980–81 (r = 0.20)* | | | | |
| Manufacturing | 272.6 | 1,362.9 | 2,493 | 0.547 | 0.109 |
| Other industry | 103.1 | 515.6 | 1,180 | 0.437 | 0.087 |
| Commerce | 100.0 | 500.0 | 1,608 | 0.311 | 0.062 |
| | *1984–85 (r = 0.18)* | | | | |
| Manufacturing | 404.0 | 2,244.3 | 3,097 | 0.725 | 0.131 |
| Other industry | 126.5 | 902.7 | 1,258 | 0.718 | 0.129 |
| Commerce | 146.5 | 813.7 | 2,367 | 0.344 | 0.062 |

a. Derived from Commissioner of Taxation, Taxation Statistics, various years.
b. $r$ is the statutory rate of allowance.
c. Derived from ABS, *Australian National Accounts*, various years.
d. Corresponds to the $t_2$ parameter used in model application in the appendix to this volume.

Table 2-2. *Average Rate on Buildings, 1980–81, 1983–84*

Values in millions of dollars

| Item | 1980–81 | 1983–84 |
|---|---|---|
| Municipal rates (Vic, WA, SA, Tas) | 723.8 | 1,035.7 |
| Land and buildings rates (70 percent of above rates) | 506.7 | 725.0 |
| Urban land value (all states) | 105,720 | 149,780 |
| Buildings value (all states, excluding public enterprises) | 178,297 | 248,736 |
| Total | 284,017 | 398,516 |
| Municipal rate per dollar of building or land | 0.00178 | 0.00182 |

Source: ABS, Taxation Revenue, various years; Herps (1981, 1985). Land valuations come from Herps.

## Household Tax Rates

Interest and dividends are taxed at households' marginal rates when received by individuals. A weighted marginal tax rate on each of these types of income from capital can be calculated using *Taxation Statistics*.[8] These rates show significantly higher tax rates on dividends than interest because dividends tend to be received by individuals with higher taxable incomes.

8. Commissioner of Taxation.

Table 2-3. *Effective Tax Rates on Interest and Dividends, Selected Years, 1980–90*

| | Dividends | | Interest | | |
|---|---|---|---|---|---|
| Years | Weighted tax rate on reported dividends ($t_c$) | Weighted tax rate on all received dividends ($t_r$) | Weighted tax rate on reported interest ($t_c$) | Weighted tax rate on all received interest ($t_r$) | Weighted tax rate on all attributed interest ($t_a$) |
| 1980–81 | 0.44 | 0.38 | 0.37 | 0.27 | 0.23 |
| 1984–85 | 0.46 | 0.41 | 0.38 | 0.27 | 0.24 |
| 1987–88 | 0.44 | 0.38 | 0.38 | 0.27 | 0.24 |
| 1989–90 | 0.46 | 0.40 | 0.37 | 0.23 | 0.23 |

Source: Unless otherwise indicated, all tables are based on author's calculations.

a. The weighted tax rate on all received dividends or interest is equal to $t_c \cdot \alpha + (1 - \alpha) \cdot (e + f) \cdot 0 + g \cdot 25$, where $\alpha$ is the proportion of taxed receipts (Commissioner of Taxation) to household receipts of that type (ABS, *Australian National Accounts*), $e$ is the proportion of unreported receipts that evade tax (assumed constant at 30 percent), $f$ is the proportion of unreported receipts received by zero rate taxpayers and legitimately not reported (assumed constant at 20 percent), and $g$ is the proportion of unreported receipts that are taxed by reducing the dependent spouse rebate (assumed constant at 50 percent).

The weighted tax rate on all attributed interest is equal to $t_r \cdot (b - c)/b$, where $b$ is total borrowing from the private sector by all financial intermediaries, and $c$ is total current deposits in major trading banks (Reserve Bank, 1985).

A comparison of interest and dividends paid with interest and dividends declared to the commissioner of taxation, however, reveals that a large proportion of such income is not directly taxed. To complicate matters further, some of this income that is not declared may in fact be taxed indirectly as it is added to dependent-spouse income and so serves to reduce the dependent-spouse rebate. In this case the effective tax rate is 25 percent. In addition, households receive some interest income in the form of untaxed services from banks. That is to say, they hold current deposits that have no interest attributed to them (although the funds are presumably lent productively by the bank), but they do receive free and untaxed account-keeping services.

Table 2-3 shows how these complexities are accounted for in this chapter. The final adjusted tax rates on dividends and interest, respectively, are the weighted tax rate on received dividends (second column of data) and the weighted tax rate on attributed interest (fifth column of data).

### Superannuation Funds

Until 1988–89, superannuation funds themselves paid no tax in Australia. They now pay tax at the rate of 15 percent on their income, with allowance given for imputation credits obtained on franked dividends. Consistency with the conventional application of the King and Fullerton model would therefore appear to require the application of a tax rate of zero (and no allowance for franking of equity income) on superannuation funds for the former period, and a tax rate of 0.15 (and credit for franked equity income) for the latter period. In this work, however, account is taken of the personal-tax provisions that apply to superannuation. These have made a significant difference to the effective tax rate on investment in superannuation funds by individuals. It is by no means true for Australia, as appears to have been true of some other countries, that personal taxation arrangements have broadly approximated expenditure-tax treatment.

Superannuation contributions may be made either by employees from taxed labor income, or by employers with payments on behalf of employees. The latter type of payments are made free of labor income tax. Withdrawal of benefits in the form of a lump sum has been taxed at varying rates over the years, generally at less than the full personal tax rate that would be borne on pension payments. In 1980–81 *employee* contributions were nominally rebatable, but in fact the rebate could be effectively used for this purpose by very few.[9] *Employer* contributions were paid out of pretax labor income, while lump-sum withdrawals were minimally taxed.[10] For most contributors this treatment was on average more generous than that under an expenditure tax.

In 1983 lump-sum payments which represented deducted employee contributions, income earned in the fund, or employer contributions became taxable at 30 percent (plus Medibank levy). Only undeducted employee contributions could be taken as a tax-free lump sum, although the first $55,000 of any lump sum was taxed at the concessional rate of 15 percent (plus Medibank levy). This treatment could broadly be summarized as being, at the margin, expenditure tax treatment for employer contributions and income tax treatment for employee contributions.

Along with changes to the taxation of fund income in 1988, taxation arrangements applying to employers' contributions and to lump-sum withdrawals were altered. Broadly speaking, 15 percentage points were lifted from taxation of lump sums of all sizes and a new tax of 15 percent was instituted on employers' contributions. This left personal taxation of superannuation funded by employers' contributions as it was, with

9. Expenditure was rebatable only to the extent that total rebatable expenditure (including non-superannuation expenditure) equaled or exceeded $1,590. The Committee of Inquiry into the Australian Financial System (1981) suggests that in 1978–79, when similar provisions prevailed, only 6.5 percent of individuals received any incremental benefits from the rebate for superannuation.

10. Five percent of the payout was included in taxable income in the year of payment.

expenditure tax treatment, and income tax treatment on most employees' contributions, but at a lower rate. More details of the calculation of tax rates on superannuation are presented in the appendix.

### Insurance Companies

In general terms, life insurance offices are taxed at the prevailing company tax rate on assessed income from investment. For the period examined here, personal taxation can essentially be ignored, since there is no taxation of payments when the policy is held for ten years or more and there were and are no effective concessions on investment.

Although taxed as companies, insurers actually received considerably varied tax treatment over this period. This most significant change was in 1988, when insurance companies were brought into the imputation system and taxed on dividend income with credit for tax paid at the company level. Before this they had had access to the intercompany dividend rebate, although because not all expenses were deductible it can be argued that some positive tax rate existed. At the same time, before the 1988 reforms, a special tax deduction of 1 percent of the actuarial value of liabilities was allowed. The effective marginal tax rates on dividend and interest income before 1988 are based on estimates provided for the Institute of Actuaries.[11] The rates used for interest are 37 percent for 1980 and 1985, and 39 percent for 1990. For dividends the rates are 2 percent for 1980 and 1985, and 39 percent for 1990.

### Unincorporated Business

Unincorporated business is taxed on the same basis as incorporated business, but at the marginal tax rate applying to the investor rather than the company rate. In this chapter it is assumed that the relevant personal tax rate is the same as that applicable to dividends from the corporate sector (see table 2-3).

### Housing

The taxation of owner-occupied housing has been unchanged throughout the period of this analysis. There is no taxation of income in the form of implicit rent (imputed rent) and interest is not deductible. When capital gains taxation was introduced in 1985, taxation of the change in

11. As quoted by Davies (1982).

the value of the principal residence was explicitly excluded. Although it is clearly necessary to allow for the taxation of interest on loan capital supplied to the owner-occupied housing sector, the proportion of the total housing stock that is financed by loans is actually very small.[12]

## Current Taxation of Corporate Source Income

Table 2-4 shows the effective tax rates calculated for 1990 in the four standard categories: industries, assets, financing methods, and owners. Inflation is assumed to be at the prevailing level of 7 percent. While these results are in the spirit of the King and Fullerton (KF) model, there are some differences in application, primarily to take account of Australia's system of imputation. Further details are provided in the appendix.[13]

The first two columns of table 2-4 show total effective tax rates. These are the results usually shown in KF applications and are relevant if it can be assumed that marginal investment decisions are principally made by residents. The remaining columns split the total tax rate into a rate applying at the level of the corporation and a rate applying to resident individuals. The rate applying to individuals would indicate the savings distortions facing residents if the returns out of corporate sector were entirely determined by the investment of foreigners; that is that marginal investments by residents had no effect in bringing more marginal investment projects into being. If that were true, the effective tax rates on investment in the Australian corporate sector would then be those applying to foreign investors, as shown in the fourth column.

The idea that foreigners determine the marginal Australian investment projects is certainly consistent with the formal results for a small open economy. However, there are reasons for thinking that it is too extreme an assumption, even for Australia. One reason is associated with results which suggest that investment is made to a far greater extent in the country of residence than might be suggested by theory.[14] Another reason has to do with the imputation system in Australia. The effect of imputation is to make company tax, as it applies to residents, akin to a withholding tax. Even if company income is reinvested, the company tax paid on it can

---

12. A value of 10 percent was obtained using the value of the housing stock from Piggott (1987) and the Reserve Bank Series, *Credit by Financial Intermediaries for Housing*.

13. The appendix also contains results calculated on different assumptions about the taxation of debt-financed assets.

14. Feldstein and Horioka (1980).

Table 2-4.   *Effective Tax Rates, Corporate Sector, 1990*[a]

Percent

| | Total | | Corporate | | Individual | |
|---|---|---|---|---|---|---|
| | | | Less imputation credits | No imputation credits | | |
| Item | New view (1) | Old view (2) | (3) | (4) | New view (5) | Old view (6) |
| Asset | | | | | | |
| Machinery | 32.1 | 38.6 | −9.6 | 21.6 | 38.4 | 44.9 |
| Buildings | 32.9 | 39.6 | −8.4 | 21.4 | 38.4 | 45.2 |
| Inventories | 46.3 | 46.3 | 0.3 | 43.7 | 46.2 | 46.2 |
| Industry | | | | | | |
| Manufacturing | 36.3 | 41.0 | −6.5 | 28.7 | 40.6 | 45.3 |
| Other industry | 33.1 | 39.3 | −8.9 | 23.2 | 38.9 | 45.1 |
| Commerce | 36.4 | 41.2 | −6.3 | 26.5 | 40.6 | 45.4 |
| Finance | | | | | | |
| Debt | 21.5 | 21.5 | −22.3 | −22.3 | 36.0 | 36.0 |
| New issues | 50.3 | 50.3 | 1.0 | 52.6 | 49.8 | 49.8 |
| Retained earnings | 40.4 | * | 0.9 | 52.6 | 39.8 | * |
| Owner | | | | | | |
| Households | 37.4 | 42.0 | −12.4 | 8.9 | 45.5 | 50.1 |
| Superannuation | 23.3 | 27.7 | −1.5 | 44.3 | 24.4 | 28.8 |
| Insurance companies | 59.0 | 66.0 | −0.5 | 48.0 | 59.2 | 66.3 |
| Overall tax rate | 36.0 | 40.9 | −6.7 | 27.2 | 40.4 | 45.3 |

* Statistically insignificant.

a. The new view of company taxation is based on the idea that personal taxes on dividends are not effective on investments from retained capital. The old view of company taxation is modeled here by assuming all investment is financed by new share issues.

The corporate tax rate in the third column is defined as $(p - x)/p$, where $p$ is the real pretax return, $x$ is equal to the interest rate $r$ in the case of debt finance, $p\theta - \pi$ in the case of franked equity returns, and $p - \pi$ in the case of unfranked returns. The personal tax wedge in the fifth and sixth column is $(x - s)/x$, where $s$ is the real after-tax return to the investor. The corporate tax wedge and the personal tax wedge do not add exactly to the total tax wedge. The corporate tax wedge in the fourth column is calculated as $x = \rho - \pi$; that is, company tax is not associated with any imputation credits.

be credited to shareholders through the issuance of franked bonus shares. In general this will mean that residents are likely to pay less total tax on an investment in an Australian company than nonresidents. Imputation credits do not get fully credited to foreigners in Australia. Instead they receive remission of dividend withholding tax on franked dividends, while continuing to pay withholding tax on unfranked dividends. They are then liable for taxation on the income in their own country, although this taxation may allow some credit for Australian taxes paid.

Given that new investment continues to be made by both foreigners and residents, it is probably most sensible to examine the incentives to invest in the corporate sector on each of the alternative assumptions that Australians and foreigners make the marginal investments. This would imply that the incentives to invest in assets and industries are provided by either the first or fourth column. As is clear from table 2-4, the patterns of effective tax-rate results are very similar for 1990. The first column shows effective tax rates under the "new view" of company taxation, while the second assumes the "old view." Similarly the fifth and sixth columns show the personal tax rate under each view. This difference in approach turns on the impact of personal taxes on earnings which are retained. The KF model has conventionally adopted the new view, and this is the perspective taken in the discussion that follows.

### Assets and Industry Distortions

Judging from the results in the first (and fourth) column of table 2-4, the Australian tax system shows remarkably little distortion by asset and industry. (As will be shown later in this chapter, this has by no means always been true.) The largest source of distortion now is between investment in inventory and investment in other physical assets. This reflects the pure nominal taxation of inventory under Australia's FIFO (first in, first out) system of taxation, and the somewhat less than nominal taxation under historical cost depreciation for plant, equipment, and buildings.

While Australia's tax-depreciation regime is now based more closely than ever on economic life, the closeness of effective tax rates on buildings and plant and equipment is perhaps a little unexpected. The actual depreciation arrangements are characterized by the use of straight-line depreciation for buildings against declining balance for plant and equipment, and the use of a loading of 20 percent on allowances for plant and equipment but none for buildings. In addition, the rates calculated here depend on the relationship between assumed actual lives and assumed allowed lives. Industry differences are principally due to asset composition, and the slight favoring of other industry reflects its relatively smaller inventory requirements.

### Finance and Owner Distortions

Under the new view of company taxation, retained earnings are generally the tax-favored form of equity finance. This is clearly true for Australia. Income that is not taxed in the company itself is assumed to add to share values. This is taxed under the capital gains tax, which in Australia is levied largely on real gains. Capital subscribed by way of new issues, however, must at some stage incur personal taxation on dividend income and so has a much higher tax rate.

These results appear to suggest a favoring of debt finance for the financing decisions of residents (first column, table 2-4). That conclusion, however, must be interpreted carefully. An important cause of this is that the weighted tax rate on interest is lower than that on equity returns. This in turn is due to three things. One is that there is a higher proportion of lower-income (and so lower tax-rate) individuals among lenders than among equity investors. Another is that much more interest income avoids taxation altogether than does equity income. The final reason is that the calculation of the rate applicable to interest receipts includes allowance for income taken in the form of tax-free services on current banking accounts.

These sources of difference are important in considering criticisms of the tax system which suggest that debt is favored for more fundamental reasons to do with the deductibility of nominal interest and the concessions inherent in the real capital gains tax. In recent work, the Bureau of Industry Economics considered these issues of tax design and showed that if residents are considered taxpayer by taxpayer, there appears to be very little bias in their incentives to offer debt or equity.[15]

The results in the third column of table 2-4 appear to imply a preference for foreign debt finance. However, it should be noted that these calculations do not take account of interest-withholding tax. If interest-withholding tax actually impinges on foreigners' decisions, then this negative effective tax rate is greatly reduced.[16]

The results by owner show that superannuation is still a very attractive method of investment on average. This is not true of investment through insurance companies. However, because these are averages, it should not be inferred that no individual will find such investment attractive.

## Corporate and Individual Tax Rates

The third, fourth, fifth, and sixth columns in table 2-4 divide total taxation into a tax rate on the company alone and a tax rate on individuals alone.

---

15. Bureau of Industry Economics (1990).

16. Bureau of Industry Economics (1990); although interest-withholding tax can be credited abroad, there are reasons for thinking that this process often is not effective. This can occur when funds are supplied via financial intermediaries, for whom the credit is much larger than the "turn" that they take (and so is wasted), or when the credit abroad is "washed out" by foreign imputation systems.

If imputation credits broadly offset corporate taxation liabilities on equity investment, then many effective tax rates (third column) are negative. The reason is that while the corporate tax rate on investments financed with equity is approximately zero, the corporate tax rate on debt is negative because the value of interest deductibility usually outweighs taxation of debt-financed assets in the company. Individual taxation (fifth and sixth columns) shows the extent of personal taxation of returns from the corporate sector. It varies with the degree of taxation of individual assets because, on the equity side, taxation in the company affects the amount of income paid out as franked dividends.[17] (Interest, however, is taxed uniformly.)

As has been noted, these results may also in some broad sense indicate the effect of taxation on incentives to supply capital to the corporate sector if marginal investments are made by foreigners. As such it is probably the comparisons among methods of finance and forms of saving that are most interesting, together with the aggregate result (the latter in terms of its comparison with other years). The most significant impact of making the assumption that residents do not make marginal investment decisions is in the effective tax rate on debt, where taxes at the corporate level can be ignored, and so overall taxes become much higher and closer to those on equity.

## Taxation of Corporate Source Income, 1985

Table 2-5 shows the effective tax rates for 1985. They are based on a model very similar to the standard PTAX (see the appendix). Because there is no imputation, it is only necessary to present a single corporate tax rate. Inflation is set at 7 percent, which is the average of the consumption deflators for 1983–84, 1984–85, and 1985–86. In general terms table 2-5 shows a marked contrast with table 2-4. Tax rates are very much more dispersed. Because this measurement of the tax system contains parameters based on the situation before the first reform of September

17. Consider an investment in inventories. Because this investment is taxed on a full nominal basis, nominal income is likely to be paid out as a dividend to allow shareholders access to imputation credits. (It should be remembered that, if required, a dividend can be paid while income is retained in the company, under the Australian tax system.) With assets that are taxed on less than a full nominal basis, some income can be retained and be taxed not as a dividend, but under the capital-gains-tax provisions as share values rise. This accounts for the differences among assets in the third and sixth columns of table 2-4.

Table 2-5.  *Effective Tax Rates, Corporate Sector, 1985*[a]

Percent

|  | Total | | | Individual | |
| --- | --- | --- | --- | --- | --- |
| Item | New view | Old view | Corporate | New view | Old view |
| Asset | | | | | |
| Machinery | 17.8 | 30.3 | −9.3 | 22.2 | 38.9 |
| Buildings | 46.8 | 56.7 | 24.5 | 27.9 | 48.7 |
| Inventories | 74.8 | 82.4 | 57.0 | 44.9 | 79.7 |
| Industry | | | | | |
| Manufacturing | 40.0 | 51.1 | 17.3 | 29.3 | 52.3 |
| Other industry | 23.1 | 34.3 | −4.1 | 24.8 | 42.1 |
| Commerce | 46.9 | 56.4 | 24.0 | 31.8 | 55.2 |
| Finance | | | | | |
| Debt | −7.4 | −7.4 | −58.0 | 32.9 | 32.9 |
| New issues | 73.9 | 73.9 | 46.5 | 60.0 | 60.0 |
| Retained earnings | 53.7 | * | 46.6 | 16.2 | * |
| Owner | | | | | |
| Households | 34.9 | 56.1 | 3.8 | 33.3 | 79.7 |
| Superannuation | 45.6 | 45.6 | 36.0 | 20.0 | 20.0 |
| Insurance companies | 61.3 | 47.7 | 40.7 | 39.4 | 8.2 |
| Overall tax rate | 41.4 | 51.8 | 18.2 | 30.0 | 52.6 |

* Statistically insignificant.

a. The new view of company taxation is based on the idea that personal taxes on dividends are not effective on investments from retained capital. The old view of company taxation is modeled here by assuming all investment is from new investment.

The corporate tax rate is defined as $(p - x)/p$, where $p$ is the real pretax return, $x$ is equal to the interest rate $r$ in the case of debt finance, and $p - \pi$ in the case of equity. The personal tax wedge is $(x - s)/x$, where $s$ is the real after-tax return to the investor. The corporate tax wedge and the personal tax wedge do not add exactly to the total tax wedge.

1985, in some ways it provides an indication of the extent of the gains for neutrality from all the tax reforms of the latter part of the 1980s. The variations in tax rates, along with possible causes, are considered in detail below.

### Assets and Industries

The asset distortions in total effective tax rates under the new view (first column, table 2-5) show perhaps the greatest variation of all. The very low rates on plant and equipment are due to the accelerated depreciation regime that applied and the presence of the investment allowance.[18] Buildings had a higher rate of depreciation than in 1990, at 4.0 percent rather then 2.5 percent, but still had a higher effective tax rate. There

18. Note that the investment allowance did, however, terminate for new investment decisions in June 1985.

were personal-tax as well as company-tax influences on this, but certainly the much higher company tax rate (49 percent rather than 39 percent) had a significant influence.

One indication of the effect of company tax is in the third column, which shows the effect of company tax alone as a tax rate. In 1990 machinery and buildings were both slightly below minus 10 percent, while inventories were roughly zero. In 1985, however, the effective tax rate on buildings, at about 25 percent, was far above that for machinery (roughly minus 10 percent), and inventories were nearly double the level on buildings. In other words, the disparity was much greater. Note that since, by chance, inflation rates are equal, there is no differential inflation impact on these results.

Since there was no imputation in 1985, it could be argued that asset and industry biases were more likely to be determined by foreign capital, on the grounds that foreigners may have had lower total taxes than residents on investment in Australia. In this case the distortions in the corporate sector are best judged by the third column. Distortions facing residents are best judged by the fourth (or fifth) column under these assumptions. On any basis, however, it is clear that the distortions among assets are still manifestly worse than in 1990. Once again the distortions in asset choice feed through to produce distortions in effective tax rates facing industries, as the second group of effective tax rates clearly shows.

*Financing and Owners*

The discrepancy between debt and equity on the basis of total effective tax rates was substantially worse in 1985 than in 1990. This reflects the concessional treatment of assets in combination with nominal interest deductibility, the high company tax rate, and for new issues, the double taxation of company income through the classical tax system. The fact that superannuation funds were tax free encouraged this bias. Their lending gained the benefit of the negative taxation of debt-financed assets in the company (third column), but equity investment was taxed in the company (third column again).

From the point of view of international capital, debt was also encouraged (third column), although this may have been attenuated (but not offset) by interest-withholding tax.[19] From the point of view of investors,

---

19. Bureau of Industry Economics (1990).

the choice between institutional and personal investment was biased, but it is difficult to make comparisons with 1990.

Superannuation funds have lower taxation of corporate source income in 1990 than in 1985, despite having their fund income taxed. This comes about because of the benefits of being given access to imputation credits. Although their income was newly taxed in 1990, the tax rate on their investment income was set at such a level as to enable them to use imputation credits on corporate equity investment, while still paying some positive tax on investment generally. This meant in effect that incentives to invest in equities were improved, while incentives to invest in everything else were reduced. The measure was obviously partly aimed at the distortion between debt and equity so clearly evident in table 2-5. The net effect of the change was to improve greatly the incentives to invest in the corporate sector.

## Taxation of Corporate Source Income, 1980

In 1980 Australia's tax system differed from that in 1985 in the following main ways: the company tax rate was 46 percent rather than 49 percent; depreciation was based on economic life (with a 20 percent loading to allowances) rather than the accelerated system; there was virtually no depreciation allowed on buildings; superannuation lump sums were essentially untaxed. The effective tax rates for 1980 are shown in table 2-6. Inflation, based on the average of consumption deflators for 1979–80, 1980–81, and 1981–82, is set at 10 percent.

One difference between 1985 and 1980 is a somewhat more even pattern of effective tax rates on assets in the earlier year because of the use of a depreciation system based more on economic life. Note, however, that higher inflation at this time has pushed up the effective tax rate on inventories, thus introducing a new disparity.

The effective tax rate on superannuation shows the benefit of more favorable tax treatment by being lower, rather than in 1985 higher, than personal taxation. A large tax bias in favor of debt remains.

## An Overview of Effective Tax Rates, 1960–90

In this section some calculations of effective tax rates for 1960 and 1970 are added to the previous results to provide some indication of the

Table 2-6. *Effective Tax Rates, Corporate Sector, 1980*[a]

Percent

| Item | Total | | | Individual | |
|------|----------|----------|-----------|----------|----------|
| | New view | Old view | Corporate | New view | Old view |
| Asset | | | | | |
|   Machinery | 50.5 | 66.4 | 30.3 | 27.1 | 62.1 |
|   Buildings | 58.9 | 74.0 | 40.0 | 30.5 | 71.0 |
|   Inventories | 89.0 | 100.6 | 74.3 | 94.4 | 240.0 |
| Industry | | | | | |
|   Manufacturing | 64.5 | 78.9 | 46.3 | 48.8 | 119.4 |
|   Other industry | 54.1 | 69.5 | 34.3 | 31.5 | 73.3 |
|   Commerce | 67.3 | 81.4 | 49.5 | 52.6 | 129.2 |
| Finance | | | | | |
|   Debt | 5.4 | 5.4 | −44.0 | 35.0 | 35.0 |
|   New issues | 96.7 | 96.7 | 68.3 | 140.0 | 139.7 |
|   Retained earnings | 69.3 | * | 68.3 | 5.2 | * |
| Owner | | | | | |
|   Households | 67.2 | 91.5 | 39.9 | 74.7 | 195.1 |
|   Superannuation | 50.5 | 50.5 | 57.4 | −34.3 | −34.3 |
|   Insurance companies | 82.4 | 69.7 | 62.4 | 82.7 | 156.8 |
| Overall tax rate | 64.7 | 79.1 | 46.6 | 48.9 | 119.5 |

* Statistically insignificant.
a. See table 2-5.

trends in neutrality over time. Features of the tax systems in 1960 and 1970 are discussed in the course of analysis of the results.

### Asset and Industry Taxation

Figure 2-1 shows the effective tax rates applying to assets. The results are shown in conventional KF form as total effective tax rates under the assumptions of the new view. Taxation is more neutral the more the results for any year converge. In 1960 there was very little inflation, 3 percent,[20] and tax rates were relatively uniform. In 1970 inflation had increased to 5 percent,[21] and the company tax rate had increased from 40.0 to 47.5 percent. These two factors help explain the marked increase in taxation of inventories. Plant and equipment, however, was by then benefiting from a 20 percent investment allowance which offset the increase in effective tax rate that would otherwise have occurred. The combination of these elements led to increased disparities in effective tax rates.

20. Calculated as the average of the private consumption deflator for 1969–70, 1970–71, and 1971–72.

21. Calculated as the average of the private consumption deflator for 1959–60, 1960–61, and 1961–62.

Figure 2-1.   *Effective Tax Rates of Assets, 1960–90*

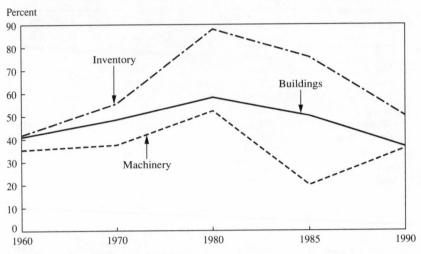

Source: All figures are based on author's calculations.

By 1980 inflation had further increased, to 10 percent, and the taxation level overall had increased. While the effects of inflation on tax burdens was probably one factor in this increase, another was the change in taxation of personal savings through institutions, about which more is said later in this chapter. The relative increase in disparities, with the much higher relative taxation of inventories, can, however, be largely attributed to the effects of inflation in conjunction with the taxation of nominal income under FIFO.

There was lower inflation in 1985. Other things equal, this would have tended to smooth out asset distortions. But the introduction of accelerated depreciation produced the very large decline in effective taxation of plant and equipment, and caused the effective tax rates to show their greatest dispersion of any year considered here.

The second half of the 1980s saw both the termination of the investment allowance and the elimination of accelerated depreciation. At the same time, imputation caused overall effective tax rates to fall.[22] The effect of all these changes was to generate the least dispersion seen at this level of asset disaggregation since the low-inflation days of the 1960s.

22. This was especially true of investment by superannuation funds, which gained the benefit of imputation credits on equity investment in exchange for relatively low (15 percent) taxation of fund income.

Figure 2-2. *Effective Tax Rates of Industry, 1960–90*

Percent

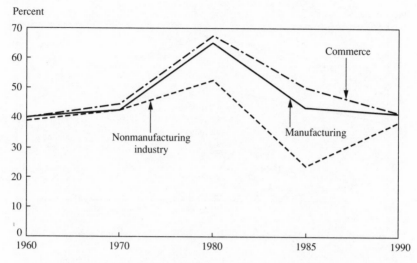

Disparities in asset taxation often feed through to produce disparities in industry taxation.[23] As figure 2-2 shows, it is generally true that the most severe nonneutralities by industry occur in the years in which asset distortions are also most severe. The relative differences among industries, however, are much less marked than in the case of assets. This reflects similar asset structures across industries. The industry that is most affected by these asset distortions is the other industry category, which broadly has relatively lower inventory requirements and a relatively higher proportion of plant and equipment.

### Financing and Ownership

The main change in effective tax rates on debt and equity, and on the two forms of equity, clearly occurred between 1985 and 1990. One cause of this was clearly imputation, which reduced taxes on new issues. It is interesting, however, in examining figure 2-3 to observe that there had in fact been a broad trend toward lower taxes on capital income before this time, probably associated with the reductions in total effective taxation associated with accelerated depreciation. This change, however, had not

---

23. Financing can also make a difference, but it tends not to in these results because financing proportions are very similar.

Figure 2-3.   *Effective Tax Rates on Finance Methods, 1960–90*

Percent

produced reductions in distortions, which were extensive until the late 1980s.

Another interesting aspect of figure 2-3 is that a large contribution to the reduction in distortion is attributable to the increase in taxation of debt finance in the late 1980s. This in turn is due to the removal of accelerated depreciation and the lowering of the company tax rate, which, respectively, increase taxation in the company of the income from debt-financed assets and reduce the value of interest deductions.

The impact of changes in the taxation of different channels for investing in the corporate sector is considered in figure 2-4. Generally speaking, neutrality is unlikely to be shown in these aggregate results, and even if it were, neutrality would be unlikely then to hold taxpayer by taxpayer. The reason is that taxation of investment through institutions varies very little with the tax rate of the individual. One consequence of this is that, simply because some institutional investment is shown to be more highly taxed than personal investment, it does not mean that no investor will find it attractive; high-rate taxpayers may well find it so.

There are nonetheless some interesting aspects to figure 2-4. One is the significant increase in tax rates on institutional investment that occurred after the effective removal of deductibility for personal contributions to institutions between 1970 and 1980. Another significant change that is evident is the fall in the effective tax rate on superannuation following the introduction of imputation in 1988.

Figure 2-4.   *Effective Tax Rates on Owners, 1960–90*

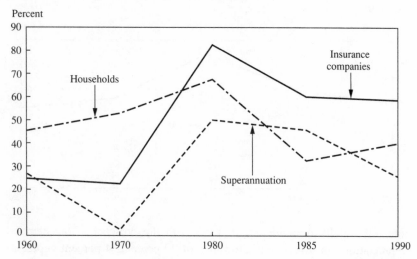

Percent

*Overall Effective Tax Rate*

Changes in the total effective tax rate reflect not just tax-parameter changes but changes in the ownership and financing of the capital stock as well. In interpreting the changes, it is worth remembering that a relatively large (but decreasing) proportion of the capital stock is financed with equity, and that retained earnings are a large part of that equity. In recent years superannuation funds have become very important holders of equity (holding almost one half) after starting the period with a tiny share (3 percent). Households have held a large proportion of the debt throughout the period.[24]

The overall effective tax rate is shown in figure 2-5. Between 1960 and 1970 the tax rate rose. This rise can be broadly attributed to the increase in the company tax rate and the increase in inflation on equity-financed assets. These increases were partly offset by an investment allowance on machinery, and the combined effect of inflation and the higher company tax rate in reducing the cost of debt finance. A shift toward debt finance also helped prevent a higher rate of increase in taxation.

The really significant change in 1980 was the elimination of deductibility for contributions to superannuation and life insurance by individuals. At the same time, the proportion of debt financing fell and inflation increased substantially. The total effective tax rate rose dramatically. That

24. Precise details of the parameters are provided in the appendix to the volume.

Figure 2-5.   *Effective Tax Rates on Overall Corporate Source Income,*
*1960–90*

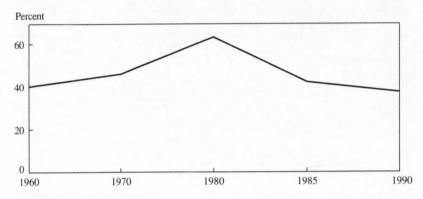

rate fell equally dramatically in 1985 with the presence of accelerated
depreciation, an investment allowance of 20 percent, 4 percent depreciation for buildings, and a lower underlying inflation rate. The proportion
of debt financing also increased, and superannuation funds increased the
proportion they held of total equity. Both factors tended to lower tax rates.

By 1990 there existed the situation which has already received a great
deal of attention: the introduction of imputation (especially important in
lowering taxation on equity investment by superannuation funds, despite
the taxation of fund income), the elimination of accelerated depreciation in
combination with a lower company tax rate, and the introduction of capital
gains taxation. The net effect has been to reduce the overall tax rate a little.

The overall effective tax rate is quite sensitive to the parameters that
are the hardest to specify precisely in this work, namely the proportions
of ownership of equity and debt and the split between debt and equity. For
this reason the changes in figure 2-5 should be considered at the broadest
level only. At this level, and except for the spike in 1980, the rates have
not shown enormous variation. As earlier sections have shown, however,
this has not meant that distortions within the tax system have remained
constant. This would appear to show the value of detailed examination
of the tax system for policy purposes.

## Unincorporated Investment and Housing

By substituting the personal tax rate for the company tax rate and
assuming no further taxation of income accruing to equity holders, it is

Table 2-7.   *Effective Taxation of Noncorporate Income, 1980, 1985, 1990*[a]

Percent

| Item | 1980 | 1985 | 1990 |
|------|------|------|------|
| Asset | | | |
|   Machinery | 36.4 | 9.3 | 37.8 |
|   Buildings | 44.9 | 36.5 | 38.0 |
|   Inventories | 70.2 | 61.9 | 58.6 |
| Industry | | | |
|   Manufacturing | 49.0 | 29.3 | 43.6 |
|   Other industry | 39.9 | 15.3 | 38.7 |
|   Commerce | 51.5 | 36.7 | 44.0 |
| Finance | | | |
|   Debt | 20.9 | 4.4 | 21.2 |
|   Equity | 56.0 | 41.1 | 54.0 |
| Overall | 49.2 | 31.1 | 43.3 |

a. Calculations based on inflation of 10 percent in 1980, and 7 percent in 1985 and 1990.

possible to generate effective tax rates for the unincorporated sector. Here it is assumed that financing of, and the asset mix in, different activities is the same as for the incorporated sector.

### Unincorporated Investment

Other things being equal, neutrality is as much an object in the unincorporated sector as in the incorporated sector. An additional interesting aspect is the extent to which nonneutralities in noncorporate investment match those in companies. Table 2-7 shows effective tax rates in the unincorporated sector. The pattern in assets is very similar to that for the incorporated sector, with a large distortion between inventory and the other assets under the high inflation in 1980, an even larger distortion in 1985 as machinery benefits from both accelerated depreciation and the investment allowance, and great reduction in distortions under the 1990 regime. The consequential effects of dispersed-asset effective tax rates on industry effective tax rates also follow the pattern of the corporate sector, with the other industry category, having low inventory and high machinery requirements, starting out of line in 1980, getting more out of line in 1985, and becoming more like the other two sectors in 1990.

The effective tax rates on financing alternatives show a pattern similar to those in the corporate sector in 1985 and 1990, with the preference for debt declining. In 1980 the situation is a little different, since in that

Figure 2-6.    *Effective Tax Rates on Noncorporate and Corporate Investment*

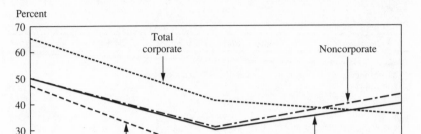

year there was a great difference between the statutory corporate tax rate (46 percent) and the tax rate in the unincorporated sector (38 percent). This difference affects the value of interest deductibility and makes the effective tax rate on debt somewhat higher relative to that on equity in the unincorporated sector.

Perhaps the question of greatest interest is the overall incentive to invest in the corporate versus the unincorporated sector. Some of the relevant information from the results calculated in this work is shown in figure 2-6. The figure shows the total effective tax rates in the unincorporated sector, and the incorporated sector. The effective tax rate on the corporate sector has also been split into a corporate tax rate (ctr) and a personal tax rate (ptr). (See "Current Taxation of Corporate Source Income," earlier in this chapter.) The noncorporate rate is below the total corporate rate in 1980 and 1985 but rises above it in 1990. This preference for corporate investment is perhaps surprising. The presence of the tax on unfranked dividends associated with Australian imputation must make the tax rate on an equity investment by an individual in the corporate sector higher than an equivalent investment in the unincorporated sector. However, the figures in the chart show the *aggregate* incentives to invest and so include taxes on debt finance and, for the corporate sector, the effects of investing through institutions. Largely because of the impact of superannuation-fund investment (which is assumed not to be made in the unincorporated sector), the results therefore show very slight aggregate preference for corporate investment in 1990.

If the corporate tax rate can be assumed to represent the incentives facing foreigners to invest in the Australian corporate sector, figure 2-6 appears to indicate that there is a tendency for corporate investment to be overexpanded relative to noncorporate investment. However, as was indicated earlier in this chapter, to assume that foreigners make all the marginal corporate investments is probably too strong an assumption. Interestingly, the personal tax rate on corporate source income follows the noncorporate rate very closely. This could be taken to indicate a lack of tax bias in Australians' choice between corporate and noncorporate investment if the Australian economy were fully open to investment from abroad.

### Owner-Occupied Housing

As there is no taxation of imputed rent in Australia and no deductibility of interest, the only taxes that affect the return to investment in owner-occupied housing are on rates and interest receipts. In addition, the proportion of debt is very low (about 10 percent), which tends to reduce the effective tax rate further. The main variables affecting the effective tax rate are thus the inflation rate (which causes nominal interest rates and taxation to rise), the proportions of interest received by different lenders, and the tax rates on those lenders. The effective tax rate of owner-occupied housing was 3.2 percent in 1980, 7.5 percent in 1985, and 12.2 percent in 1990. These figures mainly show the effect of increased taxation of superannuation funds. The figures are perhaps more notable for their absolute level than for their changes over time. They are clearly very low relative to taxes on investment in industry.

## Inflation and Taxation—the Income-Tax Issue of the 1990s

Inflation has the effect of reducing the present value of depreciation allowances. Other things equal, this leads to an increase in effective tax rates on depreciable assets in the company. At the same time, inflation increases the nominal interest rate. At the company level this increases the size of the deduction for interest, but it also increases the taxation of lenders who pay tax on nominal interest receipts. The net effect is partly dependent on the relative level of statutory tax rates in the company and

Figure 2-7.    *Effective Tax Rates under Inflation*

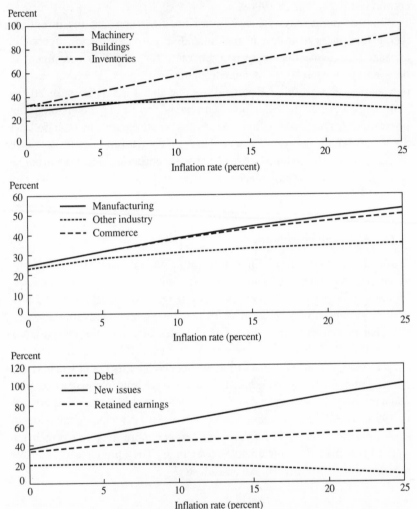

on lenders. The other important effect of inflation, as has been stressed throughout this chapter, is on taxation of inventories under FIFO.

Figure 2-7 shows the effective tax rates in the various categories of interest at different rates of inflation. The total effective tax rate on corporate source income in Australia rises with inflation. At the same time, distortions generally get worse as inflation increases. For assets, this worsening is due to the full nominal taxation of inventories combined with less than nominal taxation of the other assets. Distortions among

Figure 2-7    *(continued)*

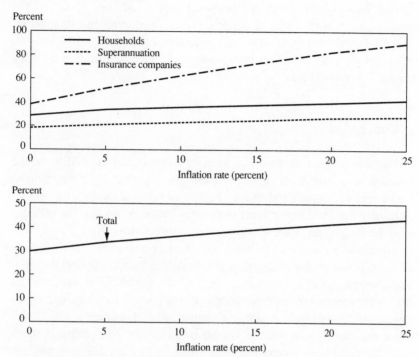

industries basically reflect the worsening at the asset level and the different asset proportions used in industries. The finance distortions show, at the extremes, the nominal taxation of income received as new issues through the imputation process, and the benefit to debt finance that occurs because the deduction for interest is taken at a higher tax rate than the subsequent taxation in the hands of lenders. Retained earnings are subject to increasing nominal taxation in the company but benefit, relatively, because the remaining income is taxed under the indexed capital gains tax. With recipients, the major difference appears to occur because insurance companies do not have the benefit of indexation in the taxation of their capital gains.

The results thus appear to indicate substantial sensitivity of the tax system to inflation. It should be noted, too, that summary results of this type can never give sufficient weight to the types of distortion likely to be introduced. Differences by asset, for example, are likely to be much more severe if disaggregated into assets of different lives.

The sensitivity of the tax system to inflation is perhaps the most important current issue in the design of taxes on capital income. These results suggest that modifications to the tax system, including full indexation, deserve further sustained attention. In terms of the results of figure 2-7, full indexation of the present tax system would give the effective tax rates shown at zero inflation.

## Conclusion

The aim of this chapter has been to examine the neutrality of the taxation of income from capital in Australia. Most attention was paid to the current tax system and to the changes in taxation through the 1980s, especially the extensive reform in the late 1980s. However, the changes over the longer run, back to 1960, were also considered.

The tax reforms of the late 1980s have had a major effect in evening out nonneutralities in the taxation of corporate (and noncorporate) income. The combination of inflation, the classical tax system, high company tax rates, allowances for investment and depreciation, and particular forms of taxation of institutions led to a high degree of disparity, which was at its most evident in the tax system of 1985. By 1990 most of those distortions had been greatly reduced. This is not to say, however, that the tax system is now ideal. There remains, for example, a strong relative incentive to invest in owner-occupied housing. Moreover, the current tax system is sensitive to inflation in several ways. Distortions by asset, industry, finance, and owner all increase with inflation. In addition, the total incentive to invest in the corporate sector as a whole increases with inflation.

It would seem, therefore, that further reform of the tax system should not be ruled out. With inflation proving stubbornly resistant to significant reduction, there would appear to be grounds for examining comprehensive indexation of the tax system. In adddition, the continuing gap between the effective taxation of owner-occupied housing and of other corporate and unincorporated investment is indicative of the problems associated with a tax system that places strong emphasis on the taxation of income from capital of (perhaps necessarily) only some assets. The desirability of moving toward further neutrality either by making income taxation more comprehensive or by reducing the burden on assets that currently are highly taxed seems clear.

## Appendix: Nonstandard Assumptions

The results shown in this chapter vary in some respects from those generated under the standard King-Fullerton program PTAX. The variations are described below.

### Financing

In all the results presented here, financing is allowed to vary by industry. This makes very little difference to the uniform financing under the conventional program PTAX.

### Imputation

There were important changes to the modeling of imputation in 1990. The PTAX approach was to have a single imputation parameter applicable to all dividends. However, this cannot be used for Australia, for the ability to frank depends on company tax paid. Unless there is trading in imputation credits, which is much less likely now than it has been,[25] such an approach would generally reduce effective tax rates by allowing excesssive credits. In addition, the Australian mechanism for franking earnings which are retained is not allowed for in PTAX.

In my work the following approach is taken (this lies behind the results in table 2-4): for investment through new issues, dividends are received either franked or unfranked. The after-tax return is then either equation 2A-1 in the case of a franked dividend or equation 2A-2 in the case of an unfranked dividend.

$$(2A-1) \qquad\qquad \rho\theta(1 - m)$$

$$(2A-2) \qquad\qquad \rho(1 - m),$$

where $\rho$ is the discount rate or internal rate of return in the company, $\theta$ is the imputation parameter, and $m$ is the personal tax rate. In equation 2A-1, dividends may be considered to have been paid out of income which has borne the full rate of company tax. (The quantity of such dividends which is paid is limited by the amount of company tax paid.) In equation 2A-2, the dividends may be considered to have borne no company tax.

25. Bureau of Industry Economics (1990).

Disregarding charges such as rates imposed outside the company tax system, franked dividends are paid from an amount of company income after company tax ($\tau$) of

(2A-3)                                $(p + \pi)(1 - \tau)$,

where $\pi$ is the rate of inflation. Using the definition of the imputation parameter, $[\theta = 1/(1-\tau)]$, the after-tax return to shareholders from these dividends is therefore

$$(p + \pi)(1 - m),$$

which is the same as the final return on unfranked dividends. For investment using retained earnings, the shareholder's return is

(2A-4)                                $f(p + \pi)(1 - m)$

for the proportion, $f$, of earnings covered by franking credits, and

(2A-5)                                $(1 - f)(p + \pi)(1 - z)$

for the rest—$(1 - f)[p(1 - z) + p]$ in the case of the indexed capital gains tax).

### Alternative Model

An alternative possibility in dealing with the situation in 1990 involves the value of debt finance. Under imputation, a payment or saving of tax at the company level is not necessarily given by the value of the dollar amount multiplied by the company tax rate. This is because of the relationship between company tax paid and personal taxation under imputation. A saving of tax, for example, means that there is less in the franking account balance and that more after-tax income in the company may be retained and therefore taxed concessionally as a capital gain to the shareholder rather than as a dividend. In effect the tax rate ($\tau'$) on income earned on debt financed assets, and the tax rate for interest deductions, is

(2A-6)                                $\tau' = m - z$

for an unindexed capital gains tax and

(2A-7)                                $\tau' = m - [pz/(p + \pi)]$

for an indexed capital gains tax. The results of this alteration are in table 2A-1.

The principal differences are a higher rate of effective taxation on debt because of the lowering of the tax rate. In general the value of interest

Table 2A-1.   *Alternative Results for 1990*

Percent

| Item | Total (new view) | Corporate (less imputation credits) | Individual (new view) |
|---|---|---|---|
| Asset | | | |
| Machinery | 37.8 | −2.4 | 39.3 |
| Buildings | 39.0 | −0.5 | 39.3 |
| Inventories | 46.4 | 0.4 | 46.2 |
| Industry | | | |
| Manufacturing | 40.6 | −1.1 | 41.3 |
| Other industry | 38.6 | −1.8 | 39.7 |
| Commerce | 40.6 | −0.1 | 41.2 |
| Finance | | | |
| Debt | 34.9 | −5.4 | 38.2 |
| New issues | 50.3 | 1.0 | 49.8 |
| Retained earnings | 40.4 | 0.9 | 39.8 |
| Owner | | | |
| Households | 45.1 | −2.6 | 46.8 |
| Superannuation | 24.8 | −0.3 | 24.6 |
| Insurance companies | 59.5 | −0.3 | 59.3 |
| Overall tax rate | 40.4 | −1.1 | 41.1 |

deductibility is greater than the taxation of income from a debt-financed asset, and this tax advantage is reduced. In addition there are some small changes among assets. These become greater as the taxation of income earned on the asset concerned becomes higher. Inventory, which is taxed on a nominal basis, has taxation of income which is equal to the value of nominal interest deductibility, and its taxation is unaffected by the tax rate at the company level.

### Superannuation

In this chapter, superannuation is treated as a form of investment by a household. This should be contrasted with the conventional KF approach, which treats superannuation as tax-free on the basis that expenditure tax treatment is common. This makes some difference to the total tax rate on superannuation and to the overall tax rate.

The tax rate applying to superannuation is the implicit subsidy or tax that would equate the final value of a unit investment to the final value achieved by existing tax concessions.[26] For employers' contributions, the final benefit may be written as $(1 + p)^n \cdot (1 - t_g)/(1 - m)$, where $p$ is the

26. As in Hills (1984).

rate of return earned by the superannuation fund, $n$ is the number of years the investment is held, $t_g$ is the tax rate on the lump sum, and $m$ is the marginal personal tax rate on income. The factor $1/(1-m)$ reflects the tax deductibility given to contributors. This treatment also applies to employee contributions in 1960 and 1970, when they were allowed tax deductibility.

The equivalent annual (negative) tax on a unit investment out of post-tax earnings under such arrangements is given by $t_f$ where

$$(2A\text{-}8) \qquad [1 + p(1 - t_f)]^n = (1 + p)^n(1 - t_g)/(1 - m)$$
$$t_f = 1 - [(1 + p)(1 - t_g)^{1/n}$$
$$(1 - m)^{-1/n} - 1]/p.$$

By 1980, employees' contributions were no longer effectively deductible for most contributors. In these circumstances, the effective tax rate on employees' contributions, $t_n$, is given by the equation

$$(2A\text{-}9) \quad [1 + p(1 - t_n)]^n = (1 + p)^n - t_g[(1 + p)^n - 1)]$$
$$t_n = 1 - \{[(1 + p)^n(1 - t_g) + t_g]^{1/n} - 1\}/p.$$

For the situation in 1988–89 and following years the return out of the company, $p$, will be reduced in all cases by superannuation tax $t_p$. In addition, employers' contributions will be subject to tax, $t_c$, at 15 percent. This gives, for employers' contributions which are invested in lending or new issues

$$(2A\text{-}10) \qquad [1 + p(1 - t_f)]^n = \{[1 + p(1 - t_p)]^n(1 - t_g)$$
$$(1 - t_c)\}/(1 - m)$$
$$t_f = 1 - \{[1 + p(1 - t_p)](1 - t_g)^{1/n}$$
$$(1 - t_c)^{1/n}(1 - m)^{-1/n} - 1\}/p,$$

and for employees' contributions

$$(2A\text{-}11) \qquad [1 + p(1 - t_n)]^n = [1 + p(1 - t_p)]^n - t_g$$
$$\{[1 + p(1 - t_p)]^n - 1\}$$
$$t_n = 1 - \Big(\{[1 + p(1 - t_p)]^n$$
$$(1 - t_g) + t_g\}^{1/n} - 1\Big)/p.$$

If the superannuation fund has shares in companies that invest out of retained earnings, the gains are subject to a real capital gains tax. The total effective tax rate on employers' contributions is derived as follows:

Table 2A-2.  *Superannuation and Insurance Parameters, Selected Years, 1960–90*

| Item | 1960 | 1970 | 1980 | 1985 | 1990 |
|---|---|---|---|---|---|
| $n$ | 20.00 | 20.00 | 20.00 | 20.00 | 20.00 |
| $m$ | 0.23 | 32.00 | 0.37 | 0.40 | 0.40 |
| $t_g$ | 0.03 | 0.03 | 0.03 | 0.30 | 0.1625 |
| $t_p$ | . . . | . . . | . . . | . . . | 0.15 |
| $t_c$ | . . . | . . . | . . . | . . . | 0.15 |
| $w_f$ | 1.00 | 1.00 | 0.32 | 0.31 | 0.31 |
| $t_i$ (interest) | 0.23 | 0.28 | . . . | . . . | . . . |
| $t_i$ (dividends) | −0.16 | −0.16 | . . . | . . . | . . . |

$$(2A\text{-}12) \quad (1 + p(1 - t_f))^n = [1 + p - (p - \pi)z]^n(1 - t_g)$$
$$(1 - t_c)/(1 - m)$$
$$t_f = 1 - \{[1 + p(1 - z) + \pi z](1 - t_g)^{1/n}$$
$$(1 - t_c)^{1/n}(1 - m)^{-1/n} - 1\}/p.$$

The total-effect tax rate on employees' contributions is derived similarly:

$$(2A\text{-}13) \quad [1 + p(1 - t_n)]^n = [1 + p - (p - \pi)z]^n - t_g$$
$$\{[1 + p - (p - \pi)z]^n - 1\}$$
$$t_n = 1 - \big([\{[1 + p(1 - z) + \pi z]^n(1 - t_g)$$
$$+ t_g\}^{1/n} - 1\big)/p.$$

The final tax on superannuation as a whole, $t_s$, is then

$$(2A\text{-}14) \quad t_s = w_f t_f + (1 - w_f)t_n,$$

where $w_f$ is the proportion of investment which receives the benefits of deductibility. The relevant parameters are given in table 2A-2.

### Life Insurance

In 1960 and 1970, contributions to life insurance were deductible. As with superannuation, this benefit is taken into account in calculating the effective tax rate on this form of investment. The effective tax rate $t_l$ is given, as before, by equating terminal benefits, where $t_i$ is the tax rate on the income from the investee company when it is received by the insurance company.

$$(2A\text{-}15) \quad [1 + p(1 - t_l)]^n = [1 + p(1 - t_i)]^n/(1 - m)$$
$$t_i = 1 - \{[1 + p(1 - t_i)](1 - m)^{-1/n} - 1\}/p.$$

## References

Australian Bureau of Statistics (ABS). *Australian National Accounts: National Income and Expenditure*. Catalogue 5204.0. Canberra: Australian Government Publishing Service (AGPS).

———. *Taxation Revenue*. Catalogue 5506.0. Canberra: AGPS.

Bureau of Industry Economics. 1990. *Does the Australian Tax System Favour Company Debt?* Business Income Taxation Paper 4. Canberra: AGPS.

Commissioner of Taxation. *Taxation Statistics*. Canberra: AGPS.

Commonwealth of Australia. 1975. *Committee of Inquiry into Inflation and Taxation* (Mathews Report). Canberra: AGPS.

———. 1981. Australian Financial System. *Final Report of the Committee of Inquiry*. Canberra: AGPS.

———. 1985. *Reform of the Australian Tax System*. Canberra: AGPS.

Davies, Peter H. 1982. "Equity Finance and the Ownership of Shares." In *Australian Financial System Inquiry—Commissioned Studies and Selected Papers*, pt. 3, 259–442. Canberra: AGPS.

Evans, Edward A. 1987. "Australia." In *World Tax Reform: A Progress Report*, edited by Joseph A. Pechman, 15–39. Brookings.

Feldstein, Martin, and Charles Horioka. 1980. "Domestic Saving and International Capital Flows." *Economic Journal* 90 (June): 314–29.

Herps, M. D. 1981. "A Study of the Official Land Valuations of the Australian States and of Their Capacity to Raise Revenues from Land Transactions." In Commonwealth Grants Commission, *Report on State Tax Sharing Entitlements, 1981*, vol. 2: *Report of Consultants*. Canberra: AGPS.

———. 1985. "Relative Capacities of States and the Northern Territory to Raise Land Revenues." In Commonwealth Grants Commission, *Report on State Tax Sharing Relativities, 1985*, vol. 2: *Appendixes and Consultants' Reports*. Canberra: AGPS.

Hills, John. 1984. *Savings and Fiscal Privilege*. London: Institute for Fiscal Studies.

King, Mervyn A., and Don Fullerton. 1984. *The Taxation of Income from Capital: A Comparative Study of the United States, the United Kingdom, Sweden, and West Germany*. University of Chicago Press.

Piggott, John. 1987. "The Nation's Private Wealth—Some New Calculations for Australia." *Economic Record* 63: 61–79.

Prest, Alan R. 1983. *Some Issues in Australian Land Taxation*. Centre for Research on Federal Financial Relations. Canberra: Australian National University Press.

Reserve Bank of Australia. 1985. *Australian Economic Statistics 1949–50 to 1984–85*. Occasional Paper 8A. Sydney.

Reserve Bank of Australia. [Annual]. *Reserve Bank Bulletin*. Sydney.

Walters, Robert, and Robert J. Dippelsman. 1985. *Estimates of Depreciation and Capital Stock: Australia*. Australian Bureau of Statistics Occasional Paper 1985/3. Canberra: AGPS.

CHAPTER THREE

# Canada

*Michael J. Daly*
*Pierre Mercier*
*Thomas Schweitzer*

THE MANNER in which investment income is taxed in Canada ought to be a matter of interest to international observers, and a matter of concern to all Canadians. A tax system that departs from neutrality by giving preferential treatment to some forms of capital income shifts the tax burden onto wage earners, consumers, and the recipients of capital income in forms that the tax system does not favor. Moreover, a nonneutral tax system diverts capital resources from their most productive uses—that is, those with the highest rates of return before taxes—into activities that are less productive but that yield greater after-tax returns because of the preferential tax treatment they enjoy. Nonneutralities also encourage taxpayers (firms as well as individuals) and their advisers to devote real resources to the discovery of ways to convert one type of income into another (for example, dividends into capital gains, or vice versa) in order to minimize their tax liabilities, a practice that in turn creates a need for further legal constraints to prevent tax avoidance. The multiplication of constraints has created an unnecessarily complex and constantly changing tax system— one that entails real costs for firms, individuals, and the tax authorities. The result is less productivity and national output, and thus lower living standards for capital owners and wage earners alike. Furthermore, the existing tax system as a whole favors current consumption over saving, a departure from neutrality that tends to discourage investment, thereby

The authors thank Richard Bird, Don Fullerton, Mervyn King, George Kuo, Jack Mintz, and David Sewell for their helpful comments. The support of the Economic Council of Canada and the assistance of the Department of Finance are gratefully acknowledged. The views expressed are solely those of the authors and, as such, have not been endorsed by either the Economic Council of Canada or the Department of Finance.

impeding economic growth and jeopardizing the future living standards of all groups in society.

One of the principal objectives of the recent steps taken by Canada's federal government to overhaul the Canadian tax structure is to increase the neutrality of the tax system in order to ensure that decisions to save and invest are based on economic rather than tax considerations. This objective is being achieved in three ways: by reducing, and in some cases removing, certain tax concessions, thereby broadening the tax base; by lowering statutory tax rates; and by implementing a consumption-based value-added tax.

The purpose of this chapter is threefold. First, using the theoretical framework developed by Mervyn A. King and Don Fullerton, marginal effective tax rates for Canada are computed, taking into account corporation, personal, and business property taxes, as well as sales taxes levied on purchases of capital inputs.[1] Although these sales taxes are especially important in the case of Canada, they have generally been ignored by studies involving the computation of marginal effective tax rates. By including such taxes in the calculations reported in this study, a more complete picture of the pattern of marginal effective tax rates in Canada is provided than that found in previous studies. The overall marginal effective tax rate is then separated into various components corresponding to each particular tax so as to determine their relative contribution to the total tax wedge as well as to the variation in total tax rates. Second, the King and Fullerton methodology for computing marginal effective tax rates is extended to noncorporate business investment and to owner-occupied housing. This enables us to determine not only the extent to which the tax system distorts the pattern of investment incentives within the noncorporate sector, but also the degree to which it discriminates against investments in the corporate sector compared to those in the noncorporate sector. Third, we evaluate the impact of recent tax reform on investment and saving incentives in Canada.

The rest of this study is organized as follows. The next section, "Theoretical Framework," contains a brief description of how the King and Fullerton methodology for deriving marginal effective tax rates is applied to Canada. The following section, "An Overview of the Canadian Tax System," summarizes the main features of the Canadian tax system, both before and after recent tax reform, together with the tax parameters

1. King and Fullerton (1984).

used to compute marginal effective tax rates. Estimates of marginal effective tax rates for Canada, including those resulting from tax reform, are reported in the following section, and the chapter ends with some concluding comments.

## Theoretical Framework

The marginal effective tax rates for Canada reported in this chapter are derived from the cost of capital, as defined by Hall and Jorgenson, using the methodology developed by King and King and Fullerton. A detailed description of the manner in which this methodology can be adapted and applied to Canada is described by Michael J. Daly, Pierre Mercier, and Thomas Schweitzer.[2]

### Marginal Effective Tax Rates

Following King and Fullerton, marginal effective tax rates on income from capital in the corporate sector are calculated for a series of hypothetical marginal investment projects, with four distinct characteristics: 1) the type of asset purchased—machinery, buildings, or inventories; 2) the industry in which the investment is made—manufacturing, commerce, or other industry; 3) the manner in which the investment is financed—debt, new share issues, or retained earnings; and 4) the category of investor supplying the funds—a household, a tax-exempt institution, or a life insurance company.

The total tax wedge, $w$, is the difference between $p$, the real rate of return on investment net of depreciation, and $s$, the after-tax real rate of return on savings used to finance the investment. Thus, the marginal effective *total* tax rate is defined as

$$(3\text{-}1) \qquad t = w/p = (p - s)/p.$$

The total tax wedge can be separated into two components: $w_1$, the corporate tax wedge (which includes business property taxes as well as sales taxes levied on capital goods); and $w_2$, the personal wedge. They

---

2. Hall and Jorgenson (1967); King (1977); King and Fullerton (1984); Daly, Mercier, and Schweitzer (1989).

are defined respectively as $w_1 = p - q$ and $w_2 = q - s$, where $q$ denotes an investment project's real rate of return after corporate income taxes, property taxes, and sales taxes, but before personal taxes. Hence,

$$(3\text{-}2) \qquad\qquad t_c = w_1/p = (p - q)/p$$

and

$$(3\text{-}3) \qquad\qquad t_p = w_2/q = (q - s)/q,$$

where $t_c$ is the marginal effective *corporate* tax rate (inclusive of property and sales taxes), and $t_p$ is the marginal effective *personal* tax rate. If property and sales taxes are excluded and only the corporation tax is involved, $t_c$ is defined as the marginal effective *corporation* tax rate.

In the case of debt-financed investment, $q = i - \pi = r$, where $i$ is the nominal market interest rate, $\pi$ denotes the expected annual rate of inflation, and $r$ is the real interest rate. For investment financed by new share issues or retained earnings, $q = \rho - \pi$, where $\rho$ denotes an investment project's rate of return net of corporation taxes, business property taxes, and sales taxes levied on purchases of capital goods.

Note that if investment is financed by domestic saving, $i$ and $\rho$ are determined domestically, and the total tax rate, $t$, reflects the incentive or disincentive to invest provided by the tax system. However, if Canada can be considered a small open economy and capital is perfectly mobile internationally, then $i$ and $\rho$ are instead determined on world capital markets. Consequently, it is the corporate tax rate, $t_c$, rather than the total tax rate, $t$, that is relevant for domestic investment decisions, while the personal rate, $t_p$, is most relevant for domestic saving decisions.[3]

The minimum rate of return (or hurdle rate) that an investment project must yield before taxes in order to provide the saver with the same net-of-tax return as he or she would receive from lending at the market rate of interest is called the cost of capital and denoted as $c$. The relation between the cost of capital and the real rate of interest can be expressed as

$$(3\text{-}4) \qquad\qquad p = c(r),$$

where $c(r)$, the cost-of-capital function, depends on the industry in which the investment is undertaken, the type of capital purchased, the method

---

3. These issues are discussed at greater length in Daly, Mercier, and Schweitzer (1989).

of finance used, the kind of saver supplying the funds, and, of course, the tax structure.

The saver's post-tax real rate of return is

$$(3\text{-}5) \qquad\qquad s = i(1 - m) - \pi,$$

where $m$ denotes the marginal personal tax rate on interest income. In the absence of tax arbitrage, the value of $s$ depends upon the manner in which real investment is financed and the type of saver providing the funds.

For the unincorporated business sector, the procedure for computing marginal effective tax rates is similar to the one used for the corporate sector. However, while we again have the same three types of asset and the same three industries, we consider only two methods of finance—debt and proprietors' equity—and one category of investor—households. Furthermore, since income from investment in the unincorporated business sector is not subject to corporate income taxes, but is instead taxed at the personal level, only the total tax wedge is computed, again taking into account business property and sales taxes levied on capital goods. For owner-occupied housing, only one asset is involved, with two possible methods of finance—debt and homeowners' equity—and again one category of investor—households. The total tax wedge in this case is computed taking into account residential property taxes as well as personal taxes.

### Cost of Capital

Following the notation used by King and Fullerton, the expression for the cost of capital net of depreciation is given by

$$(3\text{-}6) \qquad c(r) = \frac{(1 + h)(1 - A)(\rho + \delta - \pi) + d_1\tau(\pi - v)}{(1 - \tau)} + w_c - \delta,$$

where $h$ denotes the rate of sales tax levied or purchases of capital goods, $A$ is the present value of any tax allowances for the investment, $\tau$ is the corporation tax rate, $w_c$ is the business property tax rate, $v$ is the rate of inventory allowance, with the dummy variable, $d_1$, taking the value of one for inventories and zero for machinery and buildings, and $\delta$ is the exponential rate of economic depreciation. The firm's discount rate, $\rho$, is related to $i$ and, therefore, to $r$.

In the case of unincorporated business investment, the cost of capital expression is the same as that given by equation 6 except that the corporation tax rate, $\tau$, is replaced by the unincorporated business proprietor's personal marginal tax rate, $n$. In effect, this means that the tax treatment of noncorporate investment income is the same as that which would be achieved with full integration of corporate and personal income taxes. The proprietor's discount rate is then substituted for the corporation's discount rate.

Investment in owner-occupied housing does not receive any tax credits or depreciation allowances. Moreover, the imputed return from owner-occupied housing is nontaxable and neither mortgage interest payments nor residential property taxes are tax-deductible. No sales taxes are levied on the purchase of a new house. The cost of capital corresponding to owner-occupied housing is, therefore,

(3-7) $$c(r) = \rho - \pi + w_p,$$

where $w_p$ denotes the residential property tax rate.

### Financing Assumption

Our main estimates of marginal effective tax rates are based on the assumption that firms finance marginal investments in exactly the same way as they financed their existing capital stock. As shown in table A-4 in the appendix to this volume, this means that only a very small proportion of marginal corporate investment is financed by new share issues. The small weight associated with new share issues is consistent with the "new" or "trapped-equity" view of corporate taxation, according to which a dividend tax is capitalized in share prices and thus cannot affect the cost of capital.

Empirical evidence gathered by James M. Poterba and Lawrence H. Summers, however, suggests that dividend taxes do have an adverse effect on investment, a finding that supports the "traditional" view of corporate taxation.[4] This finding may be explained by the fact that the "new" view ignores the signaling function of dividends. The nonneutrality of dividend taxation with respect to investment decisions may also be attributed to the possibility that, although the new view may be appropriate for mature corporations, the traditional view is probably more indicative of the sit-

4. Poterba and Summers (1983).

uation faced by new or recently established corporations, because such firms depend more heavily on new share issues to finance their investments. Hence, marginal effective tax rates are also computed for the corporate sector under the assumption that the part of marginal investment financed with equity consists exclusively of new share issues. Obviously, under the traditional view, changes in the taxation of dividends have a greater impact on marginal effective tax rates, and changes in the taxation of capital gains have a smaller impact on marginal effective tax rates, than is the case if the new view prevails.

## An Overview of the Canadian Tax System

Although introduced by the federal government in 1917 as a temporary measure to defray the costs associated with the First World War, income taxes were never abandoned. Instead they became a permanent feature of the Canadian tax system. The importance of the personal tax has grown to such an extent that it is now the main source of revenue for federal and provincial governments combined, accounting for 34.5 percent of total tax receipts in 1985, compared with 19.5 percent in 1955. In contrast, whereas the corporation tax yielded almost 19.5 percent of total tax revenue in 1955, thirty years later its share of receipts had dropped to 8.5 percent. The contribution of sales and excise taxes to total revenue also fell, from 36.5 percent in 1955 to 22.9 percent in 1985. Over the same period, property taxes as a proportion of total tax revenue dropped slightly, from 11.4 to 9.3 percent.

Since World War II, Canada's income tax system has undergone numerous changes, many of which have concerned the taxation of capital income and have been aimed at promoting saving and investment. In 1949, following three years of study, a wholly revised federal Income Tax Act was adopted. Among other things, the new legislation introduced the present system of capital cost allowances (CCAs) based on the declining balance method, as well as a dividend tax credit. Tax-deductible registered retirement savings plans (RRSPs) were introduced in 1957 to encourage personal saving for retirement.

The most important event in the evolution of the country's income tax system was establishment of the Carter commission, which published its report in 1966, after almost five years' study of Canada's tax system. This landmark in Canadian tax history resulted in some major revisions to the Income Tax Act in 1972. While focusing much of its attention on fairness, the report also addressed a number of issues pertaining to the taxation of capital income, among them the adoption of a more comprehensive concept of income, closer integration of corporate and personal income taxes, and the achievement of greater neutrality in taxation through the elimination or reduction of incentive provisions. Strict adherence to these general principles would have required full taxation of capital gains (which were previously exempt), full crediting of corporate income tax against personal income tax for shareholders, elimination of many incentive features of the corporation tax, and an overhaul of the taxation of international income. Although in 1969 the government released a white paper embracing many of the Carter commission's ideas, public resistance resulted in 1972 in considerably watered-down legislation. This legislation required taxpayers to include half of realized capital gains in their taxable income, revised and extended an existing credit for corporation taxes against personal income, eliminated several incentive features of the corporation tax, and reduced the top personal income tax rate. The legislation also repealed federal gift and death taxes, an action followed in later years by all provinces.

The acceleration in the rate of inflation after 1972 also resulted in major tax changes aimed at indexing the tax system. Personal income tax exemptions and tax brackets were indexed to the consumer price index (CPI) starting in 1974, thus preventing the rapid inflation of the middle-to-late 1970s and early 1980s from raising real tax burdens by pushing taxpayers into higher tax brackets. Furthermore, part of the rationale for the $1,000 deduction for interest income, which was introduced in 1974 and subsequently extended to cover dividends and capital gains, was a desire to shelter from taxation the inflation-premium component of interest for low-income taxpayers. Concern over the impact of inflation on the taxation of businesses prompted the government to provide some relief from the taxation of inflationary inventory profits that were created by first in, first out (FIFO) accounting methods; in 1977 the federal government introduced an income tax deduction equal to 3 percent of the value of inventories held at the beginning of the tax year. The adverse impact of inflation on corporate cash flows was also a factor behind the enhancement of the investment tax credit and capital cost allowances.

All these developments, together with other changes in both the structure and rates of tax, reveal four distinct trends with respect to the corporation and personal tax systems during the 1970s and early 1980s.

First, Canadians witnessed an increasing degree of integration between corporate and personal income taxes through the dividend tax credit.[5] Second, notwithstanding the Carter commission's emphasis on the desirability of a comprehensive income tax, there was a gradual shift away from a tax system based on annual income to one based on a hybrid of income and expenditure, owing mainly to the rapid growth in tax-exempt saving through registered pension plans and RRSPs, and to the $1,000 investment income deduction. Third, the preferential corporation tax rate on profits derived from manufacturing and processing in Canada, the three-year write-off for expenditures on machinery and equipment by firms engaged in manufacturing and processing, and the increased use of the investment tax credits introduced in 1975 all reflected a trend toward encouraging investment in certain activities by means of the tax system. This too was contrary to the views expressed by the Carter commission. Finally, in an attempt to adjust the capital income tax system for the effects of inflation, a number of measures were introduced, notably the $1,000 personal investment income deduction, the enhancement of the investment tax credit and capital cost allowances, the 3 percent inventory allowance, and indexed security investment plans (ISIPs).[6] These and other features of the corporation and personal tax structures are discussed at greater length in the remainder of this section.

## The Tax System in 1985

THE CORPORATION TAX. In 1985 the federal statutory corporation tax rate was 36 percent. Manufacturing income was taxed at the rate of 30

---

5. The additional burden on distributed profits imposed by the corporation tax is measured by $\theta(1 - \tau)$, where $\theta$ denotes the opportunity cost of retained earnings in terms of gross dividends forgone, and $\tau$ is the rate of corporation tax. This measure of integration is known as the ACID test statistic (see King, 1977, p. 57). A value of zero implies complete confiscation of dividend income by the corporation tax, while a value of unity means that the corporation tax imposes no tax on dividends over and above the level of personal taxation. For large manufacturing and nonmanufacturing companies, respectively, the ACID test statistic rose from values of 0.80 and 0.72 in 1972 to 0.90 and 0.81 in 1977, and remained at roughly the same values until 1987. The increase in value was due to the increase in the dividend tax credit from 33 1/3 percent to 50 percent of grossed-up dividends in 1977.

6. ISIPs were introduced in 1983 to allow full indexation of capital gains realized on the disposition of shares in Canadian companies. Little use was made of these plans, however, and they were withdrawn in 1985 when the $500,000 personal lifetime exemption for capital gains was announced. Consequently, the estimates or marginal effective tax rates for 1985 reported later in this chapter ignore such plans.

percent, however, and for the first $200,000 of income of Canadian-controlled private corporations, small business rates of 10 percent and 15 percent, respectively, were applicable to manufacturing and nonmanufacturing. Additional taxes are levied by provinces, again with reduced rates usually for small businesses and sometimes for manufacturing. The typical provincial rate in 1985 was approximately 14 percent. Companies face different statutory tax rates, therefore, depending on their size, the province in which they are located, and the nature of their production activities. Consequently, as shown in appendix table 3A-1, overall corporation tax rates, $\tau$, vary considerably from one industry to another.

Tax incentives and other deductions mean, however, that a corporation's effective tax rate on investment income is usually well below the statutory rate. Accelerated capital cost allowances enable firms to write off certain investments for tax purposes long before the end of the assets' economic lives. For example, machinery used in the manufacture and processing of goods (CCA class 29) could be written off after only three years, even though its economic life is estimated at over eighteen years. By contrast, the tax lives of buildings corresponded more closely to their economic lives. In addition, investment tax credits (ITCs) were available for new investments of specific types at rates that varied by type of asset, by industry, and by region (see table A-3 in appendix to this volume). Moreover, certain types of inventories qualified for a 3 percent allowance. Finally, interest payments on corporate debt are considered as a business expense so that they are deductible from profits for corporation tax purposes, whereas the costs of equity finance are not deductible. As a result, the corporation tax is levied only on income from investment financed by equity.

BUSINESS PROPERTY TAXES. Property tax rates also vary by type of asset and across industries, as shown in table 3A-1. Business property taxes are levied mainly on land and buildings, with machinery being free of such taxes except insofar as it is used to service buildings. Although no precise estimates were available concerning the proportion of machinery involved in such servicing, it is probably fairly small. Hence, in our calculations the property tax rates given in table 3A-1 are assumed to apply only to buildings (after adjusting for the taxes paid on land).

SALES TAXES. In 1985, federal sales taxes applied to all goods manufactured in Canada or imported into Canada. They were levied not only on goods for final domestic consumption but also on machinery and equipment used in the production of domestic goods and on intermediate inputs. Provincial sales taxes, which are imposed at the retail level, are also levied on machinery and equipment and intermediate inputs in a manner similar to that for federal sales taxes. The federal and provincial sales taxes on machinery and equipment thus partly offset the preferential treatment of those assets under the corporation tax. According to the most recent estimates available, which are for 1980, 13.3 percent of federal sales taxes and 8.6 percent of provincial sales taxes were levied on business purchases of capital inputs; 35.5 percent and 28.5 percent of federal and sales tax revenues, respectively, were derived from intermediate inputs.

The sales tax rates applicable to machinery are reported in table 3A-1. Note that the marginal effective tax rates reported later in this chapter do not take into account sales taxes levied on intermediate inputs used in the production of capital goods. According to Chan-Yan Kuo, Thomas C. McGirr, and Satya Poddar, in the case of materials used in the construction of buildings, the effective total sales tax rate was 5.5 percent in 1980.[7]

THE PERSONAL TAX: HOUSEHOLDS. Nonneutralities in the personal taxation of income from capital can also influence saving and investment decisions. As shown in table 3A-2, the tax treatment of income from corporate investment varies depending upon the manner in which investments are financed (debt, new share issues, or retained earnings) and the tax status of the saver supplying the funds for the investment (households, tax-exempt institutions, or life insurance companies). Interest is earned on debt-financed investments, whereas investments financed by new share issues and retained earnings yield income in the form of dividends and capital gains, respectively.

In the case of households, interest is taxed at the marginal rate, $m$. To compensate in part for the fact that dividends are paid to shareholders out of a corporation's after-tax profits, dividends received by Canadian taxpayers from taxable Canadian corporations are grossed up at the rate $\theta$ for personal tax purposes, and then a tax credit at the rate of $(\theta - 1)$ is applied. The dividend tax credit thus reduces the marginal personal tax rate on dividends from $m$ to $\hat{m}$, where $\hat{m} = \theta m - (\theta - 1)$. In 1985 the value of $\theta$ was 1.5. This in effect meant that for every dollar of dividends actually paid out, the shareholder was deemed to have received a gross

7. Kuo, McGirr, and Poddar (1988).

dividend of $1.50 and to have already paid taxes on that gross dividend at the rate of 33.3 percent.[8]

Capital gains are only taxed upon realization. As a result of such tax deferral, the effective accrued tax (EAT) rate on capital, $z$, is less than the statutory rate, $z_b$. Moreover, in 1985 this statutory rate was, in effect, only half of a capital gains recipient's marginal tax rate because only half of realized capital gains were subject to tax.

The extent of the nonneutralities in the tax treatment of various types of investment income among households differs according to the income tax bracket of the investor. According to the Department of Finance's tax simulation model,[9] dividend tax credit and the $1,000 investment income deduction having been taken into account, the marginal personal tax rate on dividends for a typical shareholder, $m_e$, was approximately 13.4 percent in 1984, the latest year before tax reform for which such information was available. Hence, a typical shareholder's interest income was taxed at the marginal personal rate, $m_e$, which was roughly 42.3 percent.[10] With only half of realized capital gains being taxable, such income was typically taxed at the statutory rate of about 21.1 percent. Assuming that one-tenth of accrued gains are realized in each year, the EAT ratio was about one-half.[11] Consequently, the effective accrued tax rate on capital gains for a typical shareholder, $z_e$, was calculated to be approximately 10.6 percent.

Interest income from corporate bonds received by households directly or indirectly through taxed intermediaries, such as banks, typically faced a marginal personal tax rate, $m_d$, of about 31.8 percent, which is less than that of a typical shareholder, $m_e$, because dividends are concentrated more heavily among persons in high income brackets than is interest income. Therefore, whereas for a typical bondholder the tax rate on interest income was 31.8 percent, that on dividends was only −2.3 percent,[12] owing to the dividend tax credit, and the effective accrued tax rate on capital gains, $z_d$, was approximately 8.0 percent.

---

8. This is an approximation. The actual amount of credit varies by province.

9. The subsequent marginal personal tax rates are generated by the tax simulation model using the 1984 tax structure and data on a sample of 1981 tax filers.

10. $m_e = [\hat{m}_e + (\theta - 1)] \div \theta = [0.134 + (1.5 - 1)] \div 1.5 = 0.423$

11. The effective accrued tax (EAT) rate, $z$, equals the statutory tax rate, $z_s$, multiplied by the EAT ratio. In 1985, $z_s = 0.5m$. The EAT ratio $= \lambda/(\lambda + s + \pi)$, where $\pi$ is the expected inflation rate (5 percent), $\lambda$ denotes the proportion of capital gains realized by investors in each period (10 percent), and $s$ is the post-tax rate of return to the investor. See King (1977, p. 74).

12. $\hat{m}_d = \theta m_d - (\theta - 1) = 1.5 \times 0.318 - (1.5 - 1) = -0.023$.

The personal tax parameters used in our calculations are summarized in table 3A-3.

THE PERSONAL TAX: TAX-EXEMPT INSTITUTIONS. Further nonneutralities arise depending upon whether or not savings are channeled through tax-exempt institutions or life insurance companies. No personal taxes are paid on income from investments financed with households' savings held by tax-exempt institutions in the form of pension funds and registered retirement savings plans. This is precisely what would happen under a personal lifetime-expenditure tax.[13] The present personal tax system is thus a hybrid with features of both an annual income tax and a lifetime-expenditure tax.

THE PERSONAL TAX: LIFE INSURANCE COMPANIES. As regards the tax treatment of income from savings through life insurance policies, one must consider the taxation of both the policyholder and the life insurance company.[14] It is assumed that the purchase of a life insurance policy does not entail any subsequent personal tax liability for the policyholder. This is the usual situation for exempt policies that are held until death and whose holders use any policy dividends to buy additional insurance. Most life insurance policies sold in Canada are exempt policies. As a result, investment income from contractual savings held by life insurance companies for households is assumed to be nontaxable when received by the policyholder.

Life insurance companies are allowed policy-reserve deductions, which ensure that any interest earned on policyholders' funds is not taxable if it is used to fund future payments to policyholders. Our model assumes that life insurance companies earn no excess profits; all the income earned on policyholders' funds is required to fund future payments. It follows that if a life insurance company invests in corporate debt, its tax rate is zero. If, instead, it invests in shares, the policy-reserve deduction is still allowed.

---

13. Implicit in our model is the assumption that the personal income tax rate against which contributions to pension schemes and RRSPs are deducted is the same as the rate at which retirement benefits are taxed when paid out. In practice, however, most individuals probably face higher tax rates during their working lives, when contributing to pension schemes and RRSPs, than when they receive retirement income. To the extent that tax rates fall after retirement, the personal tax rate on income from pension and RRSP funds is negative rather than zero. Consequently, our subsequent calculations probably overstate the marginal effective tax rate on capital income for this category of saver.

14. A more detailed discussion of these and other aspects of life insurance can be found in Hoffman and Macnaughton (1989).

This means that the tax system allows an implicit tax credit payable to life insurance companies for dividends and retentions.

The policy reserve deduction can be viewed as the equivalent of a dividend tax credit at the rate $(\phi - 1)$, as defined in table 3A-2, so long as insurance companies are fully taxable (and dividends are nondeductible for companies distributing them). We estimate that in 1985 insurance companies' statutory rate, $\tau_I$, was 49.7 percent.[15] Realized capital gains were taxed at half that amount, which meant that capital gains received by life insurance companies on policyholders' funds were taxed at the effective accrued rate $z_I = 5.7$ percent.[16] Using policyholders' funds to invest in equity can, therefore, reduce the corporation tax that life insurance companies pay on their income from other activities. Together with the relatively low personal tax rate assumed to apply to policyholders, this meant that income from equity held by life insurance companies was heavily subsidized under the 1985 tax system.

Substituting the values for $\tau_I$ and $z_I$ into the expression in the third column of table 3A-2, we find that the tax rates corresponding to interest, dividends, and capital gains received by households via life insurance companies were 0 percent, $-100$ percent, and $-87.5$ percent, respectively.

UNINCORPORATED BUSINESS. The tax base for unincorporated businesses is exactly the same as that for corporations. Rather than being taxed at the corporation rate, however, unincorporated business income is taxed at proprietors' personal rates. According to the Department of Finance's tax simulation model, in 1984 the marginal personal tax rates (combined federal and provincial) on unincorporated business income, $n$, were 40.6 percent, 32.9 percent, and 35.4 percent, respectively, for manufacturing, other industry, and commerce.

OWNER-OCCUPIED HOUSING. Owner-occupied housing, which accounts for just over two thirds of Canada's residential housing stock, enjoys favorable tax treatment relative to investment in the business sector. The

15. This rate is calculated by adding the 36.0 percent federal rate to a weighted average provincial rate of 13.7 percent. The latter is calculated by weighting the general provincial corporation tax rates by the provincial distribution of premiums collected by life insurance companies. Not that we ignore provincial premium taxes, which, according to Hoffman and Macnaughton (1989, p. 281), are levied at an average rate of 2 percent.

16. $Z_I$ is computed in exactly the same way as $z$ in note 11 except that $z_s = 0.5\tau_1$. The EAT rate for life insurance companies was found to be 0.23.

imputed income derived from home ownership (that is, the rental value) is not subject to tax, nor are capital gains realized upon the sale of a taxpayer's principal residence. In addition, local property tax rates are lower for residential housing than for nonresidential structures. On the other hand, whereas interest payments on debt-financed investments in the business sector are tax deductible, mortgage interest payments are not. The interest received on funds channeled through financial institutions to finance mortgages is, like any other interest income, subject to personal tax. No sales tax is levied on the purchase of a house. Federal and provincial sales taxes are paid, however, on materials and capital goods used in the construction of a house, but these taxes were not taken into account in our calculations.

### Recent Tax Reform Measures

The forerunner of the current tax reform measures was a discussion paper tabled with the 1985 federal budget.[17] The paper proposed a number of significant changes in the corporation tax. Notable among these proposals were: abolition of the investment tax credit (ITC), except in a few special cases (for example, a credit would still be available for scientific research expenditures); removal of the 3 percent inventory allowance; a reduction in capital cost allowances; and a cut of 7 percentage points in the basic federal statutory corporation tax rate. Moreover, plans to phase in a $500,000 lifetime personal exemption for capital gains were announced in the budget itself. In addition, the budget included announcement of an increase from 10 percent to 11 percent in the general rate of federal sales tax, to take effect in 1986.

1986 FEDERAL BUDGET. Subsequent to the 1985 discussion paper, and as a preliminary to the government's 1987 white paper on tax reform, the 1986 federal budget announced several measures intended to reduce the variation in marginal effective corporation tax rates.[18] The measures included: the phasing out of the investment tax credit by 1989 except in a few special cases and designated areas; immediate elimination of the inventory allowance; and a gradual reduction in statutory corporation tax rates over a three-year period starting in 1987. In addition, the dividend tax credit was reduced from 50 percent to 33 1/3 percent, which became

17. Canada, Department of Finance (1985).
18. Canada, Department of Finance (1986).

effective on January 1, 1987. Furthermore, a 3 percent surtax was imposed on corporate and personal incomes, and the general federal sales tax rate was raised from 11 percent to 12 percent.

1987 WHITE PAPER AND THE 1988 FEDERAL BUDGET. Far broader measures designed to achieve a greater degree of tax neutrality were proposed in the 1987 white paper, which was to be implemented in two stages.[19] The first stage involved a gradual overhaul of the corporate and personal income tax systems. The second stage envisaged replacement of the existing federal sales tax with a broad-based value-added tax that extends to the retail level and exempts business inputs and exports.

Implementation of the first stage of tax reform, as laid out in the white paper, was announced in the 1988 federal budget. More specifically, the basic federal statutory corporation tax rate was reduced from 36 to 28 percent on July 1, 1988. The tax rate applicable to manufacturing was gradually reduced from 30 percent to 23 percent in 1991, and the small business rate reduced to 12 percent. The special tax deduction that further reduces the corporation tax rate for small manufacturers was, however, eliminated so that the tax rate on these small businesses rose on July 1, 1988, from 8 percent to the 12 percent rate proposed for small businesses generally. At the same time, the incentive embodied in capital cost allowances was curtailed. In particular, the three-year write-off previously accorded to investment in manufacturing machinery was reduced to a 25 percent declining balance rate. In addition, the taxable proportion of corporate capital gains was increased from its previous level of one-half to two-thirds in 1988, and to three-quarters in 1990. Moreover, a new tax was applied to dividends from preferred shares, if the earnings of the payer corporation are nontaxable, and a 15 percent tax was levied on investment income accruing to fund insurance liabilities of life insurance companies.

At the personal level, federal tax rates were reduced to three brackets: 17 percent on the first $27,500 of taxable income, 26 percent on the next $27,500, and 29 percent on any additional taxable income. These reductions were accompanied by the elimination of a large number of exemptions and deductions, many of which were converted into tax credits. The dividend tax credit was further reduced, to 25 percent. The lifetime capital gains exemption was fixed at $100,000 except in the case

19. Canada, Department of Finance (1987, p. 2).

of farmland and small business shares, both of which became eligible for a $500,000 lifetime exemption. However, the proportion of an individual's capital gains that is taxed increased from the previous level of one-half to two-thirds in 1988, and to three-quarters in 1990 and subsequent years.

1989 FEDERAL BUDGET. Further changes affecting the taxation of income from capital were announced in the 1989 federal budget.[20] The personal income surtax on all individuals was raised from 3 percent to 5 percent, and an additional 3 percent surtax was applied to individuals with income over $70,000. The budget also contained a new tax on the corporate sector, the large corporations tax, which is levied at the rate of 0.175 percent on capital in excess of $10 million employed in Canada by corporations. This new tax is creditable against the existing 3 percent corporate surtax, so that corporations are now, in effect, subject to the greater of the two taxes. The total revenues raised by the large corporations tax and the corporate surtax combined was expected to be equal to the revenue that would be raised by a 10 percent corporate surtax. In addition, the general federal sales tax rate was increased from 12 percent to 13.5 percent pending its replacement with a more broadly based tax on goods and services.

THE GOODS AND SERVICES TAX. At the time of the 1989 federal budget, the government also declared its intention to replace the existing federal sales tax in 1991 with a goods and services tax (GST) on most goods and services consumed in Canada.[21] Originally, a 9 percent GST was envisaged, but the rate actually implemented was 7 percent.[22] A zero rate of tax applies to a limited range of items, such as basic groceries, prescription drugs, and medical devices. Furthermore, tax credits are allowed in full for the taxes paid or payable on inputs. As a consequence, business inputs, including capital, are effectively free of GST. Moreover, to mitigate the burden of the tax on low-income households, the GST has been accompanied by a more generous refundable tax credit for families with net incomes below a certain threshold (with the credit being reduced by $5 for every $100 of net income in excess of the threshold), and a system

20. Canada, Department of Finance (1989a).
21. Canada, Department of Finance (1989b, pp. 31–61).
22. Canada, Department of Finance (1989c, p. 3).

of rebates for taxes paid on the purchase of a new house priced below $450,000.[23] As part of the 7 percent GST package, the government also announced that, effective January 1, 1991, the federal surtax levied on high income individuals would be raised from 3 percent to 5 percent, and the large corporation tax rate increased from 0.175 percent to 0.2 percent.

## Estimates of Marginal Effective Tax Rates

Estimates of marginal effective tax rates on income from corporate and noncorporate investments in Canada are reported in tables 3-1 through 3-12. These estimates are based on the "fixed-$p$" assumption, whereby all investment projects earn a 10 percent real pretax rate of return net of depreciation.

### Corporate Sector

PRINCIPAL RESULTS (1985). using the capital stock, financing, and ownership weights summarized in table A-4 in the appendix to the volume, weighted averages of marginal effective tax rates have been computed for the same twelve broad categories of investment examined by King and Fullerton in the 1984 study. Estimates of the marginal effective tax rates associated with these types of investment in 1985 (before the May budget) are shown in table 3-1, based on a 5 percent expected annual inflation rate. (The actual rate in 1985 was 4 percent, but was 5 percent in 1990.)

The most striking feature of table 3-1 is the enormous variation in tax rates across assets, industries, methods of finance, and owners. Column 1 shows that when sales, property, corporation, and personal taxes were all taken into account, machinery was taxed less than inventories, which in turn were taxed much less than buildings. Investments in manufacturing were the most lightly taxed, and those in "other industry" were taxed the most heavily. Investments financed by debt received much more favorable tax treatment than did investments financed by new shares

---

23. For homes priced at or below $350,000, the rebate is 2.5 percentage points of the tax; and for homes priced between $350,000 and $450,000 the rebate is calculated on the basis of the following formula:

$$Rebate = \$8,750 \times \frac{(450,000 - house\ price)}{100,000}.$$

Table 3-1. *Marginal Effective Tax Rates, Fixed-p, Corporate Sector, Canada, 1985*[a]

Percent

| | | | Corporate | | Total | | |
|---|---|---|---|---|---|---|---|
| Item | Total (1) | Personal (2) | Including sales and property taxes (3) | Excluding sales and property taxes (4) | Excluding sales and property taxes (5) | Excluding sales tax (6) | Excluding property taxes (7) |
| Asset | | | | | | | |
| Machinery | 30.4 | 22.2 | 8.2 | −4.5 | 19.5 | 19.5 | 30.4 |
| Buildings | 50.7 | 19.1 | 31.6 | 12.1 | 34.0 | 50.7 | 34.0 |
| Inventories | 41.8 | 21.4 | 20.4 | 20.4 | 41.8 | 41.8 | 41.8 |
| Industry | | | | | | | |
| Manufacturing | 32.2 | 21.1 | 11.2 | 2.8 | 25.0 | 29.5 | 27.8 |
| Other industry | 47.6 | 19.3 | 28.3 | 13.5 | 34.9 | 42.2 | 40.3 |
| Commerce | 45.1 | 22.3 | 22.8 | 5.9 | 30.8 | 37.8 | 38.2 |
| Methods of finance | | | | | | | |
| Debt | 19.0 | 39.5 | −20.5 | −37.3 | 6.0 | 13.1 | 11.9 |
| New share issues | 55.5 | 10.4 | 45.2 | 35.5 | 46.8 | 51.7 | 50.6 |
| Retained earnings | 53.6 | 8.3 | 45.3 | 35.8 | 44.4 | 49.6 | 48.4 |
| Owner | | | | | | | |
| Households | 48.5 | 27.3 | 21.2 | 9.0 | 38.6 | 44.1 | 43.0 |
| Tax-exempt institutions | 13.2 | 0.0 | 13.2 | 0.1 | 0.1 | 7.3 | 5.9 |
| Insurance companies | −26.3 | −22.9 | −3.4 | −18.4 | −43.6 | −34.1 | −35.8 |
| Overall tax rate | 40.0 | 20.9 | 19.0 | 6.6 | 29.3 | 35.2 | 34.0 |
| Tax wedge | 4.0 | 2.1 | 1.9 | 0.6 | 2.9 | 3.5 | 3.4 |
| Weighted standard deviation | 29.1 | 23.9 | 36.9 | 38.9 | 30.2 | 31.1 | 29.2 |

Source: All tables are based on authors' calculations.

a. These estimates are based on a 5 percent expected annual inflation rate. Under the fixed-$p$ assumption, all investment projects earn a 10 percent real pretax rate of return net of depreciation.

or retained earnings. Finally, investments financed by savings channeled directly from households to corporations were taxed a great deal more than investments financed by savings channeled indirectly to corporations through tax-exempt institutions or insurance companies. Investments financed by the latter were in fact subsidized.

As column 4 of table 3-1 shows, the corporation tax system was responsible for most of the variation in marginal effective tax rates among assets, types of finance, and industries, even though it accounted for a relatively small proportion of the total tax wedge—that is, the difference between the before-tax and after-tax rates of return. The corporation tax wedge, exclusive of both property and sales taxes, was 0.6 percentage point, whereas the personal tax wedge was 2.1 percentage points. The wide variation in marginal effective corporation tax rates was caused largely by the investment tax credit and accelerated capital cost allowances, both of which heavily favored machinery, by the tax-deductibility of interest payments, and incomplete integration of corporate and personal income taxes, all in combination with high statutory corporation tax rates. The fact that manufacturing industries and small businesses were subject to lower statutory corporation tax rates than nonmanufacturing industries and large corporations also contributed to tax rate variance.

Although the personal tax accounted for more than one-half the total tax wedge, it was much less important than the corporation tax as a source of variation in marginal effective tax rates (see column 2 of table 3-1).[24] The personal tax system contributes to the variation in tax rates in two ways: by treating different forms of investment income differently and by treating different types of investors differently. But some of the features of the personal tax system that cause such differences mitigate some of the effects attributable to the corporation tax. For instance, interest income received by households is taxed upon receipt and thus partially offsets the deductibility of interest payments for corporation tax purposes. Moreover, preferences for dividend income and capital gains in the personal tax system partly make up for the lack of corporate deductions for the costs of equity finance. Thus, the personal tax tends to counteract the bias in favor of debt financing caused by the corporation tax. The result is that the variation in marginal effective tax rates attributable to both the personal tax and the corporation tax (30.2) was substantially less than the variation attributable to the corporation tax alone (38.9).

As pointed out earlier, federal and provincial sales taxes levied on purchases of capital goods were borne entirely by machinery, with commerce and other industry being most affected. A comparison of columns 1 and 6 in table 3-1 reveals that sales taxes raised the marginal effective total tax rate on income from investments in machinery from 19.5 to 30.4 percent, thereby bringing it somewhat more into line with the rates on income from investments in buildings and inventories. Hence, the main effect of sales taxes was to offset partially the preferential treatment accorded to machinery by the corporation tax through accelerated depre-

---

24. Our calculations assume that a typical household investing in corporate bonds faces a marginal personal tax rate of 31.8 percent, whereas a typical shareholder faces a rate of 42.3 percent. The rate for shareholders is higher because dividends are concentrated more heavily than interest income among persons in high-income brackets. Hence, the variation in effective tax rates is caused in part by the fact that marginal personal tax rates rise with income. It follows that further disaggregation of households by income groups would lead to more variation in effective tax rates.

ciation allowances and the investment tax credit. When sales taxes were added to corporation, business property, and personal taxes, the variation in marginal effective tax rates, as measured by the standard deviation, dropped from 31.1 to 29.1. It follows that eliminating capital expenditures from federal and provincial sales tax bases, or replacing sales taxes with a value-added tax that exempts capital inputs, increases the variation in marginal effective tax rates, unless the capital cost allowances granted to machinery are reduced. (Note that no account is taken here of the fact that a consumption-type VAT would also exempt intermediate inputs that are used in the production of capital goods, notably buildings.)

A comparison of columns 1 and 7 of table 3-1 shows that municipal business property taxes increased the marginal effective tax rate on buildings relative to machinery and inventories. Again, commerce and other industry were most affected. Consequently, when business property taxes were added to corporation, sales, and personal taxes, the variation in marginal effective tax rates dropped slightly, from 29.2 to 29.1.

IMPACT OF INFLATION ON MARGINAL EFFECTIVE TAX RATES. Inflation increases marginal effective tax rates in some cases and decreases them in others. The result of these contradictory tendencies is a broadening of the range of variation in marginal effective tax rates—a result that increases the distortion of investment decisions by taxes. The tendency of inflation to increase the variation in marginal effective tax rates is especially pronounced with respect to the corporation tax.

As inflation erodes the real value of capital cost allowances, for instance, it tends to increase marginal effective corporation tax rates on depreciable capital such as machinery and buildings. In addition, inflation tends to increase the nominal value of inventories. Because firms must use first-in, first-out (FIFO) inventory accounting for tax purposes, the difference between the current sales price and the acquisition cost of inventories represents taxable profits. Thus, inflation tends to increase nominal taxable profits and, consequently, the marginal effective corporation tax rate. As partial compensation, firms were formerly permitted an inventory allowance of 3 percent, but this allowance was withdrawn by the February 1986 federal budget.

As an offset, inflation increases nominal interest rates and hence interest payments on corporate debt. Since interest payments are deductible from taxable income, inflation decreases corporation taxes paid on debt-financed investments. At the same time, however, inflation tends to increase nominal interest receipts, resulting in payment of higher personal taxes. The two effects are not equal, however. Averaged over all investors, the marginal personal tax rate on interest income was approximately 24.1 percent,[25] whereas an averaging of corporation tax rates (taking into account the special rates for manufacturing and small business, as well as the different provincial rates), showed a range of 35.23 percent in commerce to 41.33 percent in manufacturing. And since income from equity-financed investments is taxed in nominal terms at both the corporation and personal levels, inflation increases the effective tax rates on dividends and capital gains. The result is encouragement for investments financed by debt rather than by new share issues or retained earnings.

Marginal effective tax rates under various expected inflation rates are reported in tables 3-2 and 3-3. The tax rates in the zero-inflation columns would obtain if the 1985 tax system had been fully indexed.[26] As shown in table 3-2, with inflation, marginal effective corporate tax rates on machinery and buildings decline, whereas tax rates on inventories increase as inflation rises above 5 percent.[27] Tax rates on debt-financed investment decline with inflation, while those on equity-financed investments increase. In all industries, marginal effective corporate tax rates decline as inflation rises.

Marginal effective personal tax rates tend to increase with inflation unless investments are channeled through life insurance companies or tax-exempt institutions. The former receive a slight subsidy, which rises with inflation; the latter are, of course, not subject to personal taxes. Table 3-3, which takes the corporate and personal tax systems together, shows that inflation increases marginal effective total tax rates for households, all industries, all types of assets, and all types of finance except debt. The result is that inflation increases the overall marginal effective tax rate. For example, the rate for the corporate sector as a whole rises from 35.5 percent with zero inflation to 44.2 percent if inflation is expected to remain at 10 percent.

Moreover, by increasing the marginal effective tax rate in some cases and decreasing it in others, inflation accentuates the variation in rates.

25. This is a weighted average for all savers.

26. Some features of the tax system were introduced to counteract the impact of inflation. In the absence of inflation, these features would probably have been withdrawn, since otherwise they would cause a considerable decline in tax revenue. Consequently, our calculations with zero inflation assume that there was no inventory allowance. We do not, however, take into account the likely reductions in income tax credits and CCAs.

27. The marginal effective corporate tax rate associated with inventories increases as inflation rises from 0 to 5 percent because the estimates with zero inflation assumed no inventory allowance.

Table 3-2. *Marginal Effective Corporate Tax Rates under Different Inflation Rates, Fixed-p, Corporate Sector, 1985*
Percent

| Item | Expected inflation rate (percent) | | |
|---|---|---|---|
| | 0 | 5 | 10 |
| Asset | | | |
| Machinery | 11.2 | 8.2 | 3.0 |
| Buildings | 36.3 | 31.6 | 23.1 |
| Inventories | 22.1 | 20.4 | 31.4 |
| Industry | | | |
| Manufacturing | 14.1 | 11.2 | 9.3 |
| Other industry | 31.4 | 28.3 | 21.8 |
| Commerce | 27.0 | 22.8 | 21.6 |
| Method of finance | | | |
| Debt | −0.7 | −20.5 | −39.4 |
| New share issues | 37.7 | 45.2 | 52.9 |
| Retained earnings | 37.6 | 45.3 | 52.9 |
| Owner | | | |
| Households | 23.6 | 21.2 | 19.1 |
| Tax-exempt institutions | 19.0 | 13.2 | 7.9 |
| Insurance companies | 9.3 | −3.4 | −15.4 |
| Overall tax rate | 22.4 | 19.0 | 16.0 |
| Weighted standard deviation | 25.4 | 36.9 | 49.8 |

Table 3-3. *Marginal Effective Total Tax Rates under Different Inflation Rates, Fixed-p, Corporate Sector, 1985*
Percent

| Item | Expected inflation rate (percent) | | |
|---|---|---|---|
| | 0 | 5 | 10 |
| Asset | | | |
| Machinery | 25.9 | 30.4 | 32.6 |
| Buildings | 47.3 | 50.7 | 50.2 |
| Inventories | 35.7 | 41.8 | 58.4 |
| Industry | | | |
| Manufacturing | 28.0 | 32.2 | 36.9 |
| Other industry | 43.0 | 47.6 | 48.6 |
| Commerce | 40.4 | 45.1 | 51.8 |
| Method of finance | | | |
| Debt | 22.6 | 19.0 | 16.0 |
| New share issues | 43.8 | 55.0 | 67.4 |
| Retained earnings | 44.1 | 53.6 | 62.2 |
| Owner | | | |
| Households | 40.7 | 48.5 | 55.9 |
| Tax-exempt institutions | 19.0 | 13.2 | 7.9 |
| Insurance companies | −3.4 | −26.3 | −48.9 |
| Overall tax rate | 35.5 | 40.0 | 44.2 |
| Weighted standard deviation | 20.8 | 29.1 | 38.4 |

Table 3-4.   *Marginal Effective Total Tax Rates before and after Tax Reform, Fixed-p, Corporate Sector, Selected Years, 1980–89*[a]

Percent

| Item | 1980 (1) | 1985 (2) | 1986 budget[b] (3) | 1988 budget (4) | 1989 budget (5) | Federal GST[c] (6) | National GST[c] (7) |
|---|---|---|---|---|---|---|---|
| Asset | | | | | | | |
| Machinery | 25.7 | 30.4 | 33.7 | 41.0 | 42.2 | 36.1 | 30.8 |
| Buildings | 48.4 | 50.7 | 50.3 | 52.7 | 53.5 | 53.6 | 53.6 |
| Inventories | 40.7 | 41.8 | 48.5 | 48.2 | 49.7 | 49.9 | 49.9 |
| Industry | | | | | | | |
| Manufacturing | 30.3 | 32.2 | 37.0 | 43.0 | 44.0 | 43.0 | 41.7 |
| Other industry | 44.0 | 47.6 | 46.9 | 49.4 | 50.2 | 47.5 | 44.6 |
| Commerce | 40.6 | 45.1 | 47.8 | 50.0 | 51.2 | 46.6 | 43.2 |
| Methods of finance | | | | | | | |
| Debt | 12.1 | 19.0 | 28.1 | 34.9 | 34.7 | 31.3 | 28.5 |
| New share issues | 55.1 | 55.0 | 67.6 | 71.1 | 73.5 | 72.1 | 70.5 |
| Retained earnings | 53.1 | 53.6 | 50.0 | 51.9 | 53.8 | 51.7 | 49.6 |
| Owner | | | | | | | |
| Households | 45.3 | 48.5 | 49.9 | 52.6 | 53.8 | 51.5 | 49.3 |
| Tax-exempt institutions | 10.7 | 13.2 | 20.0 | 22.9 | 23.5 | 20.2 | 17.3 |
| Insurance companies | −29.8 | −26.3 | −14.9 | 28.0 | 28.2 | 24.7 | 21.9 |
| Overall tax rate | 36.9 | 40.0 | 42.6 | 46.6 | 47.7 | 45.2 | 42.9 |
| Weighted standard deviation | 30.7 | 29.1 | 24.5 | 19.4 | 20.2 | 21.2 | 22.6 |

a. Estimates are based on a 5 percent expected annual inflation rate.
b. Includes $500,000 personal lifetime capital gains exemption.
c. Goods and services tax.

Although inflation has contributed less to the variation than the investment tax credit and accelerated capital cost allowances, it should be borne in mind that one factor behind the enhancement of these incentives during the 1970s and early 1980s was a desire to counteract inflation's adverse impact on corporate cash flows. Thus ad hoc tax policy responses to inflation, as well as inflation itself, have contributed to the wide variation in marginal effective tax rates.

COMPARISON WITH 1980. Column 1 of tables 3-4, 3-5, and 3-6 reports marginal effective tax rates for 1980, which can be compared with the 1985 tax rates shown in column 2. For purposes of comparison, the 1985 capital stock, financing, and ownership weights were also used to calculate the 1980 tax rates so that any changes in tax rates since 1980 are the result of changes in the tax system rather than changes in the pattern of investment. While the pattern of tax rates changed very little between 1980 and 1985, there was a trend toward higher taxation of income from corporate investment.

Table 3-5. *Marginal Effective Corporate Tax Rates before and after Tax Reform, Fixed-p, Corporate Sector, Selected Years, 1980–89*[a]

Percent

| Item | 1980 (1) | 1985 (2) | 1986 budget (3) | 1988 budget (4) | 1989 budget (5) | Federal GST (6) | National GST (7) |
|---|---|---|---|---|---|---|---|
| Asset | | | | | | | |
| Machinery | 4.3 | 8.2 | 15.1 | 21.8 | 22.8 | 15.5 | 9.3 |
| Buildings | 30.3 | 31.6 | 34.1 | 35.4 | 35.8 | 35.9 | 35.9 |
| Inventories | 20.6 | 20.4 | 31.0 | 29.1 | 30.4 | 30.7 | 30.7 |
| Industry | | | | | | | |
| Manufacturing | 10.3 | 11.2 | 20.0 | 25.1 | 25.8 | 24.5 | 23.0 |
| Other industry | 25.6 | 28.3 | 30.5 | 31.8 | 32.7 | 29.1 | 25.7 |
| Commerce | 19.2 | 22.8 | 28.3 | 29.6 | 30.6 | 25.0 | 21.0 |
| Methods of finance | | | | | | | |
| Debt | −25.0 | −20.5 | −9.6 | −1.1 | −1.8 | −6.3 | −9.9 |
| New share issues | 44.7 | 45.2 | 48.1 | 47.5 | 49.4 | 47.2 | 45.1 |
| Retained earnings | 44.7 | 45.3 | 48.2 | 47.6 | 49.4 | 47.3 | 45.1 |
| Owner | | | | | | | |
| Households | 19.2 | 21.2 | 27.0 | 29.1 | 30.0 | 26.9 | 24.2 |
| Tax-exempt institutions | 10.7 | 13.2 | 20.0 | 22.9 | 23.5 | 20.2 | 17.3 |
| Insurance companies | −6.9 | −3.4 | 5.4 | 33.6 | 34.3 | 31.1 | 28.5 |
| Overall tax rate | 16.9 | 19.0 | 25.1 | 28.2 | 29.0 | 25.9 | 23.2 |
| Weighted standard deviation | 38.6 | 36.9 | 31.9 | 26.5 | 27.7 | 29.2 | 30.7 |

a. Estimates are based on a 5 percent expected annual inflation rate.

Table 3-6. *Marginal Effective Personal Tax Rates on Corporate Source Income, Fixed-p, New View, Selected Years, 1980–89*

Percent

| Item | 1980 (1) | 1985 (2) | 1986 budget (3) | 1988 budget (4) | 1989 budget (5) | Federal GST (6) | National GST (7) |
|---|---|---|---|---|---|---|---|
| Asset | | | | | | | |
| Machinery | 21.4 | 22.2 | 18.6 | 19.2 | 19.4 | 20.6 | 21.5 |
| Buildings | 18.1 | 19.1 | 16.2 | 17.3 | 17.7 | 17.7 | 17.7 |
| Inventories | 20.1 | 21.4 | 17.5 | 19.1 | 19.3 | 19.2 | 19.2 |
| Industry | | | | | | | |
| Manufacturing | 20.0 | 21.1 | 17.0 | 17.9 | 18.2 | 18.5 | 18.7 |
| Other industry | 18.4 | 19.3 | 16.4 | 17.6 | 17.8 | 18.4 | 18.9 |
| Commerce | 21.4 | 22.3 | 19.5 | 20.4 | 20.6 | 21.5 | 22.2 |
| Methods of finance | | | | | | | |
| Debt | 37.1 | 39.5 | 37.7 | 36.0 | 36.5 | 37.6 | 38.4 |
| New share issues | 10.4 | 10.4 | 19.5 | 23.6 | 24.1 | 24.9 | 25.4 |
| Retained earnings | 8.4 | 8.3 | 1.8 | 4.3 | 4.4 | 4.4 | 4.5 |
| Owner | | | | | | | |
| Households | 26.1 | 27.3 | 22.9 | 23.5 | 23.8 | 24.5 | 25.1 |
| Tax-exempt institutions | 0.0 | 0.0 | 0.0 | 0.0 | 0.0 | 0.0 | 0.0 |
| Insurance companies | −22.9 | −22.9 | −20.3 | −5.6 | −6.1 | −6.4 | −6.6 |
| Overall tax rate | 20.0 | 20.9 | 17.5 | 18.4 | 18.7 | 19.3 | 19.7 |

THE IMPACT OF TAX REFORM. The impacts on marginal effective total tax rates of the 1986, 1988, and 1989 federal budgets and of the GST are also shown in table 3-4. The corresponding impacts of tax reform on marginal effective corporate tax rates and marginal effective personal tax rates are reported in tables 3-5 and 3-6, respectively.

Column 3 of tables 3-4, 3-5, and 3-6 captures the combined effect of the main changes announced in the 1986 budget (as summarized earlier in this chapter), had they been fully implemented. These estimates also take into account the $500,000 lifetime capital gains exemption proposed in the 1985 budget. Judging by the weighted standard deviation, the outcome would have been a substantial reduction in the dispersion in tax rates, and therefore greater tax neutrality. On the other hand, the overall marginal effective total tax rate on corporate investment would have increased from 40.0 percent to 42.6 percent, and the overall marginal effective corporate tax rate from 19.0 percent to 25.1 percent, thereby increasing the disincentive to invest in the corporate sector.

Column 4 of tables 3-4, 3-5, and 3-6 shows the pattern of marginal effective tax rates resulting from the measures involved in the first stage of tax reform, as implemented in the 1988 federal budget (see "1987 White Paper and the 1988 Federal Budget"). Again the outcome is less variance in tax rates. There is also a more significant increase in the overall taxation of marginal investment in the corporate sector, however, which would tend to discourage such investment.

As shown in column 5 of tables 3-4, 3-5, and 3-6, the measures announced in the 1989 federal budget (see "1989 Federal Budget") and fully taking effect in 1990 not only increased the overall taxation of marginal investment in the corporate sector, but also reversed some of the reduction in the dispersion in tax rates accomplished by the 1986 and 1988 budgets.

The main feature of the second stage of the tax reform, as envisaged in the 1987 white paper, entailed the implementation of the broad-based goods and services tax (GST) in 1991. One of the principal advantages of such a tax is that, unlike the previous federal manufacturers' sales tax and current provincial sales taxes, capital goods and other intermediate inputs are exempt. Since the burden of federal and provincial sales taxes levied on purchases of capital goods was borne entirely by machinery, however, such taxes tended to offset the corporation tax system's bias in favor of investments in machinery that is attributable to accelerated CCAs. It follows, therefore, that replacement of the federal sales tax with the GST increases the dispersion in marginal effective tax rates, as shown in column 6 of tables 3-4 and 3-5. Hence, unless further steps are taken to reduce the generosity of CCAs permitted by the corporation tax, stage two of tax reform could undo some of the tax neutrality accomplished in stage one. Not surprisingly, removal of sales taxes on purchases of capital goods reduces the overall taxation of capital income. The impact of replacing provincial as well as federal sales taxes with a national GST (as originally envisaged in the 1987 white paper) is shown in column 7 of tables 3-4, 3-5, and 3-6. Hitherto, only Quebec had replaced its provincial sales tax with a provincial GST.

Since, according to the traditional view of dividend taxation, a larger proportion of marginal investment is financed through new share issues, insofar as dividends are taxed more easily than capital gains at the personal level, marginal effective personal tax rates, and therefore marginal effective total tax rates, will be higher than those computed on the basis of the new view of dividend taxation. Moreover, the increased taxation of dividends as a consequence of the reductions in the dividend tax credit from 50 percent to 33 1/3 percent in 1986 and from 33 1/3 percent to 25 percent in 1988 assumes greater importance under the traditional view than under the new view, while reduced taxation of capital gains is of lesser importance. As dividends and capital gains were taxed at roughly the same effective personal rate in 1985, there is little difference between the marginal effective tax rates computed for that year under the two different views. But as shown in tables 3-7 and 3-8, the increases in marginal effective tax rates between 1985 and 1990 (prior to implementation of the GST in 1991) is much more pronounced under the traditional view of taxation than under the new view, which is reflected in tables 3-4, 3-5, and 3-6. (Note that marginal effective corporate tax rates are the same under both the traditional view and the new view.)

Overall, although tax reform has narrowed the dispersion in tax rates in the corporate sector, some important discrepancies remain. Capital cost allowances are still more generous for investments in machinery than for those in buildings, and the latter continues to bear the brunt of municipal business property taxes. New investments financed by debt are taxed less heavily than those financed by equity, and whereas in 1985 investments financed by new share issues and retained earnings were taxed at roughly the same rate, as a result of tax reform, investments financed by new share issues are now taxed more heavily than those financed by retentions. Moreover, firms still face different federal corporation tax rates, depending on their size and the nature of their production activities. Consequently,

Table 3-7. *Marginal Effective Total Tax Rates before and after Tax Reform, Fixed-*p*, Corporate Sector, Traditional View, Selected Years, 1980–89*[a]

Percent

| Item | 1980 (1) | 1985 (2) | 1986 budget[b] (3) | 1988 budget (4) | 1989 budget (5) | Federal GST (6) | National GST (7) |
|------|------|------|------|------|------|------|------|
| Asset | | | | | | | |
| Machinery | 27.2 | 31.8 | 44.0 | 51.9 | 53.3 | 48.0 | 43.3 |
| Buildings | 49.2 | 51.5 | 58.8 | 62.2 | 63.2 | 63.5 | 63.5 |
| Inventories | 41.5 | 42.6 | 56.6 | 57.5 | 59.1 | 59.5 | 59.5 |
| Industry | | | | | | | |
| Manufacturing | 31.7 | 33.7 | 47.5 | 54.3 | 55.6 | 54.8 | 53.6 |
| Other industry | 45.0 | 48.5 | 56.1 | 59.5 | 60.8 | 58.3 | 55.8 |
| Commerce | 41.2 | 45.7 | 54.9 | 57.9 | 59.2 | 55.2 | 52.1 |
| Methods of finance | | | | | | | |
| Debt | 12.1 | 19.0 | 28.1 | 34.9 | 34.7 | 31.3 | 28.5 |
| New share issues | 55.1 | 55.6 | 67.6 | 71.2 | 73.5 | 72.1 | 70.5 |
| Retained earnings | ... | ... | ... | ... | ... | ... | ... |
| Owner | | | | | | | |
| Households | 46.8 | 50.0 | 61.7 | 65.4 | 67.0 | 65.1 | 63.3 |
| Tax-exempt institutions | 10.7 | 13.2 | 20.0 | 22.9 | 23.5 | 20.2 | 17.3 |
| Insurance companies | −33.8 | −30.3 | −18.7 | 23.4 | 23.3 | 19.7 | 16.8 |
| Overall tax rate | 38.0 | 41.0 | 51.9 | 56.7 | 58.0 | 55.8 | 53.8 |
| Weighted standard deviation | 31.7 | 30.0 | 29.6 | 25.3 | 26.4 | 27.7 | 28.9 |

a. Estimates are based on a 5 percent expected annual inflation rate.
b. Includes $500,000 personal lifetime capital gains exemption.

after tax reform new investment in manufacturing continues to be taxed less heavily than that in commerce and other industry. Finally, the tax system remains extremely susceptible to inflation. As shown in tables 3-9 and 3-10, the dispersion in marginal effective tax rates still increases substantially with inflation.

At the same time, the changes in the taxation of investment income owing to tax reform entail a number of additional drawbacks. The overall impact is to increase the marginal effective tax rate applicable to the corporate sector as a whole, which tends to discourage new investment. Furthermore, the corporate and personal income tax systems are less integrated after tax reform than before.[28] This is of little consequence according to the new view of dividend taxation. But if one adheres to the traditional view of dividend taxation, reduced integration of corporate

28. The degree of integration, as measured by the ACID test statistic, for large nonmanufacturing companies, falls from 0.810 in 1985 to 0.740 after tax reform and drops from 0.900 to 0.809 in the case of large manufacturing companies.

Table 3-8.   *Marginal Effective Personal Tax Rates on Corporate Source Income, Fixed-p, Traditional View, Selected Years, 1980–89*

Percent

| Item | 1980 (1) | 1985 (2) | 1986 budget (3) | 1988 budget (4) | 1989 budget (5) | Federal GST (6) | National GST (7) |
|---|---|---|---|---|---|---|---|
| **Asset** | | | | | | | |
| Machinery | 22.9 | 23.6 | 28.8 | 30.0 | 30.5 | 32.5 | 34.0 |
| Buildings | 18.8 | 19.8 | 24.7 | 26.8 | 27.4 | 27.5 | 27.6 |
| Inventories | 21.0 | 22.3 | 25.6 | 28.3 | 28.7 | 28.8 | 28.8 |
| **Industry** | | | | | | | |
| Manufacturing | 21.4 | 22.5 | 27.5 | 29.2 | 29.8 | 30.3 | 30.6 |
| Other industry | 19.3 | 20.1 | 25.5 | 27.6 | 28.1 | 29.2 | 30.0 |
| Commerce | 22.1 | 23.0 | 26.6 | 28.3 | 28.6 | 30.1 | 31.2 |
| **Method of finance** | | | | | | | |
| Debt | 37.1 | 39.5 | −37.7 | 35.8 | 36.5 | 37.6 | 38.4 |
| New share issues | 10.4 | 10.4 | 19.4 | 23.6 | 24.1 | 24.9 | 25.4 |
| Retained earnings | ... | ... | ... | ... | ... | ... | ... |
| **Owner** | | | | | | | |
| Households | 27.6 | 28.8 | 34.6 | 36.3 | 37.0 | 38.2 | 39.1 |
| Tax-exempt institutions | 0.0 | 0.0 | 0.0 | 0.0 | 0.0 | 0.0 | 0.0 |
| Insurance companies | −26.9 | −27.0 | −24.2 | −10.1 | −11.0 | −11.4 | −11.7 |
| Overall tax rate | 21.1 | 22.0 | 26.7 | 28.5 | 29.0 | 30.0 | 30.6 |

Table 3-9.   *Marginal Effective Total Tax Rates under Different Inflation Rates, Fixed-p, Corporate Sector, 1989 Budget*

Percent

| Item | Expected inflation rate (percent) 0 | 5 | 10 |
|---|---|---|---|
| **Asset** | | | |
| Machinery | 36.1 | 42.2 | 46.2 |
| Buildings | 49.1 | 53.5 | 54.4 |
| Inventories | 33.4 | 49.7 | 65.7 |
| **Industry** | | | |
| Manufacturing | 36.0 | 44.0 | 50.0 |
| Other industry | 45.0 | 50.5 | 52.8 |
| Commerce | 42.0 | 51.2 | 58.9 |
| **Method of finance** | | | |
| Debt | 32.1 | 34.7 | 35.1 |
| New share issues | 54.9 | 73.5 | 90.7 |
| Retained earnings | 44.0 | 53.8 | 61.2 |
| **Owner** | | | |
| Households | 43.8 | 53.8 | 61.8 |
| Tax-exempt institutions | 25.5 | 23.5 | 19.2 |
| Insurance companies | 29.1 | 28.2 | 24.4 |
| Overall tax rate | 40.1 | 47.7 | 53.2 |
| Weighted standard deviation | 14.3 | 20.2 | 28.1 |

Table 3-10.  *Marginal Effective Corporate Tax Rates under Different Inflation Rates, Fixed-p, Corporate Sector, 1989 Budget*
Percent

| | Expected inflation rate (percent) | | |
|---|---|---|---|
| Item | 0 | 5 | 10 |
| Asset | | | |
| Machinery | 24.1 | 22.8 | 19.3 |
| Buildings | 39.3 | 35.8 | 28.7 |
| Inventories | 20.3 | 30.4 | 40.6 |
| Industry | | | |
| Manufacturing | 24.6 | 25.8 | 25.0 |
| Other industry | 34.7 | 32.7 | 27.3 |
| Commerce | 29.6 | 30.6 | 30.2 |
| Method of finance | | | |
| Debt | 10.6 | −1.8 | −17.0 |
| New share issues | 40.7 | 49.4 | 56.3 |
| Retained earnings | 40.7 | 49.4 | 56.3 |
| Owner | | | |
| Households | 29.3 | 30.0 | 28.4 |
| Tax-exempt institutions | 25.5 | 23.5 | 19.2 |
| Insurance companies | 31.8 | 34.3 | 34.6 |
| Overall tax rate | 28.7 | 29.0 | 27.0 |
| Weighted standard deviation | 18.7 | 27.7 | 39.1 |

and personal income taxes exacerbates the increase in the marginal effective total tax rates on corporate investment resulting from tax reform.

### The Noncorporate Business Sector

Fixed-$p$ calculations of marginal effective tax rates for the noncorporate business investments are reported in table 3-11. These tax rates are computed for the same broad categories of asset and industry examined in the corporate sector. The capital stock weights and debt-equity ratios used are identical to those used for the corporate sector, because it was not possible to obtain separate data for each of the two sectors. In any case, use of the same capital stock weights and debt-equity ratios enables us to compare the tax treatment of corporate and noncorporate business investment. The only form of equity finance available to unincorporated businesses other than debt is proprietors' equity. It is assumed that neither tax-exempt institutions nor insurance companies invest in unincorporated businesses.

The pattern of marginal effective tax rates among industries and assets in the noncorporate business sector in 1985 was very similar to that found

Table 3-11.  *Marginal Effective Tax Rates, Fixed-*p, *Noncorporate Sector, 1980, 1985, 1989*[a]

Percent

| Item | 1980 | 1985 | 1989 budget | Federal GST |
|---|---|---|---|---|
| Asset | | | | |
| Machinery | 25.8 | 30.3 | 42.4 | 36.2 |
| Buildings | 47.0 | 48.4 | 51.9 | 51.9 |
| Inventories | 40.2 | 42.5 | 51.3 | 51.3 |
| Industry | | | | |
| Manufacturing | 29.4 | 31.8 | 43.7 | 42.4 |
| Other industry | 41.5 | 44.5 | 48.9 | 45.7 |
| Commerce | 42.6 | 46.2 | 52.9 | 48.3 |
| Method of finance | | | | |
| Debt | 29.2 | 34.9 | 46.2 | 43.1 |
| Retained earnings | 41.1 | 42.1 | 48.6 | 46.1 |
| Owner | | | | |
| Households | 36.3 | 39.2 | 47.6 | 44.9 |
| Overall tax rate | 36.3 | 39.2 | 47.6 | 44.9 |

a. These estimates are based on a 5 percent expected annual inflation rate.

in the corporate sector. However, although investments financed by debt were again taxed less than those financed by equity, the difference was much smaller than that found in the corporate sector. As a result, the dispersion in marginal effective tax rates was much smaller than that existing in the corporate sector and is also much less sensitive to inflation. Finally, the overall marginal effective tax rate faced by unincorporated business was slightly lower than that applied to corporations.

Tax reform has had an impact on the taxation of investment income in the noncorporate business sector similar to that found for the corporate sector. As shown in table 3-11, the dispersion in marginal effective tax rates is much lower and the overall tax rate higher after tax reform. The increase in the overall tax rate faced by unincorporated business investment, however, is substantially greater than the increase faced by corporate investment, if one adheres to the new view of dividend taxation. Consequently, whereas before tax reform, unincorporated business investment was taxed slightly less than corporate investment, the overall marginal effective tax rates faced by the corporate and noncorporate business sectors are roughly the same after tax reform. By contrast, according to the traditional view of dividend taxation, the discrepancy between overall marginal effective tax rates in the corporate and noncorporate sectors increases as a consequence of tax reform.

Table 3-12. *Marginal Effective Tax Rates for Owner-Occupied Housing, Fixed-p, 1980, 1985, 1989*[a]

Percent

| Item | 1980 | 1985 | 1989 budget | Federal GST |
|---|---|---|---|---|
| Method of finance | | | | |
| Debt | 51.2 | 56.1 | 57.2 | 61.0 |
| Equity | 10.7 | 12.3 | 12.3 | 18.0 |
| Overall tax rate | 15.4 | 17.4 | 17.5 | 23.0 |

a. Estimates are based on a 5 percent expected annual inflation rate.

### Owner-Occupied Housing

Marginal effective tax rates for investment in owner-occupied housing are reported in table 3-12, taking into account a residential property tax rate of 1.07 percent in 1980 and 1.23 percent in 1985, and assuming that the marginal personal tax rate on mortgage interest receipts is the same as the tax rate on interest income used in computing marginal effective tax rates for the corporate and noncorporate business sectors. The marginal effective tax rates for owner-occupied housing reflect the fact that, in 1984, 88.4 percent of the housing stock was financed with owners' equity and the remaining 11.6 percent was financed by mortgages.

As shown in table 3-12, with a 5 percent expected annual inflation rate, the marginal effective tax rate on owner-occupied housing rose by 2 percentage points between 1980 and 1985. This increase was due mainly to the rise in the residential property tax rate. According to our calculations, the tax changes contained in the 1986, 1988, and 1989 federal budgets increased the taxation of owner-occupied housing very slightly. Since our calculations show that the overall tax rate on marginal investment in both the corporate and noncorporate business sectors increases substantially more than the tax rate on newly constructed housing as a consequence of tax reform, it follows that new investment in housing has been further encouraged relative to that in businesses. By contrast, the federal GST substantially increases the tax rate on investment in owner-occupied housing compared to business investment, thereby reducing the tax system's bias in favor of the former.[29]

29. Note that the marginal effective tax rate computed for owner-occupied housing does not take into account federal and provincial sales taxes levied on materials and capital goods used in the construction of a house. Such indirect levies, if shifted forward, are equivalent to federal and provincial tax rates on the average purchase price of a new house of roughly 5.1 percent and 4.4 percent, respectively. The

## Conclusion

Although recent tax reform measures in Canada have in some respects resulted in a more neutral tax treatment of investment and saving, a number of important nonneutralities remain. Some nonneutralities have even been exacerbated by tax reform. The tax system in Canada therefore still constitutes a serious potential source of distortions in investment and saving decisions.

More specifically, the tax system remains biased in favor of new investments in certain types of assets such as machinery and equipment and against those in buildings and inventories, and companies' federal statutory tax rates still vary depending on the size and the nature of their production activities. Moreover, the continuing double taxation of equity income owing to the incomplete integration of personal and corporate income taxes means that the tax system is still biased against equity-financed investments in the corporate sector. The tax system also continues to discriminate against savings supplied by households directly or indirectly through taxed intermediaries and in favor of savings channeled through pension funds, RRSPs, and life insurance companies, albeit to a lesser extent than previously. In addition, new investment in housing is still encouraged relative to that in corporate and noncorporate businesses. As a consequence, marginal effective tax rates continue to vary widely depending on the type of asset acquired, the industry in which the investment is made, the manner in which the investment is financed, the tax status of the saver supplying the funds, and whether the investment is made in the business sector or in housing.

It is also noteworthy that the upward movement in marginal effective tax rates since 1985 as a result of tax reform has increased the disincentive to new investment and to saving in the economy as a whole.[30] Such an outcome is undesirable because Canada continues to be heavily dependent

---

GST results in the removal of the 5.1 percent indirect federal tax, and its replacement with a direct federal tax averaging roughly 5.8 percent on the price of a new house once allowance is made for the proposed rebates. If these indirect taxes are taken into account, the marginal effective tax rate on owner-occupied housing rises from 26.2 to 26.8 percent once the GST is implemented.

30. These calculations do not take into account increases in limits on tax-deductible contributions to registered retirement savings plans. More specifically, in 1987 the annual limit was raised from $5,500 to $7,500. In addition, plans were announced to further relax that limit in stages, so that in 1995 individuals who are not members of employer-sponsored pension schemes would be able

on foreign saving to finance domestic investment, and new investment is an essential ingredient in the considerable restructuring of the Canadian economy that is required in the wake of the Canada–United States free trade agreement.

Finally, because the tax system is not indexed, it remains extremely susceptible to inflation. Hence, a resurgence in inflation could undo much, if not all, of the neutrality gains achieved as a result of the implementation of measures contained in the 1986 federal budget and the 1987 white paper, and leave the way open for the same kind of ad hoc response that accentuated, rather than mitigated, the increased variation in marginal effective tax rates caused directly by inflation during the 1970s and early 1980s.

As pointed out repeatedly by numerous reports and academic studies, many of the foregoing nonneutralities could be greatly alleviated, if not eliminated altogether, by levying the corporation tax on cash flows and the personal tax on lifetime expenditures. Under a cash-flow corporation tax, all investment outlays on machinery and buildings could be immediately expensed, so that such investments would be treated in the same way as other nonfinancial expenses, while interest expenses would no longer be deductible. A lifetime expenditure tax would permit individuals to save as much as they wish in the form of tax-deductible assets, such as RRSPs, and non-tax-deductible assets, with income from the latter being nontaxable.

---

to contribute up to 18 percent of their earned income to an RRSP, up to a maximum of $15,500. Unfortunately, there is no reliable evidence concerning the impact of changes in RRSP contribution limits to the proportion of personal saving in RRSP versus nonregistered forms. Needless to say, insofar as a larger proportion of investment is financed by tax-deductible saving, the increase in the marginal effective total tax rate resulting from tax reform will be less than that suggested by our calculations.

Table 3A-1.  *Specific Tax and Inventory Parameters Used in the Calculations for Canada, Selected Years, 1980–89*

| Item | 1980 | 1985 | 1986 federal budget | 1988 federal budget | 1989 federal budget | Federal GST package |
|---|---|---|---|---|---|---|
| Corporation tax rate$(\tau)$[a] | | | | | | |
| Manufacturing | 0.4320 | 0.4133 | 0.3842 | 0.3526 | 0.3684 | 0.3716 |
| Other industry | 0.3964 | 0.4033 | 0.3840 | 0.3458 | 0.3619 | 0.3652 |
| Commerce | 0.3690 | 0.3523 | 0.3328 | 0.3034 | 0.3173 | 0.3201 |
| Insurance companies' tax rate $(\tau_1)$[a] | 0.4959 | 0.4973 | 0.4772 | 0.4257 | 0.4453 | 0.4493 |
| Opportunity cost of retained earnings in terms of gross dividends forgone $(\theta)$ | 1.5 | 1.5 | 1.33 | 1.25 | 1.25 | 1.25 |
| Personal tax rate on noncorporate business income $(n)$[b] | | | | | | |
| Manufacturing | 0.406 | 0.406 | 0.414 | 0.365 | 0.369 | 0.369 |
| Other industry | 0.329 | 0.329 | 0.336 | 0.321 | 0.326 | 0.326 |
| Commerce | 0.345 | 0.345 | 0.352 | 0.335 | 0.339 | 0.339 |
| Proportion of inventories taxed under FIFO $(v)$ | 1.0 | 1.0 | 1.0 | 1.0 | 1.0 | 1.0 |
| Corporate wealth tax rates $(w_c)$[c] | | | | | | |
| Machinery | | | | | | |
| Manufacturing | 0.0 | 0.0 | 0.0 | 0.0 | 0.0 | 0.0 |
| Other industry | 0.0 | 0.0 | 0.0 | 0.0 | 0.0 | 0.0 |
| Commerce | 0.0 | 0.0 | 0.0 | 0.0 | 0.0 | 0.0 |
| Buildings | | | | | | |
| Manufacturing | 0.0227 | 0.0227 | 0.0227 | 0.0227 | 0.0227 | 0.0227 |
| Other industry | 0.0177 | 0.0184 | 0.0184 | 0.0184 | 0.0184 | 0.0184 |
| Commerce | 0.0290 | 0.0351 | 0.0351 | 0.0351 | 0.0351 | 0.0351 |
| Inventories | | | | | | |
| Manufacturing | 0.0 | 0.0 | 0.0 | 0.0 | 0.0 | 0.0 |
| Other industry | 0.0 | 0.0 | 0.0 | 0.0 | 0.0 | 0.0 |
| Commerce | 0.0 | 0.0 | 0.0 | 0.0 | 0.0 | 0.0 |
| Sales tax rate $(h)$[d] | | | | | | |
| Machinery | | | | | | |
| Manufacturing | 0.0313 | 0.0327 | 0.0353 | 0.0353 | 0.0373 | 0.0194 |
| Other industry | 0.0957 | 0.1005 | 0.1102 | 0.1102 | 0.1175 | 0.0522 |
| Commerce | 0.1215 | 0.1285 | 0.1427 | 0.1427 | 0.1533 | 0.0577 |
| Buildings | | | | | | |
| Manufacturing | 0.0 | 0.0 | 0.0 | 0.0 | 0.0 | 0.0 |
| Other industry | 0.0 | 0.0 | 0.0 | 0.0 | 0.0 | 0.0 |
| Commerce | 0.0 | 0.0 | 0.0 | 0.0 | 0.0 | 0.0 |
| Inventories | | | | | | |
| Manufacturing | 0.0 | 0.0 | 0.0 | 0.0 | 0.0 | 0.0 |
| Other industry | 0.0 | 0.0 | 0.0 | 0.0 | 0.0 | 0.0 |
| Commerce | 0.0 | 0.0 | 0.0 | 0.0 | 0.0 | 0.0 |

a. Includes the federal corporate income surtax of 3 percent introduced in the 1986 federal budget, and the large corporations tax announced in the 1989 federal budget.

b. Includes the federal personal income surtax of 3 percent introduced in the 1986 federal budget.

c. This is the business property tax rate.

d. These tax rates are based on 1984 data when the general federal sales tax rate was 9 percent. The sales tax rates for 1985, 1986, 1988, and 1989 were obtained by scaling up the 1984 rate by 10/9, 12/9, 12/9, and 13.5/9, thereby reflecting the increases in the general rate.

Table 3A-2. *Tax Rates for Different Types of Income and Investor*

| | Type of investor | | |
|---|---|---|---|
| *Type of income* | *Household* | *Tax-exempt institution* | *Life insurance company* |
| Interest | $m$ | 0 | 0 |
| Dividends | $\theta m - (\theta - 1)$ | 0 | $-1$ |
| Capital gains | $z$ | 0 | $\phi z_l - (\phi - 1)$ |

$m$ denotes marginal personal tax rate on interest income

$\theta$ denotes the rate at which dividends are grossed up

$\theta - 1$ denotes the dividend tax credit rate

$\phi = 1/(1 - \tau_l)$, where $\tau_l$ is the statutory corporation tax rate on life insurance companies in 1985 and 1986, but $\phi = 1/(1 - \tau_l + 0.15)$ after the introduction of the 15 percent tax on life insurance companies' investment income, announced in 1988

$z$ denotes effective accrued personal tax rate on capital gains realized by households

$z_l$ denotes effective accrued tax rate on capital gains realized by life insurance companies.

Table 3A-3. *Tax Parameters, by Source of Finance, Selected Years, 1980–89*

| Item | 1980 | | | 1985 | | | 1986 federal budget | | | 1988 federal budget | | | 1989 federal budget | | | GST package | | |
|---|---|---|---|---|---|---|---|---|---|---|---|---|---|---|---|---|---|---|
| | Debt | New shares | Retained earnings | Debt | New shares | Retained earnings | Debt | New shares | Retained earnings | Debt | New shares | Retained earnings | Debt | New shares | Retained earnings | Debt | New shares | Retained earnings |
| **Household wealth tax rates ($w_p$)** | | | | | | | | | | | | | | | | | | |
| Households | 0.0 | 0.0 | 0.0 | 0.0 | 0.0 | 0.0 | 0.0 | 0.0 | 0.0 | 0.0 | 0.0 | 0.0 | 0.0 | 0.0 | 0.0 | 0.0 | 0.0 | 0.0 |
| Tax-exempt institutions | 0.0 | 0.0 | 0.0 | 0.0 | 0.0 | 0.0 | 0.0 | 0.0 | 0.0 | 0.0 | 0.0 | 0.0 | 0.0 | 0.0 | 0.0 | 0.0 | 0.0 | 0.0 |
| Insurance companies | 0.0 | 0.0 | 0.0 | 0.0 | 0.0 | 0.0 | 0.0 | 0.0 | 0.0 | 0.0 | 0.0 | 0.0 | 0.0 | 0.0 | 0.0 | 0.0 | 0.0 | 0.0 |
| **Tax rates on interest ($m$)[a]** | | | | | | | | | | | | | | | | | | |
| Households | 0.291 | 0.423 | 0.423 | 0.318 | 0.423 | 0.423 | 0.324 | 0.431 | 0.431 | 0.323 | 0.425 | 0.425 | 0.326 | 0.434 | 0.434 | 0.326 | 0.437 | 0.437 |
| Tax-exempt institutions | 0.0 | 0.0 | 0.0 | 0.0 | 0.0 | 0.0 | 0.0 | 0.0 | 0.0 | 0.0 | 0.0 | 0.0 | 0.0 | 0.0 | 0.0 | 0.0 | 0.0 | 0.0 |
| Insurance companies | 0.0 | 0.0 | 0.0 | 0.0 | 0.0 | 0.0 | 0.0 | 0.0 | 0.0 | 0.0 | 0.0 | 0.0 | 0.0 | 0.0 | 0.0 | 0.0 | 0.0 | 0.0 |
| **Tax rate on capital gains ($z_s$)[b]** | | | | | | | | | | | | | | | | | | |
| Households | 0.211 | 0.211 | 0.211 | 0.211 | 0.211 | 0.211 | 0.067 | 0.067 | 0.067 | 0.105 | 0.105 | 0.105 | 0.107 | 0.107 | 0.107 | 0.108 | 0.108 | 0.108 |
| Tax-exempt institutions | 0.0 | 0.0 | 0.0 | 0.0 | 0.0 | 0.0 | 0.0 | 0.0 | 0.0 | 0.0 | 0.0 | 0.0 | 0.0 | 0.0 | 0.0 | 0.0 | 0.0 | 0.0 |
| Insurance companies | 0.248 | 0.248 | 0.248 | 0.249 | 0.249 | 0.249 | 0.239 | 0.239 | 0.239 | 0.319 | 0.319 | 0.319 | 0.334 | 0.334 | 0.334 | 0.337 | 0.337 | 0.337 |

a. Includes federal personal surtaxes.
b. Includes federal surtaxes.

# References

Canada. Department of Finance. 1985. *The Corporate Income Tax System: A Direction for Change*. Ottawa: Canadian Government Publishing Centre (CGPC).

———. 1986. *Budget Papers*. CGPC.

———. 1987. *The White Paper: Tax Reform, 1987*. CGPC (June).

———. 1989a. *Budget Papers*. CGPC (April).

———. 1989b. *Goods and Services Tax: Technical Paper*. CGPC (August).

———. 1989c. *Goods and Services Tax*. CGPC (December).

Daly, Michael J., Pierre Mercier, and Thomas Schweitzer. 1989. *The Taxation of Income from Capital in Canada*. CGPC.

Hall, Robert E., and Dale W. Jorgenson. 1967. "Tax Policy and Investment Behavior." *American Economic Review* 57 (June): 391–414.

Hoffman, Lorey A., and Alan Macnaughton. 1989. "Life Insurance and Tax Reform." In *Economic Impacts of Tax Reform*, edited by Jack Mintz and J. Whalley, 255–85. Toronto: Canadian Tax Foundation.

King, Mervyn A. 1977. *Public Policy and the Corporation*. New York: Wiley.

King, Mervyn A., and Don Fullerton, eds. 1984. *The Taxation of Income from Capital: A Comparative Study of the United States, the United Kingdom, Sweden and West Germany*. University of Chicago Press.

Kuo, Chan-Yan, Thomas C. McGirr, and Satya Poddar. 1988. "Measuring the Non-Neutralities of Sales and Excise Taxes in Canada." *Canadian Tax Journal* 36 (May–June): 655–70.

Poterba, James M., and Lawrence H. Summers. 1983. "Dividend Taxes, Corporate Investment, and 'Q.'" *Journal of Public Economics* 22 (November): 135–67.

CHAPTER FOUR

# France

*Julian S. Alworth*
*François Bourguignon*

IN RECENT YEARS the overall tax burden in France has attained a level comparable to that of the most heavily taxed countries in Scandinavia. And yet the marginal and average taxes on most households' capital income have dwindled to virtually nil and the corporate tax burden has declined sharply. Indeed, as far as capital income is concerned, the base of French income taxes diverges markedly from the comprehensive concept of income. At the personal level, the combination of a very high allowance for capital income under the personal income tax system, a high exemption limit for capital gains tax, the taxation of many types of capital income at source, and a wide number of savings incentives has meant that for the majority of taxpayers the return on most types of financial instruments is nearly tax free. At the corporate level, during the second half of the 1980s, greater flexibility in the use of depreciation allowances and lower tax rates reduced the average and marginal tax burden by about 10 percentage points. By contrast, at least on paper, the burden of wealth taxes levied by central and local government became somewhat higher at the corporate level and, more recently, at the personal level.

This chapter examines the incentives to save and invest in the French private sector. Much of the study is concerned with attempting to summarize for analytical purposes the complex provisions of the tax code. The interaction between the various components of the tax system is quantified via effective tax-rate measures derived by Mervyn A. King and Don Fullerton,[1] and adapted to take account of the institutional details specific to France. In addition to the taxation of income originating in the corporate

The authors are grateful to Michael J. Daly and P. Skinner for helpful comments on a draft of this chapter.

1. King and Fullerton (1984).

sector, consideration is also given to the taxation of owner-occupied housing and of unincorporated businesses.

The structure of this chapter is as follows. In the first section we summarize the main trends in the composition of tax revenues during the past three decades. In the second section we examine the tax treatment of corporate income under the company tax and local taxes on wealth in some detail and also describe the principal investment incentives. An overview of the personal tax system, including a summary of provisions covering insurance companies, is given in the third section. In the fourth section we summarize the changes in the composition and financing of investments that have taken place in recent years. The final two sections include the discussion of the effective tax rates computed according to King and Fullerton, and some concluding remarks.

## The Composition of Tax Revenues

During the past twenty-five years there has been a pronounced increase in the overall tax burden in France (see table 4-1). Between 1965 and 1988 the ratio of tax revenues to gross domestic product (GDP) rose from 35 percent to nearly 45 percent, a ratio exceeded only by those of Scandinavia and the Netherlands. The increase in the tax burden was associated with each of the oil price shocks, characterized by an upward ratchet effect, and accompanied by a shift in the composition of revenues. There was a pronounced decline in the relative importance of excise and transactions taxes and of "other" duties, whereas there was a steep increase in social security contributions, which between 1970 and 1988 expanded from 13 to 19 percent of GDP.

Social security contributions in relation to GDP are currently higher in France than in any other member country of the Organization for Economic Cooperation and Development (OECD), whereas personal income taxes are relatively unimportant, providing only 12 percent of total revenues. However, payroll taxes for social security (*prélèvements sociaux*), comprising employers' and employees' contributions, are important principally because they are used to directly finance health care and family benefits (*allocations familiales*), in addition to old-age pensions.

As far as income from capital is concerned, receipts from withholding taxes on capital income (*prélèvements libératoires*) and the local personal

Table 4-1.  *Sources of Tax Revenues in France, Selected Years, 1965–88*

Percent share of total receipts unless otherwise specified

| Revenue sources | 1965 | 1970 | 1975 | 1980 | 1985 | 1988 |
|---|---|---|---|---|---|---|
| Taxes on personal income, including | 10.6 | 12.0 | 12.3 | 12.9 | 12.8 | 12.1 |
| Withholding tax on capital income | ... | 0.5 | 1.1 | 1.3 | 1.2 | 1.1 |
| *Taxe d'habitation* | ... | 1.2 | 1.7 | 1.3 | 1.3 | 1.3 |
| Taxes on corporate income[a] | 5.3 | 6.3 | 5.2 | 5.1 | 4.5 | 5.2 |
| Social security contributions | 34.2 | 36.3 | 40.6 | 42.7 | 43.3 | 43.3 |
| Wealth taxes | 4.3 | 3.5 | 3.4 | 3.5 | 4.4 | 4.8 |
| Value-added taxes | 20.1 | 25.5 | 23.1 | 20.9 | 19.7 | 19.4 |
| Excises, specific duties, and other taxes on transactions | 18.3 | 12.7 | 10.2 | 9.5 | 10.0 | 10.1 |
| Other | 7.3 | 3.8 | 5.2 | 5.3 | 5.3 | 5.1 |
| Total receipts (billion of francs) | 169.1 | 278.3 | 541.7 | 1,171.4 | 2,089.5 | 2,510.3 |
| GDP (billions of francs) | 490.2 | 793.5 | 1,467.9 | 2,808.3 | 4,700.1 | 5,658.6 |
| Total revenues/GDP (percent) | 34.5 | 35.1 | 36.9 | 41.7 | 44.5 | 44.4 |

Source: OECD (various years).
a. *Impôt sur les sociétés* and other taxes.

tax on dwellings (*taxe d'habitation*) have risen in lockstep with other taxes and therefore continue to account for a constant proportion of total tax revenues. Receipts from corporation tax have also remained constant, amounting to about 5 percent of total tax revenues.

The value-added tax, which was introduced in France in 1954, thirteen years before it was introduced in any other industrial country, is the second most important source of tax revenue and accounts for about 20 percent of total receipts. France is also unique in its treatment of excise duties, which are widespread but generate comparatively little revenue. Finally, France is the only major industrialized country to have introduced, suspended, and reimposed a personal net-wealth tax during the last forty years.

## Corporate Business Taxation

In this section, the tax treatment of corporate income under the company tax and local taxes on wealth is examined.

*Corporate Tax*

Corporate income tax (*impôt sur les sociétés*) is payable by all limited-liability companies (*sociétés à responsabilité limitée*), limited partnerships with shares (*sociétés en commandite par actions*), permanent establishments (branches) of foreign companies, and cooperatives. With very few exceptions, the definition of taxable income for the corporate and noncorporate sectors is the same, the revenues and costs of companies being determined under the laws governing income tax. However, some companies (ranging from mutual funds to new firms) and sectors (such as real estate, forestry, and communications) are subject to special provisions.

In France, unlike in most other countries, income tax is calculated on a territorial basis. Only French source income is subject to tax.[2] Income received from abroad is taxed only when it is distributed by a French company to its shareholders.

From 1965 to 1985, the tax on corporate profits (*impôt national sur les bénéfices des sociétés*) was levied at a rate of 50 percent. The tax rate was subsequently lowered to 45 percent, 42 percent, 39 percent and 37 percent for profits generated in the calendar years 1986, 1988, 1989, and 1990, respectively. Accordingly, in the simulations the value of the corporate tax rate $\tau$ was 0.5 for 1980 and 1985, and 0.37 for 1990.

Corporate income tax is not graduated, but small firms may elect to be taxed on a special lump-sum (*à forfait*) basis if they follow a simplified accounting system and have a turnover of less than a specified amount. In 1990 these ceilings were Fr 500,000 for industrial and commercial enterprises and Fr 150,000 for companies in the services sector. Since the 1970s there has been a very steady decline in the number of companies choosing to be taxed on a lump-sum basis, partly because the limits on the value of turnover have not been modified. In 1984 only 43 percent of firms were taxed under this special regime, compared with 78 percent in 1975. The share of total corporate turnover subject to this simplified regime declined even more dramatically between 1975 and 1984, from 32 to 10 percent.[3]

---

2. The main exceptions to this rule are when a company elects to be taxed on its consolidated accounts, or when subsidiaries are established in jurisdictions deemed by the French tax authorities to be tax havens. Credit for foreign taxes on income is granted up to the rate of French company tax and any excess is allowed as a credit carried forward. A tax credit is also permitted in respect of withholding tax levied in a country with which France has concluded a double-taxation agreement.

3. Conseil des Impôts (1987).

As regards the tax treatment of losses, companies are allowed to carry them forward for five years and also since 1984 to carry them back for three years, subject to certain restrictions. Operating losses resulting from depreciation may be carried forward indefinitely if the depreciation is reported as being deferred for tax purposes. However, loss-making companies are subject to an annual minimum tax which varies with the level of turnover.

### Dividend Relief

In 1965 France adopted the imputation system of dividend relief at the shareholder level. Under this system, when profits are distributed, shareholders receive an amount in cash $C$ in respect of which a personal tax $s$ is deemed to have been paid. Hence gross dividends $(G)$ for purposes of computing personal income tax and dividend relief are given by $G = C/(1 - s)$. A tax credit (*avoir fiscal*) equal to $sC/(1 - s)$ is granted to shareholders against their personal income tax liability of $mC/(1 - s)$. At present 50 percent of cash dividends are deductible against personal tax and the value of $s = 1/3$.[4] The benefits of the tax credit are available only to French residents, although under some tax treaties (for example, with Germany) the tax credit is extended to foreign shareholders.

While dividend relief is independent of the amount of corporate taxes paid, the benefits are available only if taxes have actually been paid on the underlying profits. Dividend distributions out of losses or tax-exempt income, including foreign-source income, are subject to a supplementary tax (*précompte mobilier*) levied at the corporate level. This equalization tax corresponds to one-third of dividends grossed up by the amount of the shareholder credit, or one-half of the cash dividends actually received by the shareholder. Application of the *précompte mobilier* offsets in full the tax credit received by shareholders on dividend payments out of franked income.

In 1980 and 1985 the value of $\theta$, the opportunity cost of dividends in terms of retained earnings, was equal to $\theta = 1/(1 - s) = 1.5$.[5] In 1989 and 1990 surtaxes of 3 percent and 5 percent, respectively, were applied to dividend distributions, which meant that the company tax rate on distributions was in actual fact 42 percent in these two years. Owing to

4. Taxable income is equal to 150 percent of cash dividends. Personal income tax is levied at progressive rates on that amount less a tax credit of 50 percent of the cash dividend.

5. King and Fullerton (1984, p. 22).

the corporate surtax in 1990, the value of $\theta = (1-\tau-\alpha)/(1-\tau)(1-s) = 1.38095$, where the rate of surtax $\alpha = 0.05$.

## Tax Allowances for Depreciation and Inventories

Tax allowances for depreciation in France are based on the historic cost of the asset. Depreciation begins when an asset comes into use, and allowances in the first year are computed as a proportion of the time for which an asset is likely to be in service.

The tax authorities have not established a fixed life for individual assets and the tax code (article 39[1-2]) allows explicitly for variation across industries and assets depending on specific economic conditions. It is commonly accepted that industrial and commercial buildings have a useful life of twenty and thirty-three years respectively, whereas the useful life of equipment (excluding vehicles) is estimated at eight years.[6] Since 1988 companies have been allowed greater discretion in the manner in which useful life is determined. In particular the tax authorities will not question depreciation allowances which diverge by less than 20 percent from the commonly accepted practices. Firms are also allowed to depreciate assets more quickly if they can prove higher rates of utilization than those specified by the code.

The standard type of depreciation is the straight-line method, but accelerated depreciation on a declining-balance basis with a switchover to straight-line is allowed for equipment with a useful life of at least three years and for buildings having a useful life of under fifteen years. The rate of declining balance is computed as a multiple of the rate of depreciation under the straight-line schedule and varies with the useful life of assets: 1.5 times the straight-line rate for assets with a useful life of three to four years; 2.0 times the straight-line rate for assets with a useful life of five to six years; and 2.5 times the straight-line rate for assets with a longer useful life.[7] Special "exceptional" depreciation provisions, in addition to the investment incentives described in the next section, apply to research-and-development expenditures and antipollution investments and to investments in certain special sectors (such as cinema, mining, and steel).

Inventories must be valued at the lower of historic cost or market value. First in, first out (FIFO), or the average-cost method, must be

---

6. Conseil des Impôts (1987); Lefebvre (1990).
7. Higher rates of declining balance are permitted for energy-saving investments.

applied. Although last in, first out (LIFO) accounting is prohibited, there is a special measure against the effects of high inflation. This adjustment consists of a six-year deferral of tax on increases in the price of inventories exceeding 10 percent.

In summary, the calculation of effective tax-rate estimates later in the chapter assumes that on average a half-year convention applies for the time at which depreciation begins, useful life is the one commonly accepted but in 1990 was reduced by 20 percent, equipment is depreciated according to the declining balance (with the exception of the special provisions covering 1983–85), and buildings are depreciated according to the straight-line method.[8] As far as inventories are concerned, the simulations assume historic cost, but for 1980 the special-deferral provision was assumed to apply because of the high rate of inflation existing at that time.

### Estimates of Economic Depreciation

There are no estimates in France of economic depreciation based on a direct sampling of useful lives derived from the secondhand values of assets. The most reliable estimates of useful lives for the capital stock utilized in industry are those computed from company accounts by Margaret Atkinson and Jacques Mairesse, and extended recently to a wider sample by Gilbert Cette and Daniel Szpiro.[9] The estimates were derived by comparing fixed investment with the stock of assets and applying various mortality distributions. On the basis of the latter study the average life of the total capital stock in manufacturing and other industry (construction only) was found to be about 12.5 and 8.5 years, respectively, for the period covered in the study. Unfortunately these studies provide no breakdown for the life of building and equipment or according to manufacturing and other industry. Independent estimates by Derek W. Blades based on expert opinion suggest that the average life of buildings in the manufacturing sector and in the construction and retail trade industries was 37 and 30 years, respectively.[10] Using these estimates and information

8. In 1983 the proportion of companies following the different depreciation procedures was as follows: 44 percent, declining balance, 52 percent, straight-line, 4 percent, the "exceptional" method. Companies making losses report somewhat less usage of declining balance depreciation than other companies. There are also significant differences in the usage of the various depreciation methods according to industry (Conseil des Impôts, 1987).

9. Atkinson and Mairesse (1978); Cette and Szpiro (1988a).

10. Blades (1983). The life of buildings in France varies markedly by sector within the manufacturing industry. See Cette and Szpiro (1988b).

on the breakdown of fixed assets between equipment and buildings contained in Cette and Szpiro, it is possible to approximate the useful life of equipment in manufacturing and other industry as 11.5 and 11.7 years, respectively.[11]

Assuming that $2/L$ approximates the rate of true economic depreciation $\delta$,[12] the values of $\delta$ for investment in equipment in manufacturing and other industry can be estimated at 0.1739 and 0.1709, respectively. Similarly the values of $\delta$ for buildings in these two sectors are 0.0541 and 0.0667, respectively. The value of $\delta$ for the services sector was estimated at 0.1700 for equipment and 0.0541 for buildings.

### Investment Grants and Incentives

Many tax incentives have been employed to encourage investment, particularly in the 1970s when, owing to the high rate of inflation, depreciation allowances were considered inadequate. The types of tax incentive for capital expenditure in France have not been uniform over different periods and have varied in their coverage.

The incentive introduced in 1975, which replaced earlier special discretionary allowances, took the form of a tax credit which could be offset against value-added tax. (For a similar scheme see the chapter on Italy in this volume.) It applied to all assets that could be depreciated according to the declining balance method (that is, equipment). The credit applied to all assets ordered between April 30, 1975, and January 1, 1976, and delivered within the following three years. The tax credit could not exceed 10 percent of investment expenditure. This incentive was changed in subsequent years to apply only to the growth in investment expenditure compared with the preceding year and was restricted only to firms having two-thirds of their capital stock invested in equipment. Because of its limited use, this investment incentive was not considered in the simulations. (A number of incentives have been applied at different times for newly established companies.)

In 1981–82, a new incentive was introduced which consisted of a tax deduction of 10 percent for capital expenditure on equipment and some commercial buildings between October 1, 1980, and January 31, 1981.

---

11. Cette and Szpiro (1988b). A much higher rate of utilization of the existing capital stock appears to have taken place in the 1980s but this does not appear to have changed the economic life.

12. King and Fullerton (1984, p. 29).

The deduction was raised to 15 percent for 1982, but this applied only if the number of employees in a company did not decline.

A new set of incentives was introduced for 1983–85. These incentives covered all capital expenditure on equipment and consisted of a first-year allowance of 40 percent for assets having a tax life of less than nine years and 42 percent for assets with a tax life of ten years. Assets having longer useful lives could receive additional deductions equal to 4 percentage points per year of tax life; that is, for a tax life of fifteen years, the first-year deduction was equal to 62 percent of the capital expenditure.

Since 1985, investment incentives have had a far more limited applicability (for example, to encourage research and development).

### Wealth Taxes

There are three types of wealth tax affecting companies. The most important one is the local enterprise tax (*taxe professionnelle*), which is similar in spirit to state corporation taxes in the United States in that it is levied on the basis of companies' payrolls and the implicit rental value of their buildings and equipment.[13] In 1985 revenue from the local enterprise tax amounted to more than Fr 65 billion, roughly the same as that from corporation tax. The second wealth tax on companies is the local tax on the implicit rental value of buildings and land (*impôt foncier*).[14] Revenue from the *impôt foncier* on companies amounted to Fr 3 billion in 1985. While the revenue from both local wealth taxes accrues entirely to the various local authorities, the taxes themselves are administered by the central government.

Subject to certain criteria limiting their yearly rate of change and to a ceiling, the rates of the *taxe professionnelle* and the *impôt foncier* are decided each year by the different local authorities (communes, departments, and, since 1989, regions). Because the tax rates differ markedly from one local authority to another (ranging, for example, for the *taxe*

13. The *taxe professionnelle* was introduced in 1975. The initial tax proposal of 1974 envisaged a "formula apportionment" of 22 percent, 46 percent, and 32 percent, respectively, for gross payrolls, for the implicit rental values of equipment and buildings, and for profits. Profits were dropped in the final version of the tax because of the difficulty of allocating profits within multiestablishment companies. The share of payroll and implicit rental values has remained constant since the introduction of the tax: buildings account for 15 percent, equipment and other assets for 40 percent, and payroll accounts for 45 percent.

14. The tax is actually levied in two parts: on buildings and on undeveloped land.

*professionnelle* from 11 to 33 percent in 1985), the average rate was chosen for the simulations. In 1981 and 1986 the average tax rates for the *impôt foncier* $(t_f)$ were 0.174 and 0.212. For the same years the rates of *taxe professionnelle* $(t_p)$ were 0.186 and 0.191 respectively.

Both the *taxe professionnelle* and the *impôt foncier* are deductible from the corporate tax base. In addition new investments benefit from a three-year and two-year deferral of the *impôt foncier* and the *taxe professionnelle*, respectively, because the taxes are levied in arrears. Since 1987 a 16 percent rebate against the tax base has been allowed for the *taxe professionnelle*.[15] Accordingly the effective nominal value of the *taxe professionnelle* is taken as $x t_p$, where $x$ is equal to 1.0 for 1980 and 1985 and 0.84 for 1990.

The tax treatment of buildings is roughly the same under the *impôt foncier* and the *taxe professionnelle*. For commercial buildings (*cadastres* or land registers), providing implicit valuations of income from property is the basis for computing the tax liability on the implicit rentals. With regard to the *impôt foncier*, this cadastral value is then reduced by 50 percent to take account implicitly of maintenance costs and depreciation. In theory the assessments of cadastral values of buildings and other structures should be revised every six years. In practice revaluations based on specific examinations of individual properties have not been carried out since 1970. At that time the cadastral value was taken as the actual rental value of a commercial building or that of a comparable property. Subsequently, a major revaluation was undertaken in 1978, but on the basis of coefficients common to all property located in specific areas. Since 1980 a set of common revaluation coefficients for the country as a whole has been published annually and used to adjust the value of taxable rentals. In spite of these assessments and adjustments, it is widely believed that the cadastral estimates used for computing taxable income undervalue actual rental income. A conservative estimate of the undervaluation of 25 percent was assumed for the purpose of determining an overall effective tax rate.[16] Taking account of this undervaluation and assuming an 8 percent nominal implicit return, a factor of 0.06 was used to convert the nominal tax rates of the *taxe professionnelle* and the *impôt foncier* (reduced by

---

15. Other rebates are allowed when companies increase the number of their employees and in certain sectors.

16. This average undervaluation conceals a very wide dispersion among local authorities that carried out the reassessments. See Conseil des Impôts (1986).

amortization) into a wealth tax equivalent, that is, the wealth tax rate on commercial buildings is approximated by $t_k = 0.06 \ (0.5t_f + xt_p)$.[17]

The tax base for the assessment of industrial buildings is determined by assuming an implicit rate of return on the value of these fixed assets carried in the balance sheets at historic cost. For buildings constructed after 1976 this rate of return is equal to 8 percent. Revaluations such as those for commercial buildings have also been carried out for industrial buildings, although for the *taxe professionnelle* these revaluations have only been partial. As for commercial buildings, under the *impôt foncier* there is also a deduction for costs. Accordingly, assuming there is no initial undervaluation of balance-sheet values, the wealth tax for industrial buildings is approximated by $t_k = 0.08 \ (0.5t_f + xt_p)$.

The *taxe professionnelle* also applies to all other company assets, including both equipment and inventory. Only commercial and industrial companies having a turnover exceeding Fr 1 million or Fr 400,000, respectively, are taxable. The tax base is equal to 16 percent (8 percent implicit rental value plus 8 percent depreciation) of the initial cost of the asset less a standard deduction of Fr 25,000. Moreover, as with buildings, since 1987 the value of the asset has been computed at 84 percent of the initial investment. No adjustment is made for inflation. The value of the wealth tax in this case can be approximated by $t_k = 0.16 \ (xt_p)$.[18]

The values of the nominal and effective tax rates on wealth deriving from the *impôt foncier* and *taxe professionnelle* are summarized in table 4-2.

---

17. This is an approximation of the correct annualized value of the wealth tax given by

$$t_k = [c(\rho + \delta)/\rho][xt_p e^{-2\rho} + 0.5t_f e^{-3\rho} - (xt_p + 0.5t_f)e^{-33\rho}],$$

where $c$ refers to the initial discount from the true market value of the property, the asset is assumed to have a tax life of thirty-three years but to depreciate exponentially at a rate $\delta$, and $\rho$ is the implicit rate of return. This formula also allows for the two- and three-year deferral of exemption from tax under the *taxe professionnelle* and the *impôt foncier* respectively. Under the present laws the difference between the approximate and exact estimates of the wealth tax is negligible.

18. An exact estimate of the wealth tax $(t_w)$ is computed by equating the present value over the tax life of the *taxe professionnelle* multiplied by 0.16 times the *gross* initial investment, with the present value of the implicit tax on the *net* capital stock depreciated at an economic rate, that is,

$$\frac{0.16xt_p(l - e^{-\rho L})}{i} = \frac{t_k}{\delta + \rho},$$

where $l$ is the useful life for tax purposes, $i$ and $\rho$ are the nominal and real rates of interest, and $\delta$ is the rate of true economic depreciation.

Table 4-2. *Average Nominal Rate of the* Taxe Professionnelle *and* Impôt Foncier *and Effective Tax Rates on Companies' Wealth, 1980, 1985, 1990*[a]

Percent

| Average nominal rate | 1980 | 1985 | 1990 |
|---|---|---|---|
| Impôt foncier | 17.40 | 21.20 | 23.00[b] |
| Taxe professionnelle | 18.60 | 19.10 | 19.50[b] |
| Effective tax rates | | | |
| Industry | | | |
| Buildings | 2.18 | 2.38 | 2.23 |
| Equipment and inventories | 2.98 | 3.06 | 2.62 |
| Commerce | | | |
| Buildings | 1.64 | 1.78 | 1.67 |
| Equipment and inventories | 2.98 | 3.06 | 2.62 |

Sources: Conseil des Impôts (1986), and authors' calculations.
a. The values for 1980 and 1985 actually refer to assessments for 1981 and 1986, respectively.
b. Estimate.

In addition to the *impôt foncier* and the *taxe professionnelle*, the third wealth tax on companies is a 1 percent registration duty (*droit d'enregistrement*) on the size of the capital of new companies. Before January 1, 1985, this registration duty also applied to any nominal increase in the capital of firms resulting from new share issues. Such increases in capital are currently exempted from the registration duty. This tax was not considered in the simulations.

## Personal Taxes

Taxable personal income in France is assessed at the household level, although adult children or other dependents may elect to file a return independently. Income is defined net of social security payments. There is a standard allowance for business expenses of 10 percent on wages and salaries, with a ceiling in 1990 of Fr 66,950, corresponding to an individual income from paid employment of Fr 669,500 or more. Alternatively, business or employment expenses may be itemized. A further so-called special allowance of 20 percent is granted on wages and salaries after the deduction of business expenses. The initial reason for this additional allowance was to reestablish some equivalence between those in paid employment, who cannot avoid or postpone payment of tax, and the self-employed, who are able to conceal a substantial part of their income. This allowance does not apply to that part of household incomes in excess of Fr 607,000. Taxable income from paid employment (as well as income from pensions) thus amounts to 72 percent of the amount actually received, except perhaps for the top centile of the population. Net income from self-employment, however, is wholly taxable.[19]

The personal income tax schedule is the usual piecewise linear function found in most other countries. There is a big difference, however, in the way in which household size is taken into account. In the French system, the marginal tax rate is not determined by the taxable income of the household, but by that income divided by the *quotient familial*, that is, approximately the number of persons in the household—the first two children counting as one person only. If $Y$ is the taxable income and $N$ the *quotient familial*, the tax $T$ to be paid is given by

$$T = Nt(Y/N),$$

where $t(\ )$ is the piecewise linear tax schedule which applies to single-person households. The marginal tax rate thus depends crucially on the size of the household. However, there is a ceiling on the amount of taxes which can be deducted because of the presence of children in a family— that is, the difference between $t(Y)$ and $Nt(Y/N)$—so that very wealthy households face a marginal tax rate given by $t'(Y)$ rather than $t(Y/N)$.

The income tax schedule corresponding to a single-person household is given in table 4-3. The average income tax rate in France is rather low (around 8 percent of primary income) because almost 50 percent of households are below the taxation threshold. However, the system is fairly progressive and the marginal tax rate increases rather quickly above the tax threshold. The maximum rate is currently 56.8 percent, but it has fluctuated widely over time. It was 60 percent in 1981, when the Socialist government came into power; it then increased to 65 percent but was reduced to 60 percent again in 1985, just before the Conservatives won the elections in 1986. It has been gradually reduced since then by both the Conservative (1986–88) and subsequent Socialist governments. Given the numerous allowances provided by the tax system for those in paid employment and the tax-credit mechanism applying to dividend payments, very few people, even among the wealthy, are actually liable for the top rate. This was certainly true at the time the maximum rate was 65 percent, whereas the total tax rate on companies' profits could not exceed 57.5 percent because of the tax credit system.

19. Owing to the size of these allowances and to tax evasion, the income tax base amounts to only about one-half of disposable income as defined in the national accounts (Conseil des Impôts, 1990).

Table 4-3.    *Income Tax Rates for Persons without Dependents, 1985, 1990*

| 1985 | | 1990 | |
|---|---|---|---|
| Taxable income (francs) | Tax rate (percent) | Taxable income (francs) | Tax rate (percent) |
| 0–15,650 | 0 | 0–18,140 | 0.0 |
| 15,650–16,360 | 5 | 18,140–18,960 | 5.0 |
| 16,360–19,400 | 10 | 18,960–22,470 | 9.6 |
| 19,400–30,680 | 15 | 22,470–35,520 | 14.4 |
| 30,680–39,440 | 20 | 35,520–45,660 | 19.2 |
| 39,440–49,550 | 25 | 45,660–57,320 | 24.0 |
| 49,550–59,950 | 30 | 57,320–69,370 | 28.8 |
| 59,950–69,170 | 35 | 69,370–80,030 | 33.6 |
| 69,170–115,250 | 40 | 80,030–133,340 | 38.4 |
| 115,250–158,510 | 45 | 133,340–183,400 | 43.2 |
| 158,510–187,490 | 50 | 183,400–216,940 | 49.0 |
| 187,490–213,280 | 55 | 216,940–246,770 | 53.9 |
| 213,280–271,740 | 60 | Over 246,770 | 56.8 |
| Over 271,740 | 65 | | |

Source: Lefebvre (1990).

## Taxation of Unincorporated Businesses

The major difference in the tax treatment of incorporated and unincorporated businesses is that the profits of the former are subject to corporate income tax, whereas the latter's profits are taxed at proprietors' personal rates. The tax base and most accounting practices are the same in both cases. Where members of households are employed and also engaged in an unincorporated business the profits of the latter (whether *bénéfices industriels et commerciaux* or the profits received by individuals engaged in professional activities, such as lawyers, doctors or architects) are simply added to other taxable income.

If no special tax advantages were granted to small corporate enterprises, incorporation for the purpose of retaining earnings would be advantageous only if the average corporate tax were below the average rate of personal income tax. Moreover, even with a tax credit of 50 percent for dividends, incorporation becomes advantageous only if the corporation tax rate is below 33 percent. However, under the present rate schedules the differences in the taxation of both types of businesses are not very great. For the highest marginal personal tax rate of 56.8 percent, the overall tax rate on dividends is 59.2 percent.

## Tax Treatment of Interest Income and Dividends

The tax treatment of households' financial investments is very mixed, has changed markedly since the early 1970s (especially after 1982), and is difficult to summarize in terms of an overall average marginal tax rate. At different times tax concessions have been used to channel funds into particular types of investment, such as housing, shares, other marketable securities, and mutual funds. They also have been used to boost the overall level of saving. More recently, the taxation of savings has been lowered, avowedly to limit capital flight after the lifting on January 1, 1990, of all remaining capital controls of foreign investments by French residents.[20] On balance, all of these measures have contributed to a marked reduction in the average and marginal taxation of income from financial assets, and much of capital income is currently exempt, de facto if not de jure, from personal income tax.

Under the personal income tax arrangements, capital income is subject to a 1 percent "solidarity" surtax, but a standard allowance is granted in respect of dividend income and interest from bonds. In 1985 these allowances, which are limited to taxpayers with annual incomes of less than Fr 320,000, amounted to Fr 3,000 and Fr 5,000 respectively.[21] Since January 1, 1988, a fixed lump sum of Fr 16,000 per household has been deductible by all taxpayers on interest income from marketable securities combined with dividends. Furthermore, any tax credits can be set off against the total tax liability.

In contrast to the Anglo-Saxon countries, in France (as in Italy and Belgium) taxpayers can often elect to be subject either to the progressive personal income tax described above or to a flat-rate final tax (*prélèvement libératoire*).[22] However, in some instances the *prélèvement libératoire* is mandatory. The rates of the *prélèvement libératoire* vary according to the type of instrument, date of issue, and maturity. All rates, however, are subject to a 1 percent surtax, the proceeds of which are used to pay family benefits, and for the period August 1 to December 31, 1990, to a further

20. The introduction of all of these measures has coincided with and possibly resulted in dramatic modifications in respect of households' portfolio decisions, particularly with regard to the allocation of new savings.

21. In 1980 both allowances amounted to Fr. 3,000. Given the average dividend and bond yields in 1985 of 3.6 percent and 12 percent respectively, these allowances covered a share portfolio of Fr 83,000 and a bond portfolio of Fr 41,700.

22. In the absence of a double-taxation agreement interest and dividends distributed to nonresidents are subject to a final withholding tax only.

1 percent exceptional levy. The tax rates described below are inclusive of these surcharges. (Nonresidents are exempt from the surcharges.)

Interest on negotiable securities issued between 1965 and 1987 is subject to a 10 percent withholding tax at source. This tax (which does not apply to interest on bank deposits) can be credited against income tax or the *prélèvement libératoire* in respect of negotiable securities traded on regulated exchanges, but is in addition to the *prélèvement obligatoire* for other instruments. Interest on all government bonds and on negotiable securities issued after January 1, 1987, is not subject to this withholding tax. For example, in 1985 the *prelévèment libératoire* on private-sector and government bonds was 26 percent. Investors could credit the 10 percent withholding tax borne by the issuer against their tax liability. In 1990 the same arrangement was applied to securities issued before 1987, but the *prélèvement libératoire* on all securities was lowered to 17 percent. For securities issued after 1987 there is no withholding tax, so the tax liability for all negotiable securities is limited to the *prélèvement libératoire*.

In addition to the flat-rate deduction and the *prélèvement libératoire*, there are numerous tax incentives under the personal income tax arrangements which are specific to individual financial instruments.

The main features of the tax treatment of interest income and dividends and of the incentives for saving, and the manner in which they have evolved over time, are summarized below.[23]

FULLY EXEMPT SAVINGS. A limited number of savings accounts enjoy full exemption from tax. These comprise certain accounts (*livrets A*) held with savings institutions (*caisses d'épargne*) and popular savings accounts (*livrets roses*). However, these accounts are strictly regulated in respect to the interest rate payable and there is a ceiling on the amounts that can be deposited.

Since January 1, 1983, individuals purchasing savings certificates (*bons de capitalisation*) or concluding contracts under a savings plan for retirement (*plan d'épargne pour la retraite*) have been allowed to accrue interest free of tax so long as the term of maturity of the contract is greater than six years. If these accounts are liquidated earlier, the tax rates are 17 percent (four to six years), 27 percent (two to four years), and 47 percent (less than 2 years). For 1990 the savings plan has been slightly modified and renamed the *plan d'épargne populaire*. Contributions to the new

---

23. In 1988 only Fr 56 billion out of a total of Fr 341 billion of measured income from capital was subject to the progressive income tax. See Conseil des Impôts (1990).

plan can be made up to a ceiling of Fr 600,000. As under the previous plan, interest and dividends are added to the principal and reinvested net of tax. The zero rate of tax applies only to accounts held for more than eight years. When the accounts are surrendered earlier, the rates of tax can be as much as 37 percent.

These arrangements have been extended to investment companies (mutual funds) since October 1, 1989 (see the section "Tax-Exempt Institutions").

SAVINGS ADMISSIBLE FOR THE *PRÉLÈVEMENT LIBÉRATOIRE.* For the purposes of determining the rate at which the *prélèvement libératoire* is levied, a distinction is made between negotiable securities tradable on regulated exchanges and savings accounts.

Interest income from bonds and other listed securities was subject to a rate of 26 percent in 1985 (which included 1 percent for social security contributions).[24] For interest income earned in 1990 this rate was lowered to 17 percent (including surcharges).

Other securities traded on a regulated exchange include certificates of deposit, Treasury bills, and commercial paper (*billets de trésorerie*). The rates are the same as those payable on interest on bonds.

Savings accounts at financial institutions comprise savings bonds (*bons*), savings deposits (*dépôts à terme*), and taxable accounts at savings institutions (*livrets fiscalisés*). The withholding tax was gradually raised, from 25 to 33 percent in 1974, to 40 percent in 1978, and to 46 percent in 1983. For 1990 the rate of tax was lowered to 37 percent.

Nondeclared income from securities, that is, any income not declared by individuals in their personal income tax return or for the *prélèvement libératoire*, is subject to a flat-rate tax of 51 percent.

As far as the parameters used in the simulations are concerned, it has been assumed in table 4-4 that the value of the *prélèvement libératoire* on marketable securities corresponds to the marginal tax rate on households' interest income. This value probably overestimates the marginal tax rate for most French households.

SAVINGS INCENTIVES. Irrespective of their amount, savings for retirement, that is, contributions to recognized pension schemes, are deductible

24. Companies that have issued these securities are obligated to withhold for tax purposes 10 percent or 12 percent of the gross amount of interest distributed. These amounts can be credited against the *prélèvement libératoire* or the personal income tax liability.

Table 4-4. *Taxation of Interest Income under the* Prélèvement
Libératoire, *1980, 1985, 1990*

| | Rate of tax (percent) | | |
|---|---|---|---|
| *Rate of* prélèvement libératoire | *1980* | *1985* | *1990* |
| Savings accounts | 40 | 46 | 37 |
| Bonds and other negotiable securities | 26 | 26 | 17 |
| "Capitalization" accounts | . . . | 0–46 | 0–37 |
| Deposits at savings institutions and "popular" accounts[a] | 0 | 0 | 0 |
| Unidentified holder of security | 51 | 51 | 52 |
| Estimated marginal personal tax rate on debt | 28 | 26 | 17 |

*Source:* Lefebvre (1990, and previous years).

a. The interest rates on these accounts are below those available on deregulated markets, and amounts deposited are subject to a ceiling. In 1980, 1985, and 1990 the interest rates were 8.5 percent, 6 percent, and 4.5 percent, respectively (for the "Livrets A"). The maximum amounts which could be held on deposit were Fr 49,000 and Fr 68,000 (1985 and 1990).

from the taxable income of individuals. However, pensions are taxed as earned income.

From 1978 to 1982, net annual share purchases by households of up to Fr 6,000 were deductible from personal income tax under the Monory Law.[25] To allow for this concession, the value of the discount rate for new share issues $\rho$ in 1980 was set at

$$\rho = i \frac{(1 - m_b)}{(1 - m_s)\theta + m_s},$$

where $m_s$ and $m_b$ are the marginal personal tax rates on dividend and interest income, respectively.[26]

### Taxation of Owner-Occupied Housing

Owner-occupied housing is affected by three sets of tax provisions: those for the personal income tax, the land tax on buildings (*taxe foncière sur les propriétés baties*), and the inhabitants' tax (*taxe d'habitation*).[27]

25. These deductions subject to a number of qualifications are still available for a much narrower group of investors.

26. See King and Fullerton (1984, p. 23).

27. Taxable income is equal to 150 percent of cash dividends. Personal income tax is levied at progressive rates on that amount less a tax credit of 50 percent of the cash dividend.

Under the personal income tax arrangements, imputed rental income on owner-occupied housing is exempt from income tax, whereas interest payments on mortgages can be partly offset by income tax payments. An annual tax credit of 20 percent of interest payable, with a ceiling of Fr 9,000 plus Fr 1,500 per dependent child, is granted on mortgages taken out before 1984 for the purchase of a principal residence. However, the relief is limited to the first ten years of the mortgage. For mortgages concluded after January 1, 1984, the tax credit has been increased to 25 percent, with the same limits on the maximum amounts, but the period during which the interest may be offset against tax has been reduced from ten to five years.

The bases for the *taxe d'habitation*[28] and the *taxe foncière sur les propriétés baties* are practically identical. They consist of 50 percent of the gross implicit rental value of dwellings, arbitrarily taken to be 8 percent of the capital cost of new buildings, or the cadastral rental value for existing dwellings. The implicit rental value depends on the characteristics of the dwelling (size, location, and quality). Tax rates, which range from 6 to 10 percent, depend on the local authorities, as does the size of the allowances, and they vary from year to year.[29] For want of better information, our calculations are based on Paris, where the tax rate was 8.5 percent in 1989. For a family without children, the rate of the *taxe foncière* on the value of a new dwelling in Paris would therefore amount to 0.34 percent (8.5 percent × 8 percent × 50 percent). New housing used as the principal dwelling is exempt from the *taxe foncière* during the early years of use. Buildings constructed before 1973 are allowed a twenty-five-year exemption; after that date the period of exemption has been reduced to fifteen years. Assuming that housing has an economic life of fifty years, the effective rate of the property tax is lowered by about one-fifth; the effective wealth tax equivalent rate of the *taxe foncière* on new dwellings in Paris can be estimated at 0.25 percent.

As already noted, the gross base for the *taxe d'habitation* is the implicit rental value of housing, but several deductions are available depending on the status of the owner-occupier. Rates for the *taxe d'habitation*, as for the *taxe foncière*, vary widely. Since tax revenues under the *taxe d'habitation* and the *taxe foncière sur les propriétés baties* are the same, it

---

28. The *tax d'habitation* accounts for about 10 percent of direct taxes paid by households, nearly 1 percent of gross personal income, and a quarter of revenues collected by local authorities.

29. There is no ceiling on the tax rates that councils can apply.

has been assumed that the effective yearly rate of wealth tax is equivalent to that of the *taxe foncière*. Accordingly, 0.50 percent is taken as a rough approximation of the overall rate of wealth tax for new owner-occupied dwellings.[30]

### Tax-Exempt Institutions (UCITS)

Contrary to the practice followed in most countries covered in the King-Fullerton study, tax-exempt institutions were not taken to include private pension funds or charitable institutions, both of which are of limited importance in France. The tax-exempt sector was taken to comprise only UCITS (undertakings for collective investment in transferable securities), known in France as OPCVM (*organismes de placement collectif en valeurs mobilières*), which benefit from a tax status comparable to that of pension funds in other countries. There are two types of UCITS: the open-ended SICAVs (*sociétés d'investissement à capital variable*) and the closed-ended FCPs (*fonds communs de placements*).

UCITS are exempt from company taxes, and see-through tax provisions generally apply to their earnings. If the dividends received by the SICAVs are distributed, the holders of SICAV shares can claim the underlying tax credit on a pro rata basis. The underlying tax credit cannot be claimed if the dividends are not distributed. Similarly any withholding taxes levied on interest from bonds cannot be reclaimed unless the proceeds are channeled to the individual bondholders.

Until 1989, UCITS were not allowed to accumulate reinvested interest tax-free but were obliged to distribute any earnings. Since 1990 any realized interest may be reinvested tax-free. Sales of shares in a UCITS which has accumulated interest are, however, subject to capital gains taxation if they exceed Fr 288,400 in a given year.

In the simulations it has been assumed that as far as interest income is concerned, UCITS were taxed at the rate of the *prélèvement libératoire* in 1980 and 1985 but were not taxed in 1990 because they were no longer obliged to distribute their income. The tax rate on the return to equity was set at 33 percent, the value of which offsets the benefit of the tax credit.

---

30. The personal wealth tax (*impôt sur les grandes fortunes*) is not taken into account by the simulations.

## Insurance Companies

In 1985, life insurance premiums up to Fr 4,000, increased by Fr 1,000 for each dependent child, were deductible against personal income tax. Premiums of up to Fr 3,250, increased by Fr 600 for each dependent child, were deductible on endowment policies.

In theory, the proceeds of the policies are taxed at the time of their realization, like other forms of deferred income such as pensions. However, tax-free reinvestment or accumulation of interest receipts has been allowed for insurance policies since 1983. In these cases the proceeds of life insurance, measured as the difference between gross revenue and premium payments, are exempt from tax, like those of other contracts where the interest is added to the principal and reinvested, if the insurance policy has a maturity of eight years or more. In practice this means that virtually all the proceeds of insurance policies are exempt from personal income tax.

Insurance companies are allowed to accumulate reserves against premiums paid as well as dividends or interest payments received on their investments. With regard to reserves, insurance companies can claim 100 percent of premiums paid in, net of commercial and management costs. In 1988, these reserves amounted to 83 percent of actual premiums. As regards earnings, companies can claim a deduction for earnings distributed to policyholders. In 1988, this amounted to approximately 40 percent of earnings and 4 percent of total reserves.

In summary, taking account of tax relief at the personal and corporate level, the effective acquisition cost of a life insurance policy is given by $(1 - m)(1 - \mu\tau)$, where $\mu$ is the percentage of premiums set aside as tax-free reserves. The post-tax return is equal to $(1 - \tau_I)(1 - m')$, where $m'$ is the present value of the deferred tax on the proceeds of the insurance policy held for ten years given by $(me^{-\rho 10})$ and $\tau_I$ is the tax on insurance companies. Assuming a real discount rate of 5 percent, $m' = 0.6m$.

Hence the effective tax rate $\tau_e$ on the policyholder's initial investment is given by

$$\tau_e = 1 - \frac{(1 - \tau_I)(1 - m')}{(1 - \mu\tau)(1 - m)}.$$

Taking account of the possibility after 1983 of accumulating and reinvesting interest payments as described earlier, whereby $m' = 0$ for investments held for longer periods and assuming $\mu = 0.83$, the value of $\tau_e$ for 1980, 1985, and 1990 was approximated for a median taxpayer having a marginal tax rate of 25 percent as 0.0598, −0.0684, and −0.1365 respectively.

### Taxation of Capital Gains and Wealth

The taxation of capital gains on shares and other negotiable securities was introduced in 1976 and modified in 1978 and 1983. The 1978 modifications introduced taxation at a flat rate and a very high exemption limit for gains realized in a particular year. As a result the present 16 percent capital gains tax applies only to gains above a specified ceiling, the value of which is reviewed every year and in 1990 corresponded to Fr 307,600. Gains made by institutional investors are exempt from tax. As a result most taxpayers pay virtually no capital gains tax.[31]

A tax on personal wealth (*impôt sur les grandes fortunes*) was introduced in 1981. It applied to all households with total assets exceeding Fr 3.5 million, at a progressive rate of 0.5 percent to 2 percent (for total assets worth more than Fr 20 million). Numerous items were exempted, however, such as works of art, productive assets in nonincorporated businesses, land rented to farmers, and forestry. In 1985, just before the tax was abolished by the conservative government that came to power in 1986, fewer than 100,000 households were liable. But the proceeds of the tax proved much smaller than expected, mostly because of numerous ways of evading part of the tax through underreporting or fictitious sales. The average tax rate on the assessment amounted to 0.5 percent.

The wealth tax was reintroduced under a new name (*impôt de solidarité sur la fortune*) by the Socialist government that came to power in 1988, the most noticeable change being the reduction of the top rate from 2.0 to 1.5 percent, and a modification in the tax schedule making it less progressive than before. The effective average marginal tax on wealth has been assumed to be equal to 0.25 percent in 1990.

## Structure of the Capital Stock and Its Ownership

Detailed data on the capital stock of the corporate sector (*sociétés et quasi-sociétés*) are compiled regularly by INSEE (Institut National de la Statistique et des Etudes Economiques — the National Institute of Statistics

31. Purchases or sale of shares and bonds traded on a stock exchange are liable to a stamp duty of 0.3 percent or 0.15 percent, depending on whether the size of the transaction exceeds or is less than Fr 1 million. Transactions carried out in over-the-counter markets are exempt from tax. This stamp duty is not considered in the simulations.

and Economic Research) and are the main source for the capital stock weights utilized in the simulations. The value of the net capital stock statistics is, as in most other countries, compiled using the perpetual inventory method.[32]

### Capital Stock Weights

The sectoral breakdown for the capital stock weights corresponds to that followed in King and Fullerton: the "manufacturing" sector excludes the mining industry; "other industry" is taken to comprise the construction, transport and communication, water, gas, and electricity industries; "commerce" includes nonfinancial services and the distribution sector.[33] The figures for the capital stock used in this study exclude the large nationalized French enterprises.

The capital stock series compiled by INSEE exclude inventories. The national accounts provide information on yearly changes in the level of inventories and since 1986 a separate disaggregation has been available for the corporate sector. Unfortunately, the breakdown by industry does not correspond exactly to that available for the capital stock: the mining industry is included in the data for manufacturing, the transport and communications industry is grouped with "services" rather than "other industry," and this latter classification includes the nationalized industries.

In spite of these drawbacks, the statistics provide a reasonably satisfactory basis for compiling information on the value of inventories outstanding. Two assumptions were made in order to derive stock data on inventories from the flow data. First, changes in inventories were assumed over the long term to be a constant proportion of output and, second, this proportion was multiplied by the average capital-output ratio recorded for each sector in the 1980s. The ratio of inventories to capital stock computed in this manner for manufacturing, other industry, and commerce amounted to 0.25, 0.41 and 0.069 respectively (table 4-5).

### Sources of Finance

The debt-equity ratios for each of the three sectors were estimated from balance sheet data for the corporate sector collected by the Bank

---

32. Ward (1976).
33. King and Fullerton (1984).

Table 4-5.  *Net Capital Stock, by Asset and Industry, at Replacement Cost, 1985*

| Item | Machinery | Buildings | Inventories | Total |
|---|---|---|---|---|
| | *Billions of francs* | | | |
| Manufacturing | 712.0 | 344.2 | 264.1 | 1,320.3 |
| Other industry | 343.4 | 301.1 | 264.2 | 908.8 |
| Commerce | 551.7 | 634.9 | 81.9 | 1,268.5 |
| Total | 1,607.1 | 1,280.2 | 610.2 | 3,497.6 |
| | *Percent shares* | | | |
| Manufacturing | 20.36 | 9.84 | 7.55 | 37.75 |
| Other industry | 9.82 | 8.61 | 7.56 | 25.98 |
| Commerce | 15.77 | 18.15 | 2.34 | 36.27 |
| Total | 45.95 | 36.60 | 17.45 | 100.00 |

Sources: Unpublished data from INSEE, Paris, and authors' calculations.

Table 4-6.  *Sources of Finance, by Industry, 1985*

Percent

| Item | Manufacturing | Other industry | Commerce |
|---|---|---|---|
| Debt | 44.0 | 44.0 | 43.8 |
| New share issues | 4.0 | 0.0 | 6.2 |
| Retained earnings | 52.0 | 56.0 | 50.0 |
| Total | 100.0 | 100.0 | 100.0 |

Source: Bank of France, Forecasting Office, Balance Sheet Data Office; and authors' estimates.

of France's Central Balance Sheet Data Office and the Direction de la Prévision (Forecasting Department).[34] The debt-equity ratio was computed for a given year by dividing the sum of total debt for all enterprises in a given sector by the value of their net equity (table 4-6).

### Ownership of Assets and Portfolio Behavior

The changes in the taxation of savings described under "Tax Treatment of Interest Income and Dividends" have been accompanied by profound changes in households' saving behavior since the end of the 1970s. On the one hand, there has been a pronounced decline in sight accounts as well as taxable and tax-exempt term deposits. In 1979 such liquid assets accounted for 80 to 90 percent of total households' savings, but by 1988 their share had declined to less than 40 percent. On the other hand, fixed-income securities and insurance products have expanded markedly and in 1988 accounted for 25 percent and 35 percent, respectively, of

34. We are grateful to M. F. Legendre, of the Direction de la Prévision, for making these data available to us.

Table 4-7.  *Structure of Share Ownership, 1975–89*

| Year | Households | UCITS[a] | Insurance companies |
|------|-----------|----------|---------------------|
| | | *Billions of francs* | |
| 1975 | 230.3 | 13.7 | 37.3 |
| 1980 | 419.0 | 31.0 | 76.0 |
| 1985 | 1,017.0 | 127.0 | 134.0 |
| 1989 | 3,212.0 | 333.6 | 346.0 |
| | | *Percent* | |
| 1975 | 81.87 | 4.87 | 13.26 |
| 1980 | 79.66 | 5.89 | 14.45 |
| 1985 | 79.58 | 9.95 | 10.49 |
| 1989 | 82.54 | 8.57 | 8.89 |

Source: Bank of France, Forecasting Office, Central Balance Sheet Office; and authors' calculations.
a. Undertakings for collective investment in transferable securities (European Community).

new savings. These developments are unfortunately not captured by the aggregate figures used for compiling the King-Fullerton weights described below.

Data on the distribution of equity ownership have been taken from the flow-of-funds statistics. However, no sectoral breakdown between the equity holdings of the different ownership categories (households, tax-exempt institutions, and insurance companies) according to financial and nonfinancial institutions is available. Accordingly, it has been assumed that the distribution of share ownership for the corporate sector as a whole does not differ from that for nonfinancial enterprises (table 4-7).

Flow-of-funds data have also been the principal source for compiling the breakdown of debt by type of owner. As in the case of shares, it has been assumed that bonds issued by nonfinancial enterprises were distributed among the various ownership categories in the same proportion as in the corporate sector as a whole.

In the case of banking debt, it was assumed that its distribution by type of ownership followed that of banks' deposits (table 4-8). Since deposits

Table 4-8.  *Debt Ownership Breakdown, 1985*

Billions of francs unless otherwise specified

| | Households | UCITS[a] | Insurance companies |
|------|-----------|----------|---------------------|
| Bank deposits | 1,060.0 | ... | ... |
| Bonds and other | | | |
| negotiable securities | 23.5 | 25.5 | 18.0 |
| Total | 1,129.5 | 25.5 | 18.0 |
| Shares (percent) | 96.3 | 2.2 | 1.5 |

Source: Authors' calculations based on Flow of Funds tables supplied by the Banque de France, Paris.
a. Undertakings for collective investment in transferable securities (European Community).

by UCITS and insurance companies are negligible, all bank deposits and accordingly all bank lending to the nonfinancial corporate sector have been allocated to the household sector.

## Estimates of Marginal Effective Tax Rates

Table 4-9 shows the summary aggregate estimates of marginal tax rates in 1985 assuming a hypothetical pretax real rate of return ($p$) equal to 10 percent (fixed-$p$). The first column of the table displays values of effective tax rates given by $(p-s)/p$, where $s$ is the after-tax real return on savings. Splitting these results between the personal and corporate effective tax rates shown in the second and third columns, respectively, provides further insights into the factors determining the level of the overall effective rates for individual components. At the corporate level, the effective tax rate is defined as $(p - \rho)/p$, where $\rho$ is the value of the endogenous discount rate used to value individual projects. At the personal level, the effective tax rate is given by $(\rho - s)/s$. The fourth and fifth columns show the marginal tax rates assuming that companies were tax-exhausted ($\tau = 0$) or that there was no wealth tax at the corporate level respectively.

These estimates of effective tax rates display five main features of the treatment of capital income in France in 1985. First, assuming a zero rate of inflation the overall average tax rate was, at 56 percent, high compared to that in other countries. Second, taxes levied at the corporate level account for about two-thirds of the marginal tax rate, the balance resulting from taxes levied at the personal level. Third, average marginal tax rates did not exhibit particularly wide dispersion when examined across sectors of activity. This is due to the relatively similar mix of financing and type of assets assumed for investments undertaken in different sectors. Indeed, there were significant differences by type of asset, source of finance, and ownership. By type of asset, inventories were the most heavily taxed (65 percent). Machinery is treated favorably, as can be seen from the third column, because of accelerated depreciation and the immediate expensing of 40 percent of new investments. Debt is by far the most tax-favored source of finance, with effective tax rates more than 20 percentage points below those of other sources of finance. As a result of the de facto exemption from capital gains taxes, retained earnings are favored over new share issues. Moreover, these simulations do not take account of registration fees and duties, which would tend to increase the cost of raising funds through new share issues even further. The ef-

Table 4-9. *Marginal Effective Tax Rates, with Zero Inflation, Corporate Sector, 1985*

Percent

| | | | | Total | |
| | | | | With complete tax exhaustion ($\tau = 0$) | Excluding wealth tax on companies |
| Item | Total | Personal | Corporate | | |
|---|---|---|---|---|---|
| Industry | | | | | |
| Manufacturing | 54.3 | 40.5 | 23.2 | 47.3 | 34.0 |
| Other industry | 58.1 | 41.0 | 29.0 | 46.8 | 39.4 |
| Commerce | 53.8 | 40.4 | 22.4 | 44.2 | 36.3 |
| Asset | | | | | |
| Machinery | 45.5 | 39.5 | 9.9 | 48.4 | 20.3 |
| Buildings | 56.9 | 40.8 | 27.1 | 41.4 | 44.1 |
| Inventories | 65.2 | 42.2 | 39.7 | 48.3 | 47.6 |
| Method of finance | | | | | |
| Debt | 40.9 | 31.3 | 14.0 | 51.7 | 16.0 |
| New share issues | 77.2 | 52.9 | 51.6 | 50.7 | 46.4 |
| Retained earnings | 67.4 | 50.2 | 34.4 | 42.2 | 52.7 |
| Owner | | | | | |
| Households | 57.2 | 43.5 | 24.2 | 51.5 | 38.5 |
| Tax-exempt institutions | 57.9 | 39.0 | 31.0 | 35.1 | 39.5 |
| Insurance companies | 32.3 | 0.5 | 32.0 | −7.1 | 4.0 |
| Overall tax rate | 56.0 | 40.6 | 25.2 | 46.6 | 36.4 |

Source: Tables 4-9 through 4-14 are authors' calculations.

fective rate of tax by type of ownership on investments through UCITS and directly by individuals was virtually the same. Owing to the benefits of deferral and provisioning, the marginal tax rates on investments channeled through insurance companies received the most favorable tax treatment.

Fourth, as shown in the fifth column, about 20 percentage points of the overall effective tax rate on capital income were accounted for by wealth taxes on investments by companies (*impôt foncier* and *taxe professionnelle*). In particular, the effective tax rate on debt-financed investments falls from 41 to 16 percent. The decline is particularly striking in the case of insurance companies, reducing their marginal tax rate to only 4 percent. By contrast, the presence of tax exhaustion is a mixed blessing. It lowers the value of effective tax rates on equity but raises the value on debt. There is also in this case a pronounced effect on investment channeled through insurance companies. Finally, a comparison of the fourth and fifth columns shows that repealing the *taxe professionnelle* and the

Table 4-10.   *Marginal Effective Tax Rates under Different Inflation Rates, Corporate Sector, 1985*

Percent

| Item | Expected rate of inflation (percent) | | |
|---|---|---|---|
| | 0 | 5 | 10 |
| Industry | | | |
| Manufacturing | 54.8 | 64.4 | 72.4 |
| Other industry | 58.1 | 71.4 | 82.6 |
| Commerce | 54.7 | 60.6 | 63.4 |
| Asset | | | |
| Machinery | 46.1 | 49.3 | 50.9 |
| Buildings | 57.3 | 62.9 | 62.9 |
| Inventories | 65.4 | 86.4 | 107.7 |
| Method of finance | | | |
| Debt | 40.9 | 40.0 | 36.1 |
| New share issues | 77.2 | 78.2 | 91.6 |
| Retained earnings | 67.4 | 87.4 | 105.5 |
| Owner | | | |
| Households | 57.5 | 69.1 | 78.8 |
| Tax-exempt institutions | 58.7 | 70.4 | 80.5 |
| Insurance companies | 33.6 | 24.4 | 12.9 |
| Overall tax rate | 56.1 | 66.3 | 74.6 |

*impôt foncier* would have a much larger impact on the cost of capital than abolishing corporation tax.

The impact of inflation on effective tax rates is shown in table 4-10. Overall effective tax rates display a positive correlation with inflation, rising from 56 percent at 0 percent inflation to nearly 75 percent at 10 percent inflation. Effective tax rates on inventories for which no adjustments are allowed for inflation rates below 10 percent and on equity-financed investments become virtually confiscatory at an inflation rate of 10 percent. The cost of debt finance declines slowly in spite of the deductibility of interest.

Table 4-11 displays the values of effective tax rates for 1980 and, if these estimates are compared with those for 1985, it appears that the overall average marginal tax rates were roughly the same in both years. However, in 1980 inflation exceeded 10 percent, whereas in 1985 it was only 5 percent. There were also other minor differences in the values of effective tax rates in 1980 and 1985. As far as assets are concerned, the accelerated depreciation measures of 1983–85 tended to widen the tax differential between machinery and buildings. Indeed, expensing of equipment provided a substantial shield against the effects of inflation

Table 4-11. *Marginal Effective Tax Rates under Different Inflation Rates, 1980*

Percent

| Item | Inflation rate (percent) | | |
|---|---|---|---|
| | 0 | 5 | 10 |
| Industry | | | |
| Manufacturing | 52.9 | 65.6 | 75.8 |
| Other industry | 55.3 | 70.3 | 83.0 |
| Commerce | 52.3 | 61.6 | 66.7 |
| Asset | | | |
| Machinery | 48.9 | 58.0 | 64.0 |
| Buildings | 51.4 | 58.0 | 58.4 |
| Inventories | 60.2 | 81.8 | 103.4 |
| Method of finance | | | |
| Debt | 40.9 | 43.8 | 43.2 |
| New share issues | 59.1 | 76.0 | 90.1 |
| Retained earnings | 63.9 | 85.0 | 104.0 |
| Owner | | | |
| Households | 55.1 | 69.3 | 80.8 |
| Tax-exempt institutions | 53.7 | 66.7 | 76.9 |
| Insurance companies | 39.0 | 40.0 | 37.4 |
| Overall tax rate | 54.0 | 66.6 | 76.8 |

on capital cost. Second, the repeal of the Monory Law, which had allowed share purchases to be offset against personal tax, raised the cost of new equity finance by more than 15 percentage points between 1980 and 1985. Third, the relative tax treatment of investments channeled through insurance companies became far more favorable as a result of the new provisions concerning the accumulation and reinvestment of interest income.

## The Noncorporate Sector and Owner-Occupied Housing

Estimates of effective tax rates for investments by the noncorporate business sector are shown in table 4-12. The calculations apply to the same broad spectrum of assets and industries as for the corporate sector. The capital-stock and source-of-finance weights are the same as those used for the corporate sector, since it was not possible to obtain weights separately for each of the two sectors. However, only households are assumed to be the ultimate investors and the only form of equity investment available is proprietors' equity. There is no tax distinction between reinvested earnings and consumption. As regards proprietors' income,

Table 4-12.  *Marginal Effective Tax Rates under Different Inflation Rates, Fixed-*p, *Noncorporate Sector, 1985*

Percent

| Item | Expected rate of inflation (percent) | | |
|---|---|---|---|
| | 0 | 5 | 10 |
| Industry | | | |
| Manufacturing | 48.4 | 54.0 | 57.2 |
| Other industry | 52.6 | 61.6 | 68.3 |
| Commerce | 48.0 | 49.9 | 47.3 |
| Asset | | | |
| Machinery | 38.5 | 37.0 | 33.0 |
| Buildings | 51.3 | 52.3 | 46.4 |
| Inventories | 60.6 | 78.6 | 96.6 |
| Method of finance | | | |
| Debt | 41.2 | 40.6 | −36.8 |
| Proprietors' equity | 56.6 | 68.2 | 77.4 |
| Households (overall) | 49.9 | 56.1 | 59.6 |

a relatively high marginal tax rate of 50.3 percent was estimated from personal income tax returns.

In 1985 the overall effective marginal tax rates appeared somewhat lower than their counterparts in the corporate sector. In the case of debt-financed investments, the marginal tax rates were nearly equivalent because the tax rate on noncorporate profits was roughly the same as that on companies' profits in that year. Equity-financed investments, by contrast, were taxed at a lower rate than the corporate sector because there was no double taxation of dividends. However, the convergence of tax rates between equity finance and debt finance did not affect the dispersion of rates by asset and industry because investments by institutional investors were not included in the simulations.

The cost of capital for new dwellings in France was approximated by

$$c = \rho - t_h,$$

where $t_h$ is the estimated wealth tax rate derived in the section, "Taxation of Owner-Occupied Housing." Effective marginal tax rates for owner-occupied housing are reported in table 4-13, assuming a value of $t_h$ of 0.5 percent in 1985 and a marginal personal tax rate of 40 percent. In the absence of information on the composition of the financing of owner-occupied housing, separate figures are shown for debt-financed and equity-financed investments.

Table 4-13. *Marginal Effective Tax Rates under Different Inflation Rates, Owner-Occupied Housing, 1985*

Percent

| | Expected rate of inflation (percent) | | |
|---|---|---|---|
| *Item* | *0* | *5* | *10* |
| Debt | 2.06 | 0.52 | −0.01 |
| Equity | 5.00 | 5.00 | 5.00 |

The low value of the effective marginal tax rate for debt-financed investments of only 2 percent at stable prices, and even lower for positive rates of inflation, assumes that households benefit from the partial deductibility of nominal interest for the first ten years of a mortgage and the absence of tax on imputed rental income. In the case of equity finance the rate of tax is equal to the income tax equivalent of the wealth tax.

### Recent Changes in Legislation

The main changes in the tax regime between 1985 and 1990 that have been taken into account for the simulation results shown in table 4-14 are as follows:

— the reduction in the rate of the *précompte libératoire* and of the effective tax rate on investments channeled via insurance companies;
— the reduction in the tax on retained earnings;
— the lowering of the useful life for fixed assets;
— the scrapping of investment incentives for equipment.

There were several notable changes in the values of the effective tax rates as a result of these reforms. First, at stable prices the overall effective tax rate declined from 56 percent in 1985 to 45 percent in 1990. At a rate of inflation of 5 percent, which was close to that prevailing in both years, the overall effective tax rate decreases from 66 to 54 percent (fourth column). Second, the bulk of the contraction in the overall tax rate took place at the personal level. As can be seen by comparing the second and third columns in table 4-14 with the second and third columns in table 4-9, the overall tax rate in the personal sector fell from 41 to 29 percent, whereas for the corporate sector the decline was from 25 to 22 percent. The pronounced reduction in the tax rates on savings and smaller

Table 4-14.  *Marginal Effective Tax Rates under Different Inflation Rates, 1990*

Percent

| | Zero rate of inflation | | | Total effective tax rate | |
|---|---|---|---|---|---|
| Item | Total | Personal | Corporate | 5 percent inflation | 10 percent inflation |
| Industry | | | | | |
| Manufacturing | 42.5 | 29.2 | 18.8 | 51.0 | 57.3 |
| Other industry | 44.7 | 29.3 | 21.8 | 53.9 | 61.7 |
| Commerce | 45.6 | 29.4 | 23.0 | 57.3 | 66.9 |
| Asset | | | | | |
| Machinery | 38.0 | 29.0 | 12.7 | 43.0 | 45.6 |
| Buildings | 40.9 | 29.1 | 16.6 | 44.7 | 44.3 |
| Inventories | 49.7 | 29.6 | 28.6 | 65.2 | 80.1 |
| Method of finance | | | | | |
| Debt | 33.2 | 19.2 | 17.4 | 34.4 | 34.0 |
| New share issues | 67.6 | 39.3 | 46.6 | 93.1 | 117.8 |
| Retained earnings | 52.7 | 37.9 | 23.9 | 67.5 | 81.1 |
| Owner | | | | | |
| Households | 45.9 | 31.7 | 20.8 | 56.7 | 65.7 |
| Tax-exempt institutions | 46.2 | 30.3 | 22.8 | 57.7 | 67.2 |
| Insurance companies | 15.2 | −10.4 | 23.2 | 5.7 | −7.1 |
| Overall tax rate | 44.7 | 29.3 | 21.8 | 53.9 | 61.7 |

decreases in wealth taxes were the principal reasons for the strong decline in the overall personal tax rates. Third, the dispersion of rates across assets narrowed markedly, particularly between buildings and equipment. Indeed, in terms of effective tax rates in the corporate sector alone, the scrapping of investment incentives and the lower useful lives meant that the effective tax rates on equipment actually rose marginally, from 10 to 13 percent. The reduction in the dispersion of rates across asset types also entailed a narrowing of the differentials in effective tax rates across industries. Finally, the reduction of the corporate tax has increased the marginal tax rate on debt-financed investments while lowering that for projects financed by equity.

Figures for 1990 on effective tax rates in the noncorporate sector which are not included in the table show a similar picture to that depicted in table 4-12. The only changes in the tax regime since 1985 for earnings in the noncorporate sector have been the repeal of the incentives on investments in equipment and the small decrease in the personal wealth tax rate. As a result there has, if anything, been a convergence of tax rates between the corporate and noncorporate sectors.

## Conclusion

At the corporate level, the taxation of capital income in France does not differ much from that in other countries. The present rate of corporation tax is, at 37 percent, marginally above that in the United Kingdom and the United States but equal to if not below the rate found in most other European countries. At present, there are no major incentives covering investment in the corporate sector, with the exception of those applying to specific industrial sectors or types of investment, such as research and development. Wealth taxes on corporate assets are not unlike those found in some other European countries.

The main distinguishing feature of the French tax system is the treatment of income from capital received by households directly or through institutional investors. As far as households are concerned, it is possible for taxpayers to elect to be taxed in a variety of ways, although all types of income are in theory taxable under personal income tax. Moreover, there are numerous exemptions and special incentives to channel savings into certain types of investment. As a result, it is difficult to assign a meaningful number to the marginal effective tax rate on households, and in all likelihood the number used in the simulations, namely the value of the *taxe libératoire*, is an overestimate of the actual-value marginal tax rate. Savings channeled through insurance companies and mutual funds are either not taxed at all or are taxed at very low rates.

Clearly, the simplification and reorganization of the tax treatment of capital income would represent an important reform of the French tax system, but changes in this area are increasingly linked to developments elsewhere in Europe.

Table 4A-1.  *Real After-Tax Return to Savings*

| Method of finance | Household | Tax-exempt institution | Life insurance company |
|---|---|---|---|
| Debt | $i(1 - m_b) - \pi - w_p$ | $i(1 - m_b) - \pi - w_p$ | $\dfrac{i(1 - \tau_I)(1 - m\prime) - \pi - w_p}{(1 - \mu\tau)(1 - m)}$ |
| New shares | $\rho\theta(1 - m_s) - \pi - w_p$ | $\rho\theta(1 - m_s) - \pi - w_p$ | $[\rho/(1 - \tau)] - \pi - w_p$ |
| Retained earnings | $\rho(1 - z) - \pi - w_p$ | $\rho(1 - z) - \pi - w_p$ | $\dfrac{\rho(1 - z) - \pi - w_p}{1 - \tau}$ |

$m_b$  Marginal personal tax rate on interest income (*prélèvement libératoire*)
$i$    Nominal interest rate
$\pi$    Inflation rate
$\rho$    Rate of return net of corporation taxes
$\theta$    Opportunity cost of retained earnings in terms of gross dividends forgone
$\tau$    Statutory corporation tax rate
$w_p$  Effective average personal wealth tax rate
$\tau_I$   Life insurance statutory tax rate
$m\prime$   Present value of marginal personal income tax on deferred (capitalized) income
$m_s$   Marginal personal tax rate on dividend income
$z$    Effective accrued tax rate on capital gains
$m$    Marginal personal tax rate of income
$z_I$   Effective accrued marginal tax rate on capital gains of insurance companies.


Table 4A-2.  *Firms' Discount Rate, $\rho$*[a]

| | | Type of investor | |
|---|---|---|---|
| Method of finance | Household | Tax-exempt institution | Life insurance company |
| Debt | $i(1 - \tau)$ | $i(1 - \tau)$ | $i(1 - \tau)$ |
| New shares[b] | $\dfrac{i(1 - m_b)}{(1 - m_s)\theta + m_s}$ | $i$ | $i$ |
| Retained earnings | $\dfrac{i(1 - m_b)}{1 - z}$ | $\dfrac{i(1 - m_b)}{1 - z}$ | $\dfrac{i(1 - m)}{1 - z_I}$ |

a. See table 4A-1 for description of symbols.
b. The value of firms' discount rate shown in the table applies to 1980 only when the Monory law was in force. For 1985 and 1990 the value of the discount rate was $i(1 - m_b)/(1 - m_s)\theta$.

# References

Atkinson, Margaret, and Jacques Mairesse. 1978. "Length of Life of Equipment in French Manufacturing." *Annales de l'Insee* 30–31 (April–September): 23–48.

Blades, Derek W. 1983. *Service Lives of Fixed Assets*. OECD Economics and Statistics Department Working Paper 4. Paris: Organization for Economic Cooperation and Development.

Cette, Gilbert, and Daniel Szpiro. 1988a. "La durée de vie des équipements industriels sur la période 1972–84." Banque de France, *Cahiers Economiques et Monétaires* 28: 3–38.

———. 1988b. "La durée de vie et l'âge moyen de l'outil de production." Institut National de la Statistique et des Etudes Economiques (INSEE), *Economie et Statistique* 208: 3–15.

Conseil des Impôts. 1986. *Huitième rapport au Président de la République: Relatif à l'imposition du capital*. Paris.

———. 1987. *Neuvième rapport au Président de la République: Relatif a la fiscalité des entreprises*. Paris.

———. 1990. *Douzième rapport au Président de la République: Relatif à l'imposition du revenu*. Paris.

King, Mervyn, and Don Fullerton, eds. 1984. *The Taxation of Income from Capital: A Comparative Study of the United States, the United Kingdom, Sweden and West Germany*. University of Chicago Press.

Lefebvre, Francis. 1990. *Mémento pratique Francis Lefebvre, Fiscal 1990*. Paris: Ed. Francis Lefebvre.

Organization for Economic Cooperation and Development (OECD). *Revenue Statistics of OECD Member Countries*. Paris.

Ward, Michael. 1976. *The Measurement of Capital: The Methodology of Capital Stock Estimates in OECD Countries*. Paris: OECD.

CHAPTER FIVE

# Germany

*Willi Leibfritz*

IN GERMANY tax treatment of capital formation has changed several times in recent decades. With the Law for Economic Stabilization and Growth (Stabilitäts- und Wachstumsgesetz) in 1967, a main goal of economic policy was to mitigate cyclical fluctuations of the economy. Temporary tax measures, including changes in depreciation allowances, were some of the proposed policy tools in the context of this law besides a Keynesian-type anticyclical public spending policy. During all three recessions that the German economy experienced subsequently (1967, 1974–75, and 1982–83), temporary reliefs for business investment were introduced, especially tax-free investment grants.

At the beginning of the 1970s, with the Investment Tax Law (Investitionszulagengesetz), tax-free investment grants were also introduced to speed up structural adjustment in various areas such as energy saving, environmental protection, and regional policy.

In the meantime, some of these investment-promotion measures have been abolished or replaced by other policy tools. Regarding the general tax system, the main changes since the late 1970s had been the reform of the corporate tax system with the introduction of full imputation in 1976 and major tax cuts in 1975 and during the period 1986–90. This most recent tax reform has been influenced by the international "new approach" of lowering tax rates and broadening the tax base. It brought the biggest income tax cut German taxpayers have seen so far, although top marginal tax rates were reduced much less than in other countries: the personal income tax rate from 56 to 53 percent and the corporate tax rate for retained earnings from 56 to 50 percent; for middle-income brackets marginal tax rates were reduced substantially. General depreciation allowances, which had been improved substantially in 1978 (equipment investment) and in 1985 (business construction), have remained unchanged. As Germany's

166

corporate tax rate for retained earnings is still the highest among industrial countries, the government plans to reduce this rate further, to 44 percent, by 1994. At the same time depreciation allowances will be reduced.

Because of its unequal burden on industry sectors and individual firms, the local business tax and the net wealth tax on corporations have been a source of contention for many years. Despite some fundamental reform proposals, only minor changes are expected for future tax reform. More radical reforms for the general tax system, such as the introduction of a cash-flow tax, are becoming more popular among economists but it is not expected that German tax policy will move in the direction of a cash-flow tax in the near future.

Since unification the main task of German economic policy has been to restructure east Germany's economy. After unification industrial production in east Germany broke down. The main reasons were the low productivity and the poor competitiveness of east German firms. This was aggravated by the fact that currency union brought a strong effective revaluation for east German exporters. In addition, the traditional trade with Eastern Europe, including the former Soviet Union, had declined sharply.

A variety of tax and subsidy measures have been taken to promote investment in east Germany and to restructure that region's whole economy.

It is striking that, despite many changes in direct and indirect taxes in the past decades in west Germany, the ratio of tax to gross national product has hardly changed. Over the past quarter century the ratio fluctuated between 23 and 25 percent. After the most recent tax cut the ratio declined from 24.3 to 23.6 percent. This ratio is only 2 to 3 percentage points higher than the ratios for the United States and Japan, which by international standards have relatively low taxes. But if social security contributions are included, the ratio of taxes to GNP increases by 14 percentage points, exceeding the ratios of the United States and Japan by 8 to 9 percentage points. Because of a rapid increase in social security contributions, this overall ratio increased by 7 percentage points during the 1970s but remained almost constant during the 1980s.

Because of higher indirect taxes and income tax progressivity, the German tax-to-GNP ratio is expected to increase. For 1995 the government is preparing a further tax increase to put the financing of the cost of unification on a sounder base.

Regarding the structure of tax revenues (excluding social security contributions), the most lucrative tax is the wage tax (34.3 percent of total tax revenues in 1989, after 30.6 percent in 1980 and 22.8 percent in 1970), followed by the value-added tax (25.3 percent of total tax revenues). The share of the corporate tax is only about 6 percent, and that of the local business tax is about 7 percent. The reason for the relatively low share of corporate tax revenues is not a relatively low effective business tax rate but rather the fact that noncorporate business has a relatively high share in the German economy.

The international comparisons of capital-income taxation reported by Mervyn A. King and Don Fullerton in 1984 showed West Germany with higher marginal effective tax rates than Sweden, the United States, and the United Kingdom. The overall marginal effective tax rate on capital income from the corporate sector was 48.1 percent, compared with 37.2 percent for the United States, 35.6 percent for Sweden, and 3.7 percent for the United Kingdom.

In this chapter the following questions are posed.

— What are the main taxes on capital formation and on the capital stock in Germany?

— How have they been changed by recent tax reforms?

— What are the marginal effective and average tax rates on capital income?

— What is the effect of the investment promotion scheme in east Germany?

## Capital Taxes

Like other countries, Germany has a variety of taxes on capital return and on the capital stock: the personal income tax, which includes taxes on interest and dividend income, but (for individuals) not on capital gains; the wealth tax on the net value of assets owned by individuals and corporations; taxes on real property in the form of houses, land, and fixed equipment; the tax on corporate and noncorporate profits; the local business tax with a profit and a capital-stock tax base; and the tax on the transfer of wealth via gifts and bequests as well as via purchases of land and of financial assets. Table 5-1 summarizes the taxes in Germany that can be labeled as taxes on capital. In the calculations of the marginal tax rates as presented later in this chapter, the taxes on capital income and on capital stock are taken into account. The effective tax rate depends not

Table 5-1. *Taxes on Capital, Germany*

| Category of tax | Tax rates |
|---|---|
| *Tax on capital income* | |
| Personal income tax | Before 1990: 22–56 percent<br>1990: 19–53 percent |
| Corporate income tax | Retentions before 1990: 56 percent<br>1990: 50 percent; 1994: 44 percent<br>Dividends 36 percent<br>Full imputation |
| Dividend income withholding<br>  tax | 25 percent (deductible from income tax) |
| Interest income withholding<br>  tax (deductible from income tax)<br>  Jan. 1–June 30, 1989<br>  Since Jan. 1, 1993 | <br><br>10 percent<br>30 percent (high tax allowances) |
| Local business profit tax | 18 percent (average); deductible from income<br>  tax base, DM 36,000 tax allowance;<br>  up from 1993 DM 48,000 |
| *Tax on capital stock* | |
| Net wealth tax | 0.6 percent on corporate wealth<br>0.5 percent on personal wealth |
| Local business capital tax | 0.7 percent average; deductible from income<br>  tax base, DM 120,000 tax allowance |
| Local land tax | 1.1 percent (average); deductible from income<br>  tax base |
| *Taxes on capital transfers*<br>Inheritance tax<br>Stock market turnover tax<br>Company equity purchase tax<br>Land purchase tax | <br><br>Until 1991 |

only on the statutory tax rates but also on the definition of the tax base. In this respect the tax base of business profits is especially influenced by depreciation allowances (table 5-2). In the following discussion an attempt is made to catch at least the most important tax factors influencing capital formation in the business sector.

Depreciation allowances were improved during the 1970s and the 1980s. As other countries such as the United States and the United Kingdom have reduced depreciation allowances, German investors are now treated relatively favorably in this respect. Only in a few other industrial countries are depreciation allowances more favorable. Furthermore, since 1990 for inventory valuation the LIFO (last in, first out) method

Table 5-2.  *Depreciation Allowances*

| Kind of investment | Method | Rate |
|---|---|---|
| Equipment | Declining balance | 3 (1994: 2.5) times the straight-line rate maximum 30 percent (1994: 25 percent) |
| Construction | Straight line or<br>4 (1994: 5) years<br>3 (1994: 6) years<br>18 (1994: 14) years | 4 percent<br>10 percent (1994: 7 percent)<br>5 percent (1994: 5 percent)<br>2.5 percent |
| Inventories | Up from 1990: last in, first out | . . . |

is allowed, which makes the German business sector less vulnerable to inflation. The government also plans to reduce the corporate tax rate on retained earnings from 50 to 44 percent by 1994 and at the same time to broaden the tax base by reducing depreciation allowances.

Past policy measures affected most of the taxes listed in table 5-1. The tax reform of 1990 mainly affected the personal income tax and the corporate tax on retained earnings. Although the various cuts in personal income tax (especially in 1975 and in 1986, 1988, and 1990) aimed at relief for labor income, the flattening of the tax rate schedule and the increase of the basic allowance also favored receivers of capital income. In 1990 the top marginal income tax rate was reduced from 56 percent to 53 percent, but marginal tax rates in middle-income brackets were reduced more.

The weighted marginal income tax on capital income declined from 44.6 percent in 1982 to 38.5 percent in 1990. In 1990 the tax allowance for capital income was increased substantially (from DM 400 for singles and DM 800 for spouses to DM 700 and DM 1,400, respectively).

Because of general evasion of tax on interest income, the government introduced a 10 percent withholding tax (*Quellensteuer*) on interest income at the beginning of 1989. The rate was relatively low (10 percent). Nevertheless, it led to substantial capital flight, especially to tax-free Luxembourg, and to a rise in interest rates. The government therefore abolished the tax. But in response to a pledge by the Supreme Court, the government had to reform taxation of interest income. In 1993 another withholding tax (*Zinsabschlagsteuer*) was introduced with a rate of 30 percent (excluding interest income of foreigners). At the same time, tax-free amounts for capital income were increased substantially (to DM

6,100 for singles and DM 12,200 for spouses). About 80 percent of previous payers of tax on interest income are below these limits and will in the future pay no tax on capital income. Nevertheless, the new withholding tax induced another flight of capital, especially to Luxembourg. This was due to irrational behavior, lack of knowledge about effects of this tax, fears among Germans of being discovered as former tax evaders, and continued tax evasion by persons in high income brackets.

With the reduction of the corporate tax rate in 1990 (from 56 to 50 percent), the overall marginal tax rate on corporate retentions, including the local business tax, was reduced from 62.8 to 58.1 percent.

## The Integrated Capital Taxation Model

The integrated capital taxation model measures the real marginal effective tax rate on the capital formation process in the business sector. It was originally developed and applied to four countries: the United States, the United Kingdom, Sweden, and west Germany.[1] Most recently this model has also been applied to other countries. The model is well described in the previous study.

### Methodology

The effective marginal tax rate on capital income is defined by

$$t = \frac{p - s}{p},$$

where $p = MRR - \delta$, and

$$\mathrm{MRR} = \frac{1 - A}{1 - \tau}(\rho + \delta - \pi) - t_w^i$$

$$s = (1 - m)i - \pi - t_w^p,$$

where $MRR$ is the gross marginal rate of return, $\delta$ is the rate of economic depreciation, $\tau$ is the marginal profit tax, $m$ is the marginal income tax rate of savers, $\pi$ is the rate of inflation, and $t_w$ is the rate of wealth tax ($t_w^i$ for investors; $t_w^s$ for savers).

---

1. King and Fullerton (1984).

The discount rate $\rho$ is different for the various sources of finance.

debt: $\rho = (1 - \tau)i$

retained earnings: $\rho = (1 - m)i$

new share issues: $\rho = \frac{1}{\theta} \cdot i$

$\theta$: tax discrimination variable between profit retentions and distributions. In the case of the German full imputation system $= 1/(1 - \tau)$.

$A$: present value of the advantage of tax depreciation and of other investment allowances.

With a comprehensive income tax system there is

$$p = r$$
$$s = (1 - m)r$$
$$p - s = rm$$
$$\frac{p - s}{p} = m = \tau.$$

With no tax system or with an investment-neutral tax system (consumption tax system) there is

$$p = r = s,$$

that is, the real marginal rate of return is equal to the real interest rate and the real return savers get on their financial assets. In this case the tax system does not drive any wedge between the marginal rate of return and the interest rate.

The tax system drives a wedge between the marginal rate of return of investment projects $p$ and the real capital market interest rate $i - \pi$, and also between the capital market interest rate and the net capital income of savers. The first part of this wedge refers to the level of the investor and the second part to the level of the saver.

Many factors influence this effective marginal tax rate (figure 5-1). Because taxes are included at both the investment and saving levels, in addition to business taxation all taxes on income and wealth of private and institutional savers are important. Because there may be variations in the tax treatment of investment goods (equipment investment, construction, and stockbuilding), different groups of savers (private households, tax-exempt institutions, and those who save via insurance companies), and different sources of business financing (debt financing and equity financing), the structure of capital formation is important. Finally, because the tax rate is defined as a real marginal tax rate, the results also depend

Figure 5.1. *Capital Taxation Model*

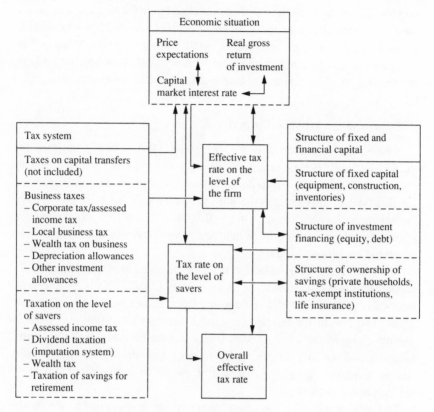

on the real interest rate and on the inflation rate, taking into account the sensitivity of the tax system to inflation.

Such a broad approach requires a variety of parameters concerning the tax system and the structure of capital formation. For some parameters the empirical finding poses no problem, as the tax code and tax statistics and other statistics provide the necessary information. But for other parameters, data are lacking and there is a good deal of uncertainty, so that estimation problems exist. This is especially the case for variables such as economic depreciation, ownership of capital, and the average marginal income tax on the various types of capital income. Tables A-1 and A-2 in the appendix to this volume show the development of the various parameters that have been used for the model calculations in the case of West Germany.

Marginal effective tax rates are calculated by types of investment, by sectors of industry, by sources of finance, and by different groups of savers for a project yielding a gross return net of depreciation of 10 percent (fixed-$p$ case). The calculations refer mainly to the corporate business sector. For comparison, marginal effective tax rates are also calculated for investment in the noncorporate business sector and for residential construction.

### Empirical Results: The Corporate Sector

Results are shown in table 5-3 for 1980, 1985, 1989, and 1990 for the fixed-$p$ case. For example, the 39.8 percent tax rate for machinery in 1990 means that with a hypothetical pretax rate of return of 10 percent for this type of investment, the ultimate saver will get 6.02 percent net capital income (which equals $0.1 - 0.0398$). The results are shown for three types of investment, three industry groups, three sources of finances, and three owners of capital.

The overall marginal effective tax rate is a weighted average of these particular subsets. It amounts to 34.1 percent in 1990. This is 7 percentage points lower than in 1989, and about 14 percentage points lower than in 1980. The reason for the decline in the rate between 1989 and 1990 is the most recent tax reform, with the reduction of the marginal income tax rates and the introduction of LIFO stock valuation. The main reason for the reduction during the first half of the 1980s is the improvement of tax depreciation allowances.

The categorization of this effective tax rate by sources of finance shows that a debt-financed fixed investment has an effective marginal tax rate of $-9.3$ percent, which means that it is subsidized, while an investment financed by retained earnings bears a high marginal tax rate of over 80 percent. Thus the German tax system is far from being a consumption tax system in which this tax rate would be zero for all types of investment and all sources of finance. However, the German system is also far from being a comprehensive income tax system in which all types of investment and all types of finance bear the same tax rate.

The reason for the large discrepancy of tax rates between a debt-financed investment and an investment financed by retained earnings is that interest payments to savers are deductible on the firm level when the corporate tax rate is higher than the income tax rate imposed on the savers' level. Only for savers who pay the top marginal income tax rate of 56 percent does a debt-financed investment bear a similar effective

Table 5-3. *Marginal Effective Tax Rates, Corporate and Personal Taxes, Fixed-p, 1980, 1985, 1989, 1990*

Percent

| Item | 1980 | 1985 | 1989 | 1990 |
|------|------|------|------|------|
| Asset | | | | |
| Machinery | 47.9 | 43.2 | 42.2 | 39.8 |
| Buildings | 43.3 | 32.9 | 31.9 | 31.6 |
| Inventories | 54.9 | 53.3 | 52.7 | 30.1 |
| Industry | | | | |
| Manufacturing | 48.8 | 42.9 | 42.1 | 34.6 |
| Other industry | 56.0 | 49.6 | 48.8 | 45.0 |
| Commerce | 42.4 | 35.4 | 34.5 | 28.4 |
| Source of finance | | | | |
| Debt | 5.2 | −3.6 | −4.8 | −9.3 |
| New share issues | 66.9 | 60.8 | 60.0 | 53.2 |
| Retained earnings | 96.6 | 93.9 | 93.4 | 83.3 |
| Owner | | | | |
| Households | 59.0 | 52.5 | 51.8 | 43.3 |
| Tax-exempt institutions | 17.5 | 12.8 | 11.8 | 9.4 |
| Insurance companies | 14.4 | 9.5 | 7.4 | 3.9 |
| Overall tax rate | 48.0 | 41.9 | 41.1 | 34.1 |

Source: Author's calculations.

tax rate, as an investment financed by retained earnings does. This model calculation neglects the fact that evasion of taxes on interest income plays an important role. Otherwise, the tax-rate differential between the sources of finance would be even larger. However, the model takes into account the fact that part of the capital is provided by tax-exempt institutions.

The tax reform of 1990 caused not only a reduction of the overall marginal tax rate, but also some narrowing of the tax-rate differential among sources of finance and among different types of investment. This decrease in the tax differential resulted from the reduction in the corporate tax rate on retained earnings.

In the early 1980s the overall effective tax rate on capital income measured by this model was relatively high by international standards. Thanks to improvements in depreciation allowances in Germany and reductions of investment-promotion schemes in the United States and the United Kingdom, the German effective tax rate is now more in line with the marginal effective tax rates than is the rate in other industrial countries such as the United States, the United Kingdom, and Japan. But Germany's tax-rate differential between various sources of finance (retained earnings and debt finance) is still wide because of a high corporate tax rate on retained

Table 5-4.  *Marginal Effective Corporate Tax Rates, Fixed-*p, *1980, 1985, 1989, 1990*

Percent

| Item | 1980 | 1985 | 1989 | 1990 |
|---|---|---|---|---|
| Asset | | | | |
| Machinery | 15.2 | 11.5 | 10.3 | 11.5 |
| Buildings | 9.3 | −1.4 | −2.6 | 1.6 |
| Inventories | 23.9 | 23.9 | 23.3 | −0.3 |
| Industry | | | | |
| Manufacturing | 16.2 | 11.1 | 10.1 | 5.2 |
| Other industry | 28.1 | 21.9 | 21.0 | 19.7 |
| Commerce | 7.6 | 1.3 | 0.2 | −2.7 |
| Source of finance | | | | |
| Debt | −46.0 | −53.6 | −55.1 | −55.0 |
| New share issues | 52.4 | 48.2 | 47.5 | 46.7 |
| Retained earnings | 83.0 | 80.1 | 79.6 | 69.4 |
| Owner | | | | |
| Households | 16.0 | 10.6 | 9.6 | 5.3 |
| Tax-exempt institutions | 14.3 | 8.8 | 7.8 | 3.7 |
| Insurance companies | 9.7 | 4.1 | 3.1 | −0.8 |
| Overall tax rate | 15.2 | 9.9 | 8.9 | 4.6 |

Source: Author's calculations.

earnings compared to the marginal income tax rate of institutional and individual savers.

Table 5-4 separates out the business-tax part of the marginal tax rate by calculating tax rates that would exist if there were only business taxes and no personal taxes on dividends, interest income, and personal wealth. The overall tax rate falls substantially, from 34.1 to 4.6 percent. As in the case of Sweden (see chapter 8), the personal tax system determines the overall effective tax rate. At a rate of inflation of 3 percent, the overall marginal rate of tax on corporate income is close to nil, but in contrast to a truly neutral system, effective tax rates differ widely by type of investment and source of finance. The 1990 tax reform reduced the tax rate for retained earnings as the corporate tax rate was lowered, but this source of investment financing is still highly taxed. For debt-financed investment, interest deductibility together with favorable depreciation brings about a negative marginal tax rate, that is, a net subsidy. The improvement of stock valuation in 1990 lowered the marginal tax rate of inventories; during 1980–85, depreciation allowances were improved for machinery and buildings.

Earlier studies showed that (in the fixed-*p* case) there was no significant relation between the rate of inflation and the overall effective marginal tax rate.[2] Some factors led the tax rate to increase with inflation, but others worked in the opposite direction. Inflation increased the effective tax rate for retained earnings and for new share issues but reduced it for debt finance. With higher inflation the deductibility of nominal interest payments against the corporate tax rate outweighed the taxation of nominal interest receipts at lower income tax rates. Because in the meantime the tax treatment of inventories was improved by allowing LIFO, the overall effective marginal tax rate declined with an acceleration of inflation. Investment financed by retained earnings and new share issues is still adversely affected by inflation.

## Empirical Results: The Noncorporate Sector

In west Germany the noncorporate business sector plays a bigger role than in other countries such as the United States and Sweden. Most large firms have the legal status of stock corporations (*Aktiengesellschaft*, or AG), and many middle-sized firms the status of corporations with limited liability (*Gesellschaft mit beschränkter Haftung*, or GmbH), that also have to pay corporate tax. Nevertheless, of total business turnover about 55 percent is made by noncorporate firms (of which 42 percent are in manufacturing). Noncorporate firms pay on their profits the personal income tax (a marginal tax rate of 19–53 percent; presumably from 1994: 44 percent on business income) and the local profit tax, which is deductible from the tax base of the income tax. In the calculation of the effective marginal tax rate an overall statutory rate of profit tax of 49 percent was used. Table 5-5 shows that the effective marginal tax rate for the noncorporate business is somewhat lower than for the corporate business. The overall marginal rate amounts to 27.7 percent in 1990, after 33.6 percent in 1989 and 39.2 percent in 1980. While debt-financed investment is not taxed at the margin, equity-financed investment is still taxed at 56.8 percent, down from 65.0 percent in 1989 and 69.5 percent in 1980.

## Residential Construction

In Germany residential construction has always been a popular field for public subsidies. Savings with special saving banks (*Bausparkassen*) have been promoted by public grants or tax deductions. In recent years

---

2. King and Fullerton (1984).

Table 5-5.  *Marginal Effective Noncorporate Tax Rates, Fixed-*p, *1980,*
*1985, 1989, 1990*

Percent

| Item | 1980 | 1985 | 1989 | 1990 |
|---|---|---|---|---|
| Asset | | | | |
|   Machinery | 36.2 | 36.4 | 32.0 | 30.4 |
|   Buildings | 37.4 | 32.1 | 27.6 | 26.1 |
|   Inventories | 45.7 | 48.3 | 44.3 | 26.6 |
| Industry | | | | |
|   Manufacturing | 39.5 | 38.4 | 34.1 | 28.0 |
|   Other industry | 45.5 | 43.4 | 39.0 | 35.2 |
|   Commerce | 36.2 | 34.2 | 29.9 | 24.4 |
| Source of finance | | | | |
|   Debt | 9.7 | 7.3 | 3.1 | −0.5 |
|   New share issues | 69.5 | 69.4 | 65.0 | 56.8 |
|   Retained earnings | . . . | . . . | . . . | . . . |
| Overall tax rate | 39.2 | 37.9 | 33.6 | 27.7 |

Source: Author's calculations.

these measures have been limited to lower-income earners. In addition,
housing investment is favored by special depreciation, family allowances,
a favorable valuation of the asset for the land tax, a favorable treatment
of imputed rental income for owner-occupied housing, and tax freedom
for capital gains. Mortgage interest payments are not deductible from the
income tax base for owner-occupied flats or houses. But during 1983–86,
as an anticyclical investment promotion measure, mortgage interests were
deductible with a maximum amount of DM 10,000.

For so-called two-family houses, mortgage interest deductibility is allowed. Tables 5-6 and 5-7 show the main elements of taxation in the
case of housing investment. The cost of capital for owner-occupied housing investment is calculated in a way similar to the way it is calculated
in chapter 8, on Sweden. Table 5-8 presents the corresponding effective
marginal tax rates for owner-occupied housing investment in the case of
a one-family house. Because depreciation allowances are limited to an
absolute amount, the marginal effective tax rate depends on the actual
cost of the house. It increases with the nondepreciable fraction. It also
depends on the sources of finance. Equity-financed housing investment
gets a subsidy up to 12.5 percent, while the tax rate for debt-financed
investment varies between about 24 percent and 33 percent. Table 5-8
shows the average effective marginal tax ratios for various debt-equity
financing ratios.

Table 5-6.  *Tax Treatment of Residential Construction, One-Family House*

| Item | Before 1987 | Since 1987 |
|------|-------------|------------|
| Income tax | No tax on imputed income No capital gains tax | |
| Mortgage interest deductibility | Temporarily (for first 3 years, with a maximum of DM 10,000 a year) | No |
| Depreciation allowance | 5 percent a year of a maximum amount of DM 200,000 during first 8 years | 5 percent a year of a maximum amount of DM 300,000 during first 8 years |
| Family allowance | DM 600 a year for each child for families with 2 or more children during first 8 years | DM 600 a year for each child for *all* families during first 8 years |
| Land tax | First 10 years free of tax | . . . |

Table 5-7.  *Tax Treatment of Residential Construction, Two-Family House, with One Flat Owner-Occupied*

| Item | Before 1987 | Since 1987 |
|------|-------------|------------|
| Income tax | On imputed rent of owner-occupied flat and actual income from rented flat | On actual income from rented flat |
| | No capital gains tax | |
| Mortgage interest deductiblility | Fully allowed | Only partially allowed (for rented flat, not for owner-occupied flat) |
| Depreciation allowance | 5 percent a year of a maximum amount of DM 200,000 during 8 years; 2 percent for additional amount and additional years *or* 5 percent during 8 years; 2.5 percent during 9–14 years; 1.25 percent during 15–50 years | For owner occupied flat: 5 percent a year of a maximum amount of DM 300,000 during first 8 years For rented flat: 7 percent during 4 years; 5 percent during 5–10 years; 2 percent during 11–16 years; 1.25 percent during 17–40 years |
| Family allowance | Same promotion scheme as for one-family house | . . . |

Table 5-8.  *Marginal Effective Tax Rate on Residential Construction,*
*with Varying Percent of the Cost of the House Depreciated*
Percent

|  | Percent of cost of house depreciated | | |
|---|---|---|---|
| Item | 0 | 50 | 100 |
| Debt | 33.8 | 29.1 | 24.2 |
| Equity | 0.0 | −6.0 | −12.5 |
| Average equity financing | | | |
| 75 percent | 8.4 | 2.7 | −3.3 |
| 50 percent | 16.9 | 11.6 | 5.9 |
| 25 percent | 25.4 | 20.3 | 15.0 |

Source: Author's calculations.

## User Cost of Capital

To analyze changes of capital costs, a time series for $p$ $(= MRR - \delta)$ is calculated in a simplified version. A cross-section analysis follows.

### Time-Series Approach

Figure 5-2 shows the development of business investment as compared with influences from the supply side, namely the user cost variable, the nominal and real interest rates, the average profit ratio and—as an influence from the demand side—the capacity utilization. The following therefore become evident.

— Since the early 1960s real capital cost (net of depreciation) has fluctuated strongly, and most of the fluctuations were due to changes in real interest rates. During the periods of recession in the mid-1970s and early 1980s, fiscal incentives (temporary investment grants) led to a sharp reduction of capital costs as compared to real interest rates.

— During the second half of the 1970s and during the mid-1980s, depreciation allowances were improved for equipment investment and for construction. This helped prevent a further increase in capital costs.

— During the past quarter century the German economy experienced four investment cycles (as measured from the first year of upswing to the trough). During most of these cycles both supply conditions and demand conditions affected investment in the same direction.

— During periods of booming investment, as in 1964–65, 1968–69, and 1985–86, capital costs were low or declining. This was also true during the more moderate investment recovery in the second half of the

Figure 5-2. *Business Investment Growth (Manufacturing Sector) and Macroeconomic Conditions, 1963–92*

DEMAND CONDITIONS

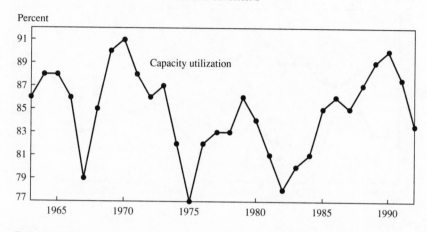

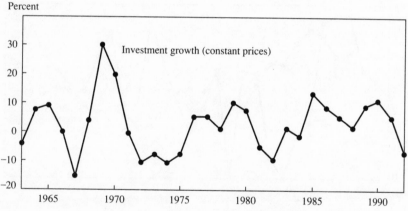

1970s. At the same time, capacity utilization, which can be taken as a demand indicator, was high or rising, as was the profit rate.

— During periods of weak investment activity, as in 1966–67, 1972–75, and 1981–82, capacity utilization was low or declining, as was the profit rate. To some extent capital cost also contributed to the investment slowdown as real interest rates were high or increasing. But in the periods of recession, 1974–75 and 1982–83, investment grants were provided to bolster investment activity by means of a reduction in capital costs.

— The investment upswing of 1989–90 was led by favorable demand and profit conditions. Both conditions were influenced by the demand

Figure 5-2    *(continued)*

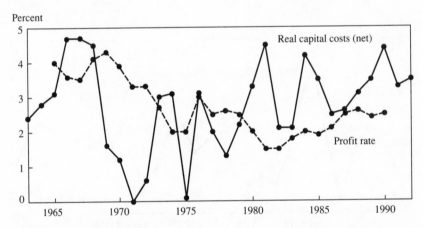

SUPPLY CONDITIONS

pull of the east German population for western products. These positive
effects more than compensated for the negative effects caused by the
higher capital costs resulting from higher real interest rates.

*Cross-Section Analyses*

Apart from temporary investment grants during past economic recessions, the government stimulates business investment in various ways.
Cross-section studies of capital costs show that because of various subsidies (such as regional policy, or the promotion of capital expenditures
for research and development and for environmental protection), all sec-

tors and branches benefit from government support, although with major differences. In sectors that exhibit public-goods characteristics and are accordingly regulated, government support is very high (railways, health care and veterinary medicine, electricity and district heating, water transportation, harbors).[3] In particular, there are four "sunset industries" (mining, steel, shipbuilding, and agriculture), which have received strong government support directly through financial aid to current production or to investment, indirectly via subsidies to the buyers of their products (as in the case of shipbuilding) or legal protectionist measures (such as tariffs and import quotas).

Therefore, the impact of investment support to the cost of capital is only one part in the total supporting framework. Furthermore, some branches of industry particularly benefit from investment grants. This is the case in fine ceramics, because of its location benefits from regional policy.

In contrast to sunset industries, relatively few resources were developed for the promotion of so-called sunrise industries such as computers and aerospace, although in the latter case subsidies have increased in recent years. (See, for example, development of the airbus.)

Taken as a whole, government intervention in sunset industries, as well as in sunrise industries, has not been very efficient. This is due either to the use of the wrong instruments (as in agriculture) or to even higher direct or indirect sectoral support of competing countries (such as shipbuilding and steel, but also high-technology sectors). Given these inefficiencies, in Germany there is much criticism of subsidies, especially those for individual sectors. But European Community member countries have different views about the appropriateness of such policies. The German government has promised to cut subsidies. While some progress has been made, there is still a long way to go. However, given persisting labor-market problems, there is much political pressure to prevent deeper cuts in subsidies.

## Investment Promotion in East Germany

With unification the west German tax system was extended to east Germany, with some exceptions. The net-wealth tax and the local capital tax will not be levied in east Germany until the end of 1995, and for

3. Gerstenberger and others (1984).

Table 5-9.  *Investment Incentives in East Germany*

| Item | Rate of promotion (percent) | Period of promotion (beginning of investment) |
|---|---|---|
| General investment grant (tax free) | 12 | July 1, 1990, until June 30, 1992 |
| | 8 | July 1, 1992, until June 30, 1994 (industry sector) |
| | | July 1, 1992, until December 31, 1992 (trade, banking, and insurance sector) |
| | 5 | July 1, 1994, until December 31, 1996 (industry sector) |
| | 20 | January 1, 1993, until December 31, 1996 (limited to East German investors in industry and craft, limited to size of investment of DM 1 million) |
| Regional investment grant (taxable) | 23, 20, 15 (maximum rates depending on type of investment) | Unlimited |
| Special first-year depreciation allowance | 50 | Unlimited |

Special loans (with reduced interest rates) by various financial institutions for small enterprises, state-owned enterprises; promotion of equity capital; state guarantees, and so on

personal income in that region there is a special allowance (DM 600 a year for single people and DM 1,200 for married couples). Also, the west German regional investment promotion scheme has been extended to east Germany and additional incentives have been introduced to promote investment in that region. (See also table 5-9).

## Policies

In regard to investment-promotion policy, the most important investment incentives are temporary general tax-free investment grants (*Investitionszulagen*) of 12 percent (between July 1, 1990, and June 30, 1992), and of 8 percent (between July 1, 1992, and December 31, 1996) for investment in the trade, financial services, and energy sectors. The period of promotion ends December 31, 1994. The investment grant is increased to 20 percent for investment in industry and crafts between December 31, 1992 and December 31, 1996, if owners of firms are of east German origin (as of November 9, 1989). Passenger car manufacturers are not favored by the general investment grant.

The general investment grant can be used in addition to special depreciation allowances:

— for regional investment grants for the whole area of east Germany (*Investitionszuschüsse*);

— for new establishments (including purchases of existing enterprises but excluding land purchases) at a maximum rate of promotion of 23 percent;

— for enlargement investment, at a maximum rate of promotion of 20 percent; and

— for restructuring, rationalization, and modernization, at a maximum rate of promotion of 15 percent.

In contrast to the general investment grant, this type of investment grant is not tax free. There is a choice between its immediate taxation as revenue or a corresponding reduction of the base for depreciation, which implies its effective taxation during the period of depreciation. Another difference from the general investment grant is that there is no legal claim to get this promotion, and its granting depends on the size of the budget and on the number of applicants.

The rates of promotion are maximum rates. The average rate of promotion (between October 1990 and the end of June 1992) of all the grants provided under this scheme is about 20 percent.

Both the general and the regional investment grants can be cumulated, although there is a maximum rate of overall promotion.

— Special first-year depreciation allowance of 50 percent on all types of fixed investment if straight-line depreciation is used.

— Special loans by European Recovery Program (ERP) fund. This fund was created after World War II to distribute U.S. aid flows from the Marshall Plan. Later the fund was used to provide favorable loans to small business. Since unification this fund also provides special loans to small and medium-size enterprises in east Germany for various purposes such as new foundations, modernization, enlargement, environment protection, and tourism.

— Promotion of equity capital for the establishment of new enterprises.

— Special promotion of the establishment of new enterprises by unemployed people (a twenty-six-week prolongation of unemployment benefits in cases where enterprises are initiated by formerly unemployed persons).

— Special loans by the Bank for Reconstruction and Development (KfW), Deutsche Ausgleichsbank, Berliner Industriebank, European Investment Bank, and other banks that get guarantees from the federal or state governments for all kinds of activities in east Germany (especially new enterprises, fixed investment, environmental protection, restructuring, modernization, and research and development).

— Special loans to restructure state-owned enterprises (by Treuhand— the agency in charge of privatizing east German industry—and KfW).

— Special loans and guarantees to improve the liquidity of state-owned enterprises (by Treuhand).

### Assessment of Investment Policies

ECONOMIC SITUATION OF EAST GERMANY AFTER UNIFICATION.  The generous tax treatment of investment in east Germany plays an important role in the modernization and enlargement of capital stock in that region. Assessment of that undertaking must take into consideration the overall state of the economy and the huge task to adapt the economy of east Germany to western standards. Economic development in east Germany— from the fall of the Berlin Wall in November 1989 to the end of 1992—has been very slow. The opening of domestic markets in connection with the immediate introduction of the deutsche mark led to completely unrealistic exchange rates for east German industry. (East German exporters had to bear an effective appreciation of about 350 percent). In addition, demand from Eastern Europe and the former Soviet Union collapsed. Furthermore, since unification, wages have been rising rapidly and should come close to those in west Germany by 1996. All this led to a collapse in industrial production in 1989–91. As a result, in east Germany a large gap emerged between distributed income and demand on the one hand and overall production on the other hand. The supply-demand gap had to be filled by imports and financed by large public transfers from western Germany. Unification therefore had a major impact on the macroeconomic financial balances. The overall German public-sector deficit increased, and with the surge of imports German trade and the current balance went from high surplus to deficit.

After the shock of unification the east German economy is now on the way to recovery. While during 1990–91 east German gross domestic product declined by 45 percent, 1992 saw a first increase by 6 percent. Economic growth is stimulated by large public investment programs and by strong tax incentives for private investors. While the construction sector and the service sector are leading the recovery, in industry there are big differences in economic activity between branches and firms. Privatization by the Treuhandanstalt is proceeding relatively successfully. Out of 11,400 units originally in public ownership, about 2,600 were not yet privatized by the end of 1992 (570 middle-size firms with 100 to 500 employees and 150 big firms with more than 500 employees). West German firms are the most active investors, and so far only a few firms have been sold to foreign investors (550–600 foreign investors, or 7 percent of total investors). Among these, European investors dominate. There are fifty to sixty U.S. investors, but by the end of 1992, Japanese firms continued to be reluctant to invest in east Germany. While the speed of privatization is relatively high, a core of big industrial enterprises remains difficult to sell. These firms are in a highly critical state and without financial aid from the Treuhandanstalt could not survive.

Although in the past there were numerous investment barriers (unclear property conditions, administrative bottlenecks), investment activity has been relatively intense from the beginning. Total investment in east Germany amounted to DM 83 billion in 1991 and DM 106 billion in 1992. During 1991 and 1992 the share of total investment in GDP was more than 40 percent. About 55 percent of this was business investment (excluding the housing sector, railways, and the postal service), about half of which was due to activity by west German firms. Nevertheless, numerous serious barriers still hinder rebuilding.

Studies show that a variety of nontax factors are stimulating investment decisions in east Germany, such as its proximity to domestic markets and position as a bridgehead to markets in eastern Europe. But tax incentives also have been important. In most cases of new establishment in east Germany, west German firms increased their total investment. But there are also cases where investment is merely shifted from west to east.

An important question remains. Will the development of investment be sufficient to create enough modern jobs? Because of rationalization and modernization, labor productivity increased between mid-1990 and the end of 1992 from one-third to about 40 percent of the west German level, but wages increased much faster, to about 65 percent. Employment in east Germany is still declining. By the end of 1992 the level of employment (excluding the various public-employment schemes) was less than 6 million people, which was 40 percent (more than 4 million people) below the preunification level. It is clear that the original employment level included much disguised unemployment and will never be reached again. About 700,000 workers have gone from east to west, almost half a million are working in the west while still living in the east, and about 800,000 have used the early pension scheme. But even to keep employment at the present level requires a continuation of the present strong investment trend. In 1992 registered unemployment in east Germany was 1.25 million, or about 16 percent, but if all the persons working in the various labor-market schemes are included, the number of unemployed was almost 2 million, or 25 percent. This high unemployment bears heavily on the mood of the population, which was used to a system in which jobs were provided by the state.

In view of this high structural unemployment there is concern that unification may be a burden that overtaxes the economic and social capability of the whole country. Furthermore, there are demands for a greater involvement of the state, in particular to prevent deindustrialization and in general to accelerate restructuring.

The government is far from following a laissez-faire policy. From the beginning of unification, measures have been taken to facilitate the transition, stimulate investment, and ease labor-market shock. The priority has been to stimulate private and public investment rather than subsidize labor costs. Concerning labor there are, however, large-scale programs for vocational training. Public transfers (including the social security system) from west to east Germany amounted to DM 160 billion in 1992, which is about DM 10,000 per capita. A good part of the overall public-sector deficit (about 3 percent of gross national product on a national-accounts basis and, if the deficit of the Treuhandanstalt is included, about 4 percent of GNP) is caused by these transfers. There is a great need to reduce the budget deficit, and the government has announced that it will follow a highly restrictive fiscal policy in future years.

There are growing demands for a more active industrial policy for east Germany to prevent deindustrialization and the loss of traditional industry locations on which the destiny of entire regions depends. Such policies bear the risk of high subsidies in shrinking sectors without guaranteeing job security in the longer term. If followed on a large scale, the policies could be a drag on future economic growth.

Table 5-10.  *Required Rate of Return (p) for Debt-Financed Equipment Investment in East Germany, Using the Special Depreciation Allowance and Various Investment Grant Combinations*[a]

Percent

| | | | General investment grant $(g_1)$ | | | | |
| | | | $g_1$ | | | | |
| | $g_2$ | $(1 - \tau)g_2$[b] | 20 | 12 | 8 | 5 | 0 |
|---|---|---|---|---|---|---|---|
| Regional investment grant | 23 | 9.7 | −13.0 | −9.1 | −7.2 | −5.7 | −3.3 |
| | 15 | 6.3 | −11.4 | −7.5 | −5.5 | −4.0 | −1.6 |
| | 10 | 4.2 | −10.3 | −6.4 | −4.5 | −3.0 | −0.6 |
| | 0 | 0 | −8.3 | −4.4 | −2.4 | −1.0 | 1.5[c] |

a. $p = \frac{1-A}{1-\tau}(+\delta - \pi) - \delta$; with $\tau = 0.58, L = 10, \delta = 0.2, \pi = 0.03, i = 0.083 = (1 - \tau)i = 0.035$.
b. Assumption: immediate taxation of the taxable grants as revenues.
c. Special depreciation allowance only.

### Marginal Effective Tax Rate for Investment in East Germany

In table 5-10 the marginal rate of return $p$ is calculated for various combinations of investment incentives for a given type of investment (fully debt financed equipment investment with an economic lifetime of ten years). If all three instruments (general investment grant, regional investment grant, and special depreciation allowance) are used, the required marginal rate of return for the investment in east Germany is always negative. Therefore there is an effective subsidy for investment in east Germany that reduces the required marginal rate of return substantially below the real interest rate, the effect depending on the size of general and regional investment grants. A prerequisite for benefiting from the generous special depreciation allowance is that there are enough overall profits by the firm. But firms can also use the German tax law to carry losses backward (two years for a maximum of DM 10 million) or forward (for an unlimited period).

Given the multitude of investment incentives, it is difficult to quantify the impact on the marginal effective tax rate for overall business investment in east Germany. The calculation in table 5-11 refers to the most important incentives, namely the above-mentioned investment grants (here an overall average net subsidy of 20 percent of investment costs is assumed), the special depreciation allowance, and the abolition of the net wealth tax and the local capital tax. Under these assumptions the investment promotion system reduces the overall effective tax rate on capital

Table 5-11.  *Marginal Effective Tax Rates on Capital from Investment in East Germany, Fixed-p, 1990*

| Item | Percent | Item | Percent |
|------|---------|------|---------|
| Asset | | Source of finance | |
| Machinery | 39.8 | Debt | −69.2 |
| Buildings | 31.6 | New share issues | 13.5 |
| Inventories | 30.1 | Retained earnings | 55.3 |
| Industry | | Owner | |
| Manufacturing | −11.6 | Households | 1.3 |
| Other industry | −12.8 | Tax-exempt institutions | −43.5 |
| Commerce | −8.3 | Insurance companies | −53.5 |
| | | Overall tax rate | −11.1 |

Source: Author's calculations.

income from investment in east Germany to −11 percent, implying a net subsidy, as against the marginal effective tax rate of 34 percent on income from investment in west Germany.

## References

Gerstenberger, W., and others. 1984. *State Intervention* (in German). Ifo-Studien zur Strukturforschung, Nr. 4.

King, Mervyn A., and Don Fullerton, eds. 1984. *The Taxation of Income from Capital: A Comparative Study of the United States, the United Kingdom, Sweden and West Germany.* University of Chicago Press.

CHAPTER SIX

# Italy

*Julian S. Alworth*
*Laura Castellucci*

THE ITALIAN tax system's first significant reforms after World War II (*riforma vanoni*) were made in the early 1950s, with the introduction of a progressive surtax on personal income and a separate tax on corporations (in addition to the existing income tax). Nevertheless, direct taxes remained relatively unimportant up to the mid-1970s, accounting for a substantially lower share of tax revenues than in other countries.[1] Undoubtedly the turning point in the postwar history of the Italian tax system occurred in 1973–74. A fully progressive personal income tax was introduced, several indirect taxes were replaced by a value-added tax, and the two-tiered system of corporate taxation was replaced by a single income tax.

Many changes have been made to the rates, bases, and administration of the taxes, but since the mid-1970s the fundamental structure of the fiscal system has remained unchanged. Reasons for some of these adjustments can be found in the interaction of macroeconomic developments and the tax system. The combination of a very high rate of inflation through the mid-1980s and significant indexation of nominal wages exacerbated fiscal drag, and several measures were taken to reduce these effects, including a significant adjustment of income tax brackets

The authors are grateful to Franco Cesari, Sergio Gambale, and especially Stefano Gorini, Giuseppe Marotta, Sergo Steve, and Giuseppe Vitaletti for discussions of previous versions of this chapter. Fabrizio Barca, Alberto Heimler, Ursula Herr, Nicola Sartor, Franca Moro, and Franco Varetto helped provide data. The simulations were carried out on programs developed with Willi Fritz. The views expressed in this chapter should not be interpreted as those of the institutions with which the authors are associated.

1. A description of the evolution of the Italian tax system is provided in Cobb and Forte (1964) and Parravicini (1971).

191

and more recently an indexation of tax brackets. Another macroeconomic factor driving changes in the tax system has been the growth of the public sector, which in the 1980s was financed by a growing deficit. Since reductions in public expenditures have been politically difficult to implement, the major means of reducing the government deficit have been to broaden the base of many taxes and to raise those perceived as providing high yields (in particular taxes on fuel). The tax system has also been used to redirect expenditure following the two successive oil shocks, with the excise duties on fuel oil consumption rising sharply.

Other problems of a more structural nature have also strained the implementation of the tax reform. Initially the tax administration had great difficulty coping with the new system, which resulted—among other changes—in the number of tax declarations rising from 5 million to 20 million. There has also been a widespread perception that income and value-added taxes, which (excluding social security contributions) provide the largest shares of tax revenue, are evaded by many taxpayers, and that taxable income is underreported, in spite of many improvements in this respect during recent years. Largely as a result of these deficiencies the tax system is regarded as inequitable. In particular, horizontal inequities between wage earners and salary earners, on the one hand, and the self-employed, on the other, are pronounced.

An indirect consequence of these perceived inequities, along with widespread tax evasion and the multitude of tax reforms, is the notable lack of discussion until recently of the effects of the tax system in terms of efficiency, even among economists. For example, estimates of deadweight loss, either for the tax system as a whole or for individual taxes, have only recently been made. Furthermore, in comparison with other countries, there has been less debate about the impact of the tax system on saving and investment decisions. This is perhaps due to the healthy growth of the Italian economy in contrast to those of other countries, as well as to a combination of Italian households' traditional propensity to save and, as we show in this chapter, to the relatively favorable tax treatment of company income. Except for the taxation of interest on government bonds, most of the public-policy debate has concentrated on the taxation of labor income—particularly, as we have already noted, the effects on the differences in treatment of wage and salary earners, on the one hand, and the self-employed, on the other—the effects of fiscal drag in times of inflation, the operation of the value-added tax, and more generally problems of tax administration, particularly those resulting from tax evasion.

The remainder of this chapter is organized as follows. The first section summarizes the main elements of the Italian tax system. Corporate business taxes and the highly intricate system of investment incentives is discussed in the second section, while the third section examines the personal income tax and the tax treatment of owner-occupied housing. Savings channeled through mutual funds and insurance companies are also discussed in this section. The data employed for calculating the weights used to compute the average marginal tax rates are discussed in the chapter's fourth section. The base year for the simulations carried out in the fifth section is 1985. Because the tax system was not significantly modified in the early 1980s, the historical comparison between 1985 and 1980 is discussed only briefly. Because of the very pronounced differences in tax treatment of investments in the Mezzogiorno—a geographical area which is subject to special laws (Economic Law for the Mezzogiorno)—we have chosen to simulate the tax rate on these investments separately. The major revisions of some aspects of the tax system, which were partly implemented in 1987 and introduced fully in 1988,[2] are discussed in the text and are simulated together with changes that were scheduled to be implemented in 1990.

## The Composition of Tax Revenues

Since the early 1970s the overall tax burden in Italy has increased dramatically and there has been an equally significant change in the composition of tax revenues. As shown in table 6-1, the ratio of total receipts to GDP rose from 30 percent in 1970 to 37 percent in 1988, a ratio comparable to that of other countries in the European Community. This sharp increase in tax revenues took place in the late 1970s, following the reform of 1973–74. At present the tax system is structured around six taxes: the personal income tax (IRPEF), the "local" income tax on unearned income (ILOR), the flat-rate tax on interest income (*imposta sostitutiva*), the corporation tax (IRPEG), the value-added tax (IVA) and the excise duties on oil products. In 1988 these six taxes accounted for roughly 85 percent of total tax revenues net of social security contributions.

A pronounced change in the relative importance of direct and indirect taxes has taken place as a result of the reform. In 1970 indirect taxes

2. Testo Unico delle imposte sui redditi, D.P.R., December 22, 1986, no. 917, henceforth referred to as Testo Unico 1986.

Table 6-1. *Sources of Tax Revenues, Italy, Selected Years, 1970–90*

Percent share of total receipts unless otherwise specified

| Revenue sources[a] | 1970 | 1975 | 1980 | 1985 | 1987 | 1988 | 1989 | 1990 |
|---|---|---|---|---|---|---|---|---|
| Income and profits | 17 | 21 | 30 | 36 | 37 | 36 | 35 | 35 |
| IRPEF | ... | 12 | 19 | 22 | 21 | 22 | 20 | 21 |
| ILOR | ... | 1 | 3 | 4 | 5 | 4 | 4 | 4 |
| IRPEG | ... | 2 | 2 | 3 | 4 | 3 | 4 | 3 |
| *Imposta sostitutiva* | ... | 3 | 5 | 5 | 4 | 5 | 5 | 5 |
| Social security contributions | 38 | 46 | 37 | 35 | 34 | 34 | 35 | 36 |
| Property[b] | 6 | 3 | 2 | 1 | 1 | 1 | 1 | ... |
| Goods and services | 39 | 29 | 31 | 28 | 28 | 29 | 29 | 29 |
| IVA | ... | 15 | 18 | 16 | 15 | 15 | 16 | 15 |
| Oil products | ... | 9 | 6 | 5 | 6 | 6 | 6 | 6 |
| Other | ... | 1 | ... | ... | ... | ... | ... | ... |
| Total | 100 | 100 | 100 | 100 | 100 | 100 | 100 | 100 |
| GDP (billions of current lire) | 67,178 | 138,632 | 387,669 | 812,751 | 979,677 | 1,079,863 | 1,192,729 | 1,306,833 |
| Share of taxes in GDP (percent) | 29.9 | 26.2 | 38.3 | 32.9 | 36.1 | 37.0 | 39.2 | 40.26 |

Sources: Ministro del Bilancio e della Programmazione Economica and Ministero delle Finanze, *Relazione generale sulla situazione economica del paese*; Banca d'Italia, *Relazione annuale* (various years); and authors' calculations.

a. IRPEF: personal income tax; ILOR: "local" income tax on unearned income; IRPEG: corporation tax; IVA value-added tax.

b. Includes taxes on gifts and inheritances, registration taxes, and INVIM (capital gains tax on real estate).

accounted for nearly 40 percent of total revenues, whereas direct taxes (income plus property taxes) were only 23 percent of total revenues. By 1985 these relative shares had been completely reversed. This turnaround can in large measure be attributed to the growing share of receipts accounted for by IRPEF, which increased from 12 to 22 percent between 1975 and 1985. The revenues from the *imposta sostitutiva*, the second most important direct tax, were particularly significant during the early 1980s, when nominal interest rates stood at record levels. In more recent years these rates rose again as a result of the extension of the tax to interest received on government bonds. The relative importance of local income taxes on both companies and individuals increased substantially, from 1 to 4 percent between 1975 and 1985. This expansion can be attributed to two successive increases in the rate of tax, to more precise assessments of taxable income, and to the growing profitability of companies in the 1980s. Tax revenues from the corporation tax were low, especially during the late 1970s and early 1980s, and have increased markedly in recent years.

The introduction in the early 1970s of the value-added tax (IVA), which has accounted for 15 to 18 percent of total tax revenues, was accompanied by a significant reduction in the number of special levies on goods and services. There are also a number of traditional excise duties, the most important of which is the indirect tax on oil products, which generates nearly 5 percent of total revenues.

Throughout this period social security contributions have been the single most important source of tax revenues. During the mid-1970s, their share of total revenues was extremely high by international standards, but given the increases that have taken place elsewhere, the relative share is presently comparable with that recorded elsewhere in the European Community (EC).

## Corporate Business Taxation

Before the tax reform of 1974, Italian companies were subject to two separate taxes on corporate income: an income tax on movable wealth, the *imposta di ricchezza mobile* (cat. B), and a tax on companies, the *imposta sulle società*, levied on a combination of corporate profits (in the previous accounting period) and net wealth. In addition, a number of surtaxes were introduced for special purposes at different periods. As regards the taxation of dividends, Italy operated a classical system with no integration of the corporate and personal taxes.[3]

### Reform of the Company Tax System

In 1974, the Italian company tax system was reformed completely. The income tax with all the special surcharges and the company taxes were replaced by two new proportional income taxes, IRPEG (*imposta sul reddito delle persone giuridiche*), a company tax levied at the national level, and ILOR (*imposta locale sui redditi*), a local income tax collected by the central government and levied at the same rate as for individuals. The tax bases for the two taxes were virtually the same,[4] and unlike in the preceding system, applied to income generated during the same year. Initially local income tax was not deductible from the company tax, and each local authority was allowed to fix its own rate of tax at levels ranging in principle between 9.4 percent and 14.7 percent. But beginning with the end of 1976, ILOR was levied at a higher uniform rate. With regard to dividends, the classical system remained in operation after the reform.

Two major changes took place in 1978. First, ILOR became deductible from the taxable income of IRPEG. Second, an imputation system was introduced for dividend distributions and phased in over a two-year period. The imputation system allows for a full crediting of IRPEG against the liability under IRPEF, but no credit for ILOR. In 1983 a balancing tax (*imposta di conguaglio*) for franked (tax-exempt) investment income including income from investments in the Mezzogiorno was introduced along the lines of the *précompte mobilier* in France. Under this system, any distribution of dividends exceeding the value of taxable income is subject to a withholding tax equivalent to the tax credit granted to individual shareholders.[5] Since 1986, a ten-year exemption from IRPEG has applied to new companies and investments located in the Mezzogiorno and in a number of other specific areas that have benefited from special

---

3. For a description of the derivation of the tax parameters before 1974 see Alworth and Castellucci (1987).

4. ILOR is not due on dividends, income subject to a final withholding tax, and income from abroad. No carryovers of losses are allowed against ILOR (see below).

5. This provision was introduced at a time in which companies were making sizable investments in tax-exempt bonds and receiving tax credits for this income. In 1984 further measures were taken to reduce tax arbitrages by limiting the amount of interest payments deductible against tax.

tax exemptions. (See the section "Tax Reliefs and Investment Grants in the Mezzogiorno," below.)

In terms of the tax parameters employed to compute the effective tax rates, the tax treatment of companies with taxable income higher than dividend distributions can be described as follows. The total tax revenue $T$ on company income $Y$, including personal taxes on gross dividends $G$, is given by

$$T = t_{IRPEG}[Y - t_{ILOR}Y] + t_{ILOR}Y + [m_s - t_{IRPEG}]G,$$

where $t_{IRPEG}$ and $t_{ILOR}$ are the *IRPEG* and *ILOR* tax rates respectively and $m_s$ is the marginal personal tax on dividends. Rearranging the terms, the values of $\tau$, the comprehensive corporate tax rate, and $\theta$, the additional dividends shareholders could receive if one unit of postcorporate tax earnings were distributed, are given by

$$\tau = t_{IRPEG}(1 - t_{ILOR}) + t_{ILOR}$$

$$\theta = 1/(1 - t_{IRPEG}).$$

Table 6-2 displays the evolution of $\tau$ and $\theta$ since 1970. Before the tax reform of 1974 the value of $\tau$ hovered around 50 percent. Following the tax reform, $\tau$ fell to 40 percent, and with the introduction of the imputation system in 1978 was lowered further to 36.25 percent. Subsequently, higher rates, 36 percent for IRPEG and 16.2 percent for ILOR, were phased in during 1982–85 and have since then remained unchanged.

Small firms follow simplified tax-accounting rules and have been subject to other special provisions since 1984. In 1985 and 1990 small-sized firms were defined for income tax purposes as those having an annual turnover of less than Lit 780 and 360 million, respectively. Taxable income for these firms is determined as the difference between all revenues and a specified list of certified expenses, as well as given percentages of gross revenues for the noncertified ones.

Very small firms with a yearly turnover of less than Lit 18 million and belonging to particular trading sectors such as retail trade and handicrafts are taxed on an even more simplified basis, with taxable income being determined by profitability coefficients on gross receipts.

### Distribution of the Company Tax Burden

Table 6-3 reports the values of revenues generated by IRPEG and ILOR since 1974, as well as the combined share of these two taxes

Table 6-2. *Company Tax Rates, 1970–90*

| Year | $t_{RM}$[a] | $t_{IS}$[a] | $t_{IRPEG}$ | $t_{ILOR}$[b] | $\tau$[c] | $\theta$[c] |
|------|------|------|------|------|------|------|
| 1970 | 0.39 | 0.165 | ... | ... | 0.4907 | 1.0 |
| 1971 | 0.42 | 0.195 | ... | ... | 0.5331 | 1.0 |
| 1972 | 0.425 | 0.195 | ... | ... | 0.5371 | 1.0 |
| 1973 | 0.41 | 0.195 | ... | ... | 0.5251 | 1.0 |
| 1974 | ... | ... | 0.25 | 0.147 | 0.3920 | 1.0[d] |
| 1975 | ... | ... | 0.35 | 0.147 | 0.4920 | 0.7[d] |
| 1976 | ... | ... | 0.25 | 0.147 | 0.3920 | 0.5[d] |
| 1977 | ... | ... | 0.25 | 0.15 | 0.40 | 0.5[d] |
| 1978 | ... | ... | 0.25 | 0.15 | 0.3625 | 0.7–1.33[d] |
| 1979 | ... | ... | 0.25 | 0.15 | 0.3625 | 1.33 |
| 1980 | ... | ... | 0.25 | 0.15 | 0.3625 | 1.33 |
| 1981 | ... | ... | 0.25 | 0.15 | 0.3625 | 1.33 |
| 1982 | ... | ... | 0.27–0.30 | 0.162[e] | 0.38826 | 1.33 |
| 1983 | ... | ... | 0.36 | 0.162[e] | 0.4637 | 1.5625 |
| 1984 | ... | ... | 0.36 | 0.162[e] | 0.4637 | 1.5625 |
| 1985 | ... | ... | 0.36 | 0.162[e] | 0.4637 | 1.5625 |
| 1986 | ... | ... | 0.36 | 0.162 | 0.4637 | 1.5625 |
| 1987 | ... | ... | 0.36 | 0.162 | 0.4637 | 1.5625 |
| 1988 | ... | ... | 0.36 | 0.162 | 0.4637 | 1.5625 |
| 1989 | ... | ... | 0.36 | 0.162 | 0.4637 | 1.5625 |
| 1990 | ... | ... | 0.36 | 0.162 | 0.4637 | 1.5625 |

Source: Authors' calculations.

a. The basic rates of *Ricchezza mobile* ($t_{RM}$) and *Imposta sulle società* ($t_{IS}$) were 25 percent and 15 percent, respectively. The numbers shown in the column include special surcharges.

b. Assumes maximum tax rate for 1974–77 period (see text).

c. Definition of $\tau$ and $\theta$:

$$1960\text{–}74 : \tau = t_{RM} + t_{IS}(1 - t_{RM}); \ \theta = (1 - w_s)$$

$$1974\text{–}77 : \tau = t_{IRPEG} + t_{ILOR}; \ \theta = (1 - w_s)$$

$$1978\text{–}90 : \tau = t_{IRPEG}(1 - t_{ILOR}) + t_{ILOR}; \ \theta = 1/(1 - t_{IRPEG})$$

d. During the period 1974–78 individuals could choose between having dividends taxed at a final flat rate or having taxes withheld and receiving a credit against personal income tax. The value of $\theta$ shown assumes that a tax credit option was chosen. If individuals chose to be taxed at a final flat rate, the value of $\theta$ would have been 0.85 during 1970–74 and 0.90 during 1974–78.

e. Including an 8 percent surcharge.

in total tax receipts and in GNP.[6] The share of taxes levied directly on companies rose between 1977 and 1988 from 5 to 9 percent. This increase took place in two successive steps, in 1982–83 and in 1986. The first step can be associated with the 10 percent increase in the IRPEG tax rate and, to a lesser extent, with the introduction of the special system

6. ILOR underwent significant revisions in 1978. The timing of tax payments was brought forward and assessments were made identical to those of IRPEF and IRPEG. This development resulted in a near doubling of tax revenues in two years.

Table 6-3. *Tax Revenues from IRPEG and ILOR on Companies,*
*1974–91*

| Year | IRPEG (billions of lire) | ILOR (billions of lire) | IRPEG + ILOR[a] as a percent of tax revenues[b] | IRPEG + ILOR[a] as a percent of GNP |
|---|---|---|---|---|
| 1974 | 131 | 40[c] | 1.0 | 0.1 |
| 1975 | 666 | 120[c] | 3.9 | 0.5 |
| 1976 | 868 | 235[c] | 4.0 | 0.6 |
| 1977 | 1,487 | 190[c] | 4.6 | 0.8 |
| 1978 | 1,311 | 1,468 | 6.0 | 0.6 |
| 1979 | 1,488 | 1,383 | 5.4 | 0.6 |
| 1980 | 2,411 | 2,128 | 6.3 | 1.2 |
| 1981 | 3,168 | 2,862 | 6.7 | 1.3 |
| 1982 | 3,636 | 3,432 | 6.1 | 1.3 |
| 1983 | 5,457 | 4,425 | 6.8 | 1.6 |
| 1984 | 8,117 | 4,941 | 7.9 | 1.8 |
| 1985 | 9,173 | 6,168 | 8.5 | 1.9 |
| 1986 | 12,090 | 8,194 | 9.3 | 2.3 |
| 1987 | 15,018 | 10,310 | 10.9 | 2.6 |
| 1988 | 13,495 | 9,636 | 8.7 | 2.1 |
| 1989 | 16,966 | 12,257 | 9.7 | 2.4 |
| 1990 | 17,216 | 12,541 | 8.8 | 2.3 |
| 1991 | 16,886 | 11,868 | 7.7 | 2.0 |

Sources: Banca d'Italia, *Relazione annuale* (various years); and authors' calculations.
a. On companies only.
b. Excluding social security contributions.
c. Authors' estimates; tax revenues from ILOR on companies not available separately before 1978.

for computing the deductibility of interest rates to take account of the possibility of investments in tax-exempt securities. The second, more pronounced, increase occurred following the change in the tax treatment of interest income whereby companies became liable for ILOR and IRPEG on interest income received from government securities which otherwise remained exempt from tax.[7] The introduction of special tax provisions for small firms and the return to higher levels of profitability by a number of major companies in the mid-1980s were other reasons contributing to the increase in tax revenues. In 1988 the drop in tax revenues may be partly attributable to wider exemption from tax granted to income earned in the Mezzogiorno.

The growth in the aggregate receipts from IRPEG and ILOR has been accompanied by a pronounced shift in the relative importance of each

7. For a description of the different tax regimes on companies in respect of their holdings of tax-exempt securities, see Di Maio and Franco (1987).

Table 6-4.   *Status of Italian Companies and Their Taxable Profits and Losses under IRPEG, 1977–87*

| | Declared status of company (percent of firms) | | | Total number of firms (thousands) | Profits and losses (thousands of billions of lire) | |
|---|---|---|---|---|---|---|
| Year | No income | Losses | Postive income | | Deductible losses | Taxable gains |
| 1977 | 48.6 | 9.2 | 42.2 | 213.5 | 11.6 | 6.5 |
| 1978 | 33.7 | 26.3 | 40.0 | 236.4 | 24.3 | 7.9 |
| 1979 | 30.6 | 27.6 | 41.8 | 245.9 | 29.2 | 10.2 |
| 1980 | 32.2 | 24.7 | 43.1 | 277.3 | 14.2 | 16.0 |
| 1981 | 30.4 | 26.5 | 43.1 | 302.5 | 15.6 | 17.0 |
| 1982 | 26.1 | 30.0 | 43.9 | 339.4 | 15.2 | 20.6 |
| 1983 | 27.7 | 33.1 | 39.2 | 373.4 | 24.1 | 23.7 |
| 1984 | 25.9 | 34.7 | 39.4 | 400.2 | 31.1 | 31.4 |
| 1985 | 27.3 | 35.0 | 37.7 | 427.8 | 20.0 | 39.4 |
| 1986 | 20.2 | 33.0 | 46.68 | 439.39 | 19.58 | 59.1 |
| 1987 | 20.4 | 20.4 | 47.6 | 467.81 | 19.46 | 58.9 |

Source: Ministero delle Finanze, *Analisi* (various years).

of these two taxes. Whereas through 1982 revenues from IRPEG were on average only 5 percent higher than tax receipts from ILOR levied on companies, more recently IRPEG has yielded 45 percent more than the corporate component of ILOR revenues.

The aggregate figures disguise somewhat the actual distribution of the tax burden among companies. Table 6-4 provides an overview of the tax base according to the status of companies paying IRPEG over the period 1977–85. One striking feature revealed by this table is that during 1984, 60 percent of companies compiling tax returns for IRPEG reported no income or losses. Moreover, this combined percentage has remained remarkably constant over time although there was a sharp increase in the number of firms recording losses after 1978, the year ILOR became deductible from the IRPEG tax base.[8]

By contrast, the lower half of table 6-4 reveals that the actual amounts of taxable gains and losses have varied markedly from year to year and that in recent years losses appear to have been declining both in absolute terms and on average for individual firms.

Table 6-5 sheds further light on the phenomenon of tax exhaustion by providing a breakdown of the losses according to the size of individual

8. The measured profitability of companies from the mid-1970s to the early 1980s was at historically very low levels. Alworth and Fornasari (1982) provide inflation-adjusted measurements of accounting profits.

Table 6-5.  *Distribution of Taxable Losses under IRPEG, by Size of Company Turnover, 1984*

| Size of turnover (millions of lire) | Number of firms as a percent of all companies reporting losses | Value of losses as a percent of the value of total losses reported | Percent of firms reporting losses in each turnover category |
|---|---|---|---|
| No turnover or unreported income[a] | 55.5 | 26.20 | 37.6 |
| 0–18 | 12.4 | 0.96 | 45.9 |
| 18–200 | 14.1 | 3.55 | 35.1 |
| 200–780 | 8.4 | 3.40 | 27.0 |
| 780–2,000 | 4.6 | 23.04 | 21.6 |
| 2,000–50,000 | 4.8 | 16.23 | 18.0 |
| Over 50,000 | 0.2 | 26.62 | 21.2 |
| Total | 100.0 | 100.00 | . . . |

Source: Authors' calculations.

a. This group comprises companies whose earnings do not result from commercial activities or that are in the process of being liquidated.

firms' turnover. As might be expected, the bulk of companies reporting tax losses in 1984 were small (90 percent had a turnover of less than Lit 780 million), but these companies accounted for only 64 percent of the recorded amounts of tax losses. In contrast to the situation in most countries, large companies in Italy reported significant losses (26.6 percent of all tax losses), and the proportion of large companies reporting losses was high (21 percent).

Apart from entailing a considerable amount of unrelieved taxes that can be carried forward under IRPEG, [9] tax exhaustion has contributed to the growth of a sizable market for tax shields, particularly in the form of the passing through of the tax benefits resulting from mergers and leasing. In the case of mergers, unlike in the United States, where "business purpose" is a serious limitation on the exploitation of tax losses, such constraints have not applied in Italy. Although there are no empirical estimates of the importance of this phenomenon, it is perceived as having been relatively widespread.[10] In recent years the authorities have moved to curb tax-motivated mergers.

9. Loss carryforwards are allowed for five years under IRPEG, but losses cannot be offset against future profits under ILOR.

10. This practice received wide publicity in the case of the privatization of Lanerossi, a major textile firm controlled by the state-owned holding company ENI, that had consistently reported sizable losses (independently of tax accounting). The valuation of Lanerossi made by a number of potential buyers, and reported in the press, included a special sub-item for the tax offset available after the

This discussion concerning the distribution of tax exhaustion among Italian companies suggests three alternative simulations to be carried out in this chapter's fourth section, "The Structure of the Capital Stock and Its Ownership": for companies paying IRPEG and ILOR, for firms paying only ILOR ($\tau = t_{ILOR}$), and for firms that are tax-exhausted under both ILOR and IRPEG ($\tau = 0$).

## Tax Allowances for Depreciation and Inventories

Firms are allowed to follow various systems of tax accounting for inventory valuation with the last in, first out (LIFO) method being the most widely employed. Accordingly, in the simulations the proportion of inventories taxed on historic cost principles, $v = 0$.

At first glance, depreciation allowances for equipment and buildings might appear particularly rigid and unfavorable. The schedules are defined by ministerial decree according to strict technical criteria, the basic method of depreciation is straight-line, and the valuation of assets is based on historic cost. Four factors, however, have played an important role in making capital consumption allowances extremely generous even in periods of high inflation: short useful lives, accelerated depreciation provisions, frequent revaluations of depreciable assets and corporate divestitures (*scorpori*).

USEFUL LIVES. Italian companies are allowed to write off most assets over relatively short periods, especially in comparison with their direct trading competitors in the European Community,[11] particularly in the case of industrial buildings and factory equipment.[12] In addition, before 1988 the actual timing of depreciation allowances was quite generous. There was a "full-year convention" and depreciation began during the fiscal year in which an asset was ordered and not when it was actually delivered or put into use. The Testo Unico of 1986 modified these provisions. A half-year convention now applies for the first year of capital consumption

---

merger. See "Fusioni. 'La scatola vouta' è di moda per attenere le agevolazioni del Fisco," *Sole 24 Ore*, August 22, 1987. The companies that are merged for the purpose of deducting tax losses are commonly known as *bare fiscali* (fiscal coffins).

11. See Alworth (1986).

12. The last determination of useful lives for tax purposes was undertaken in 1974. It is widely acknowledged that the tax authorities implicitly shortened tax lives to less than what they would be according to normal wear and tear in order to provide a form of implicit tax incentive to companies.

allowances, and depreciation begins only from the time at which an asset enters operation.

ACCELERATED DEPRECIATION. The second element that has helped make capital recovery provisions particularly favorable is the system of accelerated depreciation that was introduced in 1958, modified slightly in 1974, and revised by the Testo Unico of 1986.[13] In 1985 the system of accelerated depreciation consisted in providing additional depreciation up to 15 percent a year during the first three years of an asset's useful life. For example, the schedule of allowances for an asset ordinarily depreciated at 10 percent a year would be as follows: 25 percent during the first three years, 10 percent for two further years, and 5 percent for the remaining year. As can be seen from this example, accelerated depreciation both increased the amount of depreciation that could be taken each year and reduced the tax lifetime.

Analytically, the present value of tax depreciation allowances for 1985, $A_{85}$, can be written as

$$(6\text{-}1) \quad A_{85} = \tau \left[ \int_0^3 (\frac{1}{L} + 0.15)e^{-\rho u} du + \int_3^{L-0.45L} \frac{1}{L} e^{-\rho u} du \right]$$

$$= \tau \left[ \frac{0.15}{\rho}(1 - e^{-3\rho}) + \frac{1}{\rho L}(1 - e^{-0.55\rho L}) \right],$$

where $\rho, u,$ and $L$ refer respectively to the discount rate used for the investment, to the specific time period, and to the useful tax life of the asset.

The first half of the bracketed expression in equation 6-1 is equal to the present value of depreciation at a rate of 15 percent for each year of the first three years. The second half of the expression is equal to the present value of straight-line depreciation at a rate of $1/L$ for the shortened lifetime of $0.55L$. Furthermore, it should be noted that for assets having a useful tax life $L$ of less than $3/0.55$, full depreciation could take place in three years or less.

The Testo Unico of 1986 modified these provisions in two ways. First, accelerated depreciation was granted at a rate of one and one-half times the straight-line value for the first three years. Second, as already mentioned,

13. The 1958 decree law (Testo Unico, 29 gennaio 1958 art. 98) revised an existing law (legge del 12 gennaio 1951, no. 25).

a half-year convention was adopted for the first capital recovery period. Taking account of these changes, accelerated depreciation allowances during the first three years of life amount to a maximum of $3.25/L$ and the useful lifetime of an asset was reduced by 3.25 years irrespective of $L$ (by contrast with the previous tax law, under which the useful lifetime was reduced by 45 percent).

Taking account of the half-year convention for the first year of depreciation, the present value of the accelerated capital recovery under the Testo Unico provisions ($A_{TU}$) can be expressed as

$$(6\text{-}2) \qquad A_{TU} = \tau \left[ \int_0^1 \frac{(1.25)}{L} e^{-\rho u} du \right.$$

$$\left. + \int_1^3 \frac{2.5}{L} e^{-\rho u} du + \int_3^{L-3.25} \frac{1}{L} \frac{e^{-\rho u}}{L} du \right]$$

$$A_{TU} = \frac{\tau}{\rho L} [1.25(1 + e^{-\rho}) - 1.5 e^{-3\rho} - e^{-\rho(L-3.25)}].$$

As a result of further changes in the finance bill for 1990, accelerated depreciation was reduced to only 100 percent of the straight-line allowances in the first three years. Accordingly, the present value of tax allowances ($A_{90}$) used in the simulations is given by

$$(6\text{-}3) \qquad A_{90} = \frac{\tau}{\rho L} [(1 + e^{-\rho}) - e^{-3\rho} - e^{-\rho(L-2)}].$$

As can be seen from table 6-6, the measures for 1986 and 1990 reduced significantly the benefits of accelerated depreciation, especially for assets with long tax lives.

REVALUATIONS OF ASSETS. In 1975 and 1983 firms were allowed for accounting and tax purposes to revalue their assets to take account of changes in the price level according to two alternative methods.[14] The first method consisted in computing the value of assets, excluding inventories and net monetary assets, according to replacement costs based on a set of coefficients compiled by the Ministry of Finance to reflect past inflation. It can be estimated that the 1983 revaluations allowed firms on average to recompute the value of their outstanding assets to reflect approximately 80 percent of the change in the consumer price index.

---

14. The actual laws providing for these revaluations are commonly referred to by the name of Minister of Finance Visentini, who signed the original decree. These revaluations have a precedent in those undertaken for buildings in the early postwar period (1948 and 1952).

Table 6-6. *Present Value of Tax Allowances as a Ratio of Initial Cost under Different Depreciation Regimes*[a]

| Type of asset | Rate of straight-line depreciation from tax laws (percent) | Tax provisions in 1980 and 1985 | | Accelerated depreciation Testo Unico (1986) | 1990 proposals |
| --- | --- | --- | --- | --- | --- |
| | | Straight-line depreciation | Accelerated depreciation | | |
| Vehicles | 20.0 | 0.8848 | 0.9317 | 0.9270 | 0.9193 |
| Electronic and mechanical office equipment | 18.0 | 0.8731 | 0.9279 | 0.9247 | 0.9122 |
| Factory machinery (mechanical industry) | 15.5 | 0.8547 | 0.9218 | 0.9173 | 0.8992 |
| Furniture and ordinary office equipment | 12.0 | 0.8178 | 0.9094 | 0.8938 | 0.8687 |
| Light construction (sheds, and so on) | 10.0 | 0.7869 | 0.8987 | 0.8688 | 0.8404 |
| Industrial buildings (chemical industry) | 7.0 | 0.7146 | 0.8727 | 0.8009 | 0.7693 |
| Industrial buildings (mechanical industry) and commercial buildings | 3.0 | 0.4867 | 0.7780 | 0.5555 | 0.5291 |

Source: Authors' calculations.
a. Discount rate = 5 percent.

Under the second, indirect, method, revaluations were undertaken by recomputing the net wealth of the company and allocating these changes arbitrarily to individual assets and liabilities. The possibility of revaluing assets under either of these two systems was exploited widely at the time the measures were first introduced in 1975.[15]

15. In principle the two systems differ because under the first method debt and equity-financed assets can be revalued, whereas under the second only equity-financed investments can be revalued.

As a result of a law passed at end-1990 companies can elect to revalue their assets. In contrast to the earlier laws the revaluations will be subject to a 20 percent tax, or depreciation allowances will have to be deferred for a three-year period.

SCORPORI. A system of corporate divestiture of firms known as *scorpori* also contributed to substantial "one-off" revaluations of firms' assets for fiscal purposes between 1977 and 1980. This divestiture consisted of creating a wholly owned subsidiary to which part of the assets of the parent company were sold at an upgraded value from those shown originally in the balance sheet. The original company became a holding company with an equity stake equal to the measured net wealth of the new subsidiary. The fiscal advantage of this operation resulted from the fact that the new company could undertake depreciation for tax purposes on the revalued assets, with the old company being able to defer, sometimes indefinitely, corporate capital gains tax on the difference between the value of the asset written down for tax purposes and its resale price.

More recently, firms have been able to revalue their assets by engaging in frequent divestitures and mergers. This has been possible because the revaluations of assets following mergers are not subject to corporate capital gains tax unless a speculative intent can be proven, that is, if the corporate reorganizations occur at intervals of less than five years and at the same time involve a significant share of the company.

There can be little doubt that opportunities for revaluation and *scorpori* have been widely exploited and that tax revenues from individual companies fell sharply after their enactment.[16] However, it is difficult to assess the precise impact of these provisions on the cost of capital and to evaluate them in terms of the King-Fullerton model.[17] If the revaluations were perfectly anticipated at the time of investment, then the Italian system could be considered as one in which companies assume that depreciation is based on replacement cost. However, if the revaluations cannot be anticipated, there are no marginal effects on investment decisions via the cost of capital. In the estimations it has been assumed that revaluations could not be anticipated; in terms of the parameters this means that depreciation allowances are not indexed.

In summary, there is no immediate depreciation ($f_2 = 0$ and $f_1 = 1$). The present value of depreciation allowances $A_d$ is given by equation 6-1 for 1980 and 1985 and by equation 6-3 for 1990.

---

16. Firms have also been allowed to defer company taxes on sales of assets if the proceeds are reinvested within a fixed-time period (art. 54, D.P.R. 597).

17. King and Fullerton (1984).

## Estimates of Economic Depreciation

A considerable amount of research in Italy has been undertaken in recent years to estimate the rate of economic depreciation for different types of assets, partly in conjunction with the more general effort to improve the system of national accounts. The original estimates of the capital stock by the central statistical office assumed a fixed useful life of assets independent of the industry in which the investment good was utilized (with the exception of the construction industry).[18] The values were fixed for all industries as follows: thirty-five years for buildings, eighteen years for plant and equipment (ten years in the construction industry), and ten years for vehicles.

The most important revisions to these original estimates were undertaken by Giuseppe Rosa, and by Rosa and Vincenzo Siesto.[19] Exploiting research in other countries as well as more detailed information for individual industrial sectors in Italy, they constructed new estimates of useful lives which differed across industries. The values of the useful lives that they obtained varied roughly between thirty and forty years for buildings, fifteen and twenty years for plant and equipment, and ten years for vehicles. Fabrizio Barca and Mariella Magnani have carried out an ex post analysis of actual useful lives of assets based on a sample of 357 manufacturing firms having more than one hundred employees.[20] As regards plant and equipment, this microeconomic study confirms on average the assumptions of Rosa and Siesto for earlier periods. Barca and Magnani also report that during the early 1980s firms appear to have anticipated the scrapping of assets as a part of a more general policy of industrial restructuring and in order to take advantage of technological change. In the case of buildings the discrepancies between the Barca-Magnani and the Rosa-Siesto estimates are more significant. In particular, Barca and Magnani show consistently shorter useful lifetimes (twenty-five to twenty-eight years) throughout the 1980s.[21]

The measurement of the capital stock in most countries is derived from straight-line depreciation schedules, whereas the cost-of-capital formulae assume that economic depreciation occurs at a rate of exponential

18. ISTAT (1976).

19. Rosa (1979); Rosa and Siesto (1985).

20. Barca and Magnani (1985).

21. These estimates are based on a narrower and less representative sample than the estimates for machinery.

decay, $\delta$. If economic depreciation is truly straight-line as computed by the national accounts (that is, assets depreciate by a constant amount $1/L$ every year), then, as shown by Mervyn A. King and Don Fullerton, the equivalent rate of economic depreciation at an exponential rate can be approximated by $2/L$.[22]

To compute the value of $\delta$, the basic economic lives described by Rosa and Siesto were adjusted for the shortening of lifetimes recorded by Barca and Magnani. We assumed that machinery depreciated at 11.9 percent (1980) and 12.6 percent (1985). In both years the rate of economic depreciation for buildings was 6.5 percent in the industrial sector and 5.7 percent for services. The 1985 depreciation rates were assumed for 1990.

### Investment Grants and Incentives

The system of regional and, to a lesser extent, general investment incentives is very intricate and difficult to quantify or summarize. Industrial policy has taken a multitude of forms varied over time and been applied with a considerable degree of discretion. Our analysis in this section represents an attempt to summarize the most important incentives, although it will not always be possible to quantify all the provisions for purposes of computing the effective rates of subsidy. It should be noted that in coming years many of the present incentives will probably be repealed in order to comply with EC directives.

TAX RELIEFS AND INVESTMENT GRANTS IN THE MEZZOGIORNO.   At present, the most important incentives involve investments in the Mezzogiorno, the southern and relatively less developed part of Italy. This area is defined as beginning a few kilometers east and south of Rome and includes Sicily and Sardinia (plus some other very small municipalities in northern Italy), and is inhabited by 35 to 40 percent of the total population of Italy. These incentives, which have taken the form of tax reductions, outright grants, and interest rate subsidies, have in some instances also been extended nationwide.

There are four types of *tax relief* for industrial firms established in the Mezzogiorno. First, until the end of 1986 the major fiscal incentive consisted of a 50 percent reduction in the IRPEG rate (corporation tax) for

22. King and Fullerton (1984, chap. 2, p. 29).

ten years on new companies established in the Mezzogiorno. Modification of this provision in March 1986 allowed new companies a full ten-year exemption from IRPEG. Second, a ten-year exemption from ILOR— commencing with the period in which a company becomes profitable— was retained for investments in the Mezzogiorno, as well as in those areas north of Rome, qualifying as "disaster areas." Third, until 1986 firms had been exempted from 70 percent of the ILOR tax charge on profits that were reinvested in industrial projects in the Mezzogiorno. Since 1986, a full exemption has been allowed for reinvested profits. Finally, significant reductions are allowed for compulsory social security contributions.

Up to 1987 the most important *nonfiscal* incentive provided to firms setting up in the south of Italy was a discretionary grant disbursed by a special ad hoc fund—the Cassa per il Mezzogiorno. In 1987 the Cassa per il Mezzogiorno was replaced by another special entity (Agenzia per la Promozione dello Sviluppo del Mezzogiorno), but funds are still committed and disbursed according to the same investment incentive programs. The actual details of these investment incentives are subject to constant change and vary substantially from case to case. The grants depend on the type, size, and location of investment. In 1985 a typical grant would amount to 40 percent of investment expenditure up to Lit 7 billion, 30 percent of the additional cost up to Lit 30 billion, and 15 percent of any further expenditure.

Table 6-7 displays the aggregate value of commitments and disbursements of funds under this program as well as the ratio of commitments to investments carried out in the Mezzogiorno and the share of investments in the Mezzogiorno as a proportion of total investment in Italy. Grants have accounted at times for more than 20 percent of the value of total investments undertaken in the Mezzogiorno, although nationally the grant has never exceeded 5 percent of investments.

The effective rate of grant for new investments $(g_M)$ in the Mezzogiorno has been computed by dividing the value of commitments at time $t$ by investment outlays in the Mezzogiorno at time $t + 1$, since disbursements of funds take place with a significant and variable lag with respect to outlays. Moreover, it is a common view that the investment decisions of firms are taken on the basis of commitments of funds. Since this measure of the investment grant has varied markedly from year to year, a five-year weighted average effective rate of grant (with the weights being derived from real investment expenditure) was used for the simulations.

Table 6-7.    *Investment Incentives Provided to Industry by the Cassa per il Mezzogiorno*

| Year | Funds (thousands of billions of lire) | | $g_M^a$ (percent) | Share of investments in Mezzogiorno as percent of total investment[b] |
|------|-------------|---------------|---------|---------|
|      | Commitments | Disbursements | | |
| 1975 | 296.9   | 198.5 | 15.2 | 31.1 |
| 1976 | 334.9   | 215.3 | 11.0 | 29.2 |
| 1977 | 330.9   | 228.3 | 12.2 | 25.7 |
| 1978 | 627.0   | 270.0 | 13.0 | 22.0 |
| 1979 | 428.0   | 377.0 | 21.7 | 20.0 |
| 1980 | 321.0   | 374.0 | 10.7 | 20.5 |
| 1981 | 562.0   | 426.0 | 7.0  | 20.5 |
| 1982 | 739.0   | 394.0 | 10.7 | 22.8 |
| 1983 | 774.0   | 523.0 | 12.9 | 23.9 |
| 1984 | 427.0   | 605.0 | 11.3 | 23.8 |
| 1985 | 987.0   | 608.4 | 5.5  | 23.7 |
| 1986 | 550.0   | 801.3 | 11.5 | 24.0 |
| 1987 | 886.5   | 776.8 | 4.1  | 22.8 |
| 1988 | 1,487.3 | 814.8 | n.a. | n.a. |

Sources: Bilanci della cassa per il Mezzogiorno and agenzia per la promozione dello sviluppo del Mezzogiorno; Istituto Nazionale di Statistica; Associazione per lo Ziluppo dell' industria nel Mezzogiorno.

n.a. Not available.

a. $g_M$ = total commitments (*t*)/investments in Mezzogiorno (*t* + 1).

b. Figures for investments for 1975–86 are taken from SVIMEZ; thereafter, from ISTAT.

Virtually all grants have gone to the industrial sector, but no breakdown is available for manufacturing and other industry. The value of $g_M$ for all industrial sectors was 0.1177 for 1980 and 0.1011 for 1985.

The cost-of-capital calculation for investments in the Mezzogiorno is complex because of the combination of grants and tax-deferral provisions. The cash flows received from an investment and hence the valuation of an individual project can be split into two parts: for the first ten years of the project and for its remaining useful life. If $\tau_1$ and $\rho_1$ denote the tax rate on corporate earnings and the nominal discount during the first ten years, and $\tau_2$ and $\rho_2$ are similarly defined for the remaining life of the project, the present value $V$ of the cash flows of an investment project in the Mezzogiorno are given by

$$(6\text{-}4) \qquad V = \int_0^{10} (1 - \tau_1) MRR e^{-(\rho_1 + \delta - \pi)} du$$

$$+ \int_{10}^{\infty} (1 - \tau_2) MRR e^{(-\rho_2 + \delta - \pi)} du$$

$$= MRR \left\{ \frac{(1 - \tau_1)[1 - e^{-(\rho_1 + \delta - \pi)10}]}{\rho_1 + \delta - \pi} \right.$$

$$+ \left. \frac{(1 - \tau_2)e^{-(\rho_2 + \delta - \pi)10}}{\rho_2 + \delta - \pi} \right\}$$

$$= \frac{(1 - \tau_2)MRR}{\rho_2 + \delta - \pi} \Omega,$$

where

$$\Omega = \left\{ \frac{(1 - \tau_1)(\rho_2 + \delta - \pi)}{(1 - \tau_2)(\rho_1 + \delta - \pi)}[1 - e^{-(\rho_1 + \delta - \pi)10}] \right\} + e^{-(\rho_2 + \delta - \pi)10}.$$

Under the present legislation for the Mezzogiorno $\tau_2 = \tau$ and hence $\rho_2 = \rho$, which corresponds to those values that apply to investments made in other parts of Italy. Up to 1986 the value of $\tau_1 = 0.5t_{IRPEG}$, whereas since then $\tau_1 = 0$. Since $\Omega > 1$ because $\tau_2 > \tau_1$ and $\rho_1 > \rho_2$, the value $(1/\Omega)$ can be interpreted as the discount on investment in the Mezzogiorno in present value terms resulting from the special tax regime during the first ten years of the investment.

The difference between $\rho_1$ on investments in the Mezzogiorno and elsewhere depends on the source of finance. In the case of retained earnings they take on the same value, whereas for debt-financed investments $\rho_1 = i(1 - \tau_1)$, where i is the nominal interest rate. For new share issues, up to 1983 there was no difference in the value of $\theta$. The introduction of a recapture provision on franked investment income (the special *imposta di conguaglio*) means that since that date $\theta = 1$ for the first ten years of the project.

To compute the cost of capital, the value of future cash flows from the project must be equated with the effective cost of the project net of the present value of grants and tax depreciation allowances A. The present value of depreciation allowances is different for the first ten years because of the different value of $\tau$ between the two periods. Accordingly, in 1980 and 1985, for the Mezzogiorno the present value of accelerated depreciation allowances $A_{85}^M$ could be written as follows:

$$A_{85}^M = \tau_1 \left[ \int_0^3 (\frac{1}{L} + 0.15)e^{-\rho_1 u} du + \int_3^{10} \frac{1}{L}e^{-\rho_1 u} du \right] + \tau_2 \int_{10}^{0.55L} \frac{1}{L}e^{-\rho_2 u} du$$

$$= \tau_1 \left[ \frac{0.15}{\rho_1}(1 - e^{-3\rho_1}) + \frac{1}{\rho_1 L}(1 - e^{-10\rho_2}) \right] + \tau_2 \frac{(e^{-10\rho_2} - e^{-0.55L\rho_2})}{\rho_2 L}.$$

Because $\tau_1$ was half the value of $\tau_2$, it was not always economically advantageous to undertake accelerated depreciation rather than to depreciate assets according to the straight-line method. The economically optimal choice depended on whether the additional depreciation in the shortened 0.45 residual years (when straight-line deductions could be taken against taxes levied at a rate $\tau_2$) were greater than the depreciation allowance at the 15 percent accelerated rate during the first three years.[23] The useful life over which the straight-line method is preferable to the accelerated depreciable method depends on the level of interest rates. At low nominal interest rates the straight-line method will generally be preferred, whereas at high rates the opposite will be true. Our simulations in the fourth section of this chapter, "The Structure of the Capital Stock and Its Ownership," take account of the endogeneity of this decision.

Following the Testo Unico of 1986 and the subsequent modification for 1990 the provisions described for the present value of accelerated depreciation allowances for 1990 in the case of the Mezzogiorno is given by[24]

$$A_{90}^M = \frac{\tau_1}{\rho_1 L}\left[(1 + e^{-\rho_1}) - e^{-\rho_1 3} - e^{-\rho_1 10}\right] + \frac{\tau_2}{\rho_1 L}\left[e^{-\rho_2 10} - e^{-\rho_2(L-2)}\right].$$

In this case, the decision to choose straight-line or accelerated depreciation depends on whether the additional two years of straight-line allowances at $\tau_2$ will exceed the value of the first three years of accelerated depreciation. Since at present $\tau_1 = 0$, firms will always prefer to depreciate their assets according to the straight-line method.

In summary, equating equation 6-4 with the effective cost of the investment given by $1 - A^M - g$, and substituting for $MRR = \rho + \delta$, the relationship between the pretax real rate of return and the firm's discount rate for the case of investments in the Mezzogiorno is given by

$$p = \frac{(1 - A^M - g)}{(1 - \tau_2)\Omega}[p_2 + \delta + \pi] - \delta.$$

NATIONWIDE SUBSIDIES. Two types of nationwide subsidies are discussed in the following paragraphs—interest subsidies and "negative IVA."

23. The exact conditions for preferring the straight-line method can be expressed as: $\frac{\tau_2}{L}(e^{-\rho_2 0.55L} - e^{-\rho_L^L}) > \tau_1[0.15(1 - e^{-3\rho_1})]$. This expression holds only for $L > 10$. For assets with a useful life of less than ten years, accelerated depreciation always attracts preferential tax treatment.

24. Assets with a useful life of ten years or less have a value of $A_{90}^M = 0$.

*Interest subsidies.* Subsidized loans have been provided to firms established in the Mezzogiorno, to small and medium-sized firms in certain sectors, and, since 1977, to companies applying to a national fund for industrial reconversion. These subsidies have been granted through special credit institutions that lend at medium and longer term (see below, under "Personal Taxation") and that finance themselves by issuing debentures. The subsidy element provided by the government consists of the difference between the market rate obtained by the special credit institutions and a subsidized rate loosely related to market conditions. A number of changes have taken place in the manner in which this specific form of incentive has been used to stimulate investment: the computation of the interest rate has been based on market rates or set independently of market conditions; variations in rate have been used for macroeconomic stabilization purposes; and the rate of interest has often been varied according to location, industrial sector, and size of firm.

Table 6-8 shows the outlays by special credit institutions on this form of financial incentive, whereas table 6-9 sets out the relationship between the subsidized interest rate and the market rate of interest on the most important subsidy programs. This form of incentive was particularly important during the 1960s and 1970s, but in recent years appears to have declined somewhat in relative importance (table 6-8). Over the years the bulk of the subsidies has gone to manufacturing.

In some of the simulations reported below under "Estimates of Effective Marginal Tax Rates," we have allowed for the possibility of investments carried out at nonmarket rates by assuming that the effective nominal interest rate deductible by the firm is equal to $i = \alpha i_{NM} + (1 - \alpha)i_M$, where $i_M$ is the market interest rate at which the special credit institutions can borrow on financial markets, $i_{NM}$ is the subsidized rate, and $\alpha$ is the share of total loans financed at subsidized rates. If $i_{NM} = i_M(1 - \beta)$, then the nominal interest rate deductible by the firm equals $i = i_M(1 - \alpha\beta)$.

Given the wide variety of criteria applicable to the computation of subsidized rates under the various incentive programs (table 6-9), we assumed that for investments in the Mezzogiorno the value of $\beta = 0.64$, whereas for the rest of Italy $\beta = 0.34$. Since no breakdown by region was available, we also assumed that the value of $\alpha$ is the same nationwide, as shown in table 6-8.

*"Negative IVA."* A further incentive which was introduced in 1977— initially only for investments in the Mezzogiorno—consists of a special

Table 6-8. *Total Lending by Special Credit Institutions at Market and Subsidized Interest Rates*

Billions of lire; numbers in parentheses are percent of total at subsidized rates

| | Manufacturing | | Other industry | | Services (commerce)[a] | |
|---|---|---|---|---|---|---|
| Year | Total lending | Lending at subsidized rates | Total lending | Lending at subsidized rates | Total lending | Lending at subsidized rates |
| 1980 | 21,575 | 11,715 (54) | 4,784 | 1,269 (27) | 17,228 | 2,367 (14) |
| 1981 | 24,663 | 12,583 (51) | 6,284 | 1,531 (24) | 20,389 | 2,739 (13) |
| 1982 | 27,898 | 14,218 (51) | 8,270 | 1,869 (23) | 24,245 | 2,863 (12) |
| 1983 | 30,045 | 15,704 (52) | 9,647 | 2,427 (25) | 29,287 | 3,267 (11) |
| 1984 | 32,227 | 17,061 (53) | 11,794 | 3,058 (26) | 34,125 | 3,695 (11) |
| 1985 | 33,752 | 18,690 (55) | 11,253 | 3,079 (25) | 36,251 | 4,550 (13) |
| 1986 | 35,720 | 19,795 (55) | 13,040 | 3,053 (23) | 39,083 | 5,748 (15) |
| 1987 | 38,988 | 21,307 (55) | 13,066 | 2,970 (23) | 45,402 | 7,181 (16) |
| 1988 | 42,946 | 22,764 (53) | 12,696 | 2,796 (22) | 53,763 | 9,149 (17) |
| 1989[b] | 48,801 | 26,997 (65) | 15,012 | 2,679 (18) | 57,303 | 11,667 (20) |
| 1990[b] | 54,639 | 28,810 (53) | 16,759 | 2,496 (15) | 68,334 | 13,683 (20) |
| 1991[b] | 58,559 | 29,367 (50) | 18,364 | 2,258 (12) | 76,158 | 14,656 (19) |

Sources: Banca d'Italia, *Relazione annuale* (various years); and Silvestri (1983).

a. "Services" excludes banking and insurance.

b. New series.

Table 6-9. *Terms of Most Important Types of Subsidized Credit*

| Type of interest subsidy | Base reference rate | Relationship of subsidy to reference rate | Percent share of total subsidized loans outstanding at end of 1986[a] |
|---|---|---|---|
| *Fondo nazionale* L.M. 183 of May 2, 1976 | Varies every six months according to the average cost of funding of SCI[b] | 36 percent for Mezzogiorno 48 percent for under-developed areas in central Italy, 72 percent elsewhere | 20.8 |
| Fund for industrial restructuring and reconversion (L. 675 of 1977) | Varies every six months according to the average cost of funding of SCI[b] | 30 percent for Mezzogiorno, 40 percent for other underdeveloped areas, 60 percent elsewhere | 7.3 |
| (L. 1101 of 1971) | Varies every six months according to the average cost of funding of SCI[b] | 38 percent throughout country | 1.5 |
| Small and medium-size firms (L. 949 of 1952 and 623 of 1959), purchase of equipment | Base rate set by Mediocredito Centrale, as above | 45 percent for Mezzogiorno, 55 percent elsewhere | 4.1 |

Source: Banca d'Italia, *Relazione annuale appendice*, table aD21.
a. Net of agricultural, residential, construction, and export credits. Total value of subsidized loans outstanding at end of 1986 = Lit 24,876 billion. Loans to "other sectors" include shipbuilding, the hotel industry, and tourism.
b. Special credit institution.

deduction which may be offset against value-added tax (IVA) of a percentage of investment expenditure on plant and machinery in manufacturing and other industry. This incentive is commonly known as the negative IVA. The statutory provisions of the negative IVA and the actual use of the incentive by companies have varied over time. Between 1977 and 1983 the tax deduction was allowed on 4 percent of expenditure on plant and equipment investments carried out in the Mezzogiorno. Between September 1982 and July 1986, an additional 6 percent deduction of investment expenditures on plant and equipment was allowed nationwide.[25] The supplementary subsidy has been abolished and at present the negative IVA applies only to investment in the Mezzogiorno (6 percent).

The study by Giuseppe Campa, which covers information on tax returns up to 1982, shows that relatively few companies have made use of this incentive, but that the rate of utilization is positively correlated with size.[26] In view of these considerations, for the nationwide simulations in respect of 1985 we have assumed $g_{IVA} = 0.06$ but assigned a value of $f_3 = 0.3$ to reflect the partial use of the incentive. For the Mezzogiorno, because of the cumulation of the 4 percent and 6 percent rates until July 1986, the value of $g_{IVA} = 0.1$ for 1985. For 1980 and 1990 in the Mezzogiorno the value of $g_{IVA} = 0.04$ and 0.06, respectively. However, in the simulations for the Mezzogiorno, since $f_3 = 1$, the value of the negative IVA to be added to the values $g_M$ in order to compute an overall value of the investment grant was $g_{IVA} \times 0.3$. The resulting values of $g$ for investment in plant and equipment in the Mezzogiorno comprehensive of all incentives were equal to 0.1297, 0.1311, and 0.1191 for 1980, 1985, and 1990, respectively.

### Wealth Taxes

Except for death duties and gift taxes, the most important wealth tax in Italy is INVIM (*imposta sull'incremento del valore degli immobili*). This is a capital gains tax on nominal increments in the value of real estate and buildings. The tax was introduced in 1974 and significantly revised in 1980. Generally it is due only if ownership is transferred by sale, inheritance, or gift. However, for companies it is levied at ten-year

25. Art. 1, Law 896, December 19, 1983.
26. Campa (1986).

intervals. The tax base is the difference between sale and acquisition cost or, in the case of companies, the difference between the current value, as written in the financial balance sheet, and the value recorded the last time the asset was taxed. Although there is no indexation of the tax base to take account of changes in the overall price level, the marginal rate of tax varies according to the length of holding period and the value of the capital gain. The first tax bracket (5 percent) applies to gains below 20 percent of the initial value of the asset multiplied by the number of years the asset is held. The highest marginal tax bracket (30 percent) applies to gains exceeding 200 percent multiplied by the number of years the asset is held. For example, if an asset doubles in price overnight but is not sold for a five-year period the marginal rate of tax on the price increase is equal to 5 percent, whereas if it were sold after a year the marginal rate of tax would be 30 percent. As already mentioned, the revaluations of assets have occurred irregularly and have therefore been considered as not affecting investment decisions. Accordingly INVIM is excluded from the simulations discussed below.

## Personal Taxation

There are two separate taxes on personal incomes: a progressive income tax and a proportional local tax on nonlabor income currently levied at a flat rate of 16.2 percent.[27] Although capital income should comprise all real and financial sources of income, there are a number of exemptions under both IRPEF and ILOR. Interest income is exempt from personal taxes and comes under a series of flat-rate levies known as *imposta sostitutiva*.

Except for the exclusion of labor and dividend income under ILOR, the determination of total gross income is the same under both taxes. The value of total gross income is an aggregate computed from separate assessments carried out under five schedules covering different broad sources of income. These five schedules are real estate, capital, labor (two subschedules apply to employees and the self-employed, respectively), entrepreneurship (unincorporated firms), and other (including certain types of capital gain). The definition of income under each of the

27. ILOR is currently a local tax in name only, since it is administered by the central government and redistributed to the local authorities but not according to regional differences in tax revenues.

separate schedules varies markedly and there are numerous exceptions to the general rules set out within each category.

The gross tax liability is obtained by applying a progressive rate schedule to total taxable income, which is obtained by subtracting allowable deductions from total gross income. With the exception of the deduction for life insurance premiums there are no incentives to save under the personal income tax. Following the 1974 reform, the tax rates on individual income were revised significantly in 1975, 1983, 1986, and 1989. The 1983 revisions consisted of a drastic reduction in the number of tax brackets (from thirty-two to nine) and the attenuation of the steep degree of tax progressivity for the middle and top income ranges. In 1989 the number of tax brackets was reduced to seven, the top marginal tax bracket was lowered from 62 to 50 percent, and the rate schedule was indexed for changes in the price level.

### Tax Treatment of Interest Income (Imposta Sostitutiva) and Dividends

The *imposta sostitutiva*, or substitution tax, on nominal interest income is a flat-rate tax which varies according to the type of investor, status of the borrower, and form of finance.[28] In the case of individual investors, the *imposta sostitutiva* acts as final payment, whereas for companies, including financial institutions, it operates as a withholding tax for which a credit is provided against tax liabilities under IRPEG.[29]

Table 6-10 shows the changes in the tax treatment of various types of debt instruments over time. Four features of the *imposta sostitutiva* stand out clearly from this table. First, as regards the status of the borrower, the tax treatment of individual assets has depended on whether the borrowing entity was private or public. Another important distinction has been between banks, which extend short-term loans, and special credit institutions, which provide finance over the medium term and long term. Second, there has been a remarkable variety of changes in the rate of tax on individual instruments over time, and from period to period these changes have often appeared haphazard. In addition, identical assets issued at different dates

28. A withholding tax also applies to dividend distributions, but for all recipients with the exception of mutual funds it operates only as prepayment of income tax.

29. Until 1984 companies were treated like individuals and the *imposta sostitutiva* was the final payment of tax.

Table 6-10. Rates of Tax on Various Financial Assets under the Imposta Sostitutiva

Month and Year from Which Rates Were in Effect

| Financial asset | Jan. 1974 | Dec. 1975 | Mar. 1976 | Jan. 1978 | July 1978 | Jan. 1981 | Oct. 1982 | Jan. 1984 | Sept. 1986 | Jan. 1988 | Jan. 1989 | Jan. 1990 | Oct. 1991 |
|---|---|---|---|---|---|---|---|---|---|---|---|---|---|
| Current-account bank deposits | 15 | 15 | 16 | 18 | 20 | 20a | 21.6b | 25 | 25 | 30 | 30 | 30 | 30 |
| Savings accounts, certificates of deposit, and postal savings | 15 | 15 | 16 | 18 | 20 | 20 | 21.6 | 25 | 25 | 25 | 25 | 25 | 25 |
| Treasury bills and bonds | ....Exempt.... | | | | | | | | 6.25c | 12.5 | 12.5 | 12.5 | 12.5 |
| Bankers' acceptances | ....No withholding tax.... | | | | | 15 | 16.2 | 15 | 15 | 15.0 | 15 | 15 | 15 |
| Bonds of special credit institutions | 10 | 10 | 10 | 10 | 10d | 10e | 10.8 | 12.5 | 12.5 | 12.5 | 12.5 | 12.5 | 12.5 |
| ENEL (electricity) and other government agencies | ....Exempt.... | | | | | | | | 6.25c | 12.5 | 12.5 | 12.5 | 12.5 |
| ENI, IRI, and financial companies | 20 | 20 | 20 | 20 | 20 | 20e | 10.8 | 12.5 | 12.5 | 12.5 | 12.5f | 12.5f | 12.5f |
| Bonds of non-financial companies | 30 | 20 | 20 | 20 | 20 | 20e | 10.8 | 12.5 | 12.5 | 12.5 | 12.5f | 12.5f | 12.5f |
| Convertible bonds | 15g | 10 | 10 | 10 | 10 | 10e | 10.8 | 12.5 | 12.5 | 12.5 | 12.5 | 12.5 | 12.5 |
| Other financial assets | 15 | 15 | 15 | 15 | 15 | 15 | 15 | 15-18h | 15-18h | 15-18h | 15-30h | 15-30h | 15-30h |

a. 21.6 percent as of December 22, 1981.
b. 25 percent as of October 2, 1981.
c. 12.5 percent on bonds and bills issued after October 1, 1987.
d. Securities issued between July 3, 1980 and September 30, 1982 were exempt.
e. Securities issued between December 31, 1980 and September 30, 1982 were exempt.
f. Companies different from the mentioned are taxed at a rate of 30 percent. Companies were exempt if the company was quoted on the stock exchange.
g. Rate of 15 percent from April 1974; previously not treated separately from other bonds.
h. "Atypical" securities, including real estate and participation certificates, are taxed at a rate of 18 percent as of October 30, 1983; from 1989 at a rate of 30 percent.

have been subject to different rates of tax. These differentials between various financial assets have had the effect of virtually eliminating particular market sectors (for example, bond issues by the corporate nonbank sector) or of encouraging financial innovation (for example, bankers' acceptances). Third, up till 1990 there was a slow but continuing trend toward heavier taxation of interest on bank deposits. In recent years there also appears to be a tendency to reduce the range of tax rates across individual instruments so that at present there are basically three rates: 30 percent on current account deposits, 25 percent on other deposits, and 12.5 percent on bonds.

Finally, special mention should be made of the much-discussed treatment of government bonds, notes, and bills that were tax-exempt for companies until 1984 and for individuals until September 1986.[30] On September 1, 1987, the rate was raised from 6.25 percent to 12 percent, to put it in line with rates for other bonds.[31]

The value of the marginal tax rate on interest income was computed by weighting the *imposta sostitutiva* applying to each of the debt instruments by the ownership proportions for the various components of debt described below. After allowance was made for indirect lending through the banking system in the form of the acquisition of securities issued by companies and special credit institutions, the marginal personal tax rate on debt was equal to 19.68 percent in 1980 and 22.49 percent in 1985. The marginal tax rate for 1990 was estimated at 16.67 percent.

Cash dividends are also currently subject to withholding tax. However, except for dividends from preferred shares and distributions to nonresidents, this withholding tax is only a prepayment of IRPEF (dividends are exempt from ILOR). In the case of preferred shares, individuals can choose between receiving a tax credit against IRPEF or paying a final withholding tax, which at present stands at 18 percent.

The average marginal personal tax rates on equity for 1980 and 1985 were computed from income tax declarations by multiplying the value of dividend income in each tax bracket by the corresponding marginal tax rate. The resulting average marginal tax rates were 43.6 percent and 49.1 percent, respectively. For 1990 it was assumed that the distribution of share ownership remained the same as in 1985, but allowance was made for the shift in tax brackets resulting from rising nominal income. To compute the changing share of income in each tax bracket, we assumed

30. There has been a lively debate in Italy over the impact of taxing government bonds on the level of interest rates. See Bernareggi (1986) and Spaventa (1987).

31. During the period under consideration, nonresidents have always been subject to a 30 percent withholding tax on interest income unless otherwise specified by a tax treaty.

that the cumulative distribution of income within each bracket was triangular. Hence, for a given percentage increase in nominal income, $\pi'$, each income bracket was assumed to lose $\pi'/(1 + \pi')$ multiplied by the existing share of total dividend income attributable to the tax bracket.

After allowing for the changes in tax bracket according to these calculations, the value of the marginal tax rate on dividends was estimated to have declined from 49.1 to 46.1 percent between 1985 and 1990.

### The Taxation of Income from Owner-Occupied Housing

Imputed income from owner-occupied housing is taxed under IRPEF and ILOR. The value of imputed income is calculated according to several parameters based on the characteristics of dwellings (quality of housing, area, number of facilities, and so forth), but these cadastral assessments of income-generating capacity have not been updated in recent years. To correct the resulting undervaluations, the fiscal authorities have devised ad hoc adjustment coefficients to the cadastral assessments that are updated at irregular intervals. Even allowing for these revaluations, it is generally accepted that imputed income is considerably underestimated. In the simulations reported below, it is assumed that the tax base is only 50 percent of the actual return on owner-occupied housing, but this is likely to be an overestimate of the tax base.

Interest on mortgages is deductible up to Lit 4 million. However, Italian families have not borrowed very heavily to finance their acquisition of housing. In 1985 the ratio of total liabilities to the stock of housing in the hands of the household sector was less than 4 percent. Other tax incentives have played a more important role. Under a series of laws passed in the 1980s virtually all new buildings constructed before 1986 were exempted from ILOR until 1997. Taking all these provisions together, the marginal tax rate for investment in housing was given by $m_H = 0.50(t_{IRPEF} + t_{ILOR})$ for 1980 and 1990. For 1985 the marginal tax rate was $m_H = 0.50[t_{IRPEF} + t_{ILOR}e^{-(\rho+\delta-\pi)10}]$. No information is available on the distribution of housing by taxable income bracket. The average marginal tax rate on IRPEF of 27 percent was assumed in the simulation. The rate of economic depreciation for owner-occupied housing was $\delta = 0.02$.

### Tax-Exempt Institutions

There are no tax-exempt institutions in Italy similar to pension funds in Anglo-Saxon countries. Mutual funds (*fondi comuni di investimento*), whose legal character was finally established in 1983 after many years of discussion, are partially tax-exempt institutions because they are not subject to IRPEF, IRPEG, or ILOR. However, the *imposta sostitutiva* applies as a final payment of tax on all receipts of investment income including dividends, which are subject to a 10 percent withholding tax. In the absence of tax credits, the after-tax return on investments in shares by mutual funds is equal to $(1 - m_s) = (1 - w_s)/\theta$, where $w_s$ is the value of withholding tax on dividends. Accordingly, in 1985 and 1990, since $w_s = 0.1$ and $\theta = 1.5625, m_s = 0.424$, which means that only investors having a marginal tax rate higher than this value would find investments through mutual funds to offer any tax advantage over individual investments. In addition, mutual funds are subject to a yearly wealth tax of either 0.1 percent or 0.25 percent, depending on whether more or less than 5 percent of the fund is invested in Italian shares. For purposes of the simulations carried out in the following section, "The Structure of the Capital Stock and Its Ownership," the value of $w_p = 0.001$ was taken for new share issues and retained earnings, whereas $w_p = 0.0025$ was taken for debt. The value of the marginal personal tax rate on debt for mutual funds was computed by weighting their holdings of various debt instruments by the relevant *imposta sostitutiva*. The value of $m$ estimated for 1985 and 1990 is 0.1259 in both cases.

### Insurance Companies

Income received by households through investment in insurance policies is subject to a complicated set of tax provisions. To describe this tax treatment, we break down the various provisions into the personal income tax deductions enjoyed by households for paying a premium, the personal taxes on the amounts paid out under the insurance policies, the corporate tax treatment of insurance companies, and the special provisions applying to corporate taxes in the case of investments by insurance companies in mutual funds.

Life insurance premiums can be deducted from taxable income under IRPEF up to a maximum amount of Lit 2.5 million. Because of the ceiling this relief may not affect savings at the margin. In all likelihood, for most individuals these tax savings will be binding, and we have assumed that the acquisition cost of a unit of life insurance is equal to $1 - m$. The values of $m$ for 1980, 1985, and 1990 were estimated for the tax declarations of policyholders at 0.2678, 0.2503 and 0.2485, respectively.

If benefits under a life insurance policy are received before death, the tax treatment depends on whether payments are taken as a lump sum or as a stream of annuities.[32] In the former case a flat rate of tax, which was equal to 12.5 percent in 1985 and 1990, applies to the difference between the capital amount accumulated and the premium paid up.[33] Assuming that a unit premium which is capitalized for $L$ periods at a nominal interest rate $i$, taxable income is equal to $e^{iL} - 1$, and after tax, the accumulated amount is given by

$$e^{iL} - 0.125(e^{iL} - 1) = 0.875e^{iL} + 0.125.$$

The annualized implicit marginal tax rate on the return to the policy holder ($\hat{m}$) can be obtained by setting this expression equal to $e^{i(1-\hat{m})L}$. Accordingly,

$$(6\text{-}5) \qquad \hat{m} = 1 - \frac{\log_e[0.875e^{iL} + 0.125]}{iL}.$$

Assuming that the insurance policy is held for ten years, the value of $\hat{m}$ for 1985 and 1990 was estimated from market interest rates as 0.0823 and 0.0736.[34]

Insurance business can be divided into two categories: life and non-life insurance. For fiscal purposes both types of business are subject to IRPEG and ILOR. In computing taxable income, insurance companies are allowed to set aside a tax-free reserve (*riserve tecniche*) equal to $\gamma$ percent of the paid-up premiums. Hence, given a statutory rate of tax, $\tau$, the effective cost for a unit of investment is equal to $1 - \gamma\tau$. The value of $\gamma$ differs according to whether investment is undertaken by life or nonlife insurance companies. In the former case, the maximum amounts of reserves that can be set aside for fiscal purposes correspond to the minimum reserves required by civil law. In 1985 the increase in reserves varied across life insurance companies from 65 to 85 percent of the premiums received.[35] For purposes of our simulation, we have assumed that

---

32. Alworth and Castellucci (1987) show that the tax treatment of annuities is more onerous than the flat-rate tax.

33. Previously, lump-sum payments from the fund were tax-free. If the insurance policy is held for more than ten years under the present law, the tax rate is reduced by 2 percent for each successive year.

34. The interest rates on insurance policies are set with the agreement of government authorities but on balance do not diverge significantly from the market rates on government bonds.

35. These estimates were provided in private discussions with members of the national association of insurers. The differences in values occur because of the nature of the insurance risks taken by various companies.

$\gamma = 0.65$. In the case of nonlife insurance companies, the value of $\gamma$ is set by law at 35 percent.

Earnings received by insurance companies are taxed at different rates $(\tau_I)$. Dividends are subject to IRPEG only, whereas interest income and capital gains are taxed under both IRPEG and ILOR. In the specific case of receipts from investments in mutual funds, life insurance companies are allowed a tax credit against their tax liability on IRPEG equal to 10 percent of net receipts after withholding tax. In addition, these returns on mutual funds are subject to a wealth tax equal to either 0.1 percent or 0.25 percent, as described in the previous section. (This case is not considered in the simulation.)

In summary, the effective acquisition cost of a life insurance policy is given by $(1 - m)(1 - \gamma\tau)$, taking account of the tax relief at the personal and company level. The post-tax return is equal to $(1 - \hat{m})(1 - \tau_I)$. Hence, the effective tax rate $\tau_e$ on the policyholder's initial investment is obtained as follows:

$$(1 - \tau_e)(1 - m)(1 - \gamma\tau) = (1 - \hat{m})(1 - \tau_I).$$

Therefore

$$\tau_e = 1 - \frac{(1 - \tau_I)(1 - \hat{m})}{(1 - \gamma\tau)(1 - m)}.$$

As a result of the low tax rates and the various subsidies granted to companies and individual taxpayers, the effective tax rate on savings channeled through insurance companies was negative in many circumstances. On equity the value of $\tau_e$ was $-0.3401$ in 1980, $-0.1214$ in 1985, and $-0.1293$ in 1990. By contrast the value of $\tau_e$ for interest payments switches from $-0.4351$ in 1980 to $0.0603$ in 1985 and $0.0536$ in 1990.

## The Structure of the Capital Stock and Its Ownership

In this section we examine the computation of the weights needed to aggregate over the various effective tax rates for the eighty-one combinations of asset type, industry, source of finance, and ownership.

### Data Limitations

There are serious conceptual problems and data limitations in linking the real and financial activities of firms on the one hand with the financial investment decisions of the ultimate beneficiaries of capital income on the other. In Italy the three most conspicuous data deficiencies are the absence of data on the distribution of capital income among individuals, the lack of an industry breakdown of debt and equity according to replacement cost or market value, and the difficulty in separating the private and public sectors. In addition, major revisions to the national accounts have called into question the validity of many statistics, including those that are used in this chapter. The first problem is currently of relatively secondary importance because capital income, except for dividend receipts, is taxed at proportional rates. As pointed out earlier in the chapter, reliable information is available on the distribution of equity holdings, and use has been made of these data to compute a weighted average tax rate on dividends.

The second problem concerns the structure of the balance sheet of the corporate sector and of enterprises more generally. No statistics published in the national accounts are available concerning the financing of firms; Bank of Italy flow-of-funds statistics are also relatively poor in providing breakdowns with respect to the source of finance of firms in the corporate sector. Moreover, these statistics do not exclude publicly owned entities from the company sector, and the use of such figures would induce a distorted impression of the composition of corporate indebtedness.

The third limitation is the most serious. Enterprises owned either directly by the state (such as ENEL, the national electricity company), or indirectly (through one of the state holding companies) have accounted for a much more sizable share of national product than in other European countries. As far as this study is concerned, these indirect holdings, which often take the form of majority shareholdings in publicly traded companies, are difficult to isolate from the rest of the corporate sector for purposes of determining the composition of capital stock. Moreover, since the government has underwritten the losses of these firms by acquiring large participations in them, especially during the late 1970s and early 1980s, it is very difficult to use flow-of-funds and national-accounts data for the purposes of reconstructing an accurate picture of the way in which private savings have been channeled to private investment. More generally, through its numerous investment promotion schemes and its participation in financial intermediation through state-owned banks and other financial intermediaries, the Italian public sector has played a discretionary role in allocating resources that cannot easily be captured by summary measurements such as effective tax rates.

Finally, the Italian national accounts were revised very significantly in 1987. As a result, data on the capital stock as well as flow-of-funds data are currently undergoing major adjustments.

### Capital Stock Weights

The most thorough and detailed estimates of the capital stock at replacement cost have been constructed according to the perpetual-inventory method.[36] The estimates include breakdowns of the capital stock by sector as well as by type of asset (machinery, buildings and vehicles). (See table 6-11.) Unpublished figures for the services sector have also been employed for computing weights for "commerce."[37] The weights of the capital stock for 1985, which were also used for the 1980 and 1990 simulations, are shown in table 6-12. To avoid including figures for those sectors in which publicly owned enterprises are predominant, we have restricted "other industry" to construction only; this has meant excluding communications and transportation from the computation of the weights.

The figures for inventories were estimated by using information contained in the Mediobanca sample of firms with those of Rosa and Siesto; inventories and fixed capital stock reported in the Mediobanca statistics were recomputed at replacement cost.[38] The ratio of these revalued mea-

Table 6-11.  *Net Capital Stock in 1986 at Current Replacement Cost, Measured at 1970 Prices*

Billions of lire

|  | Sector | | | |
|---|---|---|---|---|
| Asset | Manufacturing | Other industry[a] | Commerce[b] | Total |
| Machinery and equipment | 11,724.1 | 743.6 | 6,401.5 | 18,869.2 |
| Buildings | 9,514.7 | 354.8 | 10,588.2 | 20,457.7 |
| Vehicles | 724.9 | 326.4 | 3,589.7 | 4,641.0 |
| Inventories | 10,937.3 | 1,684.9 | 3,987.2 | 16,609.4 |
| Total | 32,901.0 | 3,109.7 | 24,566.6 | 60,577.3 |

a. Construction and public works only (utilities, transportation, and communications have been excluded because mostly public-sector enterprises).
b. Commerce only (other services excluded because significant share in public sector).

36. Rosa (1979); Rosa and Siesto (1985).
37. We are grateful to Alberto Heimler, of Confindustria, Rome, for providing us with these statistics.
38. Mediobanca (1987); Rosa and Siesto (1985); Alworth and Fornasari (1982).

Table 6-12. *Proportion of Capital Stock, by Asset and Industry, 1985*

| Asset | Sector | | | |
| --- | --- | --- | --- | --- |
| | *Manufacturing* | *Other industry*[a] | *Commerce*[b] | *Total* |
| Machinery and equipment | 0.2055 | 0.0177 | 0.1649 | 0.3881 |
| Buildings | 0.1571 | 0.0059 | 0.1748 | 0.3377 |
| Inventories | 0.1806 | 0.0278 | 0.0658 | 0.2472 |
| Total | 0.5431 | 0.0513 | 0.4055 | 1.0000 |

a. Construction and public works only (utilities, transportation, and communications have been excluded because mostly public-sector enterprises).
b. Commerce only (other services excluded because significant share in public sector).

sures was used to obtain a measure of inventories. It has unfortunately not been possible to obtain separate figures for the corporate sector, but that sector accounts for the bulk of total investments.

### Sources of Finance

Italian companies do not publish balance sheets based on replacement-cost values of their investments, and the national statistical office does not produce such computations. In order to estimate the breakdown between debt and equity finance for Italian companies, the balance-sheet data published by Mediobanca for a sample of private companies that undertake roughly 15 to 20 percent of total gross investment were revalued at replacement cost.[39]

These adjustments were accomplished in two steps. First, the net capital stock was revalued by assuming arbitrarily that at the time these statistics were begun in 1968 the reported value of the capital stock accounted for roughly 85 percent of its true value. This percentage was chosen as a rough approximation for past undervaluations of the capital stock due to inflation and for depreciation above the value of economic depreciation. Second, since no breakdown by type of asset is available from the published accounts, in order to construct a new series for the capital stock economic depreciation was assumed to take place at 10 percent, which was roughly equivalent to the weighted average of economic depreciation across buildings, machinery, and vehicles. The estimated value of the capital stock was then computed on the basis of the perpetual-inventory method.

39. Mediobanca (1987).

Table 6-13.   *Capital Stock and Leverage of Private-Sector Companies, 1968–86*

Billions of lire unless otherwise specified

| Year | Balance-sheet value of capital stock (1) | Estimated value of capital stock at replacement cost (2) | Total indebt-edness[a] (3) | Measures of leverage (percent) | | |
|------|------|------|------|------|------|------|
| | | | | Col. 2/ col. 1 (4) | Col. 3/ col. 1 (5) | Col. 3/ col. 2 (6) |
| 1968 | 6,670 | 7,479 | 3,663 | 112 | 55 | 49 |
| 1969 | 7,328 | 8,533 | 4,137 | 116 | 56 | 48 |
| 1970 | 8,671 | 10,643 | 5,276 | 123 | 61 | 50 |
| 1971 | 9,478 | 12,050 | 6,263 | 127 | 66 | 52 |
| 1972 | 9,635 | 12,886 | 7,163 | 134 | 74 | 56 |
| 1973 | 10,563 | 15,421 | 7,809 | 146 | 74 | 51 |
| 1974 | 13,666 | 21,531 | 10,367 | 158 | 76 | 48 |
| 1975 | 16,293 | 25,592 | 12,551 | 157 | 77 | 49 |
| 1976 | 18,845 | 30,402 | 13,878 | 161 | 74 | 46 |
| 1977 | 21,513 | 36,502 | 16,322 | 170 | 76 | 45 |
| 1978 | 23,846 | 40,677 | 17,557 | 171 | 74 | 43 |
| 1979 | 29,044 | 47,981 | 20,108 | 165 | 69 | 42 |
| 1980 | 35,647 | 58,665 | 24,569 | 165 | 69 | 42 |
| 1981 | 39,642 | 68,464 | 28,519 | 173 | 72 | 42 |
| 1982 | 47,299 | 77,020 | 30,129 | 163 | 64 | 39 |
| 1983 | 48,712 | 83,046 | 32,849 | 170 | 67 | 40 |
| 1984 | 52,011 | 90,010 | 35,588 | 173 | 68 | 40 |
| 1985 | 54,077 | 96,803 | 34,918 | 179 | 65 | 36 |
| 1986 | 55,868 | 101,494 | 33,707 | 182 | 60 | 33 |

Sources: Mediobanca (1987); and authors' calculations.
a. Bonds, borrowing from special credit institutions, net bank debt, and reinvested deferred income.

The total value of the capital stock was obtained by adding to this adjusted measure of total fixed investments the value of inventories.[40] The ratio between the revalued capital stock and the measure reported in the balance sheets published by Mediobanca is shown in the second column of table 6-13. As expected there has been a growing discrepancy between these two measures owing to the very high level of inflation during the late 1970s and early 1980s. At the end of 1986 the estimated replacement cost value of the capital was roughly 80 percent higher than the balance-sheet measure. It should also be noted that revaluations of balance sheets, which were allowed under the two Visentini laws, had the effect of temporarily redressing the trend in the mid-1970s and early 1980s.

40. The ratio of inventories to the total measure of the capital stock revalued according to this criterion proved to be considerably more stable than a similar ratio obtained employing the original balance-sheet data.

The actual measure of leverage in the Italian private corporate sector is difficult to compute because of the significant degree of financial flow that occurs between nonfinancial companies. In particular, more than 40 percent of companies' gross indebtedness is in the form of trade credit or other forms of credit from other nonfinancial companies. To avoid this problem, company indebtedness was taken to comprise debentures, medium- and long-term credits received from the special credit institutions, net bank borrowing (advances less cash and deposits), and the *fondi di quiescienza* (deferred income payments).

As can be seen from column 5 of table 6-13, according to the book value of the capital stock the ratio of debt to total capital has varied between 55 and 77 percent. A more accurate assessment of the degree of indebtedness can be observed in column 6, which reports the ratio of debt to the estimated replacement cost value of the capital stock. We have used the latter, considerably lower measure in our simulations.

By and large, issuance of new equity has been a marginal source of finance, particularly if account is taken of share repurchases. Between 1976 and 1983 new share issues almost never exceeded repurchases. Some positive net issuing activity, however, took place in the following three years (1984–86). As a result, the weights assigned to new share issues as a marginal source of finance were 0.0 for 1980 and 0.005 for both 1985 and 1990.

### The Ownership of Equity

Proportions for equity ownership were obtained from the flow-of-funds data of the Banca d'Italia. However, neither the industrial composition of equity nor the breakdown of the equity issued by nonfinancial companies according to the final investor could be determined.

A striking characteristic of the shareholdings of Italian firms is the very pronounced degree of interlocking ownership of shares within the corporate sector. In contrast to other countries where this phenomenon occurs, such as Germany and Japan, only a small percentage of the corporate ownership of shares can be attributed to financial institutions. In 1985 nonfinancial companies accounted for roughly 72 percent of the holdings of total shares outstanding issued by firms in Italy.

In terms of outstanding amounts, the household sector holds the bulk of shares purchased by final beneficiaries. Only a minuscule component of these purchases can be attributed to nonprofit institutions such as pension

Table 6-14.    *Ownership of Italian Shares, 1980–88*

Thousands of billions of lire

| Year | Amount outstanding | | |
|------|------------|-------------|--------------------|
| | Households | Mutual funds | Insurance companies |
| 1980 | 21.9 | ... | ... |
| 1981 | 26.4 | ... | ... |
| 1982 | 20.7 | ... | ... |
| 1983 | 25.4 | ... | ... |
| 1984 | 33.8 | 0.2 | 2.8 |
| 1985 | 73.0 | 5.3 | 7.9 |
| 1986 | 135.3 | 17.0 | 12.4 |
| 1987 | 98.6 | 13.6 | 11.4 |
| 1988 | 114.3 | 14.0 | 14.2 |

Source: Banca d'Italia, *Relazione annuale appendice*, table aD37.

funds and foundations, which are important institutional investors within the household sector in other countries.

While mutual funds' and insurance companies' holdings of equity are small relative to the total outstanding amounts of shares, these entities have been major purchasers of shares in recent years. Table 6-14 shows that the share of total equity (net of intercorporate holdings) held by mutual funds expanded between 1983 and 1988 from zero to nearly 15 percent.

### The Ownership of Debt

In analyzing the ownership of debt, account must be taken of the various distinct debt instruments that companies employ to finance themselves and the manner in which final investors channel private savings to firms.

The composition of debt finance in Italy is not uniform across companies, and different statistical sources provide somewhat contrasting information. Flow-of-funds statistics across all enterprises show that more than 54 percent of total outstanding company indebtedness (excluding the *fondi di quiescienza*) was in the form of liabilities to special credit institutions. The shares of bond and bank lending were 16 percent and 30 percent, respectively. The Mediobanca-wide sample of private companies shows roughly similar proportions, although the share of bond finance is significantly lower.[41] By contrast, publicly owned companies have relied

41. Mediobanca (1987). The large bond indebtedness in the enterprise sector of the flow-of-funds statistics probably results from the inclusion of the publicly owned holding companies, which are partly excluded from the Mediobanca sample.

Table 6-15.   *Private-Sector Enterprises' Composition of Gross Outstanding Debt, Selected Years, 1968–86*
Billions of lire; proportions in parentheses

| Year | Bonds | Special credit institutions | Net bank borrowing | Total | Reinvested deferred income fund |
|------|-------|------------------------------|--------------------|-------|----------------------------------|
| 1968 | 621 | 1,183 | 948 | 2,752 | 550 |
|      | (0.23) | (0.43) | (0.34) | | |
| 1970 | 554 | 1,509 | 1,964 | 4,027 | 758 |
|      | (0.14) | (0.37) | (0.49) | | |
| 1975 | 318 | 4,491 | 4,419 | 9,228 | 2,163 |
|      | (0.03) | (0.49) | (0.48) | | |
| 1980 | 633 | 9,153 | 8,228 | 18,014 | 4,287 |
|      | (0.04) | (0.51) | (0.46) | | |
| 1985 | 1,980 | 14,458 | 8,674 | 25,112 | 7,176 |
|      | (0.08) | (0.58) | (0.35) | | |
| 1986 | 2,108 | 14,585 | 6,652 | 23,345 | 7,592 |
|      | (0.09) | (0.62) | (0.28) | | |

Sources: Mediobanca (1987).

much more heavily on short-term bank lending, which accounts for more than 75 percent of their debt.

There are also pronounced differences with respect to the relative importance of the *fondi di quiescienza*. Flow-of-funds statistics reveal that only 17 percent of external indebtedness was in this form, whereas for private companies the share was more than one third.

Over time, as shown in table 6-15, there have been pronounced changes in the composition of debt finance of private companies. During the 1960s and early 1970s, bond finance was relatively important, but with the sharp rise in interest rates that occurred in the early 1970s there was a shift toward bank loans, which at times accounted for more than 50 percent of total company debt. The 1980s saw the expansion of lending via special credit institutions, although, as noted earlier, in comparison with earlier periods a somewhat smaller share of this borrowing was at subsidized rates (table 6-16).

## Estimates of Effective Marginal Tax Rates

Table 6-17 displays the marginal tax rates for the fixed-$p$ case, in which each of the hypothetical projects is assumed to earn a pretax return of 10 percent a year and inflation is assumed to be zero. Each row of table 6-17

Table 6-16.  *Debt Ownership Proportions in 1985 and 1980*

| Item | Households | Mutual funds | Insurance companies | Total |
|---|---|---|---|---|
| | | 1985 | | |
| Debentures issued by companies | 0.0684 | 0.0058 | 0.0046 | 0.0788 |
| Debentures issued by special credit institutions | 0.5377 | 0.0082 | 0.0299 | 0.5758 |
| Bank borrowing (net) | 0.3427 | 0.0003 | 0.0024 | 0.3454 |
| Total | 0.9488 | 0.0143 | 0.0369 | 1.000 |
| | | 1980 | | |
| Debentures issued by companies | 0.0339 | 0 | 0.0012 | 0.0351 |
| Debentures issued by special credit institutions | 0.4963 | 0 | 0.0118 | 0.5081 |
| Bank borrowing (net) | 0.4525 | 0 | 0.0043 | 0.4568 |
| Total | 0.9827 | 0 | 0.0173 | 1.000 |

Source: Tables 6-16 through 6-24 are authors' calculations.

corresponds to a particular subset of the full eighty-one combinations. For example, the row for buildings gives the weighted average marginal tax rate over the twenty-seven possible combinations containing buildings.

Column 1 shows the effective marginal tax rates when companies and individuals are taxed in full and at the same time benefit from all available subsidies. The overall tax rate is 21 percent, but as in most other countries for which such simulations have been carried out, there is a great variation in tax rates across industries, assets, methods of finance, and ownership. Investments in manufacturing, which receive significant incentives, are the least taxed, and those in "other industry" are taxed the most heavily. Favorable depreciation allowances explain the very low effective tax rate on machinery relative to buildings and especially inventories. Investments financed by debt are actually subsidized by the tax system, whereas the effective tax rates on new share issues and retained earnings are far above the average effective tax rate. Finally, savings channeled by households through tax-exempt institutions bear the heaviest tax burden, whereas insurance premiums are heavily subsidized.

Columns 2 and 3 display the clear bias between the tax treatment of the return on savings at the personal and corporate level. The marginal tax rate at the corporate level has been computed as $(p - x)/p$, where $x$ is the real value of the firm's discount rate $(\rho - \pi)$ for equity-financed investments and the real rate of interest $(i - \pi)$ for debt-financed investments.

Table 6-17. *Marginal Effective Tax Rates, with Zero Inflation, 1985*
Percent

| | | | | Total | | | |
|---|---|---|---|---|---|---|---|
| Item | Total | Personal | Corporate | With complete tax exhaustion ($\tau = 0$) | With partial tax exhaustion ($\tau = t_{LLOR}$ = 0.162) | Excluding interest rate subsidies | Excluding negative IVA |
| Industry | | | | | | | |
| Manufacturing | 18.7 | 33.9 | −22.9 | 10.5 | 13.7 | 23.6 | 21.0 |
| Other industry | 25.6 | 34.3 | −13.2 | 12.9 | 17.6 | 27.4 | 27.6 |
| Commerce | 22.9 | 34.0 | −17.4 | 14.7 | 17.7 | 24.1 | 22.9 |
| Asset | | | | | | | |
| Machinery | 8.3 | 34.9 | −39.1 | 11.0 | 10.7 | 12.0 | 11.7 |
| Buildings | 20.5 | 34.3 | −20.7 | 13.3 | 15.9 | 23.5 | 20.5 |
| Inventories | 38.8 | 34.4 | 7.3 | 12.8 | 21.9 | 41.7 | 38.8 |
| Method of finance | | | | | | | |
| Debt | −10.8 | 21.8 | −41.7 | 14.1 | 7.6 | −1.9 | −8.9 |
| New share issues | 56.3 | 43.2 | 23.0 | 59.6 | 63.6 | 56.3 | 57.0 |
| Retained earnings | 38.6 | 43.2 | −8.1 | 11.2 | 19.9 | 38.6 | 39.6 |
| Owner | | | | | | | |
| Households | 23.8 | 37.1 | −21.1 | 18.4 | 20.7 | 27.3 | 25.1 |
| Tax-exempt institutions | 31.8 | 39.1 | −12.0 | 10.5 | 17.5 | 32.9 | 32.9 |
| Insurance companies | −23.4 | −8.0 | −14.3 | −61.8 | −49.2 | −21.4 | −21.3 |
| Overall tax rate | 20.8 | 34.1 | −20.2 | 12.3 | 15.5 | 24.0 | 22.1 |

Similarly, the effective marginal personal tax rate is equal to $(x - s)/x$, where $s$ is the post-tax return to savers. The personal tax system more than accounts for the total tax wedge on the return to savings, whereas at the corporate level there are heavy subsidies for nearly all types of investment. Equity-financed investments are subject to the heaviest burden in spite of the near-perfect integration of the personal and corporate taxes; interest income, which is taxed for the most part through withholding taxes, is treated somewhat more lightly than equity under the personal tax. Savings channeled through insurance companies are the only ones to benefit from a tax subsidy at the personal level; however, these subsidies do not feed through very significantly into the other breakdowns of effective tax rates because of the low weight received by insurance companies. It is also interesting to note that the personal tax system does not create a bias among investments in various sectors or assets. At the corporate level, there is a wide variation in marginal effective corporation tax rates which is caused by the system of investment incentives and interest subsidies. On the one hand, machinery, manufacturing, and debt-financed investments are heavily subsidized. On the other hand, investments financed by new share issues are taxed the most heavily. The effect of dispensing with either interest rate subsidies or negative IVA is shown in columns 6 and 7. Debt-financed investments in manufacturing are affected most by the repeal of these provisions; however, depreciation allowances for machinery continue to favor these investments over those in other assets.

The value of the effective tax rates for the case in which companies are not allowed to use their tax allowances because of complete tax exhaustion ($\tau = 0$) or because they are subject only to ILOR ($\tau = t_{ILOR} = 0.162$) is shown in columns 4 and 5 respectively. In both cases the recapture provision applies to dividend distributions (*imposta di conguaglio*), so that $\theta = 1$ for households. In addition, for mutual funds as a result of the lower value of $\theta$ the marginal personal tax rate on equity falls to nearly 10 percent. In the case of both complete and partial tax exhaustion, the overall effective tax rate declines, but this is the net outcome of a contrasting development. On the one hand, the tax shield against debt is taken away or reduced sharply. This results in a shift of the effective tax rate on debt-financed investments changing from $-10.8$ to $7.6$ ($\tau = 0.162$) and $14.1$ percent ($\tau = 0$). The most notable impact of the lifting of the tax shield is on investments in machinery. Nevertheless, the existence of interest-rate subsidies and the relatively low marginal tax rates on interest income received by households still leave debt-financed investments

Table 6-18.  *Marginal Effective Tax Rates under Different Inflation Rates, Corporate Sector, 1985*
Percent

| Item | Expected rate of inflation (percent) | | |
|---|---|---|---|
| | 0 | 5 | 10 |
| Industry | | | |
| Manufacturing | 18.7 | 17.5 | 15.0 |
| Other industry | 25.6 | 24.2 | 22.1 |
| Commerce | 22.9 | 25.7 | 26.5 |
| Asset | | | |
| Machinery | 8.3 | 11.7 | 13.7 |
| Buildings | 20.5 | 23.4 | 23.6 |
| Inventories | 38.8 | 31.7 | 24.7 |
| Method of finance | | | |
| Debt | −10.8 | −30.2 | −51.7 |
| New share issues | 56.3 | 78.9 | 100.7 |
| Retained earnings | 38.6 | 50.1 | 60.5 |
| Owner | | | |
| Households | 23.8 | 26.1 | 27.0 |
| Tax-exempt institutions | 31.8 | 38.4 | 43.6 |
| Insurance companies | −23.4 | −50.6 | −80.2 |
| Overall tax rate | 20.8 | 21.2 | 20.0 |

taxed at a low overall rate. On the other hand, the effective tax rate on investments financed through retained earnings falls 50 percent or more. In particular, the lower taxes on equity income received by mutual funds sharply reduce their effective tax rate on capital income.

Inflation has a mixed impact on the structure of effective tax rates (table 6-18). First, in 1985 the average overall marginal tax rate was insensitive to the inflation rate. The overall tax rate increased from 20.8 percent at zero inflation of 21.2 percent at 5 percent inflation, and declined to 20 percent at 10 percent inflation. The sensitivity to inflation, however, varied by type of asset, industry, source of finance, and ownership. The negative correlation was strongest for inventories, manufacturing, debt finance, and insurance companies. Conversely, the effective tax rate increased markedly with inflation for investments financed through mutual funds and by new share issues.

A second notable feature was the pronounced difference in the impact on the effective tax rate on different assets. In the case of machinery and buildings, this difference can be attributed to the short tax life for machinery and equipment and to the existence of a grant in the form of negative IVA provided for machinery. For the rates of inflation shown in table 6-18 and indeed for rates of inflation up to 20 percent, the effective tax rates on different assets do not vary with inflation (except for the LIFO tax treatment of inventories, which entails a negative correlation with inflation). However, the increase in the rate of inflation results in an increase in the dispersion of effective tax rates across individual projects.

Third, as was to be expected, the effective subsidy to debt finance surges with the rate of inflation, whereas the effective tax rate on equity finance and particularly new share issues rises markedly with the rate of inflation. For new share issues, even in the absence of inflation the relatively high marginal tax rate on dividends means that the effective tax rate exceeds the nominal tax rate on undistributed profits. Finally, as regards the various ownership categories, the rate of subsidy for insurance companies gets magnified by inflation. The difference between the effective tax rate on households and tax-exempt institutions can be attributed to the high proportion of investments in equity reported by mutual funds.

Marginal tax rates in 1985 were very similar to those prevailing in 1980 (table 6-19). At zero inflation, in 1980 the overall marginal tax rate was 18.8 percent, only two percentage points less than five years later, and at higher inflation rates the differences narrow markedly. The most striking difference between the two years concerns the effective tax rates on investment channeled through insurance companies. In 1980 the rate of subsidy was higher than that recorded for 1985 because no tax was levied at the personal level on insurance policies. The impact of this subsidy on the overall effective tax rates was very small because of the very low weight of insurance companies. The only other small differences between the effective tax rates in the two years result from the absence of negative IVA on machinery, the lower weight of subsidized loans, and the higher marginal personal tax rate on dividend income which were in effect in 1980.

### Effective Tax Rates on Investment in the Mezzogiorno

A second set of simulations of effective tax rates was carried out for investments in the Mezzogiorno (table 6-20). The values of the effective tax rates are considerably lower than those reported for the rest of Italy and show a pronounced overall negative correlation with the rate of inflation. The table also shows some of the potential relative impact of the tax incentives on different forms of investments. For example, investments in buildings are much more favorably treated than more standard investments—in part because of the lower tax rate on company profits

Table 6-19.  *Marginal Effective Tax Rates under Different Inflation Rates, Corporate Sector, 1980*
Percent

| Item | Expected rate of inflation (percent) | | |
|---|---|---|---|
| | 0 | 5 | 10 |
| Industry | | | |
| Manufacturing | 17.8 | 18.3 | 17.9 |
| Other industry | 23.0 | 23.3 | 23.3 |
| Commerce | 19.6 | 23.2 | 25.6 |
| Asset | | | |
| Machinery | 10.5 | 14.1 | 16.8 |
| Buildings | 17.7 | 21.4 | 23.2 |
| Inventories | 32.0 | 28.6 | 25.3 |
| Method of finance | | | |
| Debt | −4.4 | −16.5 | −29.8 |
| New share issues | 59.7 | 85.8 | 111.4 |
| Retained earnings | 35.5 | 47.2 | 58.0 |
| Owner | | | |
| Households | 19.6 | 21.7 | 22.9 |
| Tax-exempt institutions | ... | ... | ... |
| Insurance companies | −84.0 | −143.4 | −205.1 |
| Overall tax rate | 18.8 | 20.5 | 21.3 |

Table 6-20.  *Marginal Effective Tax Rates under Different Inflation Rates, Mezzogiorno, Fixed-p, 1985*
Percent

| Item | Inflation rate (percent) | | |
|---|---|---|---|
| | 0 | 5 | 10 |
| Industry | | | |
| Manufacturing | 8.363 | −18.177 | −39.987 |
| Other industry | 1.750 | −5.873 | −15.844 |
| Commerce | 9.526 | −7.390 | −24.366 |
| Asset | | | |
| Machinery | −5.861 | −30.596 | −53.665 |
| Buildings | 14.037 | −0.183 | −12.946 |
| Inventories | 21.976 | 13.723 | 5.583 |
| Method of finance | | | |
| Debt | 9.880 | −5.092 | −19.066 |
| New share issues | 12.451 | −1.539 | −14.644 |
| Retained earnings | −37.655 | −86.900 | −134.666 |
| Owner | | | |
| Households | −53.602 | −114.376 | −173.300 |
| Tax-exempt institutions | 63.805 | 97.954 | 126.388 |
| Insurance companies | 40.362 | 47.110 | 54.517 |
| Overall tax rate | 6.448 | −11.064 | −27.550 |

during the first ten years, but also, more significantly, because of the very favorable investment grant. The effects of the investment incentives on machinery are perverse. At low rates of inflation, the partial loss of the tax shield on debt results in higher marginal effective tax rates than in the rest of Italy. As inflation rises, the effective rate is driven down sharply by an increase in the value of the discount on new capital goods invested in the Mezzogiorno. The estimates for the Mezzogiorno also reveal a considerably lower effective tax rate for debt as a result of the much larger interest rate subsidies available through the special credit institutions, but retained earnings are also taxed more favorably because of the ten-year deferral of tax payments of ILOR.

## The Noncorporate Sector and Owner-Occupied Housing

The procedure for the computation of marginal effective tax rates on investments carried out in the noncorporate sector is similar to the one used for the corporate sector. However, only two methods of finance were considered, debt and proprietors' equity, and one category of investor, households, although in theory households could channel funds to the noncorporate sector indirectly through insurance companies. It was not possible to obtain separate data for investments in the noncorporate sector, so the weights used for corporate investment were assumed; the weighted averages shown in the table should, consequently, be treated with caution (table 6-21).

The pattern of effective marginal tax rates across industries and assets in the noncorporate sector is similar to that found for the corporate sector. The principal difference is the lower rate of tax and the much greater sensitivity to the rate of inflation. This is due to the tax treatment of debt finance in these simulations: interest payments by proprietors are set against their tax rate, which is nearly double the rate at which savers, who have lent the money, are taxed. The tax rate on proprietors' equity is also well below that on retained earnings and new share issues.

The marginal effective tax rates on owner-occupied housing (table 6-22) take into account the undervaluation of income from housing, which, as already mentioned, has been estimated at 50 percent of true imputable income. Deductibility of interest from personal income tax is considered, although only a small part of the housing stock owned by households is financed by mortgages.

Inflation has a negative impact on the effective tax rates because the adjustment coefficients to changes in property prices are not automatic. If

Table 6-21. *Marginal Effective Tax Rates under Different Inflation Rates, Fixed-*p*, Noncorporate Sector, 1985*
Percent

| Item | Expected rate of inflation (percent) | | |
|---|---|---|---|
| | 0 | 5 | 10 |
| Industry | | | |
| Manufacturing | 10.4 | 2.7 | −6.6 |
| Other industry | 18.0 | 9.7 | 0.6 |
| Commerce | 14.7 | 11.4 | 5.8 |
| Asset | | | |
| Machinery | −2.3 | −4.4 | −8.4 |
| Buildings | 12.1 | 9.3 | 3.0 |
| Inventories | 33.9 | 18.8 | 3.8 |
| Method of finance | | | |
| Debt | −12.2 | −33.8 | −57.9 |
| Proprietors' equity | 26.4 | 29.4 | 30.8 |
| Owner | | | |
| Households | 12.5 | 6.6 | −1.2 |
| Overall tax rate | 12.5 | 6.6 | −1.2 |

Table 6-22. *Marginal Effective Tax Rates under Different Inflation Rates, Owner-Occupied Housing, 1980, 1985, 1990*
Percent

| Year | Expected rate of inflation (percent) | | |
|---|---|---|---|
| | 0 | 5 | 10 |
| 1980 | 9.3 | 8.4 | 7.3 |
| 1985 | 7.2 | 6.6 | 6.1 |
| 1990 | 9.3 | 8.4 | 7.3 |

the coefficient were indexed to inflation, the taxation of owner-occupied housing would show a positive relationship with inflation. The lesser values for 1985 reflect the ten-year deferral provision applied on ILOR tax payments in that year.

### Recent Changes in Legislation

In this section we consider the effects of the following recent changes: the modification of the system of depreciation allowances in the Testo Unico which was implemented in 1987 (and subsequently amended); the abolition of negative IVA; the lowering of taxes on personal income, particularly of the *imposta sostitutiva*; and modifications in the distribution

Table 6-23.  *Marginal Effective Tax Rates under Different Inflation Rates, 1990*

Percent

| | Zero rate of inflation | | | Total effective tax rate | |
|---|---|---|---|---|---|
| | | | | 5 percent | 10 percent |
| Item | Total | Personal | Corporate | inflation | inflation |
| Industry | | | | | |
| Manufacturing | 25.2 | 29.0 | −5.4 | 23.3 | 19.3 |
| Other industry | 28.2 | 29.5 | −1.8 | 25.7 | 22.3 |
| Commerce | 31.2 | 29.6 | 2.2 | 33.9 | 33.4 |
| Asset | | | | | |
| Machinery | 14.7 | 29.3 | −20.6 | 18.2 | 19.6 |
| Buildings | 35.5 | 29.3 | 8.8 | 38.8 | 36.9 |
| Inventories | 36.7 | 29.2 | 10.5 | 27.6 | 18.5 |
| Method of finance | | | | | |
| Debt | −5.2 | 15.7 | −24.9 | −28.1 | −54.6 |
| New share issues | 59.5 | 40.0 | 32.5 | 81.4 | 101.8 |
| Retained earnings | 46.4 | 40.0 | 10.7 | 59.2 | 70.1 |
| Owner | | | | | |
| Households | 30.3 | 32.3 | −3.0 | 32.0 | 31.3 |
| Tax-exempt institutions | 41.9 | 38.3 | 5.9 | 50.9 | 57.8 |
| Insurance companies | −6.1 | −5.9 | −0.2 | −29.6 | −56.8 |
| Overall tax rate | 27.8 | 29.3 | −2.1 | 27.7 | 25.1 |

of wealth across assets.[42] The principal effects of these changes, as can be seen by comparing table 6-17 with table 6-23, are to increase the overall effective tax rate roughly 7 percentage points at zero inflation. This increase is the net outcome of two partly offsetting movements. On the one hand, there is a decline in the overall effective rate of subsidy at the corporate level, from 20 percent in 1985 to 2 percent. On the other hand, the overall effective rate of tax at the personal level contracts from 34 to 29 percent. At the corporate level there is a dramatic increase in the effective tax rate on buildings (from −21 to 9 percent), which are the assets most affected by the new depreciation schedules (table 6-6). Commerce and other services are the sectors in which investments in buildings carry the largest weight, a fact mirrored in the very sizable increase in the tax rates (nearly 20 percentage points).

As regards manufacturing and other industry, the lifting of negative IVA for investments in machinery contributes to roughly the same increase

42. A law recently ratified by Parliament introduces capital gains tax for 1991. Taxpayers can elect to be taxed yearly at 25 percent on their net realized gains or at 21 percent on a presumptive gross gain.

in effective tax rates as the change in depreciation schedules. Another net outcome at the corporate level of all these changes is that the difference between effective tax rates considered from the point of view of the sources of finance has tended to narrow somewhat, although debt finance remains by far the most tax-favored. At the personal level, the shift in companies' borrowings from the banks to the special credit institutions and to a lesser extent to bonds is responsible for a lower rate of the *imposta sostitutiva*. This results in a roughly equivalent contraction in the effective personal rate of tax on debt-financed investments from 22 percent in 1985 to 16 percent. Similarly, the small reduction in the marginal taxation of dividends entails a decline in the personal tax on equity-financed investments. On balance, the taxation of households falls from 37 percent in 1985 to 32 percent.

In 1990 the overall effective tax rate appears rather insensitive to different levels of the rate of inflation below 10 percent, but declines quite markedly beyond this level. This finding is similar to that observed for the tax laws of 1985. At the 10 percent inflation level the distribution and actual value of effective tax rates is very similar to that recorded in 1985. The principal differences recorded between the years concern, on the one hand, the much higher effective tax rates for buildings and commerce in 1990, and, on the other hand, the much lower values for inventories.

## Conclusion

Although our study is far from exhaustive, we can draw several tentative conclusions about the taxation of income from capital in 1985. First, on balance, effective tax rates in Italy are low, particularly if the corporate sector is treated in isolation. These low rates occur because of a combination of high depreciation allowances, major interest-rate subsidies, and low taxes on interest income received by households directly or through insurance companies. Second, the combination of these provisions makes the tax system rather insensitive to changes in the rate of inflation; it is as if income from capital were indexed for inflation. Third, since local income taxes do not receive a tax credit and dividends are treated rather unfavorably compared with other forms of receipts of capital income, the effective tax rate on projects financed through new share issues is always the highest, particularly when there is tax exhaustion under IRPEG.

These conclusions need to be modified somewhat in light of changes in the tax system that have taken place since 1985. The balance between the taxation of capital income at the corporate and personal levels has been redressed largely through a significant scaling back of many favorable tax provisions at the company level. Nevertheless, the tax burden on capital income produced in the private sector is borne entirely at the personal level whereas, at the company level, investments are still subsidized. This dichotomy will acquire a greater importance as Italian savers and investors become more exposed to the international capital markets.

Very different findings apply to projects carried out in the Mezzogiorno, which account for one-third of total investments and are heavily subsidized. It is difficult to determine whether, in practice, the Mezzogiorno should be treated separately from the rest of the country, because tax arbitrages with investments in other areas (particularly through intracompany transfer pricing transactions) are said to be common. If account had been taken of these subsidies in the computation of aggregate effective tax rates, the taxation of capital income in Italy would have been by far the lowest in Europe.

Table 6A-1. *Real After-Tax Return to Savings*

| Method of finance | Household | Tax-exempt institution | Life insurance company |
|---|---|---|---|
| Debt | $i(1 - m_b) - \pi$ | $i(1 - m_b) - \pi - w_p$ | $\frac{i(1-\tau_I)(1-m_I)-\pi}{(1-\mu\tau)(1-m)}$ |
| New shares | $\rho\theta(1 - m_s) - \pi$ | $\rho\theta(1 - m_s) - \pi - w_p$ | $[\rho/(1 - \tau)] - \pi$ |
| Retained earnings | $\rho - \pi$ | $\rho - \pi - w_p$ | $\frac{\rho-\pi}{1-\tau}$ |

$m_b$    Marginal personal tax rate on interest income
$i$    Nominal interest rate
$\pi$    Inflation rate
$\rho$    Rate of return net of corporation taxes
$\theta$    Opportunity cost of retained earnings in terms of gross dividends forgone
$\tau$    Statutory corporation tax rate
$w_p$    Effective average personal wealth tax rate
$\tau_I$    Life insurance statutory tax rate
$m_I$    Present value of marginal personal income tax on deferred (capitalized) income
$m_s$    Marginal personal tax rate on dividend income
$z$    Effective accrued tax rate on capital gains
$m$    Marginal personal tax rate of income.

# References

Alworth, Julian S. 1986. "Taxation and the Cost of Capital: A Comparison of Six EC Countries." In *Tax Coordination in the Economic Community*, edited by Sijbren Cnossen, 253–83. Deventer: Kluwer.

Alworth, Julian S., and Laura Castellucci. 1987. "The Taxation of Income from Capital in Italy (1960–1986)."

Alworth, Julian S., and Franco Fornasari. 1982. "Profits in Italian Industry: Methodological Notes and Empirical Estimates, 1969–1980." *Rivista di Politica Economica Selected Papers*, 3–40.

Barca, Fabrizio, and Mariella Magnani. 1985. "Ristrutturazione e disinvestimento anticipato nella medio-grande industria italiana." *Contributi all'analisi economica del servizio studi* 1. Roma: Banca d'Italia.

Bernareggi, Gian Maria. 1986. "Effetti della tassazione dei titoli pubblici in Italia." *Economia Pubblica*, April–May.

Banca d'Italia. 1986a. "Gli effetti della modifica dell'IRPEF." *Bollettino Economico* 7: 1–10.

——. 1986b. "La ricchezza delle famiglie in Italia (1975–85)." *Bollettino Economico* 7: 11–24.

——. *Relazione annuale*. Rome.

Campa, Giuseppe. 1986. "L'esperienza dell'IVA negativa negli anni 1977–82." In *Politiche tributarie e struttura industriale in Italia*, edited by Antonio Ledone, 19–40. Bologna: Il Mulino.

Cobb, Charles J., and Francesco Forte. 1964. *Taxation in Italy*. Chicago: Commerce Clearing House.

Di Maio, Antonio, and D. Franco. 1987: "Gli effetti delle imposte sulla convenienza a detenere titoli pubblici in Italia 1974–86." *Moneta e Credito* 40 (March): 75–103.

Guerra, Maria Cecilia. 1989. *Imposte e mercati finanziari*. Bologna: Il Mulino.

Istituto Nazionale di Statistica (ISTAT). 1976. *Annuario di Contabilità Nazionale*, vol. 6.

Mediobanca. 1987. *Dati cumulativi di 1603 società italiane*. Milano: Mediobanca.

Ministero delle Finanze. *Analisi delle dichiarazioni dei redditi presentate dalle persone giuridiche*.

Parravicini, Giannino. 1971. *Lineamenti dell'ordinamento tributario: Con appendice sul bilancio dello stato*. Milan: Giuffré.

Rosa, Giuseppe. 1979. *Lo stock di capitale nell'industria Italia: Nuove stime settoriali e territoriali*. Rome: Centro Studi Confindustria.

Rosa, Giuseppe, and Vincenzo Siesto. 1985. *Il capitale fisso industriale: Stime settoriale e verifiche dirette*. Bologna: Il Mulino.

Silvestri, Paolo. 1983 "Agevolazioni sul credito e contributi in conto capitale (1964-1979)." In *Trasferimenti dello stato alle imprese industriali negli anni settanta*, edited by Pippo Ranci, 17–33. Bologna: Il Mulino.

Spaventa, Luigi 1987. "Effetti della tassazione dei titoli pubblici in Italia: Una nota." *Economia Pubblica*, January–February.

# CHAPTER SEVEN

# Japan

*Toshiaki Tachibanaki*
*Tatsuya Kikutani*

THE JAPANESE "miracle" of rapid economic growth in the postwar period and Japan's quick recovery from the oil crises of the 1970s have attracted many researchers. A high level of investment activity and a high rate of personal savings were two major causes of the so-called miracle.[1] It is possible that tax policies in Japan were helpful in achieving these goals. This chapter focuses on capital income taxation, one of many tax policy instruments, and investigates its effect on the cost of capital.

Mervyn A. King and Don Fullerton offered a comprehensive study of the capital income taxation for four countries—the United Kingdom, Sweden, West Germany, and the United States.[2] John Shoven and Toshiaki Tachibanaki, and Tatsuya Kikutani and Tachibanaki, applied King and Fullerton's method to Japan, using the Japanese tax code and institutional specifications.[3] The former looked at 1980; the latter examined the historical development starting in the 1960s. The purpose of this chapter is to extend these previous two analyses in several respects. First, new results for 1985 and 1990 are added. Second, some empirical results obtained in the previous studies are reinterpreted from different perspectives. Third, since Japan had an important tax reform in the field of interest-income taxation in 1988 and a major tax overhaul in the field of corporate in-

Earlier versions of this chapter were presented at a conference on the cost of capital at Harvard University in 1987; at a symposium, Steuerreform in der Bundesrepublik Deutschland und Japan, in Berlin in 1989; and at the annual conference of the Japan Society of Public Finance in Tokyo in 1991. The authors are grateful to Toshihiro Ihori, Robert Jones, Willi Leibfritz, and Jan Södersten for their useful comments.

1. See, for example, Tachibanaki (1988).
2. King and Fullerton (1984).
3. Shoven and Tachibanaki (1988); Kikutani and Tachibanaki (1990).

come taxation, together with the introduction of a value-added tax in 1989, simulations are attempted as a means of examining these reforms.

Detailed examinations of Japanese tax codes in relation to the taxation of capital income may be found in the previous studies. Nevertheless, it may be useful to briefly summarize their results.

For corporate sectors, some items should be investigated: the tax rate on corporate income, at both the national and the local levels; the reduction in the tax rate for dividend payout to avoid double taxation, which is known as the *two-rate system;* and the enterprise tax, which is one of the most important local taxes, and which is deductible in calculating the next year's taxable income. Also in need of investigation are the wealth tax, which is deductible in calculating the current year's taxable income and normal and special depreciation allowances (special depreciation is a form of accelerated depreciation that allows the first-year depreciation by the constant proportion of the acquisition cost; this first-year depreciation recently has lost some importance). In addition, tax-free reserves and allowances need to be considered. Although policies for reserves and allowances are aimed at reducing the tax burdens of corporations, they actually defer only tax payments. Finally there is the first in, first out (FIFO) accounting method applied to inventory. It is interesting to note that there have been no major reforms with respect to these items since the drastic reforms undertaken during the immediate postwar period. Since then, only various tax parameters and the legal lifetimes of machinery have been reformed by the Japanese government.

For household sectors, comprehensive income taxation was a principle in the period of the Shoup reform after World War II. This system can be described by the Haig-Simon principle, which states that all sources of income are summed up, and then taxed on this sum. After that period the principle of comprehensive income taxation was eroded, which meant that households were able to choose between comprehensive income taxation and separate taxation on each source of income. Moreover, tax-free saving accounts within a certain limitation were allowed in order to promote higher savings. This system was widely abused, and the effective tax rate on interest income was lowered significantly. In April 1988 this tax-free saving account was abolished as a result of the widely recognized abuses, and a separate 20 percent withholding tax rate was introduced for application to interest income.

As for the taxation of dividend income, a taxpayer was allowed to choose a separate tax rate. Moreover, part of the dividend received was deductible from taxable income. These arrangements were introduced for the purpose of weakening the double taxation on dividend income. The most important feature of capital-income taxation is the fact that the effective tax rate on capital gains from stockholding has been nearly zero for households except in cases of voluminous and frequent transactions. It should be pointed out, however, that as the banking sector is included in the household sector, the effective tax rate on capital gains is not zero but positive. The banking sector engages in large and frequent transactions in both stocks and equities in Japan. The effective tax rate on capital gains in the banking sector was calculated under several assumptions.[4]

## The Effective Marginal Tax Rate on Capital Income

Kikutani and Tachibanaki estimated the effective marginal tax rates in 1961, 1970, and 1980 based on the fixed-$p$ case.[5] The tax wedge ($p - s$), where $p$ is the before-tax real rate of return on one unit of investment net of depreciation and $s$ is the after-tax real rate of return to the saver that supplied the finance for one unit of investment. The effective marginal tax rate is calculated by $t = (p - s)/p$, which varies depending on the asset type, industrial sector, source of finance, and owner of the returns. Detailed explanations of the various asset types, industrial sectors, sources of finance, and ownership categories are given in the studies by King and Fullerton, Shoven and Tachibanaki, and Kikutani and Tachibanaki.

A total of eighty-one hypothetical projects can be made by considering three categories for each of the four characteristics. The overall mean tax wedge, $\bar{w}$, is calculated by $\bar{w} = \sum_{k=1}^{81}(p_k - s_k)\,\alpha_k$, where $\alpha_k$ is the capital stock weight of the $k$th combination. It is possible to calculate not only the overall mean tax wedge divided by $p$ but also the conditional mean marginal tax rates. Finally, changes in the marginal effective tax rates occur not only when the value of tax parameters is changed but also when the weights described above are changed.

The effective rate is calculated, assuming that the before-tax rate of return to a one-unit investment is 10 percent. This is called the fixed-$p$ case. Since it was found previously that the estimated effective tax rate in Japan was insensitive to the value of $p$, provided that the value of $p$

4. Kikutani and Tachibanaki (1990).
5. Kikutani and Tachibanaki (1990).

would be higher than 8 percent, a hypothetical value, 10 percent, should be acceptable in the fixed-$p$ case. It would be possible to calculate the effective tax rate for a given real interest rate $r$. In some cases, however, the value of the discount factor turned out negative in Japan. Therefore, the fixed-$r$ case is not adopted.

### Results for 1985

Table 7-1 shows the estimated marginal effective tax rates for each category, and the overall means for 1985. Since taxable incomes are usually measured in nominal terms, the effective tax rate is influenced by the rate of inflation unless taxes are fully indexed to inflation. Thus, various inflation rates are considered, including 0 percent, 5 percent, 10 percent and 1.43 percent (the average of actual annual inflation rates in 1981–85). This actual figure is the average of consumer and wholesale price indexes. The low value shows that the rate of inflation in recent years has been much lower than in the 1970s.

The overall effective marginal tax rate is equal to 28.8 percent in 1985 with no inflation. This value is nearly equal to the value in 1980. There are two major changes in the tax parameters for the corporate sector between 1980 and 1985. The first is the increase in the corporate income-tax rate (mainly for retained earnings) from 40.0 to 43.3 percent, and the second is the increase, from 30.0 to 33.3 percent, in the tax rate for dividends paid. The share of debt financing in the manufacturing and commerce sectors also increased during the period. Debt financing in Japan reduces a corporation's tax burden as described in Shoven and Tachibanaki, and in Kikutani and Tachibanaki. Those effects, namely a change in tax parameters and a change in the source of financing, produced an unchanged value of the effective tax rate on capital income, by canceling each other out.

Table 7-1 shows that the overall tax rate decreases drastically with increases in the rate of inflation. This is one of the most notable features of capital income taxation in Japan, and is confirmed in the international comparison given by Shoven and Tachibanaki and by Kikutani and Tachibanaki.

It may be useful to summarize why this feature appears in relation to inflation in Japan. Normally, the interest paid by a firm is deductible from the calculation of taxable income. Therefore, a deduction lowers the cost

Table 7-1.  *Marginal Effective Tax Rates in Japan under Different Inflation Rates, Fixed-p, 1985 and Selected Previous Years*

Percent

| Item | Inflation rate (percent) | | | |
|---|---|---|---|---|
| | 0 | 5 | 10 | Actual |
| | *1985* | | | |
| Asset | | | | |
| Machinery | 26.7 | 17.6 | 4.4 | 24.6 |
| Buildings | 26.1 | 14.5 | −3.1 | 23.7 |
| Inventories | 37.2 | 18.4 | −1.1 | 32.0 |
| Industry | | | | |
| Manufacturing | 28.1 | 17.0 | 2.0 | 25.5 |
| Other industry | 30.2 | 16.6 | −1.3 | 26.8 |
| Commerce | 29.4 | 16.0 | −1.1 | 26.1 |
| Source of Finance | | | | |
| Debt | −2.1 | −39.4 | −81.5 | −12.1 |
| New share issues | 55.6 | 67.7 | 77.9 | 59.3 |
| Retained earnings | 55.7 | 65.5 | 71.9 | 59.0 |
| Owner | | | | |
| Households | 27.4 | 13.7 | −4.1 | 24.1 |
| Tax-exempt institutions | 25.3 | 11.4 | −5.8 | 21.8 |
| Insurance companies | 36.2 | 31.7 | 24.4 | 35.3 |
| Overall tax rate | 28.8 | 16.7 | 0.6 | 25.9 |
| | *1961* | | | |
| Overall tax rate | 27.2 | . . . | . . . | 24.7 |
| | *1970* | | | |
| Overall tax rate | 22.0 | . . . | . . . | 15.0 |
| | *1980* | | | |
| Overall tax rate | 28.7 | 18.2 | 4.7 | 9.6 |

Sources: Results for 1961, 1970, and 1980 based on Kikutani and Tachibanaki (1989); results for 1985 based on authors' estimates.

of capital. Interest incomes received by the household sector, which deposits savings in banks, must be taxed at the tax rate $m$. The cost of capital is then reduced by $(\tau - m)$ with debt financing when all other parameters are held constant. Normally, $\tau > m$ is observed in the real world. The larger is the difference, the larger is the decrease in the effective tax rate associated with a given amount of debt financing. This is demonstrated by the following partial derivative, which is derived easily by ignoring other effects such as depreciation allowances: $dt/d\pi = -(\tau - m)/(1 - \tau)p$, where $\pi$ is the rate of inflation. Japan had a high value of $\tau$ and a low

Table 7-2.  *Marginal Effective Tax Rates under Different Inflation Rates, Assuming Share of Debt Finance Is Zero and Proportion of New Share Issues and Retained Earnings Is Held Constant*
Percent

| | Inflation rate (percent) | | |
|---|---|---|---|
| *Asset* | *0* | *5* | *Actual* |
| Machinery | 54.3 | 66.0 | 58.1 |
| Buildings | 54.2 | 64.3 | 57.8 |
| Inventories | 61.4 | 67.3 | 63.4 |

Source: Authors' calculations.

value of *m* relative to those in other industrialized countries. This is the main reason that the effective tax rate is a decreasing function of inflation.

The role of debt financing has been far more important than that of the other sources in Japan. Thus, this characteristic reinforced the effect of debt financing on lowering the burden of capital income, which is shown by the lower value of the overall mean when the inflation rate is high.

That feature, however, is no longer applicable because the rate of inflation in Japan has been very low in recent years. Japan no longer enjoys a lower effective tax rate on capital income. This is an interesting observation, and it will be interesting to see how Japanese firms react to this change. The federation of Japanese employers has already started to complain about the high tax burden for firms.

The result in table 7-1 can be examined more carefully by focusing on each category. With respect to the asset type it is found that inventories show a high rate. This is due mainly to the fact that depreciation allowances are not taken into consideration for inventory investments. For machinery and buildings the amount of depreciation allowance is evaluated on a historical cost basis. When the rate of inflation is high, the real value of depreciation is lowered. Thus it is likely that the effective tax rate would increase. The empirical results in table 7-1, however, show the opposite outcome. This is largely due to the effect of debt financing. More specifically, since a relatively high rate of investments for machinery and buildings has been financed by debt, the effect of debt financing has been stronger than the effect of lower inflation rates. Table 7-2 is presented to confirm this argument. It shows the result of a simulation under the assumption that the amount of debt is zero and the proportion of new share issues and retained earnings is kept constant. It shows that the effective tax rates for all assets are increased.

Table 7-3.  *Marginal Effective Tax Rates under Different Inflation Rates, Assuming Source of Finance for Tax-Exempt Institutions and Insurance Companies Is Same as That for Households*
Percent

| | Inflation rate (percent) | | |
| Item | 0 | 5 | Actual |
|---|---|---|---|
| Owner | | | |
| Households | 30.4 | 19.2 | 27.8 |
| Tax-exempt institutions | 20.0 | 1.6 | 15.2 |
| Insurance companies | 24.7 | 10.4 | 21.1 |
| Overall tax rate | 25.0 | 10.4 | 21.4 |

Source: Authors' calculations.

For the ownership category it is interesting that the effective tax rates for tax-exempt institutions are only marginally lower than those for households. Initially this fact may be surprising because the effective marginal tax rates for tax-exempt institutions in other countries are much lower than those for households. This difference arises from a somewhat unusual feature of the finance structure in Japan. Since equity holdings are relatively more important for tax-exempt institutions than they are for households, debt does not strongly affect the former's tax rate.

Table 7-3 presents evidence to support this conjecture. It shows a simulation under the assumption that the proportional allocation of available funds to debt and other sources is the same for both tax-exempt institutions tions and insurance companies, as well as for households. We find that the effective tax rates for tax-exempt institutions and insurance companies are lower than those for households. This simulation also suggests one reason why the marginal effective tax rate for insurance companies is high. Insurance companies in Japan hold a relatively high proportion of equities.

Table 7-4 is presented to support the above argument. It shows that the weight of tax-exempt institutions, among the various owner categories, is much lower in Japan than in other countries, but the weight of insurance companies is significantly higher. This may reflect the fact that the role of enterprise pension programs is relatively minor in Japan. The majority of tax-exempt institutions in the United Kingdom and the United States are pension funds and related institutions. However, since the growth rate of enterprise pension programs has recently been higher in Japan, a different story may be told in the future.

Table 7-4.   *Share of Debt and Equity by Various Owners, Japan, United Kingdom, United States, 1980, 1985*

| Country, year, category | Households | Tax-exempt institutions | Insurance companies |
|---|---|---|---|
| Japan, 1985 | | | |
| Debt | 0.8781 | 0.0323 | 0.0896 |
| Equity | 0.7182 | 0.0457 | 0.2360 |
| Japan, 1980 | | | |
| Debt | 0.8586 | 0.0196 | 0.1216 |
| Equity | 0.7615 | 0.0333 | 0.2051 |
| United Kingdom, 1980 | | | |
| Debt | 0.7180 | 0.1370 | 0.1450 |
| Equity | 0.4350 | 0.4070 | 0.1570 |
| United States, 1980 | | | |
| Debt | 0.6094 | 0.2371 | 0.1534 |
| Equity | 0.7433 | 0.2154 | 0.0412 |

Sources: Results for Japan based on authors' estimates; results for the United Kingdom and United States based on King and Fullerton (1984).

## Past Results

Because we made a detailed evaluation of historical changes in the estimated effective marginal tax rates in our earlier study, we give here only a brief summary of historical changes. But we also present some new findings not found in that previous study.[6]

The last three rows in table 7-1 show that there was only a minor fluctuation in the effective tax rates. It is interesting to note that the effective tax rate in the absence of inflation was lowest in 1970, a period of rapid economic growth. There are several reasons for this low tax rate. First, nominal corporate tax rates were low, especially the dividend tax rate.[7] Second, the effect of special depreciation allowances, and of tax-free reserves and allowances, was relatively stronger. Third, the role of debt financing was important on average for all industries.

The effective tax rate was the lowest in 1980 for the actual inflation-rate case, mainly because of the high inflation rate of the 1970s. Incidentally, the inflation rate was 8.25 percent in 1980, 3.19 percent in 1970, and 1.28 percent in 1960. Moreover, the degree of reduction in the effective tax rate is dramatic as the rate of inflation increases. This feature was also observed in 1985, as noted earlier. It was concluded that the main cause

6. Kikutani and Tachibanaki (1990).
7. Kikutani (1988).

for the negative relationship between effective tax rates and inflation was the Japanese way of debt financing. During the period of relatively high inflation the cost of capital may have been reduced significantly, and so raised the degree of investment activity due mainly to the lower effective tax rate on capital income. Although there are many detrimental effects of inflation, one of the few advantages resulting from it was the lower effective tax rate on capital income, which may have helped the Japanese macroeconomy during and after the oil crises of the 1970s. Unlike in Japan, an increase in the effective tax rate along with an increase in the inflation rate was observed in the United States. This may be one cause of the relatively poor performance of the American economy during that period. This interpretation of the different experience of the Japanese and American economies is only speculation and merits a more careful examination.

### International Comparison

Table 7-5 presents results for five countries, namely the United Kingdom, Sweden, West Germany, the United States, and Japan. Only a few important comments are made here to minimize repetition. Under zero inflation the largest change in the effective tax rate occurs in the United Kingdom, mainly because of the frequent changes in the tax code, as pointed out by King.[8] West Germany and Japan show only minor changes in the effective tax rates. Although the effective tax rate in West Germany had been higher by about 17 to 24 percentage points than that in Japan,

Table 7-5.  *Marginal Effective Tax Rates for Five Countries under Different Inflation Rates, Fixed-p, 1960, 1970, 1980*
Percent

|  |  | Inflation rate (percent) | | | | | | | | |
|  | Actual inflation rate | 1960 | | | 1970 | | | 1980 | | |
| Country |  | 0 | 10 | Actual | 0 | 10 | Actual | 0 | 10 | Actual |
|---|---|---|---|---|---|---|---|---|---|---|
| United Kingdom | 13.6 | 35.3 | 50.4 | 53.8 | 7.4 | 27.7 | 33.6 | 12.6 | 6.6 | 3.7 |
| Sweden | 9.4 | 22.6 | 34.6 | 33.9 | 24.3 | 42.7 | 41.6 | 12.9 | 37.0 | 35.6 |
| West Germany | 4.2 | 49.4 | 50.4 | 52.5 | 46.7 | 45.7 | 49.1 | 45.1 | 46.1 | 48.1 |
| United States | 6.77 | 44.9 | 48.3 | 48.4 | 43.8 | 47.4 | 47.2 | 32.0 | 38.4 | 37.2 |
| Japan | 8.25 | 27.2 | 3.3 | 8.1 | 22.0 | -3.2 | 1.8 | 28.7 | 4.7 | 9.6 |

Sources: Results for countries other than Japan based on King and Fullerton (1984); results for Japan based on authors' estimates.

8. King (1977).

Table 7-6. *Parameter Values for the Corporate Tax Rate (τ) and the Effective Tax Rate on Interest Income (m), Five Countries, 1980*

| Country | τ | m | τ − m |
|---|---|---|---|
| United Kingdom | 52.0 | 30.55 | 21.45 |
| Sweden | 34.9 | 49.20 | −14.30 |
| West Germany | 62.0 | 39.80 | 22.20 |
| United States | 49.5 | 28.40 | 21.10 |
| Japan | 52.6 | 11.44 | 41.17 |

Sources: Results for countries other than Japan based on King and Fullerton (1984); results for Japan based on authors' calculations.

these two countries showed higher rates of economic growth than did other Organization for Economic Cooperation and Development (OECD) countries. The effective tax rates in Sweden and the United States decreased considerably in 1980 because of the major tax reforms enacted in the two countries.

Following is an examination of the effective tax rates for the actual inflation rates. (The Japanese case has already been examined.) Table 7-6 shows the difference between the corporate tax rate and the effective tax rate on interest incomes for various countries. This table is useful in understanding the influence of inflation. The United Kingdom is interesting because inflation raised the effective tax rate until 1970 and lowered the tax burden in 1980, as in Japan. One important reason for this switch is that immediate depreciation (or first-year write-off) had a strong influence in 1980.[9]

West Germany shows a very minor effect of inflation, as does the United States. Sweden's case is opposite to Japan's because in Sweden inflation raises the effective tax rate significantly. As table 7-7 shows,

Table 7-7. *Sources of Finance, Five Countries, 1980*

Percent

| Country | Debt | New share issue | Retained earnings |
|---|---|---|---|
| United Kingdom | 19.3 | 4.4 | 76.3 |
| Sweden | 52.2 | 2.0 | 45.8 |
| West Germany | 43.6 | 4.9 | 51.5 |
| United States | 33.8 | 4.9 | 61.3 |
| Japan | 46.1 | 4.4 | 49.5 |

Sources: Results for countries other than Japan based on King and Fullerton (1984); results for Japan based on authors' estimates.

9. King and Fullerton (1984).

Title 7-8.   *Marginal Effective Tax Rates under Different Inflation Rates, Corporate Sector, Japan and the United States, Selected Years, 1961–85*

Percent

| Country and year | Inflation rate (percent) | | |
|---|---|---|---|
| | *0* | *10* | *Actual* |
| Japan | | | |
| 1961 | 19.8 | −16.4 | 15.7 |
| 1970 | 14.0 | −23.2 | 3.2 |
| 1980 | 19.7 | −17.2 | −10.0 |
| 1985 | 19.2 | −22.1 | 14.4 |
| United States | | | |
| 1980 | 17.1 | 1.0 | 7.7 |

Source: Table 7-8 through table 7-17 are authors' calculations.

the role of debt financing is only slightly more important in Sweden than in Japan. At first glance the result for Sweden may appear to be strange. As table 7-6 shows clearly, the effective tax rate on interest income in Sweden is extremely high, while the corporate tax rate is relatively low. Consequently, $\tau - m$ is negative in Sweden, and the effective tax rate on capital income decreases as the rate of inflation increases.

### Decomposition of Effective Tax Rates

In this part we examine the contribution of the corporate sector and the personal sector to the total effective marginal tax rate. This enables us to examine whether the Japanese tax system, particularly regarding capital income, encourages savings and discourages investment. At the same time, we compare the corporate and personal sectors in Japan with those in the United States. This comparison provides a basis for the next section's analysis of international capital mobility between Japan and the United States.

Table 7-8 shows a simulation result under the condition that taxes on the personal sector are removed. The table presents overall effective tax rates, which can be regarded as the tax rates on the corporate sector. Under the zero inflation rate the effective rate in 1970 was lower while the rates in other years were roughly the same. This confirms the previous assertion that the low effective tax rate in 1970 was lower than in other years because of the low tax rate on the corporate sector.

A comparison of the rates for Japan and the United States for 1980 shows that Japan's rank is higher by 2.6 percentage points. Given the current sources of financing, it is possible to conclude that Japan discourages investment somewhat more strongly than the United States does. If the U.S. share of debt financing is used, the effective tax rate for the Japanese corporate sector at the zero inflation rate is 30.2 percent, which is twice the American rate. Although the Japanese rate in 1985 is almost the same as in 1980, the rate in the United States after 1981 would be lower than in 1980 because the Reagan administration adopted the Economic Recovery Tax Act in 1981. The 1986 tax reform in the United States, however, changed the tax system significantly. It is likely that this reform again increased the tax burden on the U.S. corporate sector.

Since higher inflation rates in both Japan and the United States lowered the effective tax rate for the corporate sector, debtors—mainly corporations that borrowed funds from banks and others—benefited significantly. The degree of the benefit in Japan is about two times higher than that in the United States. The effective tax rate in Japan, for example, for the actual rate of inflation is −10 percent. This is a subsidy to the corporate sector by the government. However, the recent inflation rate in Japan is very low, and the effective tax rate for the actual inflation rate is 14.4 percent. As noted previously, the United States has had two major tax reforms recently. It would be interesting to compare the current effective tax rate for the corporate sector in Japan and the United States on the basis of actual inflation rates.

Table 7-9 shows the effective tax rates for the personal sector. Under the zero inflation rate, Japan has a 5.7 percentage point lower tax rate in 1980 than the United States. Thus Japan encourages savings more strongly than the United States. As the rate of inflation increases, the effective rates in

Table 7-9.   *Marginal Effective Tax Rates under Different Inflation Rates, Personal Sector, Japan and the United States, Selected Years, 1961–85*
Percent

| | Inflation rate (percent) | | |
|---|---|---|---|
| *Country and year* | *0* | *10* | *Actual* |
| Japan | | | |
| 1961 | 7.4 | 19.7 | 9.0 |
| 1970 | 8.0 | 20.0 | 11.8 |
| 1980 | 9.2 | 21.9 | 19.6 |
| 1985 | 9.5 | 22.7 | 11.5 |
| United States | | | |
| 1980 | 14.9 | 37.4 | 29.5 |

both countries increase. This implies that the cost imposed on creditors is smaller in Japan than in the United States—a situation, as noted, largely due to Japan's low effective tax rate on interest incomes. If the U.S. tax rate on interest incomes in 1980 were to be applied, the Japanese effective tax rate for the personal sector would be 17.1 percent for the zero inflation rate, and 38.2 percent for the actual inflation rate. These values are higher than the corresponding U.S. values, and confirm our explanation.

### Capital Mobility and Marginal Effective Tax Rates

This section investigates the implication of the low effective tax rate on interest income in Japan compared with that in the United States. Note that international capital mobility has been an important phenomenon recently. In other words, the effective marginal tax rates are evaluated for an open economy with capital mobility.

Tax laws, which attempt to avoid international double taxation, are prepared in both Japan and the United States. When a firm in one country collects investment funds from a second country, it is normal practice for the firm to pay tax on returns from the investment to its own country, and to pay personal tax in the second country.

Several parameters are specified before we examine the tax system under international capital mobility.

— *TJC:* the effective marginal tax rate for the corporate sector in Japan.

— *TAC:* the effective marginal tax rate for the corporate sector in the United States.

— *TJP:* the effective marginal tax rate for the personal sector in Japan.

— *TAP:* the effective marginal tax rate for the personal sector in the United States.

A total of four cases can be devised by combining the locations of the firm and of the supplier of funds.

1.  A firm in Japan collects funds in Japan: *TJC* plus *TJP*.
2.  A firm in Japan collects funds in the United States: *TJC* plus *TAP*.
3.  A firm in the United States collects funds in Japan: *TAC* plus *TJP*.
4.  A firm in the United States collects funds in the United States: *TAC* plus *TAP*.

The rank of the combined effective marginal tax rates for the four cases is examined. Although our method is simpler and less sophisticated than that used by Julian S. Alworth, who investigated the effect of international capital mobility on the cost of capital,[10] our result will be useful in understanding the effect of international taxation.

It is necessary to consider the weight of four categories—assets, industries, sources of finance, and ownerships—to calculate the overall effective tax rates for the two countries. We apply the capital stock weight in the fund-supplying country for the assets and industries and apply the share of sources of finance and the share of ownerships also in the fund-supplying country.

We evaluate only the zero-inflation case because of the wide difference in actual inflation rates between Japan and the United States in 1980. Based on results from previous sections, $TJC > TAC$ and $TJP < TAP$ may be observed. The results in table 7-5 suggest the following inequality: $TJC + TJP < TAC + TAP$. These inequalities lead us to the following rank: $3 < 1 < 4 < 2$. It implies that a firm located in the United States that collects funds or imports capital from Japan pays the lowest tax rate. Conversely, a firm in Japan that collects funds or imports capital from the United States pays the highest tax rate. This ranking is consistent with current international capital mobility between the two countries, namely a net capital outflow from Japan to the United States. The current account disequilibrium and the difference in interest rates between the two countries are also important reasons for the net capital outflow from Japan to the United States. The result in this chapter adds a third factor, namely the difference in the effective tax rates. Incidentally, when we look at the case of the actual inflation rate, the ranking is changed to $1 < 2 < 3 < 4$. This suggests that the role of inflation cannot be ignored in examining the effect of tax differences on international capital mobility. It is true, nevertheless, that the case of zero inflation rate is more useful in understanding the implications of the tax code differences between Japan and the United States.

Finally, the condition in 1985 is examined. In the United States this corresponds to the post-ERTA period. First, $TJC > TAC$ continues to hold, with the difference widening. Since the ERTA aimed at reducing the tax burden of the corporate sector, keeping the tax rate of the personal sector fairly constant, $TJP < TAP$ must also continue to hold. At the same time, King and Fullerton estimated that the overall effective tax rate

10. Alworth (1987).

after the ERTA was 21.4 percent for the zero inflation rate.[11] This value is lower than the Japanese rate in 1985. Combining the above results, it is possible to formulate the following ranking: $3 < 4 < 1 < 2$. The change in the ranking of 1 and 4 is the only difference between 1980 and 1985. Also, the effective tax rate in the case of 3 in 1985 must be much lower than the rate in 1980. These findings suggest that the ERTA encouraged capital outflows from Japan to the United States.

### Owner-Occupied Housing

In this section we estimate and discuss the effective tax rate for investment in owner-occupied housing. Because the tax system for residential housing construction is complicated in Japan, we need to explain the estimation procedure in some detail. Our method of estimation is based on K. Iwata, I. Suzuki, and A. Yoshida, as well as on King and Fullerton.[12] Six features of the tax system are explained: (1) no tax is levied on imputed rents; (2) no depreciation is considered; (3) no income allowance is provided for either the payment of interest on mortgage or for the tax payment on wealth (a local tax); (4) a tax allowance is provided for a new housing purchase to encourage owner-occupied housing; (5) a reduction of the wealth tax is possible; and (6) a land-acquisition tax (a local tax) is levied on new land.

We must take account of features 4, 5, and 6 in calculating the effective tax rate. The calculation of $p$ is

$$p = (1 - A)(\rho + \delta - \pi) - w_c - \delta,$$

where $A$ is the reduction of the tax payment due to features 4, 5, and 6. The amount of $A$ is given by the sum of $K$ (due to 4) and $G$ (due to 5), less $F$ (due to 6). In other words, $A = K + G - F$ is satisfied. We now explain $K, G,$ and $F$ briefly.

With respect to $K$, two conditions are imposed to qualify for a tax allowance. One concerns the floor area of the house, and the second concerns the unit cost of the house. We assume that both these conditions are satisfied to calculate the reduction in the wealth tax. Two different allowances are provided, namely a 50 percent reduction for the part (up to 100 m$^2$) of the floor area for the first three years of a wooden house,

---

11. King and Fullerton (1984).
12. Iwata, Suzuki, and Yoshida (1987); King and Fullerton (1984).

and for the first five years for a nonwooden house, respectively. Thus, $K$ is

$$K = \frac{1}{2}\left[\alpha \int_0^5 w_c e^{-\rho t} dt + \beta \int_0^3 w_c e^{-\rho t} dt\right]$$

$$= \frac{w_c}{2\rho}[\alpha(1 - e^{-5\rho}) + \beta(1 - e^{-3\rho})],$$

where $\alpha$ and $\beta$ are the proportion of nonwooden houses and of wooden houses, respectively.

With respect to $G$ three conditions are imposed: the duration of the mortgage, the value of the house, and the floor area. Two tax allowances are provided for the first three years. The first is 1.0 percent of the debt outstanding for a housing loan prepared by private banks and the second is the 0.5 percent for the Japan housing loan corporation (public) system. Thus, $G$ is

$$G = 0.01 \int_0^3 B_s e^{-\rho s} ds + 0.005 \int_0^3 B_s^* E^{-\rho s} ds$$

$$= 0.01 \, B_0\left[(1 - Q)\frac{e^{3(i-\rho)} - 1}{i - \rho} - \frac{Q}{\rho}(e^{-3\rho} - 1)\right]$$

$$+ 0.005 \, B_0\left[(1 - Q^*)\frac{e^{3(j-\rho)} - 1}{j - \rho} - \frac{Q^*}{\rho}(e^{-3\rho} - 1)\right],$$

where $Q = e^{in}/(e^{in} - 1)$, $Q^* = e^{jn}/(e^{jn} - 1)$, $i$ is the interest rate for a private bank, and $j$ is the one for the JHLC (public) system. $B_s$ and $B_s^*$ are the debts outstanding after $s$ years, and $B_0$ and $B_0^*$ are the initial debts. The superscript asterisk signifies the JHLC system; $n$ is the duration.

Finally, we assume that the effective tax rate on land-acquisition tax is zero because large reductions are provided to offset this tax in reality. Therefore, $F = 0$ can be reasonably assumed.

The nominal discount rate for each financial source in housing investment is calculated analogous to usual investments, with some modifications. The current work took account of several specific features of the Japanese financial system for housing loans. These modifications and specificities are not described in this chapter out of space considerations.

Table 7-10 shows the estimated effective marginal tax rates for owner-occupied housing for 1985 and 1990. For debt financing, the effective tax rates are negative. Moreover, the difference between housing loans

Table 7-10.  *Marginal Effective Tax Rates under Different Inflation Rates, Owner-Occupied Housing, Fixed-p, Japan, 1985, 1990*

Percent

| | Inflation rate (percent) | | | | | |
| | 1985 | | | 1990 | | |
| Item | 0 | 5 | 10 | 0 | 5 | 10 |
|---|---|---|---|---|---|---|
| Debt | | | | | | |
| Private | −1.8 | −0.8 | −0.3 | −1.6 | 0.1 | 1.4 |
| Public | −43.2 | −65.4 | −87.6 | −45.0 | −65.5 | −86.5 |
| Equity (self-finance) | −9.7 | −16.2 | −22.6 | −17.0 | −29.5 | −42.0 |
| Overall | −19.7 | −29.9 | −40.1 | −22.9 | −34.4 | −46.1 |

prepared by private banks and housing loans prepared by the public corporation is enormous because the effective interest rate at the JHLC is considerably lower than the interest rate at private banks. There is a strong subsidy to housing investment by public authority in Japan. For equity financing (self-financing), the effective tax rate is also negative, mainly owing to a reduction in the wealth tax because of the housing purchase. This reduction is also applicable to debt financing. The overall effective tax rate is negative largely because of the contribution of debt financing, in particular by the JHLC, and partly because of the contribution of equity financing. It is concluded that housing investment is heavily subsidized.

There is a minor difference between 1985 and 1990 with respect to the effective tax rates. There are three main reasons. The first is the introduction of a tax on interest incomes. The second is the change in the number of years of tax allowance in housing investment, namely from three to six years. The third is the introduction of a value-added tax. These changes marginally altered the values of the marginal tax rates for owner-occupied housing. However, detailed discussions are avoided because the effects of these changes can be understood straightforwardly.

## Simulations of Tax Reform

In recent years, Japan has had two major tax reforms. The first abolished tax-free savings accounts in April 1988, and the second introduced a value-added tax together with reforms of both personal income and corporate income taxes in April 1989. Because the overall impact of the reforms on the Japanese economy is very important, we evaluate both reforms.

### Increase in the Tax Rate on Interest Incomes

Japanese tax rates on interest and dividend incomes have been low for a long time. A typical example is tax-free savings accounts. In their 1988 study Shoven and Tachibanaki explained in detail how Japan achieved these low tax rates. There were criticisms of tax-free savings accounts because abuses of them had been quite common, in particular by wealthy households. In April 1988 the new tax code was introduced, abolishing tax-free savings accounts and introducing a separate withholding tax rate for households' interest income. However, tax-free savings accounts are still allowed for people age 65 and older, and savings for house purchases are still tax-free, with some limitations.

Table 7-11 shows simulation results for the case in which a separate 20 percent tax rate on interest income with the 1985 parameter values was introduced. At the zero inflation rate the overall marginal effective tax rate is increased by 4.0 percentage points. In particular, the effective tax rate for debt finance increases by 8.6 percentage points, and for households by 5.1 percentage points. These figures suggest that introducing a nonzero effective tax rate on interest income had a substantial impact, raising the effective tax rate on capital income. As the rate of inflation rises, the rate of increase in the effective tax rate on capital income becomes larger. For example, the overall tax rate increases by 7.4 percentage points at the 5 percent inflation rate. The rate for debt financing increases by 16.0 percentage points, and for households by 9.5 percentage points. Recently, the rate of inflation in Japan has been low. Thus, the simulation assuming a 5 percent inflation rate exaggerates the impact.

### Tax Reform of April 1989

The April 1989 tax reform was the most important tax reform in Japan since the Shoup reform after World War II. The main features of the 1989 reform are the introduction of a 3 percent value-added tax, the reduction of the burden of the personal income tax and simplification of the tax schedule, the reduction of the inheritance tax, the gradual reduction of the corporate income tax, and the introduction of a capital gains tax for households. Since the reduction in corporate tax rates is the most interesting means of evaluating firms' behavior, it is examined in this section. The other reforms are examined later.

Figures on the left-hand side in table 7-12 show the tax rates at the national level on corporate income. As the table shows clearly, there are

Table 7-11.  *Marginal Effective Tax Rates under the Abolition of Tax-Free Saving Accounts, with Different Inflation Rates*
Percent

| | Inflation rate (percent) | | | | | |
|---|---|---|---|---|---|---|
| | 0 | | 5 | | Actual | |
| Item | Before abolition | After abolition | Before abolition | After abolition | Before abolition | After abolition |
| Debt | −2.1 | 6.5 | −39.4 | −23.4 | −12.1 | −1.4 |
| Household | 27.4 | 32.5 | 13.7 | 23.2 | 24.1 | 30.4 |
| Overall | 28.8 | 32.8 | 16.7 | 24.1 | 25.9 | 30.9 |

two kinds of reforms. One is a reform in which the tax rate declines gradually. In the second the tax rates on retained earnings and dividends paid are equalized in 1990. Japan adopted a two-rate system to avoid double taxation; that is, a lower rate was applied for dividends paid than for retained earnings. However, this two-rate system was phased out, and it is possible to say that Japan has adopted the classical system.

Table 7-12 suggests the following findings. Abolishing the two-rate system has a smaller impact than reducing the basic rate under the zero inflation rate. The effective tax rate in 1990 is lowered by only 1.6 percentage points from the rate in 1985. This closely reflects the case of the actual inflation rate, which was 1.43 percent. However, when the inflation rate becomes high enough, such as 5 or 10 percent, the effective tax rate is actually increased.

Table 7-12.  *Reduction in Corporate Tax Rates and Marginal Effective Tax Rates under Different Inflation Rates, 1985, 1988, 1989, 1990*
Percent

| | | Inflation rate (percent) | | | |
|---|---|---|---|---|---|
| Year | Tax rate[a] | 0 | 5 | 10 | Actual |
| 1985 | 43.3 33.3 | 28.8 | 16.7 | 0.6 | 25.9 |
| 1988 | 42.0 32.0 | 28.4 | 17.2 | 2.3 | 25.7 |
| 1989 | 40.0 35.0 | 27.8 | 18.0 | 4.7 | 25.5 |
| 1990 | 37.5 37.5 | 27.2 | 18.8 | 7.4 | 25.2 |

a. Top number in each year is tax rate on retained earnings (basic rate); bottom number is tax rate on dividends paid.

Table 7-13.  *Reduction in Corporate Tax Rates (Basic Rates) and Marginal Effective Tax Rates under Different Inflation Rates*
Percent

| | Inflation rate (percent) | | | |
|---|---|---|---|---|
| Item | 0 | 5 | 10 | Actual |
| 1985 rate | 28.8 | 16.7 | 0.6 | 25.9 |
| Reduction by | | | | |
| 2.5 percentage points | 28.0 | 17.6 | 3.7 | 25.5 |
| 5.0 percentage points | 27.3 | 18.3 | 6.3 | 25.1 |
| 7.5 percentage points | 26.5 | 19.0 | 8.5 | 24.8 |
| 10.0 percentage points | 25.8 | 19.4 | 10.5 | 24.4 |

Table 7-13 is presented to support this finding. It shows how the effective tax rate changes when the tax rate on dividends paid is lowered by 2.5, 5.0, 7.5, and 10.0 percentage points. The simulation in table 7-13 suggests the following two interesting results.

First, for the zero inflation rate the effect of a decrease in the basic tax rate on a decrease in the effective rate is only about one-third of the reduction in the basic rate. This occurs largely because a reduction in the corporate tax rate reduces tax deductions due to depreciations and the tax-deductible interest paid. These effects obviously lower the benefit of debt financing. Hence, it is necessary to implement a larger decrease in the basic tax rate for the corporate sector in order to lower the tax burden.

Second, when the inflation rate is high enough, it is likely that the effective marginal tax rate is, in fact, increased rather than decreased. The higher the rate of inflation, the higher is the rate of increase in the effective tax rate. Although inflation lowers the effective tax rate on capital income, a decrease in the corporate tax rate cancels out this effect when the rate of inflation is sufficiently high.

We will examine the reason for this result more formally. A simple mathematical calculation, by ignoring depreciation allowances, tax-free reserves and allowances, FIFO accounting, and the corporate wealth tax, yields

$$dt/d\tau = (1 - m)(\delta - \pi)/p(1 - \tau)^2,$$

where $\delta$ is the economic depreciation rate. The equation suggests that the effective tax rate decreases with a decrease in $\tau$ (the corporate tax rate) when $\delta > \pi$. However, the effective tax rate increases with a decrease in $\tau$ when $\delta < \pi$. The value of $\delta$ for machinery in Japan is about 0.067 to 0.091 and for buildings is about 0.02 to 0.025. Thus even a lower

Figure 7-1.    *Effect of a Decrease in the Corporate Tax Rate*

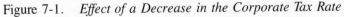
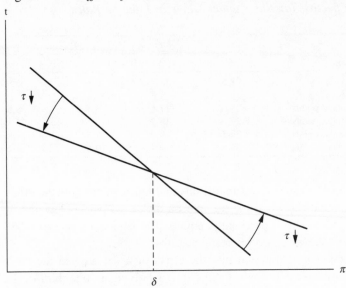

t : effective tax rate
$\pi$: inflation rate
$\tau$: corporate tax rate
$\delta$: economic depreciation rate.

inflation rate gives the possibility of an increase in the effective tax rate when $\tau$ is decreased. Moreover, the following equation is obtained:

$$\partial^2 t / \partial \tau \partial \pi = -(1 - m)/ p(1 - \tau)^2 < 0.$$

The effect of $\pi$ and $\tau$ on the effective tax rate is shown in figure 7-1. When the corporate tax rate is lowered, the line moves counterclockwise if the inflation rate is about 2.5 percent. When the inflation rate was higher in the 1970s, this mechanism did not work. Thus, an increase in the corporate tax rate during relatively high inflation years would not increase the effective tax rate but would lower it considerably. Recently, the rate of inflation has been very low. Therefore, the decrease in the corporate tax rate has lowered the effective tax rate on capital income.

### Results for 1990

The marginal effective tax rates for 1990 are presented in table 7-14. The calculation for 1990 takes account of the 1988 and 1989 tax reforms examined previously. Therefore, it includes the effect of these tax reforms.

Table 7-14.  *Marginal Effective Tax Rates under Different Inflation Rates, Fixed-p, 1990*

Percent

| | Inflation rate (percent) | | | |
|---|---|---|---|---|
| Item | 0 | 5 | 10 | Actual[a] |
| Asset | | | | |
| Machinery | 34.5 | 29.4 | 20.8 | 33.5 |
| Buildings | 32.6 | 25.3 | 12.6 | 31.3 |
| Inventories | 42.0 | 28.3 | 13.8 | 38.2 |
| Industry | | | | |
| Manufacturing | 34.7 | 27.8 | 17.3 | 33.2 |
| Other industry | 37.1 | 28.2 | 15.6 | 35.1 |
| Commerce | 36.0 | 27.3 | 15.1 | 34.0 |
| Source of Finance | | | | |
| Debt | 10.9 | −17.0 | −48.8 | 3.5 |
| New share issues | 60.9 | 76.7 | 91.0 | 65.6 |
| Retained earnings | 56.6 | 66.2 | 72.5 | 59.8 |
| Owner | | | | |
| Households | 35.2 | 26.9 | 15.0 | 33.4 |
| Tax-exempt institutions | 28.1 | 15.2 | −0.8 | 24.8 |
| Insurance companies | 38.3 | 34.4 | 27.8 | 37.5 |
| Overall tax rate | 35.4 | 27.7 | 16.5 | 33.7 |

a. 1.43 percent in 1985.

However, some of the key variables, such as the capital stock, are kept unchanged, partly because the data were not available when this work was undertaken. Thus, it should be understood that the result for 1990 is based on hypothetical parameters and is highly preliminary.

Table 7-14 shows the estimated effective marginal tax rates for 1990. The overall tax rate increased from 28.8 percent in 1985 to 35.4 percent in 1990 for the zero inflation rate. Thus, the increase is about 6.6 percentage points. Employing the 1.43 percent inflation rate, the increase is about 7.8 percent. Since the rate of inflation was very low in the 1980s, the effect of inflation was very minor.

Four main tax reforms affected the results for 1990. The first was the introduction of a tax on interest incomes, that is, the abolition of tax-free saving accounts. The second was the introduction of a value-added tax. The third was the reduction in the corporate tax rate to 37.5 percent at the national level. The fourth was the abolition of the discriminatory corporate tax treatment against dividends paid. The third factor lowers the effective tax rate, while the remaining three factors raise it. We previously examined the first and third factors carefully, and found that the first factor (the abolition of tax-free savings accounts) was crucial. Thus, the increase in the overall effective tax rate in 1990 is attributed to the first factor. However, the other factors should not be ignored, given that they had some influence. Because the results for 1990 are highly preliminary, no further comments are added.

### Traditional View versus New View

We perform a simulation on the traditional view and the new view with respect to the tax treatment of dividends. Table 7-15 presents results for the traditional view, and table 7-16 presents results for a case under the new view with an assumption of 5 percent inflation. Many studies suggest that the traditional view gives a higher effective tax rate than the new view under normal circumstance, as many studies suggest. Japan is not an exception to this rule, as shown by the two tables. Therefore, no further comments are added.

### Noncorporate Sector

It is interesting to compare the corporate sector and the noncorporate sector with respect to the marginal effective tax rates. The only form of equity finance available to noncorporate business firms is proprietors' equity. Also, it is assumed that neither tax-exempt institutions nor insurance companies invest in noncorporate firms. The tax system for the noncorporate sector in Japan is very complicated. Thus a separate study is needed to obtain comprehensive results for the noncorporate sector. This chapter provides preliminary results under several stringent assumptions about both types of firms' behavior and tax codes. These assumptions are not provided here out of space considerations.

Table 7-17 gives estimated results for 1990. Several observations on the corporate sector can be made based on this table and table 7-14. First, under zero inflation the overall effective tax rate for the noncorporate sector is lower by about 10 percentage points than for the corporate sector. This result occurs because the statutory tax rate on noncorporate business income is lower and because several favorable tax treatments exist for the noncorporate sector. Second, the effect of inflation is negligible for the noncorporate sector, because the effective tax rate does not decrease when the rate of inflation increases. As emphasized before, increases in inflation lowered the tax burden of incorporated firms for various reasons.

Table 7-15. *Marginal Effective Individual Tax Rates on Corporate Source Income, 5 Percent Inflation, Traditional View, 1980, 1985, 1990*
Percent

| Item | 1980 | 1985 | 1990 |
|---|---|---|---|
| Asset | | | |
| Machinery | 24.0 | 23.0 | 28.0 |
| Buildings | 24.3 | 23.4 | 28.9 |
| Inventories | 23.5 | 22.5 | 28.2 |
| Industry | | | |
| Manufacturing | 24.6 | 23.5 | 28.4 |
| Other industry | 22.9 | 22.0 | 28.2 |
| Commerce | 23.8 | 22.8 | 28.5 |
| Source of Finance | | | |
| Debt | 22.7 | 23.6 | 38.0 |
| New share issues | 25.0 | 22.6 | 20.0 |
| Owner | | | |
| Households | 26.8 | 26.2 | 33.2 |
| Tax-exempt institutions | 1.8 | 1.9 | 1.6 |
| Insurance companies | 13.9 | 12.9 | 11.8 |
| Overall tax rate | 23.9 | 23.0 | 28.4 |

Table 7-16. *Marginal Effective Individual Tax Rates on Corporate Source Income, 5 Percent Inflation, New View, 1980, 1985, 1990*
Percent

| Item | 1980 | 1985 | 1990 |
|---|---|---|---|
| Asset | | | |
| Machinery | 15.7 | 16.2 | 22.6 |
| Buildings | 15.8 | 16.5 | 23.4 |
| Inventories | 15.3 | 16.1 | 22.9 |
| Industry | | | |
| Manufacturing | 15.0 | 16.2 | 22.6 |
| Other industry | 16.9 | 16.4 | 23.7 |
| Commerce | 15.2 | 16.4 | 23.3 |
| Source of Finance | | | |
| Debt | 22.7 | 23.6 | 38.0 |
| New share issues | 25.0 | 22.6 | 20.0 |
| Retained earnings | 8.1 | 9.3 | 9.2 |
| Owner | | | |
| Households | 17.8 | 19.3 | 27.8 |
| Tax-exempt institutions | 0.9 | 1.1 | 1.0 |
| Insurance companies | 7.3 | 5.6 | 5.4 |
| Overall tax rate | 15.6 | 16.3 | 23.0 |

Table 7-17.  *Marginal Effective Tax Rates under Different Inflation Rates, Noncorporate Sector, Fixed-p, 1990*

Percent

| Item | Inflation rate (percent) | | | |
| --- | --- | --- | --- | --- |
| | 0 | 5 | 10 | Actual[a] |
| Asset | | | | |
| Machinery | 25.0 | 26.4 | 27.0 | 25.5 |
| Buildings | 22.9 | 23.7 | 23.1 | 23.3 |
| Inventories | 26.0 | 24.7 | 23.4 | 25.6 |
| Industry | | | | |
| Manufacturing | 23.9 | 24.5 | 24.4 | 24.3 |
| Other industry | 26.0 | 26.9 | 26.7 | 26.4 |
| Commerce | 24.6 | 25.1 | 24.8 | 24.9 |
| Source of Finance | | | | |
| Debt | 20.4 | 18.4 | 15.4 | 20.0 |
| Proprietors' equity | 28.0 | 31.0 | 33.1 | 29.0 |
| Owner | | | | |
| Households | 24.5 | 25.1 | 24.9 | 24.8 |
| Overall tax rate | 24.5 | 25.1 | 24.9 | 24.8 |

a. 1.43 percent.

Noncorporate firms do not enjoy this benefit, because they are treated differently from incorporated firms. Third, the effective tax rate on proprietors' equity is considerably lower than that on new share issues and retained earnings for obvious reasons. However, this rate is still somewhat higher than that on debt.

## Conclusion

The purpose of this chapter was to estimate the marginal effective tax rate on capital income in Japan and to draw several policy implications from these estimated tax rates. We emphasized an international comparison with Japan.

We presented the result of the effective tax rate on capital income in 1985 and found that there was no significant change in the estimated results between 1980 and 1985. Next, an analysis of international capital mobility between Japan and the United States suggested that tax factors, in the personal tax rate and in the corporate tax rate, might be responsible for explaining the current international capital mobility between the two countries, in addition to nontax factors.

Also we presented several simulation results in regard to the recent tax reforms in Japan. The abolition of tax-free savings accounts is likely to raise the effective marginal tax rate on capital income. An examination of the corporate tax rate suggested that a reduction does not necessarily lower the effective tax rate on capital income. This is particularly true when the inflation rate is high. In other words, a reduction in the corporate tax rate may not always lower the tax burden of corporations in Japan.

## References

Alworth, Julian S. 1988. *The Finance, Investment, and Taxation Decisions of Multinationals*. Oxford: Basil Blackwell.

Iwata, K., I. Suzuki, and A. Yoshida. 1987. "Cost of Capital of Investment in Owner-Occupied Housing and Tax System." *Keizai Bunseki* 107 (in Japanese).

Kikutani, Tatsuya. 1988. "On the Features of the Taxation of Income from Capital in Japan: Historical Change and International Comparison of the Effective Marginal Tax Rate." In *ACTA Humanistica et Scientifica, Universitatis Sangio Kyotiensis*. Social Science Series 18 (March): 61–99 (in Japanese).

Kikutani, Tatsuya, and Toshiaki Tachibanaki. 1990. "The Taxation of Income from Capital in Japan: Historical Perspectives and Policy Implications." In *Productivity Growth in Japan and the United States*, edited by Charles Hulten, 267–93. University of Chicago Press.

King, Mervyn, A. 1977. *Public Policy and the Corporation*. London: Chapman and Hall.

King, Mervyn A., and Don Fullerton. 1984. *The Taxation of Income from Capital: A Comparative Study of the United States, the United Kingdom, Sweden and West Germany*. University of Chicago Press.

Shoven, John, and Toshiaki Tachibanaki. 1988. "The Taxation of Income from Capital in Japan." In *Government Policy towards Industry in the United States and Japan*, edited by John Shoven, 51–96. Cambridge University Press.

Tachibanaki, Toshiaki. 1988. "Government Policies, The Working of Financial Market, Saving and Investment in Japan." In *Factors in Business Investment*, edited by Michael Funke, 204–31. Springer-Verlag.

# CHAPTER EIGHT

# Sweden

*Jan Södersten*

TWO CIRCUMSTANCES have been of primary importance for the structure and development of capital income taxation in Sweden in recent decades. First is the rapid growth of both local and central government revenue raised through taxes and social security contributions. During the postwar period total revenue rose from 25 percent of gross domestic product (GDP) in 1955 to 50 percent at the beginning of the 1980s.[1] This development was accompanied by ambitious attempts to redistribute incomes through transfer programs and steeply progressive personal income tax schedules.

Second, Sweden is a small open economy where the development of the tradables sector is seen to be of crucial importance to economic welfare. When balance-of-payments deficits arose in the mid-1960s for the first time in the postwar period, expansion of industrial investment received great emphasis in policymaking. There was a liberalization of the rules of fiscal depreciation and the special Swedish scheme of subsidizing investment, the investment funds system, was put to more frequent use. The external imbalances were much increased by the oil crises a decade later and by the concomitant rapid wage increases and the exchange-rate policies of the second half of the 1970s. The long-term policy of eliminating the balance-of-payments deficit remained one of stimulating industrial growth by various and increasingly generous investment incentives to companies.

The international comparisons of capital income taxation for 1980 reported by Mervyn A. King and Don Fullerton placed Sweden in a middle position.[2] The overall effective marginal tax rate on capital income from the corporate sector was 35.6 percent in 1980, compared with 37.2 percent for the United States, 48.1 percent for West Germany, and only 3.7

1. OECD (1992).
2. King and Fullerton (1984).

270

percent for the United Kingdom.[3] This may seem a surprising result, considering that the total tax yield in Sweden, when measured relative to GDP, by far surpasses that of the other three countries. However, the result must be viewed in the light of the double objective of Swedish tax policy—to levy high taxes on households for fiscal and redistributional reasons and to provide generous investment incentives to companies. Household taxes on dividends and interest receipts were by far the highest in Sweden. The corporate tax system, on the other hand, did provide a net subsidy to marginal investments, thereby reducing the overall wedge between pretax and post-tax rates of return to a level comparable to that of the other countries.

In Sweden, the beginning of the 1980s witnessed some important changes in attitudes, among them a growing concern about possible detrimental effects of high marginal tax rates. More emphasis was placed on efficiency and incentives and less on the goal of an equitable distribution of income. A manifestation of this change was the agreement in 1981 between two of the three parties in the nonsocialist coalition government and the opposition Social Democratic party to a reform of the individual income tax. The reform was enacted by Parliament in 1982 to be fully implemented by 1985. It was initially designed to cut marginal income tax rates for the majority of full-time wage earners to a maximum of 50 percent, while simultaneously limiting the value of interest deductions for earners in the higher marginal rate brackets (greater than 50 percent) to 50 percent.

The principle of combining cuts in tax rates with a broadening of the tax base introduced through the 1982–85 tax reform received increasing attention in the subsequent debate. Many of the nation's economic problems, for example, the extremely low level of household savings and the evolving labor shortage, were seen as intimately related to the existing structure of taxation. It was also claimed that the high statutory tax rates encouraged tax evasion and tax avoidance and made it necessary to introduce increasingly complicated tax rules. In Sweden, as in other countries, there was a widespread belief that the tax system diverted savings into "unproductive" investments in various forms at the expense of financial

3. The tax rate for Sweden in 1980 was actually only 29.2 percent. The higher number (35.6 percent) reported in the King and Fullerton study (1984, p. 135) is due to a misspecification of the cost of capital for inventories in the original computer program. All tables appearing in this chapter are produced using a corrected version of the program.

assets used to channel savings into business investment in fixed capital. Residential investment in owner-occupied housing was also considered to be favored by the tax system.

The corporation tax attracted criticism along similar lines. The tax breaks offered companies through various tax allowances, including accelerated depreciation, were to a large extent contingent on growth in real investment, so that stagnant firms paid the full statutory tax on their profits. While this once was believed to promote growth, the debate of the late 1980s stressed, rather, that the high rates of profits retention required to take advantage of accelerated depreciation actually hindered or slowed down the necessary structural readjustments of industry. According to this line of argument, the direction of corporate tax reform should be one of combining a lower statutory tax rate with a broader tax base.

In June 1989 three royal commissions jointly presented a proposal for a far-reaching reform of the nation's tax system. After considerable political negotiations, the new tax rules were enacted by Parliament in June 1990, to be implemented by January 1, 1991. The reform was designed to be revenue-neutral and involved substantial cuts in statutory tax rates and a broadening of the tax base, accomplished by eliminating or narrowing the extensive range of deductions and loopholes available to both households and companies. The U.S. Tax Reform Act of 1986 and its international followers are the obvious sources of inspiration for this reform, but it also has its roots in the above-mentioned reorientation of the Swedish tax policy debate that had already started in the early 1980s.

The drastically lowered and flattened bracket rates for the individual income tax will result in an estimated revenue loss of some 60 billion kronor (Skr)—equivalent to 6 percent of GDP. Almost half of this loss will be covered by increased revenue from a new system of taxing capital income and housing. The second main source of "financing" for the reform, with some Skr 14 billion of increased revenue, is a broadening of the value-added tax to include goods and services previously exempted or granted lower rates. Elimination of loopholes and preferential rules for taxing earned income is estimated to yield additional revenue of almost Skr 9 billion. The remaining revenue needed is expected to accrue through what has been labeled dynamic effects of the tax reform.

For dividends, interest income, and capital gains, a new proportional tax is introduced, replacing the system of taxing income from capital under the regular individual income tax. Corporations will find their statutory tax rate cut in half. To maintain an unchanged level of revenue, the proposal includes a revocation of the time-honored scheme of stimulating investment, the investment funds system, and also the possibility to undervalue stocks of inventories.

The purpose of this chapter is to measure and compare the incentives to save and invest afforded by the tax system in 1980 and 1985 and by the rules enacted for 1991. The focus of interest is the corporate sector of the economy, but some estimates are also provided for owner-occupied housing and for the noncorporate business sector. In particular, this makes it possible to determine the magnitude of the intersectoral distortions on resource allocation imposed by the tax system. The size and character of these distortions has been one of the key issues in current tax debate and also in the work of the tax commissions.

This chapter is organized as follows. In the section following this introduction, "Major Changes in Tax Legislation between 1980 and 1985," I describe the development of capital income taxation in Sweden between 1980 and 1985. The next section, "Empirical Results for 1985," gives estimates of effective marginal tax rates for 1985 with a brief comparison with 1980.[4] The treatment of the investment funds system in these estimates poses special problems and these are dealt with in some detail in the next section, "The Investment Funds System." The 1991 rules of capital income taxation are explained in the following section, "A New Tax System," and I provide estimates of the effects of these on the incentives to save and invest. In the next section, "Noncorporate Investment," I attempt to determine the extent to which the old and the new tax systems discriminate against investments in the corporate sector compared with those in the housing sector.

Evaluating capital income taxation by way of computing effective tax rates is necessarily a difficult and ambiguous exercise. Under "Noncorporate Investment" I put the estimates of the previous sections in some perspective by pointing to a few of the problems involved. The King-Fullerton (henceforth K-F) method of estimating effective tax rates, which is used in this chapter, captures all taxes that determine the wedge between the pretax rate of return on real investment and the post-tax return to the saver. Yet in an open economy taxes may have rather different effects on domestic savings than on domestic investment, and aggregated measures of effective tax rates may therefore hide important information. Under "Problems of Measurement and Interpretation" I attempt to

4. Full details of the 1980 results are given in the Swedish country chapter of King and Fullerton (1984). See also Södersten and Lindberg (1983), which, in addition to the Swedish country chapter, provides a brief summary of the King-Fullerton study.

distinguish between taxes on investment and taxes on savings, and I provide estimates of the effective marginal tax rate on investment. The standard K-F estimates assume that firms minimize their corporate tax payments by taking advantage of all available tax allowances. I discuss the difficulties with this assumption considering that the Swedish corporate tax combines generous tax allowances with provisions that effectively restrict firms in their use of such allowances. I also explore the consequences of departing from this standard assumption. I conclude with "A Summing Up."

The standard input parameters used for the estimates of effective marginal tax rates are given in the appendix tables to this volume.

## Major Changes in Tax Legislation between 1980 and 1985

A detailed description of the taxation of income from capital in the corporate sector of Sweden in 1980 is given in chapter 4 of King and Fullerton. The purpose of this section is to highlight features of the 1985 tax code that were new. Table 8-1 summarizes the changes in tax parameters from 1980 to 1985.

Between 1980 and 1985, the structure of the regular corporation income tax was basically unchanged. In 1980 companies paid both local and national income taxes and the total statutory tax rate averaged approximately 57 percent. By 1985, however, the local corporation tax was abolished and the national statutory tax rate was set at 52 percent. Some of the tax allowances available in 1980 had been eliminated or become less generous. In 1980 firms were offered an extra investment allowance for both the local and national tax assessments. The rate was set at 20 percent for machinery and equipment and at 10 percent for buildings. Regular fiscal depreciation rules were not affected, and with a (total) statutory tax rate of 57 percent these allowances were equivalent to investment grants of 11.4 percent and 5.7 percent for machinery and buildings, respectively. No such additional investment allowances or grants were available in 1985. For inventories, profits are calculated according to the principle of first in, first out (FIFO). Thus taxable income is overstated because of inflation. As an offset to this, a deduction was allowed in 1980 up to a maximum of 60 percent of the value of purchase of inventories. This deduction was limited to 50 percent in 1985.

Finally, in 1985 the rules of the investment funds (IF) system were modified. The IF system allows each firm to reduce tax payments by al-

Table 8-1.  *Summary of Changes in Swedish Tax Parameters, 1980, 1985*

| Item | 1980 | 1985 |
|---|---|---|
| Tax rates on interest ($m$) for households | | |
| Debt | 0.49 | 0.44 |
| Equity | 0.64 | 0.59 |
| Personal wealth tax rates ($w_p$) for households | | |
| Debt | 0.006 | 0.007 |
| Equity | 0.017 | 0.021 |
| Statutory rate of corporation tax ($\tau_s$) | 0.57 | 0.52 |
| Proportion of inventories with immediate depreciation ($f_2$) | 0.6 | 0.5 |
| Investment grant($f_3g$) | | |
| Machinery | 0.114 | 0.0 |
| Buildings | 0.057 | 0.0 |
| Central Bank, IF deposit rate (b) | 0.5 | 0.75 |

Source: Author's calculations for all tables.

locating up to half its pretax profits to an investment fund—which appears as an entry on the balance sheet. To obtain this tax reduction, the firm must deposit a certain fraction of the fund allocation interest-free at the Central Bank. This deposit is repaid to the firm when its IF are used for investment. Before 1984 the deposit rate was below the statutory corporate tax rate. IF allocations therefore provided an attractive alternative to paying profits tax even if the funds were never again used for investment. By the 1985 rules, however, the deposit rate was raised to 75 percent, well above the corporate tax rate of 52 percent. Firms that allocated profits to their investment funds therefore had to pay a "fee" of 23 percent in exchange for expected future benefits when the funds would be used.

The wage earners' funds introduced in Sweden in 1984 meant a dramatic step toward increased complexity in the taxation of the corporate sector. Firms were required to contribute to the financing of the funds by paying a 20 percent profit-sharing tax (PST), which was applied to a base that differed from the regular corporation tax base in important aspects. The new PST was operated parallel to the corporation tax, which meant an extremely complicated double system of taxing corporate income.

The base of the PST was obtained by reducing taxable corporate income as defined in the regular tax code by corporate tax payments and certain adjustments for inflation. These adjustments allowed firms extra deductions for the loss in real value on regular (historic-cost) depreciation allowances and for inventory profits corresponding to the rise in the general price level, but they also required the inclusion of inflationary gains on debt. Further adjustments meant that the 50 percent deduction for the value of inventory purchases was disallowed, as were the so-called Annell deductions (which are made when new shares are issued). The PST so determined was deductible against the base of the corporation tax for the following year. This provision therefore made the two parts of the new total system of taxing corporate profits interdependent.

The reform of the personal income tax decided on by Parliament in 1982 took full effect in 1985. The new tax schedule reduced the average marginal income tax of household investors in debt instruments from an estimated 49 percent in 1980 to 44 percent in 1985. For equity investors the average marginal tax rate fell from 64 to 59 percent.

Household taxation of investment income also was affected by concessions to special forms of savings first introduced at the end of the 1970s. The so-called tax savings schemes, discussed in the King and Fullerton study, were interrupted by the new Social Democratic government but reintroduced in 1984 under new names and with some changed rules. According to the new rules, households were granted a tax-free return on savings channeled into special bank accounts and special funds for shares, with an upper limit in 1985 on monthly savings of Skr 800 for the two schemes combined. These new rules are ignored in this chapter, however, for two reasons. First, the flow of deposits into the special bank accounts was not a source of finance of corporate investment, since by the new rules the deposits were rechanneled to the Bureau of the Public Debt for the purpose of financing public-sector borrowing. Second, the savings on the special funds for shares were still in 1985 relatively unimportant as a source of finance, contributing to 1.5 percent of the flow of equity funds (gross retained earnings and new share issues) into the corporate sector.

A new turnover tax on shares was introduced in 1984, and the rules in force in 1985 required both the seller and the buyer of a share to pay a tax of 0.5 percent of the value of the share. All categories of investors are subject to the tax. Assuming that investors expect capital gains to accrue at the nominal rate of 10 percent a year and assuming a holding period of ten years, this sales tax is equivalent to an extra tax on realized capital gains of 1.1 percent.

Wealth taxation in Sweden applies to individuals only. The new 1985 schedule levied a zero rate on net wealth (assets less liabilities) below

Skr 400,000, a 1.5 percent rate on wealth between Skr 400,000 and Skr 600,000, 2 percent between Skr 600,000 and Skr 800,000, 2.5 percent between Skr 800,000 and Skr 1,800,000, and 3 percent on wealth exceeding Skr 1,800,000.

For 1980 I estimated the marginal wealth tax rate on equity to be 1.7 percent, compared with 0.6 percent on holdings of debt. These numbers were obtained by combining the marginal rates for each class of net wealth with data on the distribution of household wealth among the classes of taxable net wealth. Using the same method, I estimated the new 1985 marginal wealth tax rate to be 2.1 percent on equity holdings and 0.7 percent on debt.

## Empirical Results for 1985

The King and Fullerton study measures the size of the wedge inserted by the tax system between the pretax rate of return on real investment and the net-of-tax return on savings. The results are expressed in terms of effective tax rates, which are defined as

$$t = \frac{p - s}{p},$$

where $p$ denotes the pretax real rate of return on an investment project net of economic depreciation, and $s$ is the real after-tax return received by the savers who supplied the finance for the investment.

The estimation of effective tax rates is based on the conventional cost-of-capital approach, linking the market interest rate to the pretax and post-tax rates of return, $p$ and $s$. In the following I compute the effective tax rate for a common value of the pretax rate of return, namely 10 percent. The results of these calculations, which I denote as fixed-$p$ results, depend in general on the particular combination of the type of asset, source of finance, industry and ultimate saver that are considered.

This study includes three types of asset: machinery, buildings, and inventories; three industry groups: manufacturing, other industry, and commerce; three sources of finance: debt, new share issues, and retained earnings; and three categories of savers: households, tax-exempt institutions, and insurance companies. This classification, which is motivated by differences in the tax treatment, results in eighty-one possible combinations of hypothetical investment projects, and I compute the marginal effective tax rate for each. For obvious reasons the presentation of these results takes the form of broad averages for particular subsets of the eighty-one combinations. In the tables I give the average effective marginal tax rate for each of the three types of assets, each of the three sources of finance, and so forth, and in computing these numbers I use the actual distribution of investment across type of asset, source of finance, and so on as weights.

This section presents the effective marginal tax rates on capital income in the corporate sector in 1985. For purposes of comparison, some calculations of effective tax rates are also presented for 1980. The results are shown in table 8-2. For example, the 22.9 percent tax rate for machinery means that the average of the post-tax rates of return received by the three categories of owners is 7.71 percent, given the actual distribution of this particular type of asset across the three industry groups, and the way in which savings were actually channeled (that is, the sources of finance used) into real investment.

At a 5 percent rate of inflation, which I take to be the actual rate of inflation in 1985, the overall marginal effective tax rate (where the average is taken across all assets, industries, sources of finance, and owners) is 33.9 percent. This is 3.5 percentage points higher than in 1980 at the then-prevailing rate of inflation, which was almost 10 percent. The tax schedule, which is implicit in the complicated tax rules studied here, changed between 1980 and 1985, however, so that for any given rate of inflation, the effective tax rate was now 10 to 15 percentage points higher. The main explanation for this tax increase is the abolition of the investment grants available to companies in 1980.

A comparison of the different columns of table 8-2 reveals the effects of inflation on effective tax rates. The Swedish tax system is not indexed and as a result the overall effective tax rate rises by one-half as the rate of inflation increases from zero to 10 percent. Though this is a remarkable result, the sensitivity to inflation is still considerably lower than in 1980. This reduced sensitivity is an additional effect of the elimination of the investment grants.[5]

In 1985, as in 1980, there is a wide dispersion in effective tax rates. The variation by source of finance and by owner is particularly striking. The variation in effective tax rate by asset is much less than in 1980,

5. For a full explanation of the tax-increasing effects of inflation, see the Swedish country chapter in King and Fullerton (1984).

Table 8-2.  *Marginal Effective Tax Rates under Different Inflation Rates, Standard Parameter Values (Excluding the Profit-Sharing Tax), 1985*

Percent

| Item | Inflation rate (percent) | | |
|---|---|---|---|
| | 0 | 5 | 10 |
| Asset | | | |
| Machinery | 18.4 | 22.9 | 29.0 |
| Buildings | 34.9 | 37.3 | 40.9 |
| Inventories | 29.4 | 41.2 | 53.2 |
| Industry | | | |
| Manufacturing | 26.0 | 31.2 | 37.1 |
| Other industry | 36.0 | 45.0 | 56.4 |
| Commerce | 25.2 | 31.9 | 39.6 |
| Source of finance | | | |
| Debt | 3.9 | 4.1 | 8.3 |
| New share issues | 54.1 | 74.6 | 95.3 |
| Retained earnings | 53.7 | 66.2 | 76.3 |
| Owner | | | |
| Households | 56.5 | 70.6 | 83.6 |
| Tax-exempt institutions | −6.7 | −14.2 | −20.2 |
| Insurance companies | 13.1 | 26.5 | 48.7 |
| Overall rate | 27.7 | 33.9 | 41.2 |
| Overall tax rate, 1980 | 12.9 | 21.2 | 30.4 |

largely because of the abolition of the special 20 percent investment allowance for investment in machinery.

I next attempt to determine the relative contributions of different tax instruments. That is, I decompose the effective tax rates of table 8-2 by calculating alternative tax rates that would exist were it not for personal taxes on dividends, interest receipts, capital gains, and wealth. To see how much of the 33.9 percent overall effective tax rate (at 5 percent inflation) is due to personal taxes, table 8-3 reports fixed-$p$ results for a simulation with no personal taxes. The overall tax rate falls dramatically, from 33.9 to −5.0 percent. While interrelations destroy the exact additivity of this decomposition, it is clear that the personal tax system completely determines the overall effective tax rate in 1985.

The second part of table 8-3 reports corresponding results for 1980. Without personal taxes, real investment would have received a substantial subsidy, as a result of the wide range of tax concessions available to the companies. This striking result explains why Sweden, despite high

Table 8-3.  *Marginal Effective Tax Rates under Different Inflation Rates, Fixed-*p, *Standard Parameter Values, Corporate Taxes Only, 1980, 1985*

Percent

| | Inflation rate (percent) | | | | | |
| | 1985 | | | 1980 | | |
| Item | 0 | 5 | 10 | 0 | 5 | 10 |
|---|---|---|---|---|---|---|
| Asset | | | | | | |
| Machinery | −8.5 | −14.2 | −18.8 | −53.4 | −54.4 | −55.1 |
| Buildings | 8.6 | −1.5 | −10.7 | 0.8 | −9.3 | −18.3 |
| Inventories | 0.2 | 0.3 | 0.4 | −4.3 | −5.6 | −5.2 |
| Source of finance | | | | | | |
| Debt | −23.7 | −37.7 | −47.7 | −47.5 | −59.5 | −67.0 |
| New share issues | 7.7 | 9.5 | 10.6 | −9.4 | −6.5 | −4.8 |
| Retained earnings | 27.3 | 31.7 | 32.9 | 14.3 | 19.0 | 20.1 |
| Overall tax rate | 0.2 | −5.0 | −9.6 | −18.5 | −22.5 | −25.9 |

personal taxes, was placed in a middle position in the King and Fullerton international comparison. It is also clear from the table, that the changes in tax legislation between 1980 and 1985 described in the previous section brought about a considerable reduction in the rate of subsidy.

The estimates of effective marginal tax rates for 1985 given in table 8-2 do not include the effects of the PST. Separate estimates show, however, that the new and very complicated tax had a rather limited impact on the effective tax rates. The overall effective tax rate rose by 1.8 percent, at 5 percent inflation. The reason for this small effect is that the PST is computed on after-tax profits and is also deductible against the corporate tax base for the following year. But in the case of new issues and for investment in inventories, there is a more marked (6 and 5 percentage points, respectively) tax increase. As explained, the PST disallows both regular deductions for inventory undervaluation and the so-called Annell deductions for dividends on newly issued shares.

## The Investment Funds System

The numbers presented in table 8-2 are based on my best estimates of the parameters of the tax system in 1985. As is usually the case, there is a considerable range of uncertainty for some of the parameter values. A major cause of this uncertainty is the investment funds system, and the purpose of this section is to discuss some of the problems involved in estimating the incentive effects of IF releases. I also provide estimates of marginal effective tax rates based on an alternative (as opposed to the standard estimates of the previous section) interpretation of the workings of the IF System in 1985.

Investments "financed" through releases of investment funds receive a substantial subsidy, comparable to that obtained from the use of free depreciation. This has led many researchers to conclude that releases of investment funds will cause a sharp reduction in the cost of capital, thus providing an inducement to invest.[6] This conventional view of the IF system is usually explained in the following intuitive way. Each firm may "allocate" $f$ percent of its profits to an investment fund and because the fund allocations are free of tax, only the share $1 - f$ of profits is taxed at the statutory rate $\tau_s$. The fund allocation is instead "taxed" at rate $b$ (the deposit rate), which is the proportion that must be paid to the Central Bank. The effective corporate tax rate, $\tau$, is therefore a weighted average of the statutory tax rate $\tau_s$ and the deposit rate $b$:

(8-1) $$\tau = \tau_s(1 - f) + fb.$$

When the funds are released by the government, firms withdraw from the Central Bank the amount $b$ per crown of investment considered to be "financed" through the system. The net cost of investment is therefore $1 - b$, and the gross cost of capital, $MRR$, will be

(8-2) $$MRR = \left(\frac{1 - b}{1 - \tau}\right)(\delta + \rho - \pi),$$

where, as in K-F, $\delta$ is the rate of economic depreciation, $\rho$ is the firm's nominal after-tax discount rate, and $\pi$ is the rate of inflation.

A closer look at the IF system makes it clear, however, that this conventional view requires some rather special assumptions. Most important, it implicitly assumes that the representative firm is able to finance all its current investment from its IF, and that, whenever the funds are released in the future, it expects to be in an excess-funds position in the sense that it will never exhaust its own fund.

When these strong assumptions are not fulfilled, the incentive effect of a fund release is much reduced. In a recent theoretical reexamination of the IF system, Jan Södersten shows that when the firm is unable to

---

6. See, for example, Bergström (1982) and Taylor (1982).

finance all its current investment through a fund release, the marginal
investment must be written off according to the regular rules of fiscal
depreciation, rather than through the IF system.[7] He derives, furthermore,
a new expression for the "effective" corporate tax rate as

$$(8\text{-}3) \qquad\qquad \tau = \tau_s(1 - f) + f(b - \beta),$$

where $\beta$ is the marginal gain to the firm from increasing the size of its
investment fund. The investment fund allocation is therefore "taxed" at
the rate $b - \beta$, which is the Central Bank deposit rate less the gain from
adding to the IF. Only in the special and extreme case where the firm
expects that in the future it will never exhaust its fund can this gain be
neglected.

The maximum value of $\beta$, however, occurs when the firm expects that
the current period of fund release will be extended indefinitely and when
the amount of money that can be released from its IF, at present and in the
future, will not be sufficient to finance all of its investments. Södersten
derives this maximum value of $\beta$ as

$$(8\text{-}4) \qquad\qquad \beta = b - \frac{\tau_s a(1 - f)}{a(1 - f) + \rho},$$

where $a$ is the declining balance rate of regular fiscal depreciation on assets "financed" by the IF. Using equations 3 and 4, this gives the effective
corporate tax rate:

$$(8\text{-}5) \qquad\qquad \tau = \tau_s(1 - f) + f\frac{\tau a}{a + \rho}.$$

This expression for the effective tax rate has a clear economic interpretation. A fraction $1 - f$ of profits will be taxed at the statutory tax rate
$\tau_s$, while the fraction $f$ will be allocated to the IF. By the assumption of
a permanent release of funds, this extra fund allocation can immediately
be used for (intramarginal) investment. The Central Bank deposit rate $b$
is therefore of no importance. There is, however, an implicit cost to the
firm of the allocation and this cost equals the increased tax payments due
to the loss of regular depreciation allowances on the subsequent assets,
financed by the allocation, that is $\tau a/(a + \rho)$. When the firm always
exhausts its IF and expects the period of fund release to be extended
indefinitely, the effect of the IF system is therefore to turn the effective tax

---

7. Södersten (1989).

rate into a weighted average of the statutory tax rate and the implicit cost of IF allocations.

This new interpretation of the IF system was first suggested and used for the 1980 estimates of marginal effective tax rates in the Swedish country chapter in King and Fullerton. The reinterpretation was motivated by the new IF policy which emerged as part of the government's response to the crisis in the Swedish economy in the second half of the 1970s. The new policy meant repeated renewals of IF releases, which in practice enabled firms during a ten-year period to use their investment funds continuously. During this period of "permanent" releases, less than an average of 20 percent of the investments of the industry groups included in the K-F study were actually financed through the IF system. These observations were the basis for assuming, for 1980, that the representative firm had to write off its marginal investments according to the regular rules of fiscal depreciation and that it expected to constantly exhaust its IF.

The new interpretation of the IF system for 1985 would imply a value of $\beta$ of 0.55 at 5 percent inflation. Although the total of IF releases in 1985 still fell short of the amount invested in the three industry groups, it is reasonable to assume that the firms' expectations about the government's future IF policy had now changed. In 1985 it was generally believed that the period of permanent IF releases was coming to an end. In terms of equation 8-3 the implication of this is a lower value of $\beta$, though there is no empirical foundation for choosing a definite number. However, as long as the amount of money released from the fund system is insufficient to finance current investment, a theoretical argument can be given to the effect that $\beta$ must exceed 0.45. As my standard assumption for 1985 I have, somewhat arbitrarily, set $\beta$ equal to 0.5. The effective corporate tax rate, as defined by equation 8-3, is then 38.5 percent (estimated at 5 percent inflation), compared with the statutory tax rate of 52 percent.

The standard case assumptions about the IF system are far from obvious, however. The share of investment actually financed through fund releases rose considerably in 1985 over the previous long-term average. It is conceivable that as a result of this rise, some firms were actually able to finance at least all their investments in buildings through the IF system. One could argue then that the marginal investment considered here should be analyzed as a weighted average across different firms, that is, firms that have exhausted their investment funds and firms that

Table 8-4.  *Marginal Effective Tax Rates under Alternative Assumptions, 5 Percent Inflation, Fixed-p, 1985*[a]
Percent

| Item | Standard case[a] | IF case[b] | No IF case[c] |
|------|------------------|------------|---------------|
| Asset |  |  |  |
| Machinery | 22.9 | 18.9 | 15.0 |
| Buildings | 37.3 | -1.3 | 33.1 |
| Inventories | 41.2 | 41.4 | 41.7 |
| Source of finance |  |  |  |
| Debt | 4.1 | -20.8 | -13.6 |
| New share issues | 74.6 | 66.0 | 77.2 |
| Retained earnings | 66.2 | 63.6 | 78.0 |
| Overall tax rate | 33.9 | 19.6 | 30.1 |

a. See table 8-2.
b. Marginal investments in buildings written off through the investment funds system.
c. No IF allocations are made and no IF release occurs.

have not. No data are available for such a weighting procedure, however. Instead, I present in table 8-4 marginal effective tax rates for the alternative assumption that investment in buildings is financed through the IF system. As in the standard case, I assume that investment in machinery is written off according to the regular rules of tax depreciation.

When the marginal investment in buildings is written off through the IF system, the net cost of investment becomes $1 - b + \beta$.[8] This differs from the conventional expression given above, because it takes into account that drawing down the size of the stock of funds is costly to the firm. Only in the extreme case, when the firm expects that it will never exhaust its funds, can this cost be neglected (that is, $\beta = 0$).

The new rules of the IF system, in effect since 1984, mean that $b > \tau_s$. The implication of this is that a "fee" of $b - \tau_s$ must be paid, per crown of IF allocation, in exchange for future benefits when the allocation can be used for investment. This future benefit is captured by the parameter $\beta$, and from equation 8-3 we find that $\beta > b - \tau_s$ for IF allocations to be worthwhile to the firm. Since in 1985, $b$ equaled 0.75 and $\tau_s$ equaled 0.52, the value of $\beta$ must exceed 0.23. Arbitrarily I have chosen $\beta = 0.35$ for the IF case of table 8-4, which is in the middle of the feasible interval 0.23 to 0.55 The effective corporate tax rate, as defined by equation 8-3, is then 0.46 (at 5 percent inflation).

8. See Södersten (1989).

The IF case assumptions have a dramatic impact on the estimated effective tax rates. Investment in buildings receives a slight subsidy, compared with a positive tax of nearly 40 percent in the standard case. There is also a slight reduction in the effective tax rate on machinery. Because of the wide range of corporate tax concessions to investment in machinery, the required rate of return on a project is a decreasing function of the corporate tax rate. As explained, the tax rate is 0.46 in the IF case and 0.385 in the standard case. We note also that in the IF case the combined effect of the subsidy to buildings and the increased corporate tax rate is to turn the tax on debt-financed investments into a substantial net subsidy.

For comparison, the third column of table 8-4 gives the marginal effective tax rates without the investment funds system. The corporate tax rate, as defined by equation 8-3, is then equal to the statutory tax rate, which is 52 percent. Because the tax rate is higher (compared with both the standard case and the IF case), the value of corporate tax concessions to machinery and buildings is increased. As a result, the marginal effective tax rates are lower than in the standard case. The combined effect of accelerated depreciation and full interest deductibility is furthermore sufficiently great to outweigh the taxation of nominal interest payments received by savers, and therefore debt-financed investments receive a net subsidy.

## A New Tax System

The tax legislation enacted by Parliament in June 1990 constitutes the most far-reaching reform of Sweden's tax system in at least forty years. The new rules for the corporate income tax are a noteworthy departure from the previous long-standing policy of stimulating business investment in fixed capital through a combination of a high statutory tax rate and generous allowances to investing firms. The statutory tax rate is reduced to 30 percent. Because the reform also included an elimination of the profit-sharing tax, this meant that by 1991 the total statutory rate would be cut almost in half.

To maintain an unchanged level of revenue from the corporation tax, this rate reduction presupposes a substantial base broadening. The possibility of deferring tax payments by inventory write-down up to 50 percent of the FIFO value will no longer be available. The investment funds system will also be discontinued. A new reserve option is introduced, however, enabling the companies to deduct up to 30 percent of the net increase of the book value of equity (including the increase in accumulated retained profits). The effect of this deduction—which takes the form of a tax-free allocation to a so-called tax equalization fund (Skatteutjämningsreserv, or SURV) appearing on the firm's balance sheet—is equivalent to a partial (30 percent) deduction for the nominal cost of equity. The SURV provision is also intended as a substitute for loss–carry backward, since accumulated SURV allocations may be used as an offset against tax losses. The corporate tax base is further broadened by the elimination of the so-called primary deductions for buildings and by the full inclusion of realized nominal capital gains on financial investments and real estate.[9]

For individuals the new tax system entails a flat-rate, 30 percent tax on dividends and interest receipts and likewise a 30 percent tax on realized— long-term as well as short-term—nominal capital gains. Again this is in marked contrast to the previous method of taxing capital income according to a progressive rate schedule as part of the individual income tax. A stated purpose of the new capital tax is to reduce the scope for tax avoidance in various forms, and obviously full nominal taxation of capital gains will considerably reduce the existing incentive to transform high-taxed regular income into low-taxed capital gains.[10]

The reform package also contains new and more uniform tax rules for institutional investors. For the category "insurance companies," which is residually defined in the K-F study to include various tax-paying institutions, dividends, interest receipts, and realized nominal capital gains will be taxed at a 30 percent statutory rate. Special rules to exempt part of capital income from tax will be replaced by the new SURV reserve option described above. The result is to reduce the tax to an effective rate of 23 percent, a slight increase over the former rules.

A noteworthy and politically controversial part of the reform is to impose a tax on the return to savings in pension funds. Depending on the type of pension fund (for example, individual or collective pension savings), the tax varies between 10 and 15 percent of the nominal return, including capital gains. Pension funds are included with the category "tax exempt institutions" and for 1991 the average marginal income tax rate

---

9. King and Fullerton (1984, p. 97).

10. Of course there is still an incentive to receive income in the form of capital gains, since the tax is due only upon realization. The effect of deferral is approximately to make the effective tax rate half that of the statutory rate. See King and Fullerton (1984, p. 23).

Table 8-5. *Marginal Effective Tax Rates under Different Inflation Rates, Fixed-p, 1991 Tax Reform Package*

Percent

| Item | Inflation rate (percent) | | |
|---|---|---|---|
| | 0 | 5 | 10 |
| | *Corporate tax only* | | |
| Asset | | | |
| Machinery | −6.6 | −11.3 | −16.7 |
| Buildings | 6.9 | 1.3 | −5.8 |
| Inventories | 4.3 | 12.5 | 20.6 |
| Source of finance | | | |
| Debt | −11.5 | −19.0 | −27.5 |
| New share issues | 1.0 | 5.8 | 11.1 |
| Retained earnings | 16.4 | 23.2 | 29.4 |
| Overall tax rate | 1.7 | 1.0 | −0.44 |
| | *Corporate and personal taxes* | | |
| Asset | | | |
| Machinery | 15.9 | 19.2 | 22.0 |
| Buildings | 27.2 | 30.1 | 31.7 |
| Inventories | 25.1 | 39.9 | 54.6 |
| Source of finance | | | |
| Debt | 10.8 | 13.9 | 16.0 |
| New share issues | 33.0 | 47.5 | 62.4 |
| Retained earnings | 35.8 | 47.0 | 57.7 |
| Owner | | | |
| Households | 38.4 | 50.5 | 62.0 |
| Tax-exempt institutions | 5.3 | 6.3 | 6.5 |
| Insurance companies | 21.2 | 30.7 | 39.5 |
| Overall tax rate | 22.8 | 29.9 | 36.2 |
| Overall tax rate, 1985 | 27.7 | 33.9 | 41.2 |

($m$ in the King and Fullerton notation) of this category is then increased from zero to 9.4 percent on equity returns and to 3.6 percent on the return to debt instruments.

Table 8-5 shows the effects of the tax reform on the incentives to save and invest. A first and noteworthy result is that the new tax rules will bring about a reduction in the overall effective tax rates, compared with their 1985 levels. (For a full comparison, see table 8-2 and 8-3.) At 5 percent inflation, the reduction is 4 percentage points. This result is entirely explained by the changes in the taxation of persons. The corporate tax wedge is on the contrary increased by 6.4 percentage points as a result of the policy of tax cuts and base broadening.

The reform package furthermore takes some steps toward achieving what has been called a level playing field. The incentive to use debt rather than equity as a source of finance is somewhat less pronounced under the new tax rules. The main explanation for this is the reduction in statutory tax rates in combination with the new SURV reserve option for equity capital, described earlier. The earlier discrimination in favor of new issues as a source of equity funds is largely eliminated at moderate rates of inflation.

Much of the variation in effective tax rates among assets remains, however, and indeed one of the stated objectives of the tax legislators was to make inventory investment less attractive. Different investors are still taxed at varying rates, though the variation is somewhat reduced. The sensitivity to inflation, finally, is still evident. A comparison between the different columns of table 8-5 shows that as the rate of inflation rises from zero to 10 percent, the overall effective marginal tax rate will increase by almost three-fifths.

## Noncorporate Investment

Reducing the variation in the taxation of the return to savings channeled into real investment in the corporate sector of the economy is obviously only part of the problem of achieving a more level playing field. Much of the Swedish tax-policy debate during the 1980s focused on possible tax discrimination against business investment compared with owner-occupied housing. The purpose of this section is to shed light on this issue by providing estimates of marginal effective tax rates for owner-occupied housing and noncorporate business investment.

Owner-occupied housing has provided a noteworthy exception to the general principle of taxing only realized income. Homeownership— including summer cottages—has been taxed on imputed income at a rate of 2 percent (with higher rates on more expensive houses) on the tax-assessed value of the house. This imputed income was included in the income tax base of the owner. Mortgage interest has been fully deductible. However, in those cases in which mortgage interest exceeded the imputed income, an additional income (a so-called guarantee amount) of 1.5 percent of the tax-assessed value of the house was added to that part of the owner's income subject to local income tax. The effect of this complicated provision was to levy a minimum tax on debt-financed investment in owner-occupied housing of 0.45 percent of the tax-assessed value. Real gains on housing have been taxed upon realization with an inclusion rate of 100 percent. Since 1981, however, indexation of the acquisition cost has been disallowed for the first four years of ownership.

The tax-assessed values were approximately 75 percent of the market values at the time they were set. The assessments were supposed to be changed at intervals of five years, but in practice the intervals have been considerably longer. The tax-assessed values in effect in 1989 were set as early as 1980; as a result, they amounted to less than half the market values. In 1985, on average, this ratio was 0.65.

In addition to the tax on imputed income, a new property tax was introduced in 1985, amounting to 1.4 percent of one-third of the tax-assessed value. After the 1982–85 tax reform, the value of interest deductions was also limited to a maximum of 50 percent.

The tax reform of 1991 also includes new rules for the taxation of homeownership. A new nondeductible property tax of 1.5 percent of the tax-assessed value replaces the old scheme of taxing imputed income (including the minimum tax provision). For new homes, however, no property tax is charged for the first five years, and for the next five years the tax rate is reduced to 0.75 percent. Mortgage interest is still fully deductible, but because the taxation of home ownership is considered part of the new capital income taxation, the value of interest deductions is limited to 30 percent. Capital gains on housing are fully taxed on a nominal basis but the legislation puts an upper limit on the tax actually paid upon realization. This limit is set at 9 percent of the proceeds from the sale of a house.

The cost of capital corresponding to owner-occupied housing is

$$(8\text{-}6) \qquad p = \rho - \pi + \lambda + \beta + w + z_v(\pi_v - \delta),$$

where, as before, $\rho$ is the nominal after-tax discount rate and $\pi$ is the rate of inflation. For equity finance, I take $\rho$ to be the owner's after-tax opportunity cost of funds, that is, $\rho = i(1 - m)$, and for debt finance I set $\rho = i(1 - m_v)$, where $m_v$ is the tax rate at which owner-occupants deduct mortgage interest. The tax on the imputed income of the house is $\lambda$, the minimum tax (applicable in the case of debt finance ) is $\beta$, and $w$ is the property tax. The last term of equation 8-6 is the capital gains tax, expressed as a fraction $z_v$ of the accruing change in the nominal value of the house. As in King and Fullerton, the real after-tax return to the saver is

$$(8\text{-}7) \qquad s = i(1 - m) - \pi - w_p,$$

where $m$ is the marginal income tax rate and $w_p$ is the (marginal) personal wealth tax rate.

I assume for my estimates that lending to housing investment is done by my three categories of ultimate savers in the same proportions as lending to the corporate sector. Equity funds, on the other hand, are assumed to come from households only, that is, from the owner-occupants themselves.

In 1985 the average marginal income tax rate, $m$, was 54.4 percent for the owner-occupants but only 18.4 percent for the lenders (estimated at 5 percent inflation). Mortgage payments were deducted at an average rate of 47.3 percent ($m_v = 0.473$). The average investor in owner-occupied housing, therefore, was not constrained by the 50 percent ceiling put on the value of interest deductions. I assume furthermore that owner-occupants expected the future tax-assessed values to average 65 percent of the market values (owing to the long intervals between reassessments). The result is that the tax on the imputed income, $\lambda$, will amount to 0.71 percent of the market value, the minimum tax, $\beta$, to 0.29 percent, and the property tax, $w$, to 0.30 percent.

For the 1991 estimates I set $m$ and $m_v$ of equation 8-6 equal to 30 percent, which is the new proportional individual tax on income from capital. The new property tax, $w_c$, which replaces both the old system of taxing imputed income and the minimum tax, is differentiated between old and new houses, as described above. Since my concern here is with the incentive effects of taxation, I model the rules for houses completed after 1991. The effect of these is to levy a zero property tax during the first five years and a tax of 0.75 percent of the tax-assessed value during the following five years, equivalent to 0.49 percent of the market value. After ten years the tax is 1.5 percent of the tax-assessed value, or 1.13 percent of the market value. This assumes, following the recommendations of the Income Tax Commission, that reassessments will be carried out annually to maintain the tax-assessed values at a level corresponding to 75 percent of the market values.

The tax on realized capital gains, finally, is written in equation 8-6 as a tax of $z_v(\pi - \delta)$ on the market value of the house. This tax was effectively zero in 1985 and 0.26 percent in 1991, estimated at 5 percent inflation and assuming a holding period of fifteen years.[11]

---

11. The base of the capital gains tax in 1985 was the difference between the selling price of the house and the acquisition cost, which was indexed to the consumer price index (CPI) after the first four years of ownership. Since I assume here that the selling price increases at the rate $\pi - \delta$, that is, at the rate of inflation less the rate of economic depreciation, the result is that the taxable capital gain will decrease as a share of the selling price after the first four years of ownership. At 5 percent inflation, a holding period of 14.3 years is sufficient to eliminate altogether the taxable capital gain.

Table 8-6. *Marginal Effective Tax Rates for Owner-Occupied Housing, under Different Inflation Rates, VAT Excluded, Fixed-p, 1985, 1991*
Percent

| | Inflation rate (percent) | | | | | |
| | 1985 | | | 1991 | | |
| Item | 0 | 5 | 10 | 0 | 5 | 10 |
|---|---|---|---|---|---|---|
| Debt | −33.0 | −59.3 | −80.1 | −13.2 | −18.8 | −27.2 |
| Equity | 31.3 | 31.2 | 33.8 | 19.4 | 21.8 | 21.8 |
| Average[a] | 8.7 | −0.5 | −6.1 | 8.0 | 7.6 | 4.6 |

a. Assumes that mortgage debt is 35 percent of the market value of the house.

Marginal effective tax rates $(t = (p - s)/p)$ for investment in owner-occupied housing are reported in table 8-6 for 1985 and 1991. Investment in owner-occupied housing financed by debt received a substantial subsidy under the 1985 tax law, and the rate of subsidy increased with the rate of inflation. The main reason for this is that mortgage payments were deducted by owner-occupants at a rate (47.3 percent) considerably higher than the rate at which they were included by holders of mortgage debt (18.4 percent). For equity-financed investments the effective marginal tax rates ranged between 31 and 34 percent, depending on the rate of inflation.

Assuming an average proportion of mortgage debt of 35 percent of the market value of owner-occupied housing, the overall effective marginal tax was then close to zero at an inflation rate of 5 percent a year. At higher inflation rates the tax system extended an overall net subsidy to housing investment. This is in sharp contrast to the results reported in table 8-2 for the corporate sector. The overall marginal effective tax rate on the return to real investment in the corporate sector in 1985 was estimated to be 37.3 percent at 5 percent inflation and as much as 46.7 percent at an inflation rate of 10 percent.

By the 1991 rules the net subsidy to debt-financed housing investments remains, but it is much reduced. The main reason for this change is that the difference between the rate at which interest payments are deducted and the rate at which interest receipts are taxed shrinks from 28.9 percentage points in 1985 to 11.7 percentage points in 1991. But for investments financed by owners' equity, the marginal effective tax rates are reduced by as much as one-third compared with their 1985 levels.

The age differentiation of the property tax has important effects on the incentive to save and invest. With an unreduced property tax, the marginal effective tax rate for owner-occupied housing would have been −7.0 percent in the case of debt finance and 31.9 percent for equity finance, estimated at 5 percent inflation.

The effective tax rates given in table 8-6 may, however, give a misleading picture of the effects of the 1991 tax reform on resource allocation. The K-F methodology ignores the value-added tax, since it is not a tax on investment. In computing their VAT liability, firms may deduct any VAT that has been levied on inputs into their products—including investment goods. For investment in owner-occupied housing, however, the matter is different. While owner-occupants need pay no tax on their "outputs," they are not able to reclaim the VAT on their inputs, that is, the construction costs of the houses. In a sense, therefore, the VAT serves as an investment tax on owner-occupied housing.

An important part of the 1991 tax reform is a broadening of VAT to include areas previously exempt or granted preferential treatment. For construction costs the VAT rate is raised from 12.87 percent (on a tax-exclusive basis) to 23.46 percent, which is the general level of the VAT. The effects of treating the VAT as an investment tax on housing investment are shown in table 8-7.

The taxation of noncorporate business firms differs from that of corporations in that no separate tax is levied on the income of the business entity. Profits of single proprietorships and partnerships are taxed only once, according to the (marginal) income tax rate of the entrepreneur. However, they are also reduced by compulsory social security contributions, part of which are completely unrelated to future benefits. The effect of this is to levy an additional tax on the profits of noncorporate business firms. This tax amounts to 18.2 percent, but since social security contributions are deductible for the income tax assessment, the effective rate is lower. The rules of fiscal depreciation, and investment grants and allowances available to corporations, have in general been available also to noncorporate firms. The investment funds system and the Annell deduction (for new share issues), however, have been confined to corporations.

Table 8-8 shows the incentives to save and invest in the noncorporate business sector afforded by the tax systems in 1980, 1985, and 1991. No data are available for the marginal income tax rate and the marginal wealth tax rate of the noncorporate entrepreneurs, and I simply use here the same rates of tax as for the average household investor in corporate equity. The estimates assume the same debt-equity ratios and the same asset and industry compositions as are assumed for the corporate sector. Lending to the sector is assumed to be done by households, tax-exempt institutions, and insurance companies, in the same proportions as lend-

Table 8-7. *Marginal Effective Tax Rates for Owner-Occupied Housing, under Different Inflation Rates, VAT Included, Fixed-p, 1985, 1991*
Percent

| | Inflation rate (percent) | | | | | |
| | 1985 | | | 1991 | | |
| Item | 0 | 5 | 10 | 0 | 5 | 10 |
|------|-----|-----|-----|-----|-----|-----|
| Debt | −12.7 | −39.2 | −59.6 | 12.0 | 7.0 | −1.4 |
| Equity | 44.1 | 44.2 | 47.2 | 41.0 | 43.9 | 43.9 |
| Average[a] | 24.3 | 15.0 | 9.8 | 30.8 | 31.0 | 28.0 |

a. Assumes that mortgage debt is 35 percent of the market value of the house.

ing to the corporate sector. Equity funds, however, are provided by the noncorporate entrepreneurs themselves.

The taxation of noncorporate investment has changed considerably in recent years, from extending a net subsidy in 1980 to levying a substantial overall tax in 1985 and 1991. The increased rate of taxation has been accompanied by a much smaller variation in effective tax rates among assets and sources of finance. The elimination of the investment grants available in 1980 and the reductions in statutory tax rates by the 1991 tax reform are the main factors behind this development. I also note that in 1991 the overall effective tax rate rises with the rate of inflation, whereas in both 1980 and 1985 an increased rate of inflation meant a lower effective tax rate.

Table 8-9 combines results from tables 8-2, 8-5, 8-7, and 8-8 to compare the incentives to save and invest in owner-occupied housing and in

Table 8-8. *Marginal Effective Tax Rates, 5 Percent Inflation, Noncorporate Sector, Fixed-p, 1980, 1985, 1991*
Percent

| Item | 1980 | 1985 | 1991 |
|------|------|------|------|
| Asset | | | |
| Machinery | −55.7 | −5.5 | 9.5 |
| Buildings | 14.9 | 18.1 | 27.2 |
| Inventories | 32.5 | 40.0 | 45.5 |
| Source of finance | | | |
| Debt[a] | −60.8 | −42.3 | 3.9 |
| Equity[b] | 62.2 | 83.6 | 53.3 |
| Overall tax rate | −2.0 | 17.8 | 27.6 |
| With zero inflation | 0.7 | 24.0 | 23.2 |
| With 10 percent inflation | −8.4 | 7.6 | 30.7 |

a. Owned by households, tax-exempt institutions, and insurance companies.
b. Owned by households only.

Table 8-9. *Marginal Effective Tax Rates, 5 Percent Inflation, Corporate and Noncorporate Sectors and Owner-Occupied Housing, by Source of Finance, Fixed-*p, *1985, 1991*

Percent

| Year and source of finance | Sector | | |
|---|---|---|---|
| | Corporate | Noncorporate | Housing[a] |
| Debt | | | |
| 1985 | 4.1 | −42.3 | −39.2 |
| 1991 | 13.9 | 3.9 | 7.0 |
| Equity | | | |
| 1985 | 66.5 | 83.6 | 44.2 |
| 1991 | 47.0 | 53.3 | 43.9 |
| Overall tax rate | | | |
| 1985 | 33.9 | 17.8 | 15.0 |
| 1991 | 29.9 | 27.6 | 31.0 |

a. Value-added tax included.

the corporate and noncorporate sectors of the economy. The estimates agree with the popular view that the old tax system favored investment in owner-occupied housing at the expense of business investment in real capital. The 1991 tax reform is also seen to bring about a marked reduction in the magnitude of the intersectoral distortions on resource allocation imposed by the tax system.

## Problems of Measurement and Interpretation

The effective tax rate as measured in the King-Fullerton study and in this chapter captures the combined effects of personal and corporate taxes. It shows the percentage reduction in the after-tax return to savings compared to the pretax return on real investment. In a closed economy, where capital is completely immobile, the effective tax rate so defined provides a useful summary index of how the tax system affects the incentives to save and invest. But when capital is mobile, breaking the link between domestic savings and investment, a tax on personal savings is no longer necessarily equivalent to a tax on corporate earnings. For example, a reduction in personal taxes could stimulate domestic savings, but the increased savings need not be invested domestically.

In a small open economy, the incentive to invest afforded by the tax system may be measured by computing the wedge between the required pretax rate of return on investment and the exogenously given market interest rate. While the corporate tax is obviously part of this wedge, personal taxes also matter when real investment is financed by retained earnings (provided that capital gains receive a preferential tax treatment). This is most easily seen from equation 2.27 in King-Fullerton, which shows the firm's after-tax discount rate: the higher the marginal personal tax rate on interest income, the lower is the discount rate for retained earnings, and, therefore, the pretax required rate of return on real investment.[12]

This mechanism is emphasized by Hans-Werner Sinn in a study of the 1986 U.S. tax reform.[13] He argues forcefully that domestic investment is likely to be discouraged both by the corporate tax increases and by the cuts in personal taxes. The personal income tax reductions favor domestic and foreign financial investments in debt instruments by households over holdings of domestic shares (where the returns are partially taxed under increased capital gains taxes). To counteract this, firms must raise their pretax rate-of-return requirements on real investments financed by retained profits.

The tax rules in force in Sweden in 1985 implied that the marginal effective tax rate on investment (that is, the wedge between the pretax rate of return on investment and the market interest rate, in percent of the pretax return) was $-27.3$ percent. This should be compared with the total overall marginal effective tax rate, as defined in previous sections (for example, measuring the percentage reduction in the post-tax return on savings compared to the pretax return on investment), which was 33.9 percent at 5 percent inflation. The striking conclusion is therefore that the 1985 tax on capital income from the corporate sector effectively is a combination of a substantial net subsidy to investment and a high tax on savings.

These numbers must be interpreted with care. To determine the importance of personal taxes on the incentive to invest in an open economy is a difficult problem, which strictly speaking cannot be resolved without either a convincing general equilibrium model or empirical estimation of capital mobility. In particular, the negative relationship proposed here between the marginal personal tax rate and the size of the investment tax wedge requires the assumption that domestic shares cannot be traded internationally. If such trade is possible, the reduced demand for

12. King and Fullerton (1984, p. 23).
13. Sinn (1987).

domestic shares from domestic savers, as a result of a cut in personal taxes on interest income, may very well be offset by an increased foreign demand. The final outcome might be a change in the ownership of the domestic capital stock with little effect on real investment and with the corporate tax as the principal determinant of the incentive to invest.

To evaluate the relative contributions of different tax instruments to the total overall effective marginal tax rate, I calculated in my discussion of empirical results for 1985 the effective tax rates that would exist were it not for personal taxes. The corporation tax was found to impose a negative wedge between the pretax and post-tax rates of return. At 5 percent inflation the effective overall marginal corporate tax rate was −5 percent. The rate of subsidy was slightly higher for higher rates of inflation.

The two alternative estimates for the effective tax on investment given here, −27.3 percent and −5.0 percent, obviously leave much uncertainty about the precise nature of the incentive to invest. That the taxation of capital income originating in the corporate sector is not detrimental to investment seems clear, however. At the margin the tax system rather extends a net subsidy to investment, though the exact size of this subsidy remains uncertain.

An important and implicit assumption behind the estimates of marginal effective tax rates reported in this chapter is that all available corporate tax allowances are claimed by the firm and that they reduce corporate tax payments, or (if pretax profits are too low) give rise to tax refunds, in proportion to the corporate tax rate. An immediate objection here is that actual tax systems do not treat gains and losses symmetrically. The Swedish corporate tax, for example, provides only for loss carry-forward, which means that firms lose interest on losses claimed against profits for later years. This asymmetrical treatment of positive and negative tax bases may reduce the value of tax allowances below what was assumed for my estimates of effective tax rates.[14]

A potentially more important problem, however, is that even firms that pay corporate tax to a large extent have unused tax allowances. Data available from a study carried out by the Business Tax Commission and covering all manufacturing firms with more than fifty employees indicate that unused tax allowances on average during 1979–85 amounted to no less than 66 percent of all available allowances (regular depreciation al-

14. See Altshuler and Auerbach (1990) for an analysis of the effects of corporate tax asymmetries.

lowances and allocations to inventory reserves and investment funds).[15] Actual payments of corporate tax averaged 16 percent of pretax profits for the same period. This high figure on unused allowances is conceivably affected by the inclusion of firms that already had exhausted their tax payments and therefore could be expected to abstain from claiming further allowances. No attempt to eliminate tax-exhausted firms is made, however. For the subset of firms with above-average rates of return on equity capital—which is less likely to include tax-exhausted firms—the average corporate tax burden was 19 percent, while 40 percent of available tax allowances were still unused. An increase in the use of allowances by 16 percentage points (from 60 to 76 percent of maximum allowances) would have been sufficient to eliminate all corporate tax payments for this group of firms.

The important question is, therefore, why do companies pay corporation tax? A possible explanation for the coexistence of positive tax payments and unused tax allowances is provided by the close and legally determined connection in Sweden between book profits and tax-accounting profits. Allocations to inventory reserves and investment funds, for example, reduce both the base of the corporate tax and the book profits. Because of the legal requirement that dividends must be paid out of current or accumulated book profits, companies that pay dividends may be constrained in their use of tax allowances.

The implications of a dividend constraint of the type suggested here have recently been studied by Vesa Kanniainen, Jouk Ylä-Liedenpohja, and Södersten.[16] A common conclusion emerging from these studies is that when the firm is constrained in its use of tax allowances, the marginal effective corporate tax rate is zero. The intuitive interpretation of this is simple: when tax allowances on existing assets have not been fully used, an additional investment project will not affect total tax payments. For comparison I recall that the overall effective marginal corporate tax rate, estimated on the assumption that all allowances are claimed by the firms, was −5 percent in 1985 (see table 8-3). On average, therefore, the alternative assumption that firms always have unused tax allowances makes a difference of 5 percentage points. But for the question whether the corporate tax distorts the firm's choice of assets and sources of finance,

---

15. Finanzdepartementet (1989).
16. Kanniainen (1986); Ylä-Liedenpohja (1983); Södersten (1989); Kanniainen and Södersten (forthcoming).

it is still more crucial. The extent to which tax allowances are used by the firms and the exact reasons for not using them seem to be a subject worthy of further study.

## A Summing Up

The average overall effective tax rate on capital income from the corporate sector was 33.9 percent in 1985, at the then-prevailing rate of inflation and for standard parameter assumptions. This is 3.5 percentage points higher than the tax rate for 1980. For any given inflation rate, however, the 1985 tax schedule implies an effective tax rate that is 10 to 15 percentage points higher than in 1980. This increase is brought about mainly through a marked reduction in the rate of subsidy extended to companies through the corporate tax system.

A striking result of the estimate for 1985 is the wide dispersion in effective tax rates. There is a systematic variation in tax rates depending on type of asset, source of finance, and category of saver. Investment in machinery is favored more than other assets, and debt finance is favored over other ways of channeling savings into real investment. Direct ownership by households is much discriminated against, compared to institutional ownership.

In the spring of 1990 the Swedish Parliament enacted the most far-reaching reform of the nation's tax system in forty years. A noteworthy finding of this study is that the new tax system will improve the incentive to save and invest in real capital in the corporate sector. At 5 percent inflation, the overall effective marginal tax rate will be 4 percentage points lower than in 1985. However, this result is entirely due to the new taxation of persons. For corporations, the marginal tax burden will be somewhat higher. The reform package furthermore takes a major step toward achieving a more level playing field. For example, the incentive to use debt rather than equity as a source of finance is much reduced under the new tax rules and much of the present discrimination in favor of institutional ownership is eliminated. An additional important effect of the tax reform is to narrow the gap in effective tax rates between corporate investment and owner-occupied housing. This is accomplished mainly by eliminating the net subsidy to debt-financed investments in housing and the preferential treatment of construction costs under the value-added tax.

# References

Altshuler, Roseanne, and Alan Auerbach. 1990. "The Significance of Tax Law Asymmetries: An Empirical Investigation." *Quarterly Journal of Economics* 105 (February): 61–86.

Bergström, Villy. 1982. *Studies in Swedish Post-War Industrial Investments.* Stockholm: Uppsala University.

Finanzdepartementet. 1989. *Utredningen om reformerad företagsbeskattning* (Report on reforming the business tax). States Official Report 34 for 1989. Stockholm: Allmänna Förlaget.

Kanniainen, Vesa. 1986. "Tax Allowances and the Optimal Investment Policy by Firms." Discussion Paper 218. Helsinki: Research Institute of the Swedish Economy.

Kanniainen, Vesa, and Jan Södersten. Forthcoming. "Costs of Monitoring and Corporate Taxation." *Journal of Public Economics.*

King, Mervyn A., and Don Fullerton, eds. 1984. *The Taxation of Income from Capital: A Comparative Study of the United States, the United Kingdom, Sweden and West Germany.* University of Chicago Press.

Organization for Economic Cooperation and Development (OECD). 1992. *Revenue Statistics of OECD Member Countries, 1965-90.* Paris: OECD.

Sinn, Hans-Werner. 1987. *Capital Income Taxation and Resource Allocation.* Amsterdam: North-Holland.

Södersten, Jan. 1989. "The Investment Funds System Reconsidered." *Scandinavian Journal of Economics* 91(4): 671–87.

Södersten, Jan, and Thomas Lindberg. 1983. *Skatt på bolagskapital.* Stockholm: Industrial Institute for Economic and Social Research.

Taylor, John. 1982. "The Swedish Investment Funds System as a Stabilization Policy Rule." *Brookings Papers on Economic Activity* 1: 1–45.

Ylä-Liedenpohja, Jouk. 1983. "Financing and Investment under Unutilized Tax Allowances." *Reports and Discussion Papers* 35. Helsinki: Pellerro Economic Research Institute.

CHAPTER NINE

# United Kingdom

*Mervyn A. King*
*Mark H. Robson*

THE ANNUAL presentation of the budget in the United Kingdom has customarily taken place in March, just before the start of the new income tax year on April 6. It is not, however, concerned with government spending, which is reviewed annually in November. Accordingly, the main focus of the budget is on methods of raising revenue and the financing consequences of the resulting deficit or surplus. Besides setting rates and allowances of the principal taxes, the budget statement is also concerned with technical tax matters and sometimes with major reforms. The annual detailed finance bill is presented to Parliament a few weeks afterward, and after debate and amendment, becomes law in late July. Some budget tax proposals only become law at this point, but most are back-dated to budget day itself: April 1 (the start of the new tax year for companies); April 6 (the new tax year for all other taxpayers); or the date of publication of the finance bill.[1]

In this institutional framework—the personal income tax is still, formally, a tax imposed for one year at a time only—changes to the tax code occur much more frequently than in many other countries of the Organization for Economic Cooperation and Development (OECD). Understandably, each chancellor wishes to make the most of what is traditionally a highlight of the parliamentary year, and "dull" budgets are the exception rather than the rule. The Conservative government was in power throughout the 1980s. It was first elected in July 1979, with a pledge to cut direct taxes. After the first year, progress in reducing marginal and average rates of personal direct taxes was slow. But whereas the structure of the tax

1. This system was changed in 1993: the budget was moved to December, with decisions on taxing and spending taken at the same time. The tax year will, however, continue to begin and end in April, so that tax decisions will be taken earlier. See Dilnot and Robson (1993) for a fuller discussion.

300

system remained unchanged throughout the first term (until 1983), the second and third terms saw radical changes to both the rates and base of taxation.

A perennial issue in tax reform is the choice between an income-based or an expenditure-based tax system. In this context, one comment from the start of the U.K. chapter in King and Fullerton is particularly worth noting in the light of the past decade's experience: "There has been a gradual move from an income-based tax system to an expenditure-based tax system, albeit an uncoordinated change based on a series of ad hoc reforms. There have been occasional hiccups, but these have usually proved temporary."[2]

While such a statement held true until the year of publication (1984), the course of the U.K. tax system was abruptly reversed that year with the first budget of Nigel Lawson, then chancellor of the exchequer in the newly reelected Conservative government. The trend toward an expenditure-based corporate tax system noted by King and Fullerton was abandoned in favor of a return to an income-based system of a type not seen in the United Kingdom for many decades. Moreover, for the first time ever the rates of corporation tax and capital allowances were determined for the four-year period ahead, that being the expected life of the Parliament. (Previously, rates of this tax had been set annually in arrears—a curious British custom readopted in 1991). Details of this complicated reform are set out later, but here we note that the most evident consequence was a progressive reduction in the marginal tax rate from 52 to 35 percent, made while many tax-exhausted companies were brought back into tax. Because of the way the reform was structured and announced, in the short term there was a boom in investment in plant, machinery, and industrial buildings, and a significant increase in both the corporate tax wedge and revenues.[3]

After the end of the transitional period in 1987, the year in which the government was elected to a third term in office, Nigel Lawson presented two more budgets before resigning in the autumn of 1989. The year 1990 heralded the first and only budget of his successor, John Major, who then became prime minister in succession to Margaret Thatcher. That budget made one significant change to taxation of personal savings, discussed later, but otherwise contained few surprises. The 1991 budget

2. King and Fullerton (1984, p. 31, note 1).
3. See Robson (1989) for full details.

presented by Major's successor as Chancellor of the Exchequer, Norman Lamont, contained some interesting changes of direction: the most important concerned the balance between local-government and central-government taxes.

Local government in the United Kingdom had traditionally been financed solely by a system of block grants from central government based on notional population needs, supplemented by local property taxes known as rates. Rates were levied on occupiers of both commercial and domestic property, on the basis of a notional rental value multiplied by a rate set for each financial year by the local authority or authorities for the area (up to three tiers). This was the only form of annual wealth tax levied in the United Kingdom. By 1979 the system had fallen into disrepute through a combination of a failure to adjust the notional rental values and the fact that only a minority of local government electors and consumers of services contributed directly to the cost of those services.

After all alternatives had been considered and rejected, the now infamous "community charge," or poll tax, was introduced in Scotland in 1989, and in England and Wales in 1990. After a revaluation, rates were retained on business property, but with the rate for each year being set by the central government rather than by each local authority. Further details of the system are discussed later under "Local Taxes," but perhaps the most dramatic feature of the 1991 budget was the announcement that as soon as a replacement property tax could be put in place, the poll tax would be abolished. For the year 1991–92, the government cut poll tax levels by £140 per person across the board; this reduction was financed by a rise in the standard rate of value-added tax (VAT) from 15.0 to 17.5 percent. The last increase in VAT had been in 1979, when the rate was almost doubled from 8 percent to finance cuts in personal income tax rates.

Table 9-1 summarizes the changes in significance (for raising revenue) of the various taxes over the period. The share of total receipts from the personal income tax declined as the share from VAT increased, a result of the switch from direct to indirect taxes to which the government was committed in 1979. Both the personal capital gains tax and the corporation tax declined in significance until the institution of various structural changes, described in detail below. A lucrative payroll tax (called the national insurance surcharge) was abolished in 1984. The decline and revival in customs and excise duties is particularly striking. For several years these were not indexed fully for inflation, although later there was

Table 9-1.   *Sources of U.K. Tax Revenue, 1979–80, 1984–85, 1989–90*
Percent

| | Share of total receipts | | |
|---|---|---|---|
| Revenue source | 1979–80 | 1984–85 | 1989–90 |
| Taxes on personal incomes | 29.1 | 25.6 | 25.6 |
| Taxes on personal capital | 2.1 | 1.4 | 2.7 |
| Taxes on corporate incomes and capital gains | 7.6 | 6.4 | 11.3 |
| Social security and payroll taxes | 21.7 | 18.5 | 17.4 |
| Local (property) taxes | 12.2 | 10.0 | 10.6 |
| Value-added tax | 10.3 | 14.4 | 15.6 |
| Customs and excises | 14.9 | 7.9 | 13.5 |
| Other taxes (including oil and gas) | 2.1 | 15.8 | 3.3 |

Sources: For 1979–80, King and Fullerton (1984, table 3-1); for other years, Board of Inland Revenue (various years).

some limited catching up and increased demand. The bulge in other taxes is almost entirely accounted for by the substantial yield from North Sea oil taxes in the early 1980s.

## The Tax System

In this section we discuss the personal income tax, the corporate tax system, tax allowances, investment grants, local taxes, wealth taxes, taxation of housing, and taxation of personal savings and investment.

### The Personal Income Tax

Of all the U.K. direct taxes, the personal income tax superficially changed the least over the period 1984–90 from the description found in King and Fullerton.

ALLOWANCES AND RATES.  By statutory provision, the personal tax-free allowances and tax bands are automatically increased in line with retail price inflation over the preceding calendar year unless a contrary decision is taken in each budget. In fact, the tendency has been to increase allowances by rather more than this amount in most years, for earnings have risen faster than prices. But on occasion (in 1990 as in 1981) the opposite has applied, particularly when it appears necessary to rein in consumer demand. The single person's allowance, which stood at £1,375 a year in 1980–81, had risen to £2,205 for 1985–86, and to £3,005 for

Table 9-2.   *Statutory Rates of U.K. Income Tax, 1980–81, 1985–86, 1990–91*

Income in pounds; rate of tax in percent

| | 1980–81 | | 1985–86 | | 1990–91 | |
|---|---|---|---|---|---|---|
| Type | Taxable income | Tax rate | Taxable income | Tax rate | Taxable income | Tax rate |
| Basic rate | 1–11,250 | 30 | 1–16,200 | 30 | 1–20,700 | 25 |
| Higher rates | 11,251–13,250 | 40 | 16,201–19,200 | 40 | 20,700 and above | 40 |
| | 13,251–16,750 | 45 | 19,201–24,400 | 45 | | |
| | 16,751–22,250 | 50 | 24,401–32,300 | 50 | | |
| | 22,251–27,750 | 55 | 32,301–41,200 | 55 | | |
| | 27,751 and over | 60 | 41,201 and over | 60 | | |

Source: *Annual Finance Acts* (various years).

1990–91, whereas if statutory indexation had been applied from 1980–81, these amounts would have been £2,065 and £2,695, respectively. There has been slow progress in reducing the basic rate of income tax, which is the marginal rate for most taxpayers (the higher rates would have produced only about 5 percent of the total income tax yield in 1985–86). It remained unchanged at 30 percent from 1979 to 1986, but more dramatically, all higher income tax rates above the first were abolished in 1988, as shown in table 9-2. Thereafter there were only two rates of income tax, 25 percent and 40 percent.[4] As figures 9-1 and 9-2 indicate, progressivity as measured by marginal and average rates changed insignificantly between 1980–81 and 1985–86, but dramatically after the 1988 change. The government has expressed its intention of reducing the basic rate still further, to 20 percent, but the date by which this reduction can be attained is undeclared and unclear.

INDEPENDENT TAXATION.   A new system of independent taxation of husband and wife was introduced in 1990–91. Previously, all a wife's income was treated like that of her husband. Although a wife was entitled to a separate single person's allowance on her earned income, her investment income was always taxed at the husband's marginal rate, and normally only one band of income at each rate of tax was allowed to the couple, just as for a single person. The exception to this rule was taxation by special election. High-income two-earner couples could opt for a band of income at each tax rate for each of them, as if they were still single, but at the cost of losing

4. A reduced rate band at 20 percent was introduced in April 1992 on the first £2,000 of taxable income.

Figure 9-1.  *Marginal Income Tax Rates, 1980-81, 1985-86, 1990-91*

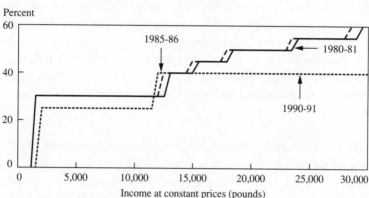

the benefit of the higher married man's tax allowance. However, this treatment was available in respect of earned income only. The wife's unearned income was treated as that of her husband in every case.

Under the new system, every married man living with his wife or supporting her still receives a higher personal allowance, although interestingly the amount was not indexed in 1991. But all the wife's income is now regarded as her own in all circumstances, with a single person's allowance available against unearned as well as earned income, and with a separate band of income taxed at the basic rate, just as if she were single. The most significant behavioral change is likely to occur in the case of those couples with investment income but with only the husband earning. Clearly they have an incentive to ensure that income-yielding

Figure 9-2.  *Average Income Tax Rates, 1980-81, 1985-86, 1990-91*

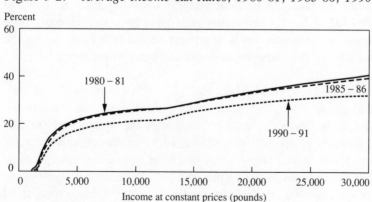

investments are held in the wife's name, at least to the extent that her own allowance can be used to cover investment income free of tax. For such couples, the marginal rate of tax on dividends, for example, could drop abruptly, from either 25 percent or 40 percent to zero. For some years yet, there will be no published data from which to assess the extent of this behavioral change, but certainly the average marginal tax rate on quoted equity and bonds held by individuals must be expected to fall as a result.

ABOLITION OF COMPOSITE RATE. A further change accompanying the introduction of independent taxation will have the effect of increasing the marginal rate for many savers. For decades in the case of building-society (savings and loan) deposit accounts, and under a similar system for bank-deposit accounts since 1985, tax has been accounted for by the institutions under what is known as the composite rate. On the basis of an annual statistical survey of the number of depositors, both taxpayers and nontaxpayers, a weighted average of zero and the basic rate of income tax was applied to all but the largest deposits by individuals with each institution, and this tax satisfied the basic rate liability. It was not refundable to nontaxpayers, but taxpayers were credited with having paid tax at the basic rate; those liable at higher rates had to pay the difference. An example may make this rather curious system clearer. For 1990–91 the composite rate was 22 percent, indicative of an approximate weight of nontaxpayers to taxpayers of 12 to 88 percent overall. On a net interest payment of £30, the institution accounted for tax of £8.46 (22 percent of the gross), but the depositor was credited with having paid tax of £10; this was irrecoverable for a nontaxpayer, but satisfied basic-rate liability at 25 percent for a taxpayer. A higher-rate taxpayer, liable at 40 percent, would have to pay a further £6 tax. This efficient means of collecting tax was abolished from 1991–92 on, so that before any consequent behavioral change, while the average marginal rate on such interest should remain the same, the marginal rate for the taxpaying majority of savers will increase.

SOCIAL SECURITY. The social security tax (known as national insurance contributions, or NICs, but in effect little more than a tax on payroll) continues to be levied on earnings, although the system has suffered several changes in structure since 1980. However, the effective rate for most employees has changed little, declining from a typical combined rate levied on employer and employee of 20.45 percent in 1980–81 to 19.45 percent in 1990–91. Under the present structure there is some relief on contributions for those making less money, but no upper-earnings limit on the employer's contribution of 10.4 percent. Traditionally NICs have been levied only on cash earnings and not on benefits in kind, so that employers have had a strong incentive to reimburse workers with perquisites rather than cash. But in 1991–92, perhaps as an experiment, the scope of which may be widened, employers' NICs were levied on the benefit to employees using company cars, as measured for income tax purposes.

INVESTMENT INCOME SURCHARGE. The surcharge of 15 percent on individuals with high unearned incomes was abolished in 1984. The highest marginal rate on income from capital therefore fell from 75 percent in 1980 to 40 percent ten years later, and the historic discrimination in the tax system in favor of earned against unearned income had been reversed, since NICs are levied on earned income alone.

PERSONAL CAPITAL GAINS. The system of taxing capital gains (formally separate from the income tax) experienced radical change over the decade of the 1980s. Since the abolition of all higher rates of income tax above the first 40 percent in 1988, capital gains of individuals are added to income and taxed at each individual's marginal income tax rate, either 25 percent or 40 percent. Previously the marginal rate had been 30 percent. Since 1988 only realized real gains over March 1982 market values are taxed, adjusted by reference to retail-price inflation, and then subject to an annual exemption limit that for 1990–91 was set at £5,000. For previous years, married couples received only one such allowance between them. Now each spouse has an allowance. The pre-1988 system charged gains over 1965 market values, with only limited indexation relief but subject to a higher annual exempt amount. However, since most realized gains are large, the average marginal statutory rate is estimated by Mark H. Robson to have risen sharply as a result of the change, from 26.4 percent in 1987–88 to 34.9 percent in 1988–89.[5]

## The Corporate Tax System

The U.K. system of corporation tax changed little during the first Conservative administration (1979–83). This was certainly not due to satisfaction with the system: on the contrary, a government Green Paper (a public

5. Robson (1988).

Table 9-3.  *Corporate Tax Rates, 1980–91*

Percent except for Θ

| Year commencing April 1 | τ (main) | τ (small profits) | Θ |
|---|---|---|---|
| 1980 | 52 | 40 | 1.429 |
| 1981 | 52 | 38 | 1.429 |
| 1982 | 52 | 30 | 1.429 |
| 1983 | 50 | 30 | 1.429 |
| 1984 | 45 | 30 | 1.429 |
| 1985 | 40 | 30 | 1.429 |
| 1986 | 35 | 29 | 1.408 |
| 1987 | 35 | 27 | 1.370 |
| 1988 | 35 | 25 | 1.333 |
| 1989 | 35 | 25 | 1.333 |
| 1990 | 34 | 25 | 1.333 |
| 1991 | 33 | 25 | 1.333 |

Sources: *Annual Finance Acts* (various years); and authors' calculations.

consultation document inviting representations) issued in 1980 bemoaned the inadequacies of the system inherited from the previous Labour government. Reform was delayed until 1984. Table 9-3 summarizes corporation tax rates over the period.

Since 1972 the United Kingdom has applied a partial-imputation tax system to corporate income. The imputation rate has always been set so as to attach to a dividend payment a tax credit equivalent to the basic rate of income tax. So, for example, if as in 1990–91 the basic rate stands at 25 percent, a dividend of £750 will be subject to a payment of advance corporation tax (ACT) of £250 by the company, which satisfies the basic rate liability of a U.K. resident shareholder. If that individual is liable at a higher rate of income tax, only the difference must be paid. A nontaxpayer (including pension funds) may have the credit refunded in full. The company is able to credit the payment of ACT against its liability to tax on an equivalent amount of profits (income or capital gains) in the same year or up to six previous years, or by carry-forward to future years.

SMALL COMPANIES.  Defined by reference only to the size of its taxable profits in any year, a small company benefits from a lower rate of corporation tax. Since 1982 the rate has been set equal to the income tax basic rate, so in that case the system is one of full imputation. In 1982–83 any company with taxable profits of less than £100,000 benefited from this relief, with a taper (and hence a higher marginal rate of 37.5 percent) on profits between £100,000 and £500,000. These two thresholds were increased to £150,000 and £750,000 in 1989, to £200,000 and £1,000,000 in 1990, and to £250,000 and £1,250,000 in 1991. Because of the reduction since 1989 in the corporation tax rate from 35 to 33 percent, the marginal rate of tax on profits lying between the two thresholds was 35 percent for 1991–92.

TAX EXHAUSTION. Under the imputation system, it is possible for a company to become "tax-exhausted" in either of two senses. First, it may simply be generating tax losses instead of profits each year, although viable on a going-concern basis or even still generating accounting profits. This was a feature of the system at the end of the 1970s, when very generous reliefs for physical investment, stock building, and nominal interest payments (at a time when real rates of interest were negative) had led to an enormous accumulation of tax losses for the corporate sector as a whole, being carried forward from year to year in nominal terms. The government's Green Paper on corporation tax, published in 1980, noted that about one-third of all companies were unlikely to pay corporation tax at all over a period of years, with a second third moving in and out of tax from year to year. However, to the extent that these companies were still able to pay dividends,they were paying advance corporation tax but without being able to offset it against future tax liabilities on profits. This is the second type of tax exhaustion: the accumulation of surplus advance corporation tax. It was possible for a company to be in this position without having tax losses, since until 1986 advance corporation tax could be offset only against corporation tax on an equivalent amount of *income*: dividends paid out of realized capital gains would still generate surplus ACT. Despite subsequent tax reform, the surplus-ACT problem remains for many U.K.-based multinationals paying dividends in the United Kingdom out of profits remitted from abroad, since for this purpose no credit is given for foreign taxes paid.

CORPORATE CAPITAL GAINS. Companies' capital gains were formerly charged to corporation tax at 30 percent, the same rate charged to individuals, but without the benefit of any annual exemption. Income losses could be offset against capital gains, but not vice versa, so that any capital losses could be carried forward only in nominal terms to offset future gains. For a company facing a marginal rate of 52 percent, it was clearly advantageous, where possible, to convert investment income into capital gains.

The various devices by which the government had attempted to combat this advantage were rendered largely unnecessary in March 1987, since from that time gains have been added to income and charged at each company's marginal rate (from 1987 to 1990 the possible rates were 25.0 percent, 37.5 percent, or 35.0 percent). Clearly this worked to the benefit of small companies, but to compensate the remainder, ACT was then allowed to be offset against tax liabilities on gains as well as income. However, it remains true that capital losses cannot reduce taxable income, and gains are indexed for inflation but income is not. We have already noted that a similar change in marginal rates was made to capital gains of individuals in 1988, and evidently such treatment was only regarded as feasible after marginal income tax rates had been reduced from their previous levels.

THE 1984 REFORMS. For companies, the reduction in marginal rates was effected by the 1984 budget. In response to public consultation following publication of the Green Paper of 1980, no clear consensus had emerged as to how the admittedly unsatisfactory company tax regime might be changed, although there was a widespread plea for stability. The radical changes in 1984 therefore came as a surprise. Until that time, the corporation tax rate had always been set one year at a time, in arrears, and had remained at 52 percent since 1973. Revenues had fallen as the tax base had become narrower, with increasingly generous reliefs. The scheme of the 1984 budget was to set rates of tax and reliefs for the four years to March 1987, reducing marginal rates while broadening the tax base. The tax rate was to fall from 52 to 35 percent, and the 100 percent first-year allowance (immediate expensing) for investment in most equipment and inventories was to be replaced by allowances closer to economic depreciation. The principal effects were expected to be to bring more companies into tax, using up accumulated tax losses quickly, to stimulate investment and revenues in the short term, and to reduce the marginal tax burden on those companies already paying tax.

### Tax Allowances for Depreciation and Inventories

As noted by King and Fullerton, the corporate tax system in 1980 was very much expenditure-based. Almost all investment in plant and machinery received 100 percent first-year allowances, the few categories that did not (such as cars) being given annual allowances on a 25 percent

reducing-balance basis. All investment in industrial buildings and structures received 50 percent initial allowances (increased to 75 percent in
1981), the balance of cost being given at 4 percent straight line over the
years immediately following first use. Land and other business buildings
had never received tax relief, on the grounds that they do not usually depreciate in nominal terms, although repair, maintenance, and replacement
costs were allowed as revenue expenditure.

All annual increases in the nominal value of stocks, real and inflationary above a figure of 15 percent of trading profits, had been relieved from
tax since 1973, in an emergency measure introduced retrospectively in
1975 during a period of unusually high inflation. This generous scheme
was modified in 1981, to provide relief only on stock increases over opening values inflated by an "all stocks index" (designed to capture average
inflation in stock prices over the period) and restricting the carry-forward
of losses generated by the relief to six years. King and Fullerton inferred
that change in this direction would be an "occasional hiccup," but in this
instance it proved to be symptomatic of more serious indigestion.[6]

At the same time rates of corporate tax were reduced for 1984 to 1987,
rates of first-year allowances were to be phased out. The remaining stock
relief was abolished immediately. Table 9-4 shows allowances available
as a proportion of cost, assuming the asset was first used in the year of
acquisition. Traditionally, changes came into effect from budget day itself,
a little earlier than April 1. Depreciation allowances on fixed investment
have never been indexed. Figures in brackets show the present value of
the full stream of depreciation allowances, as a proportion of cost, at
a discount rate equal to the rate of inflation for the year to the budget
month. Although not forward-looking, these figures give a rough idea of
the loss in value of allowances due to the delay in receiving credit for
cost against tax payments.

Initial allowances on construction of mine works, oil wells, and so
forth, and on hotels, remained in place at their respective rates of 40
percent and 20 percent until 1986, when they were abolished. The
only expenditure that has been spared the conversion to quasi-income-tax

6. For further discussion of the two stock relief schemes, see King and Fullerton (1984, pp. 43–
45). King and Fullerton assumed for 1980–81 that the new scheme was effective. The transition date
was November 14, 1980, and some years later it was found that, because of the way in which the
transitional relief was applied in practice, almost all companies were able to benefit from the old relief
for the accounting period straddling the transition date. We have therefore departed from King and
Fullerton with the benefit of hindsight to assume the old scheme in force for 1980–81.

Table 9-4. *Depreciation Allowances, 1980–92*

Percent

| Year | Inflation (1) | Plants and machinery (NPV) | | Buildings and structures (NPV) | |
|---|---|---|---|---|---|
| | | (2) | (3) | (4) | (5) |
| 1980–81 | 19.8 | 100 | 83.5 | 54 | 59.9 |
| 1981–82 | 12.6 | 100 | 88.8 | 79 | 83.2 |
| 1982–83 | 10.4 | 100 | 90.6 | 79 | 85.7 |
| 1983–84 | 4.6 | 100 | 95.6 | 79 | 93.0 |
| 1984–85 | 5.3 | 75 | 90.9 | 54 | 83.5 |
| 1985–86 | 6.1 | 50 | 85.0 | 29 | 67.6 |
| 1986–87 | 4.2 | 25 | 85.5 | 4 | 61.0 |
| 1987–88 | 4.0 | 25 | 86.2 | 4 | 62.5 |
| 1988–89 | 3.5 | 25 | 87.8 | 4 | 66.1 |
| 1989–90 | 7.9 | 25 | 76.0 | 4 | 43.2 |
| 1990–91 | 8.1 | 25 | 75.5 | 4 | 42.3 |
| 1991–92 | 8.2 | 25 | 75.2 | 4 | 41.8 |

Source: Tables 9-4 through 9-10 are authors' calculations.
Column 1: Annual retail price inflation for March immediately preceding each year.
Column 2: Balance of cost allowed at 25 percent in each following year on reducing balance basis.
Column 3: Net present value of allowances applying discount rate in column 1 and assuming one-year lag between cost outlay and benefit of first allowance.
Column 4: Balance of cost allowed at 4 percent in each year, including year of first use, on straight-line basis.
Column 5: Same as column 3.

treatment is that which takes place in depressed geographic areas designated enterprise zones. Starting in some cases in 1981, for ten years since designation, all business buildings (that is, including offices and other commercial buildings that otherwise would receive no allowances) in these zones continue to receive the benefit of 100 percent immediate cost write-off. While not particularly significant when first-year allowances stood at up to 79 percent on industrial buildings, the differential benefit of this relief following the 1984 changes has been great.

In the corporate sector, companies paying tax at the main rate received the benefit of declining marginal tax rates against the disadvantage of withdrawn accelerated depreciation allowances. Because the changes were announced in advance, there was an unsurprising investment boom over the period. Tax-paying companies that forestalled investment projects could benefit from higher capital allowances, against higher current rates of tax, in the knowledge that future returns would be taxed at a lower marginal rate. Foresight poses a difficulty for the conventional cost of capital methodology, which is myopic, and as a result will tend to overstate the true cost of capital over a transitional period of this sort. Difficult issues arise, as discussed in detail in Robson, to which the interested reader is referred.[7] However, for the sake of consistency we ignore the problem here and stick to convention. Only the results for 1985 are significantly affected. The implicit assumption for that year is that information on the tax regime for following years was not exploited. For 1990–91, similarly we assume that the retrospective reduction in the corporation tax rate from 35 to 34 percent was foreseen and expected to remain in force for following years. From April 1991 the rate of corporation tax was in fact reduced to 33 percent.

In the noncorporate sector and for small companies, withdrawal of depreciation allowances from 1984 was not compensated by lower tax rates. The incentive to forestall for such firms would therefore have been more limited but still significant.

## Investment Grants and Incentives

HISTORY OF CHANGES. The present system of regional incentives in Great Britain was introduced by the Industry Act of 1972, but has undergone many radical changes since 1980. The two major schemes were regional development grants[8] and regional selective assistance. Regional development grants (RDGs) provided largely automatic assistance at fixed rates for qualifying investment in particular areas of the country. Regional selective assistance (RSA) provided discretionary grants to projects in particular areas where, at least in principle, the projects would not have proceeded without the grant.

In July 1979 the government announced the first changes in its policies concerning incentives for regional development, primarily involving reductions in the regions eligible for special incentives in two stages effective from August 1, 1980, and August 1, 1982. In 1983 emphasis changed when the government expressed its belief that although regional selective assistance was for the most part effective and economical, regional development grants were not, being heavily biased toward capital-intensive projects and not linked to the creation of new jobs. A new scheme of regional development grants was announced in November 1984, making grants project related rather than asset related, and linking grants to the creation of new jobs.

7. Robson (1989).
8. King and Fullerton (1984, sect. 3.2.5).

But in January 1988 the government announced that the new scheme of automatic grants would be closed to applications after March 31, 1988. This was a further policy shift away from automatic grants and toward discretionary ones. On March 29, 1988, it was announced that a new scheme of discretionary regional assistance, regional enterprise grants, would start from April 1 providing assistance for firms with fewer than 25 employees in the development areas only, specifically to encourage capital investment and innovation.

Northern Ireland has always had an entirely different system of grants. Although a small part of the United Kingdom, Northern Ireland is highly significant for this purpose because its economic situation has been so poor since 1972 that the proportion of grants made there far outweighs its significance in terms of population and economic activity. The total amount of each type of grant paid over the period from 1972 to the April 1988 changes was as follows:

| *Great Britain* | *Millions of pounds* |
|---|---|
| Regional development grants | 5,991 |
| Regional selective assistance (grants) | 1,101 |
| Other discretionary grants | 216 |
| Loans/equity (before repayments and interest) | 128 |
| *Northern Ireland* | |
| Standard capital grants | 513 |
| Other selective assistance (grants) | 71 |

REGIONAL DEVELOPMENT GRANTS. Under the original scheme (RDG I), qualifying investment in development areas and special development areas received grants of 20 percent and 22 percent, respectively. Qualifying activities comprised such things as providing new buildings and adapting existing buildings, and providing new plant and machinery on qualifying premises. In addition, building and works expenditure in designated intermediate areas were eligible for grants of 20 percent until August 1, 1980, at which date the rate of grant in development areas was reduced from 20 to 15 percent. RDG I was asset based, not project based, and intentionally directed at capital investment in manufacturing industries.

RDG I was officially ended on November 28, 1984. The new scheme of regional development grants (RDG II) was available only to projects that would create new capacity, extend existing capacity, or "effect a change in a product, process, or service." Virtually all manufacturing activities qualified, except for the extraction of metalliferous ores and the installation of electrical equipment, as did diverse service activities. Under the new scheme there were no longer special development areas but only development areas. Intermediate areas did not qualify for regional development grants. There was an explicit attempt to link grants to the creation of new jobs, so that many projects in the service industry qualified under RDG II that had not under RDG I. Applicants could choose to receive a grant based either on the level of capital expenditure or on the number of net new jobs the project created. The capital grant was provided at a rate of 15 percent, up to a limit of £10,000 for each net new job created. However, firms with fewer than 200 employees did not face this cost-per-job limit as long as their total project expenditure was less than £500,000. The job grant was £3,000 for each net new job created, although for manufacturing and certain projects in the service sector the grant was limited to 40 percent of initial investment in the project.

REGIONAL SELECTIVE ASSISTANCE. Regional selective assistance (RSA) is a discretionary, project-related grant. It is normally given as a capital grant, although other forms are available. For example, training grants can be awarded, for which the maximum grant is 40 percent of the cost of materials and the wage costs of instructors and trainees: but in addition, there is a matching contribution from the European Social Fund, so that up to 80 percent of eligible training costs may be covered. In the past, soft loans and equity stakes were common, but they ceased in 1983. Separate series are published for grants under these different heads, and grants based on capital expenditure have been by far the largest part of the RSA scheme since 1977. In 1987–88, £140.0 million out of total payments of £148.7 million under RSA was for capital-project grants.

Payments of RSA grants are made after the firm makes the necessary expenditures. Typically, the first payment comes after one-third of expenditure on fixed assets has been made. After that, claims and payments are usually made annually, as the project progresses.

ENTERPRISE ZONES. In part, the system of RDGs was replaced by the experimental enterprise zones. Starting in 1981, several small depressed areas of the United Kingdom were designated under this scheme to encourage development. For a ten-year period, all business buildings in the zones enjoyed a holiday from local authority rates, and received 100 percent capital allowances (whether or not they qualified under the normal rules as industrial buildings). There were also greatly simplified planning procedures. The scheme attracted particular attention after the removal of 75 percent accelerated allowances for industrial buildings in 1984, although there has also been a considerable amount of office development, most spectacularly on London's Isle of Dogs. However, a recent Department of Environment study suggested that most of the fiscal benefits had been capitalized in land prices and rents, and the scheme is not being extended.

METHODOLOGY. Unlike tax reliefs and grants under RDG I, the remaining grants are discretionary, and so a difficulty arises regarding which to take account of in computing average marginal tax rates, including grants. King and Fullerton proposed to "make a conservative assumption about the grants firms expect would be forthcoming on additional investment projects," adding, "We shall ignore *all* discretionary grants and analyze only grants paid at fixed statutory rates on well-defined activities."[9] Only RDG I meets this criterion and as a result it was acknowledged that the level of grants, even at the margin, would be understated. But the procedure was defended on the grounds that RDG I was "far and away the most important and dependable form of assistance to investment provided through channels other than the tax system." While this is no longer true, the procedure does have the merit of being easily understood, and so is adopted here. It should be borne in mind that, particularly for 1990–91, the corporate tax wedge taking account of all grants paid would be lower than that presented here. By how much is difficult to assess for various reasons: the data are not published in a form well suited for this purpose, and in particular lags between offer and payment dates are long and variable.

We have also ignored enterprise zones, given the very small geographical area covered. The data on grant rates for 1980–81 used in King and Fullerton have been updated with the benefit of later, improved official data.

### Local Taxes

Despite extensive public debate over local-authority taxation in the United Kingdom, the only local tax on business property continues to be "rates," the tax on the benefit of occupation of immovable property assessed by reference to a notional rental value. However, the major change from 1990 in England and Wales (introduced a year earlier in Scotland) is that, after a revaluation of commercial property rental values, the rate of

---

9. King and Fullerton (1984, p. 50).

tax on rental value is now determined nationally at a uniform rate instead of by each local authority. Simultaneously, rates have been abolished on occupation of domestic property and replaced by a "community charge" or poll tax. The amount of this tax is fixed by each local authority and levied on all adult residents, subject to a very limited number of exemptions and rebates of up to 80 percent for the poorest individuals. Each authority's spending is financed by the central government grant, its share of the uniform business rate, and its community-charge proceeds. Because in most cases revenue from the community charge was designed to represent around a quarter of local revenues, there is a high gearing effect. A local authority desirous of increasing spending by 10 percent must raise its community charge by about 40 percent; any authority doing so would be likely to have its target charge "capped" (set at a lower amount) under powers retained by the central government.

In the first year of operation, most authorities levied an annual charge in the range of £250–£450. But following a widespread campaign of civil disobedience, after authorities had announced their charges from 1991–92, it was announced on budget day 1991 that all authorities would receive a subsidy of £140 a head on the basic charge—which resulted in some cases in no levy for the year. The charge was scheduled to be scrapped in 1993, to be replaced by a new form of property tax intended to be a function of both the capital value of the property, assessed in one of about eight bands, and the number of inhabitants. Although at the time of writing the details are far from clear, it appears that there will be standard multipliers for each of the bands of capital value (say, A to G) applied to a domestic tax rate for the year set by each local authority, with a discount at a standard rate (25 percent is suggested) for all single-person households. An element of wealth tax will therefore be restored to the system. It seems likely that the central government will retain the power to cap local authorities' revenue raised from this source and hence spending. No further changes are proposed to the uniform business rate.

## Wealth Taxes

At present there are no personal wealth taxes in the United Kingdom, and apart from rates, no corporate wealth taxes. The new post-1975 system of taxing capital transfers that was described in King and Fullerton again suffered radical changes in 1986, when the capital transfer tax was misleadingly renamed the inheritance tax. In fact for the most part it continues to be a tax on death estates, levied by reference to donor and not donee. As is the case with the pre-1975 estate duty, gifts made within seven years of death come within the charge at lower rates, but no other lifetime transfers are taxed. The schedule of rates has been changed in every recent year, and in 1988 the tax was converted from a scheme of progressive marginal rates ranging from 30 to 60 percent, to a flat-rate tax at 40 percent, the same as the higher rate on income and capital gains. Since this tax only applies when the value of the death estate and transfers within seven years exceeds £128,000 (for 1990–91) after the various exemptions, relatively few people are caught and the yield is small.

Treating rates on commercial property as a wealth tax, King and Fullerton suggested assuming an even distribution of the burden across the noncorporate and three industrial sectors, to arrive at a universal figure of 2.46 percent on buildings for 1980–81. However, the denominator in arriving at this number is the ill-defined value of the private net capital stock in buildings other than dwellings. Subsequent data revision suggests a slightly higher figure of 2.7 percent, increasing to 3.5 percent in 1985–86. This upward drift, however, was then halted by the introduction of rate capping (central-government intervention to prevent many local authorities from raising their rates and spending by as much as desired). Because of revaluation and the switch to the uniform business rate, the position for 1990–91 is highly unclear, since there are large redistributional effects between sectors and regions. Because the rationale behind the uniform business rate was to raise equivalent revenues, we have provisionally assumed an average figure of 3.5 percent for this year also.

### Taxation of Housing

The tax treatment of owner-occupied housing in the United Kingdom is generous. Whereas all interest receipts are taxed, almost all interest payments by individuals for nontrade purposes are not deductible. The principal exception is interest paid on a mortgage on a first home, up to a ceiling of £30,000. This limit is not indexed: it was increased from the original amount of £25,000 in 1984, but its real value has otherwise been allowed to decline with inflation. Until 1988 this limit was applied to each individual (treating married couples as one person), but it is now applied to each property. The unusually long lag between announcement and imposition of this change—more than four months—contributed to a boom in house prices in 1988.

Contrary to popular belief, deductibility of mortgage interest does not of itself introduce a distortion in favor of owner occupation. In fact, the owner of a mortgaged property who decides to rent rather than occupy will receive a deduction for interest in full, without a ceiling. It is the absence (since 1962) of a charge on imputed rents that differentiates an owner-occupier from a landlord. A cross-party political consensus has come to regard residential mortgage interest relief as anomalous. Accordingly, there are now three important differences in the interest regime as between owner-occupied and rented domestic property. First, interest relief on loans for home improvements rather than purchase was also abolished in 1988. Second, in most cases relief on home mortgages is given for basic rate tax at source, under the system known as MIRAS (mortgage interest relief at source). Anyone who has a MIRAS mortgage pays interest net of basic rate tax, and for nontaxpayers the subsidy is not reclaimed by the government. Conversely, any nontaxpayer who has the misfortune to have a mortgage outside MIRAS—say, from a private lender—cannot benefit from this subsidy. Third, although interest relief at marginal rates, over and above the basic rate, was previously given through a higher-rate taxpayer's tax assessment or by adjusting deduction of tax at source on earnings, such higher-rate relief has been withdrawn since April 1991. The main privileges afforded to owner occupation are that since 1965 there has been no tax on imputed rental income, whereas landlords are charged tax on gross rentals, net of expenses, as investment income; and capital gains on an individual's only or main residence are exempt from tax.

Investment in owner-occupied housing yields a return to the owner in the form of housing services. The owner both supplies the funds and consumes the return. The marginal rate of return equals the marginal cost of housing services, which excluding depreciation and repairs is the sum of the income that the owner sacrifices by investing in his house rather than in alternative assets, plus mortgage interest (net of relief) minus the capital gain on the house. Let the annual rate of consumer price inflation be denoted by $\pi$, the real rate of increase of house prices by $\pi_H$, the marginal tax rate by $m$, the rate of property taxes on housing by $t_H$, and the pretax real rate of interest by $r$—this is assumed equal on both mortgages and alternative investments. If mortgage interest is tax deductible at the marginal rate and capital gains are tax exempt, then the capital cost of housing services or equivalently the value of $p$ is given by $p = (1 - m)r - \pi_H - m\pi + t_H$. In the absence of a personal wealth tax on other assets, the post-tax rate of return on savings is $(1 - m)r - m\pi$. Hence, $w = p - s = t_H - \pi_H$. In other words, leaving to one side the property tax on housing and the differential rate of increase of the price of houses, the tax wedge on investment in owner-occupied housing is zero. A nonzero wedge derives only from the combination of three factors. The first two are the property tax and real capital gains on housing. In both the United Kingdom and the United States, property tax gains and real capital gains are broadly offsetting. The third factor is that, for some taxpayers, relief for mortgage interest is available at a rate different from their marginal tax rate. This occurs in the following four circumstances:

| Marginal income tax rate | Marginal rate of interest relief | Source of discrepancy |
|---|---|---|
| Nil | Basic | MIRAS subsidy |
| Basic | Nil | Loan over £30,000 |
| Higher relief from 1991–92 | Basic | No higher rate |
| Higher | Nil | Loan over £30,000 |

Since it seems unlikely that the limit of £30,000 will be increased, the number of mortgagors enjoying no marginal tax relief on interest—and hence likely to suffer a positive tax wedge—is also increasing.

## Taxation of Personal Savings and Investment

As already noted, a desire to improve tax neutrality has led to changes to corporate taxation in the direction of a comprehensive income tax. However, at the personal level, while several notable tax breaks have similarly been restricted or withdrawn, two factors have given rise to movement in the opposite direction. Concern over the low and declining personal savings rate in the United Kingdom, along with a desire to achieve wider share and bond ownership by individuals, has led to a number of schemes exempting personal savings from income tax or capital gains tax. There are four principal schemes whose features are particularly interesting, but before considering these, one should note that during the 1980s the generous reliefs available for traditional forms of savings were restricted. For example, premiums paid on life insurance policies enjoyed relief at half the basic rate of income tax until 1984, when relief was abolished, and the tax treatment of the policyholders' funds has since been reformed to increase the tax yield. Although the tax treatment of pensions remains highly generous, with full tax relief on contributions paid and on income and capital gains of the funds, the tax-free lump sum that can be taken on retirement has now been capped at a level that is unlikely to be increased in line with earnings.

THE BUSINESS EXPANSION SCHEME (BES).  An attempt to encourage external equity participation in small businesses, the business expansion scheme grew out of a business start-up scheme introduced in 1981. In essence, an individual taking an equity stake in a business with whose management he or she is unconnected may claim up-front income tax relief on the amount invested. If the equity is withdrawn within five years, so is the relief. When introduced, relief could be claimed against a top marginal income tax rate of 75 percent, but as the top rate has fallen to 40 percent, so has the relative attractiveness (and generosity) of the scheme. Aimed at risky enterprises, the scheme has been narrowed in scope in an attempt to exclude asset-backed companies (such as those holding real property, antiques, or fine wines), with one notable exception. In an attempt to revive the ailing market for domestic rented property—whose demise has been in large part due to the generous tax treatment of owner-occupiers—there is now a BES scheme for assured tenancies, that is, rental of domestic property outside rent control.

PERSONAL EQUITY PLANS (PEPs).  An entirely different approach was adopted to encourage equity investment in personal equity plans. In the United Kingdom, share ownership had been increasingly dominated by institutions such as pension and life insurance funds, which enjoyed tax breaks at the expense of direct investment by individuals. Since 1986 individuals have been allowed to invest in one PEP each year, with no up-front relief but no tax on dividends or capital gains. Given the relatively high annual exemption for capital gains, it is the relief of dividends from income tax that is the more significant attraction, but because PEP shares can only be held through approved managers, administration costs are high. The terms have been relaxed in successive budgets, increasing the amount that can be invested, reducing the minimum holding time, and allowing partial investment via collective funds such as unit trusts. For 1990–91, the annual limit was £6,000, up to half of which could be held in collective funds. Because the scheme operates independently of individual tax returns, the data are of poor quality and are nonexistent at a disaggregated level. We do know from official statistics that, up to April 1991, 1.47 million plans had been taken out representing £3.88 billion invested over four years; but some of this amount may subsequently have been withdrawn, and most individuals continuing to participate will have taken out plans in several (if not all) years to date.

TAX-EXEMPT SPECIAL SAVINGS ACCOUNTS (TESSAs).  A new tax-exempt form of saving aimed at small savers, the tax-exempt special savings account, was introduced with effect from January 1, 1991. Each individual may invest up to £3,000 in the first year and £1,800 in later years in an interest-bearing bank or building-society account and receive tax-free income, provided the funds are not withdrawn until 1996. (If they are withdrawn, so is all tax relief.) The nature of the scheme makes it easy for it to be rolled forward year by year if the government so chooses, before 1996 arrives. Like PEPs, TESSAs are a very simple scheme that bypasses the normal Inland Revenue reporting mechanisms. Each individual's unique national insurance number is used as a safeguard to ensure that only one account is opened, and the income does not have to be reported on tax returns. However, as in the case of PEPs, this very simplicity makes it impossible to judge the take-up of the schemes on a disaggregated basis, since the data will not appear in the annual published Survey of Personal Incomes compelled from tax-return data.

THE UNITED KINGDOM BOND MARKET.  As a contrasting example of how *not* to manage the introduction of a simple tax break, the new system of taxing bonds and other securities, also introduced in the 1984 reforming budget, is instructive. In an attempt to stimulate the flagging U.K. bond market, the concept of "qualifying corporate bonds" was introduced, exempting from capital gains tax sterling bonds issued by U.K. companies and quoted on a recognized exchange. (The requirement to be quoted was withdrawn in 1989, largely to prevent claims for capital losses.) This would of course have made deeply discounted bonds highly attractive, where the issuer could obtain relief for the discount, at least on redemption, on the grounds that it represented accrued interest, but the holder would enjoy a tax-free capital gain. So at the time, a new system of taxing deep-discount securities was introduced, on securities issued at a discount of more than 15 percent or 0.5 percent a year. The regime charged the holder income tax on the discount-realized redemption, but allowed relief to the issuer on an accruals basis, and hence created a useful asymmetry in tax timing.

This scheme could, however, not be applied to securities on which the redemption proceeds were uncertain, for any reason. So in 1989 penal "deep gain securities" rules were introduced, applying to securities *whenever issued* on which under the terms of issue the amount payable on redemption *might* constitute a deep gain (defined as for deep-discount securities). The holder was taxed on the gain on redemption, with the issuer receiving no corresponding relief at all. Only two exceptions were provided, subject to stringent conditions: for qualifying indexed and qualifying convertible securities. At the cost of a vast amount of unsatisfactory legislation, the purpose of the original relief has surely been almost entirely thwarted. Indeed, the position is ironically similar to that prevailing in 1984 for life insurance premium relief, when the antiavoidance legislation had grown so large that it was considered better to abolish the relief entirely.

## King-Fullerton Tax Rates for 1980–81, 1985–86, and 1990–91

This section provides a discussion of the King-Fullerton methodology as applied to tax rates at three junctures since the onset of Conservative government in 1979.

### Personal and Corporate Tax Wedges

The tax wedge on investment has been defined as the difference between the pretax rate of return on an investment project and the post-tax rate of return on the saving that financed the project. In some cases it may be useful to disaggregate the total wedge into two components, the corporate tax wedge and the personal tax wedge:

$$w = w_c + w_p.$$

A disaggregation of this kind is most informative when the corporate wedge is a function only of corporate tax rates and the personal wedge is a function of personal tax rates. Unfortunately, independence of the two wedges does not hold, and it is not in general possible to write the wedge in separable form. That is,

$$w(t_c, t_p) \neq w_1(t_c) + w_2(t_p).$$

This means that there is no unambiguous way to define the personal and corporate wedges. One way is to define the corporate wedge as the difference between the total wedge and the value that the wedge would take if all the corporate tax rates were set to zero (with the latter defined as the personal wedge). Call this definition A:

$$w(t_c, t_p) = w(0, t_p) + w_c.$$

An alternative method—definition B—would be to define the corporate wedge as the value of the total wedge under the assumption that all personal tax rates were set to zero, with the personal wedge being defined as the residual:

$$w(t_c, t_p) = w(t_c, 0) + w_p.$$

The difference between these two can best be illustrated by means of a simple example. Consider the case in which a project is financed by new equity, there is no inflation, and the corporate tax system provides no imputation relief for dividends. The post-tax return to saving, $s$, is related to the pretax return on the project, $p$, by

$$s = (1 - m)(1 - \tau)p,$$

where $m$ is the marginal rate of personal income tax and $\tau$ is the rate of corporate income tax. The total wedge is

$$w = [\tau(1 - m) + m]p,$$

and the two definitions of the component wedges are

(A) $\qquad\qquad w_c = \tau(1 - m)p \qquad w_p = mp$

(B) $\qquad\qquad w_c = \tau p \qquad w_p = m(1 - \tau)p.$

The choice between these two definitions is a matter of convenience. In both cases one of the wedges is a function of both personal and corporate taxes. The numbers presented in this book correspond to definition B, which does, however, have the consistency property that when personal tax rates are zero, the personal wedge is also zero.

### New View versus Traditional View

The new view is essentially that profits inside the corporate veil are trapped and cannot be released to the personal sector without payment of the tax burden associated with dividends. Hence this tax burden is capitalized in stock prices, and the cost of capital is that for a regime of retained earnings. Only when retained earnings were exhausted and the agency or bankruptcy costs of debt were sufficiently high would new equity finance be the optimal source of funds. The basic tables shown below adopt the King-Fullerton approach of computing a weighted average of the three sources of funds: debt, retained earnings and new equity.

The tables headed traditional view assume that equity finance comprises new equity only.

### Interpretation of Results

In view of the degree and nature of changes to the tax system since 1980, a decision was taken not to attempt to recalculate the weights used in King and Fullerton to obtain average marginal rates. To do so properly would involve difficult questions, including methodological considerations. For example, as a result of the various new schemes described above, an increasing amount of personal savings is being held in tax-free form outside the customary system of personal tax returns, both by continuing taxpayers and by the newly created cohort of nontaxpaying wives. One could approach this phenomenon either by altering average marginal personal tax rates directly, or by increasing the weight afforded tax-exempt institutions, since in many ways the new forms of saving resemble tax-free pension funds. These are interesting issues, but rather than cloud the fundamental matter here, we have chosen to abstract from them. The changes since 1980 demonstrated in the tables are therefore the result of tax factors alone.

Tables 9-5 to 9-9 have been compiled using definition B of the corporate and personal wedges: that is, the corporate wedge is "pure" and the personal wedge is the residual, reflecting changes in corporate as well as personal tax rates. Figures 9-3 to 9-5 show the corporate and total tax rates for each combination.

Considering the total tax wedge first (table 9-5), in the first five years there is a striking increase in all the rates (as a result of both the 1984 corporation tax reforms and the withdrawal of grants), as well as less variation across projects. In the next five years the overall wedge increases slightly, but some wedges increase while others decrease. This is a result of the interaction between completing the transition to the new corporate tax regime, and lower personal tax rates. Table 9-6 bears out the effects of the corporate tax reforms over this period, with all tax wedges increasing except for commerce, where the effect of the lower marginal rate dominates the withdrawal of the small amount of capital allowances available for hotels.

Table 9-8 must be treated with caution. Although it appears that personal tax rates declined sharply between 1980–81 and 1985–86, we noted in table 9-2 and figure 9-1 that this was not so. The apparent decline is a consequence of our adopting definition B to separate the component wedges, and owes more to corporate tax changes over the period. In

Table 9-5.  *Average Marginal Effective Tax Rates, 5 Percent Inflation,*
*Fixed-p, Selected Years, 1980–91*

Percent

| Item | 1980–81 | 1985–86 | 1990–91 |
|---|---|---|---|
| Asset | | | |
| Machinery | −31.2 | 15.7 | 24.3 |
| Buildings | 43.5 | 57.9 | 60.2 |
| Inventories | −2.9 | 60.3 | 52.1 |
| Industry | | | |
| Manufacturing | −19.4 | 32.9 | 39.0 |
| Other industry | 5.6 | 32.8 | 35.9 |
| Commerce | 37.0 | 53.5 | 50.3 |
| Source of finance | | | |
| Debt | −52.1 | 26.0 | 28.1 |
| New share issues | −10.5 | 22.2 | 26.3 |
| Retained earnings | 12.9 | 42.8 | 46.1 |
| Owner | | | |
| Households | 7.0 | 43.3 | 46.6 |
| Tax-exempt institutions | −12.9 | 30.1 | 34.5 |
| Insurance companies | 2.8 | 43.6 | 43.1 |
| Overall tax rate | −0.7 | 38.6 | 41.8 |

Table 9-6.  *Average Marginal Effective Corporate Tax Rates, 5 Percent*
*Inflation, Fixed-p, Selected Years, 1980–91*

Percent

| Item | 1980–81 | 1985–86 | 1990–91 |
|---|---|---|---|
| Asset | | | |
| Machinery | −67.0 | −5.4 | 8.0 |
| Buildings | 20.4 | 43.9 | 49.7 |
| Inventories | −34.2 | 46.8 | 39.8 |
| Industry | | | |
| Manufacturing | −53.3 | 14.7 | 24.8 |
| Other industry | −24.2 | 14.5 | 21.2 |
| Commerce | 12.7 | 38.9 | 37.8 |
| Source of finance | | | |
| Debt | −157.8 | −36.8 | −15.9 |
| New share issues | −61.2 | −10.1 | 4.1 |
| Retained earnings | 2.3 | 38.0 | 40.5 |
| Owner | | | |
| Households | −45.5 | 14.9 | 23.1 |
| Tax-exempt institutions | −12.9 | 30.1 | 34.5 |
| Insurance companies | −29.5 | 22.2 | 28.7 |
| Overall tax rate | −31.4 | 21.4 | 28.0 |

Figure 9-3.  *Total and Corporate Average Marginal Tax Rates, by Combination, 1980-81*

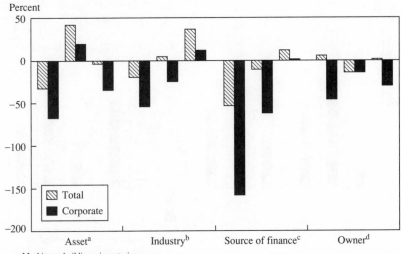

a. Machinery; buildings; inventories.
b. Manufacturing; other industry; commerce.
c. Debt; new share issues; retained earnings.
d. Households, tax-exempt institutions; insurance companies.

Figure 9-4.  *Total and Corporate Average Marginal Tax Rates, by Combination, 1985-86*

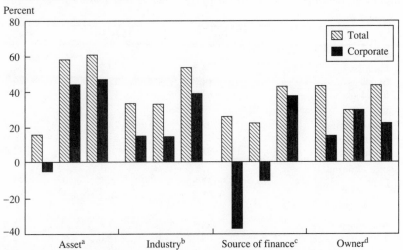

a. Machinery; buildings; inventories.
b. Manufacturing; other industry; commerce.
c. Debt; new share issues; retained earnings.
d. Households, tax-exempt institutions; insurance companies.

Figure 9-5. *Total and Corporate Average Marginal Tax Rates, by Combination, 1990-91*

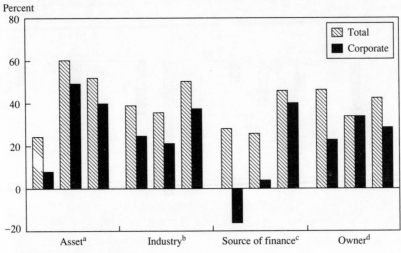

Percent

a. Machinery; buildings; inventories.
b. Manufacturing; other industry; commerce.
c. Debt; new share issues; retained earnings.
d. Households, tax-exempt institutions; insurance companies.

Table 9-7. *Average Marginal Effective Corporate Tax Rates, 5 Percent Inflation, Traditional View, Fixed-p, Selected Years, 1980–91*

Percent

| Item | 1980–81 | 1985–86 | 1990–91 |
|---|---|---|---|
| Asset | | | |
| Machinery | −124.8 | −49.7 | −24.3 |
| Buildings | −14.2 | 13.9 | 26.2 |
| Inventories | −83.2 | 17.2 | 14.5 |
| Industry | | | |
| Manufacturing | −107.4 | −23.8 | −3.7 |
| Other industry | −70.6 | −24.1 | −8.0 |
| Commerce | −23.8 | 7.2 | 12.2 |
| Source of finance | | | |
| Debt | −157.8 | −36.8 | −15.9 |
| Equity | −61.2 | −10.1 | 4.1 |
| Owner | | | |
| Households | −88.5 | −17.6 | −1.5 |
| Tax-exempt institutions | −68.3 | −12.0 | 2.6 |
| Insurance companies | −78.6 | −14.9 | 0.5 |
| Overall tax rate | −79.8 | −15.2 | 0.2 |

Table 9-8.  *Average Marginal Effective Personal Tax Rates, 5 Percent Inflation, Fixed-p, Selected Years, 1980–91*

Percent

| Item | 1980–81 | 1985–86 | 1990–91 |
|------|---------|---------|---------|
| Asset | | | |
| Machinery | 35.9 | 21.1 | 16.3 |
| Buildings | 23.1 | 13.9 | 11.0 |
| Inventories | 31.3 | 13.5 | 12.3 |
| Industry | | | |
| Manufacturing | 33.9 | 18.2 | 14.2 |
| Other industry | 29.8 | 18.3 | 14.6 |
| Commerce | 24.2 | 14.6 | 12.5 |
| Source of finance | | | |
| Debt | 105.7 | 62.8 | 44.0 |
| New share issues | 50.7 | 32.3 | 22.3 |
| Retained earnings | 10.6 | 4.8 | 5.6 |
| Owner | | | |
| Households | 52.5 | 28.4 | 23.5 |
| Tax-exempt institutions | 0.0 | 0.0 | 0.0 |
| Insurance companies | 32.3 | 21.4 | 14.5 |
| Overall tax rate | 30.7 | 17.2 | 13.8 |

Table 9-9.  *Average Marginal Effective Personal Tax Rates, 5 Percent Inflation, Traditional View, Fixed-p, Selected Years, 1980–91*

Percent

| Item | 1980–81 | 1985–86 | 1990–91 |
|------|---------|---------|---------|
| Asset | | | |
| Machinery | 73.3 | 47.1 | 31.6 |
| Buildings | 43.7 | 30.6 | 20.9 |
| Inventories | 62.2 | 29.8 | 23.4 |
| Industry | | | |
| Manufacturing | 68.6 | 40.4 | 27.3 |
| Other industry | 58.8 | 40.4 | 28.2 |
| Commerce | 46.4 | 32.4 | 23.9 |
| Source of finance | | | |
| Debt | 105.7 | 62.8 | 44.0 |
| Equity | 50.7 | 32.3 | 22.3 |
| Owner | | | |
| Households | 10.4 | 63.2 | 43.7 |
| Tax-exempt institutions | 0.0 | 0.0 | 0.0 |
| Insurance companies | 66.6 | 46.3 | 32.6 |
| Overall tax rate | 61.3 | 38.2 | 26.4 |

the latter period the result is genuine. Only retained earnings show an increase, as a result of the changes to the capital gains tax system.

While these results in the direction of less distortion between investment projects are striking, they mask a second important effect of the 1984 reforms. Since they reflect the position for taxpaying companies only, they do not reflect the fact that many companies that were tax-exhausted in 1980 have been using up their tax losses as a result of the withdrawal of stock relief and accelerated capital allowances, and many have begun to pay corporation tax. In this way, distortions between corporations as well as between particular projects have been reduced.

### The Noncorporate Sector

In the United Kingdom the noncorporate sector accounts for a negligible amount of economic activity in the three considered sectors of manufacturing, other industry, and commerce. Apart from large professional partnerships, the only significant area of noncorporate activity is agriculture, farming, and fisheries. Table 9-10 shows the result of changes over the decade for particular projects in this sector, which has a separate regime of capital allowances for buildings and structures, but is otherwise treated in the same way as the corporate sector, apart, of course, from being taxed at personal rather than corporate rates. In 1980 an investment in machinery or inventories was treated with perfect neutrality, with immediate expensing and symmetry of treatment between interest payable and interest receivable. Investment in agricultural buildings received only a 24 percent allowance in the first year, followed by 4 percent straight-line; in 1986 the higher first-year allowance was withdrawn, which resulted in a marked increase in the effective tax rate.

Table 9-10. *Average Marginal Effective Tax Rates, 5 Percent Inflation, Noncorporate Sector (Farming), Fixed-p, Selected Years, 1980–91*

Percent

| Asset | 1980–81 | 1985–86 | 1990–91 |
|---|---|---|---|
| Machinery | | | |
| Debt | 0.0 | 18.3 | 19.6 |
| Equity | 0.0 | 19.6 | 20.7 |
| Buildings | | | |
| Debt | 18.9 | 17.0 | 29.1 |
| Equity | 20.0 | 18.1 | 30.4 |
| Inventories | | | |
| Debt | 0.0 | 59.0 | 47.9 |
| Equity | 0.0 | 61.8 | 50.0 |

Neutrality disappeared with the withdrawal of stock relief and the removal of accelerated depreciation, which for the noncorporate sector was not compensated by a reduction in the marginal tax rate. Personal rates fell slightly over both periods, as reflected in the lower tax rate on buildings in 1985–86 as against 1980–81, and on machinery and inventories in 1990–91 as against 1985–86. Differences in the rates shown for debt and for equity arise solely from differing estimates of the average marginal personal tax rates of debt and equity holders, which in this illustration have been taken to be the same as those used in generating the previous tables.

## Issues for the Future

As the tables demonstrate, the system of taxing capital income in 1990–91 was far more satisfactory as measured by the yardstick of tax distortion than that in place in 1980–81. It also raised considerably more revenue, because tax losses brought forward were absorbed, but more important because inflation has remained at a stubbornly high level. When stock relief was abolished, it was suggested that it would be unnecessary in the future as the government achieved its objective of eliminating inflation. As the tables show, even at a constant inflation rate of 5 percent, without indexing for cost of inventories or capital allowances on fixed investment, effective tax rates remain high.

There are, therefore, frequent calls by industrialists for the reintroduction of some such relief, most commonly proposing a higher rate of first-year allowance for investment in plant and machinery than the current 25 percent. But as table 9-6 clearly shows, this type of investment remains relatively favorably treated. The Conservative government would most likely be much more interested in reducing marginal rates, having stated its intention to reduce the basic rate of income tax to 20 percent in the longer term. As in 1991 there may also be an accompanying cut in the marginal corporation tax rate, by international standards already low at 33 percent, which has provided a useful stimulus to inward investment.

In the personal sector it seems like that the scope of special schemes to encourage saving will widen, particularly if interest rates continue to fall sharply. The future of the capital gains tax is perhaps more puzzling. A top marginal rate of 40 percent on individuals seems rather high, b is compensated for by indexation relief. This in turn creates a distorti between income and capital gains that remains marked at recently exp rienced levels of inflation. In due course the system of national insura

contributions seems likely to become more closely integrated with income tax (at least in all but name) if current trends continue.

At the corporate level, the most pressing issue is that of surplus advance corporation tax (ACT). When a U.K. resident pays a dividend to group shareholders, it accounts for ACT, which can be offset against corporation tax on an equivalent amount of profits. When those profits have been remitted from overseas subsidiaries, U.K. corporation tax will be reduced by credit for overseas taxes paid, but ACT is not reduced correspondingly and hence has to be written off as irrecoverable. This has become a difficulty for most U.K.-based multinationals, and makes the United Kingdom unattractive relative to other European Community countries (especially the Netherlands) as a central location for multinationals with a significant proportion of non-U.K. shareholders. Over the next few years it will be interesting to see if, as intra-EC withholding taxes are abolished and cross-border reorganizations are facilitated, competition between EC member states effectively forces changes to domestic tax law. In addition to this question of whether foreign tax credits should be imputed to dividends and so reduce the ACT charge, there is a related issue of whether companies' capital gains should be imputed to capital gains on the underlying shares. At present, unless gains realized in a company are first stripped out by means of a dividend, there is an effective double tax charge if the shareholder disposes of his or her shares. But to pay ACT on the dividend may also cause a tax penalty to be levied if it cannot be relieved. However, the mechanics of such an imputation system might be difficult to administer.

## References

*Annual Finance Acts*. London: Her Majesty's Stationery Office (HMSO).

Board of Inland Revenue. *Inland Revenue Statistics*, and *Annual Report of the Commissioners of Customs and Excises*. London: HMSO.

Dilnot, A. W., and Mark H. Robson. 1993. "UK Moves from March to December Budgets." *Fiscal Studies* 14:78-88.

King, Mervyn A., and Don Fullerton, eds. 1984. *The Taxation of Income from Capital: A Comparative Study of the United States, the United Kingdom, Sweden and West Germany*. University of Chicago Press.

Robson, Mark H. 1988. "Estimating Tax Rates on Income from Capital in the UK from Official Statistics." London School of Economics Financial Markets Group, Discussion Paper 28.

Robson, Mark H. 1989. "Measuring the Cost of Capital When Taxes Are Changing with Foresight." *Journal of Public Economics* 40 (June): 261-92.

# CHAPTER TEN

# United States

*Don Fullerton*
*Marios Karayannis*

THE REVENUE from capital income taxation as a fraction of total government revenue has been declining in the past thirty years. Nevertheless, the academic literature has been paying increasing attention to the subject of capital income taxation, primarily because of the effects on investment incentives. In a perfectly competitive world with no uncertainty, and in the absence of any taxes, equilibrium would require that investment projects at the margin receive just the interest rate paid to savers at the margin. In general, however, the government uses the tax system both to generate revenue and to stimulate investment and productivity. As a consequence, the returns to savers and investors diverge, and the incentives facing them are obscured.

A careful investigation of these incentive effects should account for corporate and personal taxes as well as for the interaction of the two. This interaction is essential because, for example, interest payments are deductible at the corporate level but are taxed in the hands of the personal sector upon receipt. Therefore, the effective tax rate becomes a combined function of personal and corporate taxes. Moreover, the relationship between investment and taxation depends on corporate financial policy and on the pattern of ownership of corporate securities. There is no unique cost of capital to the corporate sector that is independent of ownership pattern or of capital structure.

We thank the participants in the Public Finance workshop at the University of Virginia, and in the International Conference on the Cost of Capital held in Cambridge, Mass., in November 1987. The research reported here is part of the NBER's research program in taxation. Any opinions expressed are those of the authors and not those of the National Bureau of Economic Research.

One study of the incentive effects of capital income taxes is the book edited by Mervyn A. King and Don Fullerton.[1] They estimated marginal effective tax rates in four countries with a common theoretical framework. Using 1980 as a reference year, they focused on the international comparisons offered by the different tax regimes. In this paper, we concentrate on a slightly different issue. We apply the King-Fullerton methodology to the U.S. economy only, for the years 1980 through 1990. This time-series approach provides an illustration of the evolution of the tax treatment of income from capital over the decade.

To maintain strict comparability of results with those of King and Fullerton for 1980, and with those of other researchers who apply the King-Fullerton methodology to additional countries in more recent years, we resist the urge to tinker with the model. We use exactly the same computer programs. We collect tax data and parameters for more recent years, but our results for 1980 exactly match those in the book. We use the same set of eighty-one hypothetical projects, the same weights, and the same assumptions about arbitrage and inflation. We therefore concentrate on tax changes only. To these calculations we add consideration of the noncorporate sector as well as owner-occupied housing.

The underlying model follows the lines of Robert Hall and Dale W. Jorgenson in finding the user cost of capital for each project.[2] The net private rate of return depends both on the source of finance used and the category of ownership of the returns. The proportional difference between the average of the pretax rate of return and the average of the post-tax rate of return weighted over all the hypothetical projects constitutes the overall marginal effective total tax rate (METTR). An alternative approach would be to measure effective tax rates by taking the ratio of observed taxes to income from existing investments. Although these average effective tax rates would reflect adequately the cash flows and tax burdens, the METTRs are intended to capture the incentives to save and invest.[3] We acknowledge the difficulties in using METTRs, as discussed, for example, by Lawrence H. Summers or David F. Bradford and Don Fullerton,[4] but we choose not to review these complex issues in this paper. Instead, we proceed with a methodology from King and Fullerton to estimate effective

1. King and Fullerton (1984).

2. Hall and Jorgenson (1967).

3. Many other differences between average and marginal effective tax rates are discussed in Fullerton (1984).

4. Summers (1987); Bradford and Fullerton (1981).

tax rates for 1980 through 1990. For each year, we provide effective tax rates for the fully phased-in version of the law as enacted.

We find that the overall marginal effective total tax rate fell from 37 percent in 1980 to 22 percent under post-transition 1981 law, and remained low until 1986, when the fully phased-in tax rate increased to 42 percent. Furthermore, it showed a moderate tendency to rise with inflation. We also find that the individual rates were distributed more uniformly in the 1986–90 period than at any other time. The biggest difference in effective tax rates, that between debt-financed projects and equity-financed projects, was substantially reduced by the Tax Reform Act of 1986.

The rest of the chapter is organized into four sections: "Methodological Framework," "Data and Parameters," "The Results," and "Concluding Remarks."

## Methodological Framework

The notation and methodology in this section follows King, and King and Fullerton.[5] Consider an economic environment in which there is perfect competition, perfect mobility, and no uncertainty. A firm contemplating a new investment project will, in equilibrium, equate the net outlay to the present value of net returns. If the cost of the project is one dollar, and the present discounted value of any grants or tax allowances on the unit of investment is A, then the net outlay is

$$(10\text{-}1) \qquad\qquad C = 1 - A.$$

Assume that this dollar invested will generate returns whose nominal value increases with inflation and decreases with the rate of depreciation. These returns are then discounted at the firm's discount rate. Then the present discounted value of the profit stream net of taxes is given by

$$(10\text{-}2) \qquad V = \frac{(1 - \tau)MRR - d\tau v\pi - (1 - \tau)w_c}{\rho + \delta - \pi},$$

where $\tau$ is the corporate tax rate, $MRR$ the marginal rate of return, $v$ the proportion of inventories on original cost-accounting—first in, first out (FIFO) as opposed to last in, first out (LIFO)—$w_c$ the corporate wealth rate, $\pi$ the inflation rate, $\rho$ the discount rate, and $\delta$ the exponential rate

5. King (1977); King and Fullerton (1984).

of economic depreciation. The dummy variable $d$ takes the value one for inventories and zero for everything else.

Now, if the rate of return net of depreciation is

(10-3) $$p = MRR - \delta,$$

and we set the net outlay $C$ equal to the present value of net returns $V$, then we can solve equations 10-1, 10-2, and 10-3 to get

(10-4) $$p = \frac{[(1 - A)(\rho + \delta - \pi) + d\tau v\pi]}{(1 - \tau)} + w_c - \delta.$$

To derive an expression for $A$, we assume that grants and allowances for investment take one of three forms: standard depreciation allowances, immediate expensing or free depreciation, and cash grants. The proportion of the cost of an asset that is entitled to standard depreciation allowances is denoted by $f_1$, and the present value of tax savings from standard depreciation allowances on a unit of investment is $A_d$. Note also that $A_d$ is the product of the statutory corporate rate, $\tau$, times the present value of allowances, $A_z$. If $f_2$ denotes the proportion of the cost of the project qualifying for immediate expensing at the corporate rate, then the tax savings from this write-off is $f_2\tau$. Finally, suppose that the proportion qualifying for grants is denoted by $f_3$ and the rate of grant (equivalent to a tax credit) is $g$. Then,

(10-5) $$A = f_1 A_d + f_2 \tau + f_3 g.$$

There is no need to restrict the sum of $f_1, f_2,$ and $f_3$ to unity since at certain times it can exceed one. For example, an investment tax credit may or may not reduce the basis for capital consumption allowances.

Suppose $r$ is the real interest rate and $i = r + \pi$ is the nominal interest rate. The relation between the nominal market interest rate and the return to the saver depends on the tax treatment of personal income. Since the tax law defines the tax base to include the receipt of nominal interest income, the post-tax rate of return of the saver is given by

(10-6) $$s = (1 - m)(r + \pi) - \pi - w_p,$$

where $m$ is the marginal personal tax rate on interest income and $w_p$ is the personal wealth rate. Then the marginal effective total tax rate can be expressed as $(p - s)/p$, the tax wedge as a fraction of the pretax returns.

To complete the model, we link the firm's discount rate to the market interest rate. This relationship will, in general, depend on the source of finance. In the case of debt finance, where nominal interest income is taxed but nominal interest payments are tax deductible,

$$(10\text{-}7) \qquad\qquad \rho = i(1 - \tau).$$

For new share issues, a potential investor would require a net rate of return equal to $i(1 - m)$, which reflects his opportunity cost. Then the project should yield a return $\rho$ such that the net of tax dividend yield equals the individual's opportunity cost, $\rho(1 - m) = i(1 - m)$. Hence, for new share issues

$$(10\text{-}8) \qquad\qquad \rho = i.$$

Finally, for retained earnings, if $z$ is the effective tax rate on accrued capital gains, the project should yield a return $\rho$ such that $\rho(1 - z) = i(1 - m)$. Thus

$$(10\text{-}9) \qquad\qquad \rho = i\frac{(1 - m)}{(1 - z)}.$$

In this case the cost of capital depends on the personal tax rates, which in general differ among stockholders according to their tax brackets. Therefore, the firm would have to equalize the net return to all these investors. We could either hypothesize a single representative investor or we could assume a Miller equilibrium in which high-tax investors hold equity only and low-tax ones hold debt only.[6] Since neither assumption conforms with reality, we instead calculate the cost of capital for retained earnings using the weighted averages of the parameters in equation 10-9, where the weights are the share-ownership proportions of the different investors.

Having summarized the model, we now examine two assumptions about arbitrage that are used in this chapter. First, the fixed-$p$ case makes no assumption about arbitrage. We assume that all hypothetical projects yield the same pretax rate of return, and we compute the post-tax return to savers for each project. In general, these post-tax returns differ across projects. This approach emphasizes differences in the tax treatment of different investments, and it provides a clear picture of the incentives offered by the tax system. Naturally, we would expect funds to flow from the low-yield (high-tax) assets toward the high-yield (low-tax) ones. This reallocation of capital among the various projects would continue until an equilibrium was established in which there would exist no further opportu-

6. See Miller (1977), and Auerbach and King (1983).

nities for mutually profitable transactions. In a second set of assumptions, the fixed-$r$ case, we assume that the real rates of return on all projects are equalized for all investors before personal taxes. Differences in personal tax rates will still generate different net rates of return across investors. We stress that when arbitrage eliminates differences among projects in the real rate of interest, there must be differences in the pretax rates of return on different investments. Hence, the tax system distorts the allocation of resources.

The choice between the fixed-$p$ and the fixed-$r$ distributions of marginal effective tax rates depends on whether one is interested in the tax schedule facing potential investors or the proportion of marginal-factor income that is taxed away. The fixed-$p$ calculations are a better guide to the schedule of tax rates levied on different combinations, but it is the fixed-$r$ distribution of marginal tax rates that would determine the welfare losses resulting from the distortionary nature of the taxation of capital income. Also the weighted averages in the fixed-$r$ case are a better guide to the ratio of additional taxed paid to additional profits earned as a result of a small increase in the corporate-sector capital stock. Although we present selected results for both assumptions, we focus mainly on the fixed-$p$ case. This emphasis corresponds to that in King and Fullerton, where the primary interest is in the effects of taxation on the incentives to invest.

As a practical matter, in the fixed-$p$ case, we take the gross rate of return, $p$, to be 10 percent. We then use equation 10-4 to calculate $\rho$, which, through equations 10-7 through 10-19, will give us an interest rate, $i$, for each case. Finally, we calculate $r$ as $i - \pi$ and substitute it into equation 10-6 to get the net rate of return. Alternatively, in the fixed-$r$ case, we begin with an $r$ of 5 percent. Substitution into equation 10-6 provides $s$, substitution into equations 10-7 through 10-19 provides the discount rate $\rho$, and substitution into equation 10-4 provides $p$.

The interaction between inflation and the tax system is one of the most important aspects of the effects of taxes on savings and investment. The expected rate of inflation enters into both the $p$ equation (10-4) and the $s$ equation (10-6). To accommodate these expectations, we calculate effective tax rates for four inflation rates. First, a zero rate provides a benchmark against which to judge other figures, and it describes the impact the tax system would have if it were fully indexed. We also look at inflation rates of 5 and 10 percent, to ensure comparability with conditions in other countries. Finally, as in King and Fullerton, we use 6.77 percent as the inflation for the United States, calculated as the average rate of increase of the price deflator for consumer and investment goods in 1970–79. Rather than update this specific figure, we use 6.77 percent again for comparability and add a column of results for 5 percent inflation. Results for any inflation rate can be approximated by interpolating between results for other inflation rates.

Each hypothetical investment under consideration is described by a unique combination of four characteristics. These characteristics include the asset in which funds are invested, the industry of the project, the way the project is financed, and the ultimate recipient of the returns. In turn, there exist three alternatives for each characteristic. More specifically, the first asset category is machinery, which includes plant, equipment, and vehicles. The second asset category is buildings, and the third is inventories. We are considering only tangible reproducible assets and thus exclude land, research and development, and other intangible assets.

The first industry is manufacturing, which consists of the SIC industry codes 13–64. Second, "other industry" contains construction, transportation, communications, and utilities. Third, "commerce" includes trade and services and corresponds to SIC codes 69 and 72–77.

The three sources of finance are debt, which includes both bond issues and bank borrowing, new share issues, and retained earnings. The three ownership categories are households, tax-exempt institutions, and insurance companies. The primary motivation for this three-part ownership classification is the different tax treatments each category receives, even though the funds are indirectly owned by households in all cases. The household category includes the household ownership of funds through taxed intermediaries such as banks. The second category includes indirect tax-exempt ownership through pension funds, the pension business of life insurance companies, and charities. Finally, the third category includes funds invested as part of contractual savings made by households through the medium of insurance companies, principally life insurance policies. In combination, with three assets, three industries, three sources of finance, and three ownership categories, there exist a total of eighty-one combinations of distinct investments that are examined.

In the third section of this chapter, "The Results," we compute the marginal effective tax rate for each combination as well as their distribution. To plot the distribution of tax rates, we need to know the proportion of investment identified with any given combination. We assume that the marginal increase in investment under consideration is proportional to the existing distribution of net capital stocks among assets and industries. Further, we assume that the saving required to finance investment is proportional to the existing ownership patterns. This enables us to determine the weights that apply to each combination. Thus, by aggregating with the appropriate weights, we can calculate marginal effective tax rates for every subset of investment projects.

To illustrate, let $k$ denote a particular combination involving debt-financed investment. There are twenty-seven such combinations. If $\alpha_k$ denotes the weight applicable to the $k$th combination, we can calculate effective tax rates for capital income generated by debt-financed investments in the following way. The mean tax wedge for this subset is

$$(10\text{-}10) \qquad \bar{w} = \sum_{k}^{27} (p_k - s_k)\alpha_k = \bar{p} - \bar{s}.$$

Then the marginal effective tax rate is

$$(10\text{-}11) \qquad \bar{t} = \frac{\bar{w}}{\bar{p}}.$$

In a similar way, we compute the rates for all the other subsets. By using the weights for all eighty-one combinations together, we get the overall mean marginal effective tax rate.

So far, the methodology follows King and Fullerton exactly, for the total effective tax rates in the corporate sector. We also recalculate these tax rates with personal rates set to zero, in order to indicate the business-tax portion of the total effective rate. Finally, in this chapter, we extend the methodology to calculations for the noncorporate sector and owner-occupied housing.[7]

For the noncorporate sector, equation 10-4 still holds, but the corporate rate $\tau$ is replaced by the personal marginal rate of the noncorporate entrepreneur, $\tau_{nc}$. Depreciation rules are the same for each asset, but allowances are discounted at the entrepreneur's net-of-tax discount rate. We consider only debt, which must earn the deductible interest cost $i(1 - \tau_{nc})$, and equity of the entrepreneur, which must earn the opportunity cost given by the interest rate taxed at the personal rate on interest receipts, $i(1 - m_d)$. In other words, we simply reset the corporate rate $\tau$

---

7. See Fullerton and Henderson (1984).

to equal $\tau_{nc}$ in equations 10-4 and 10-7, set the weights on tax-exempts and insurance companies to zero, set the weight on new share issues to zero, and calculate the discount rate for equity from equation 10-9, where $z$ is zero.

For owner-occupied housing, the investment receives no allowances but earns a return that is not subject to tax. The expression for $p$ reduces to

$$(10\text{-}12) \qquad\qquad p = \rho - \pi + (1 - \lambda\tau_h)w_h,$$

where $w_h$ is the rate of property tax, $\tau_h$ is the rate for deductions of the homeowner, and $\lambda$ is the fraction of homeowners who itemize deductions. The discount rate, $\rho$, for debt is $i(1 - \tau_h)$, and the discount rate for equity of the homeowner is the opportunity cost of funds that could earn $i(1 - m_d)$.

## Data and Parameters

Two tax reform acts in the 1980s have affected the treatment of the various assets and the distortions introduced by the tax system. The Economic Recovery Tax Act (ERTA) of 1981 reduced personal rates and assigned lifetimes for assets to a smaller number of classes. These lifetimes were shorter for the most part, so the present values of depreciation allowances were greater. The Tax Reform Act (TRA) of 1986 reduced personal rates, decreased the statutory corporate rate from 0.46 to 0.34, and repealed the investment tax credit. In the interim years, a few other adjustments of the tax code took place. All these policy changes are described below.

The capital stock weights are derived from studies by Jorgenson and Martin A. Sullivan, and by Barbara M. Fraumeni and Jorgenson, calculated by the perpetual inventory method for the year 1977.[8] We use the same weights as those in King and Fullerton. As shown in table 10-1, about 44 percent of the capital stock is used in manufacturing, 25 percent is in commerce, and the remaining 31 percent is in the other industry category. More than half (54 percent) of the total corporate capital, excluding land, is in buildings, whereas inventories and equipment share the rest equally.

---

8. Jorgenson and Sullivan (1981); Fraumeni and Jorgenson (1980).

Table 10-1. *Proportions of Corporate Capital Stock, by Asset and Industry, United States*

| Asset | Manufacturing | Other industry | Commerce | Total |
|---|---|---|---|---|
| Machinery | 0.0867 | 0.0965 | 0.0415 | 0.2247 |
| Buildings | 0.2167 | 0.1970 | 0.1248 | 0.5385 |
| Inventories | 0.1350 | 0.0176 | 0.0842 | 0.2368 |
| Total | 0.4384 | 0.3111 | 0.2502 | 1.0000 |

Sources: King and Fullerton (1984). Aggregation from unpublished data described in Jorgenson and Sullivan (1981) and in Fraumeni and Jorgenson (1980).

Table 10–2. *Source of Finance Proportions for Each Industry*

| Industry | Debt | New share issues | Retained earnings | Total |
|---|---|---|---|---|
| Manufacturing | 0.1981 | 0.0592 | 0.7427 | 1.000 |
| Other industry | 0.4847 | 0.0381 | 0.4772 | 1.000 |
| Commerce | 0.3995 | 0.0443 | 0.5562 | 1.000 |

Source: King and Fullerton (1984), as derived and described in the text.

As seen in table 10-2, three-fourths of the financing for investments in manufacturing comes from retained earnings, and only 20 percent comes from debt.[9] These proportions are more equal in commerce (40 percent debt and 55 percent retained earnings) and other industry (48 percent each). These proportions also come from King and Fullerton, so that we can replicate the results for 1980 before drawing comparisons to later years.[10]

The proportions of debt and equity holdings of each ownership category are shown in table 10-3. Households and tax-exempt institutions hold

Table 10-3. *Proportional Holdings of Debt and Equity for Each Ownership Category*

| Owner | Debt | Equity |
|---|---|---|
| Households | 0.6094 | 0.7433 |
| Tax-exempt institutions | 0.2371 | 0.2154 |
| Insurance companies | 0.1534 | 0.0412 |
| Total | 1.0000 | 1.0000 |

Sources: King and Fullerton (1984), as derived and described in the text.

9. We use COMPUSTAT data to calculate market values of debt and equity in each industry, as described in Gordon and Malkiel (1981), and King and Fullerton (1984).

10. The low 5 percent proportion for new share issues reflects flow of funds data on actual financing and is consistent with the low weight on dividend taxes in the new view of Auerbach (1979), Bradford (1981), and King (1977). New investment might have to use proportionately more new share issues, however, reflecting the old view of dividend taxes.

almost equal proportions of debt and equity, while insurance companies hold mostly debt. To enable concentration on tax changes by themselves, we allowed none of these weighting parameters to vary during the time period. The following subsections describe the other parameters and features of the tax code that do change during 1980–90.

### The Corporate Rates

The top federal statutory rate of 0.46 is used for marginal corporate income for all years until 1986. State corporate taxes are deductible at the federal level, and the weighted average of the states' top brackets is 6.6 percent. Therefore, $\tau$ is $0.46 + 0.066(1 - 0.46)$, or 49.5 percent. The 1986 act lowered the top statutory corporate tax rate of 0.34, so the same calculation provides a combined rate of 38.3 percent. Although most corporations do not reach the top statutory rate bracket, the bulk of corporate capital is held by those that do.

### Property and Wealth Taxes

Thousands of local jurisdictions set their own statutory property tax rates. Using data from the Advisory Commission on Intergovernmental Relations, Jorgenson's 1977 capital stock matrix, and estimated tax payments in 1977, we calculate the following average tax rates for businesses. For equipment and inventories $w_c$ is 0.00768, and for structures $w_c$ is 0.01126. These rates are assumed to hold for all years. The same business tax rates are used in the noncorporate sector, but Fullerton and Yolanda Kodrzycki Henderson use a higher rate of $w_h = 0.01837$ for owner-occupied housing. We assume that $\lambda = 0.7$ of these property taxes are deductible.[11] Finally, the personal wealth tax rates ($w_p$) are taken to be zero throughout. This parameter could be used for estate taxes, but these are a very small source of revenue in the United States, and the Economic Recovery Tax Act of 1981 raised the estate tax exemption to $600,000.

### The Personal Tax Rates

The data on marginal tax rates for households are made available from the Treasury and the TAXSIM simulations of the National Bureau

---

11. Fullerton and Henderson (1984).

Table 10-4. *Personal Marginal Tax Rates for Households, 1980–90*[a]

| Item | 1980 | 1981–85 | 1986–90 |
|---|---|---|---|
| Wages | 0.324 | 0.312 | 0.271 |
| Interest[b] | 0.284 | 0.258 | 0.224 |
| Dividends | 0.475 | 0.396 | 0.320 |
| Realized capital gains | 0.140 | 0.118 | 0.220 |
| Noncorporate income | 0.281 | 0.245 | 0.208 |
| Housing deductions | 0.329 | 0.300 | 0.260 |

Sources: Calculations from the National Bureau of Economic Research tax simulation (TAXSIM) model and the U.S. Department of Treasury. See text.
a. Combined federal and state marginal tax rates.
b. Tax rates for interest income have been adjusted for financial intermediation. See text.

of Economic Research (NBER).[12] The procedures of the NBER model are described in studies by Martin S. Feldstein and Daniel J. Frisch and by Daniel R. Feenberg and Harvey S. Rosen.[13] Essentially, it weights marginal rates for 25,000 households by each different source of income. Table 10-4 provides a summary of the various rates for each year. The first row shows tax rates on wage income for comparison purposes only. The second row shows the statutory rates applicable to interest income. These include an additional 0.05 to account for sate taxes. Also, financial intermediaries hold corporate debt but do not pay interest on demand deposits. Instead, they provide services to depositors, a form of return to households that is not subject to tax. We therefore multiply the combined federal and state rate by the ratio of interest-bearing direct and indirect loans of households to corporations divided by total direct and indirect loans of households to corporations. This ratio was calculated to be 0.8738 in King and Fullerton.[14] Implicit here is the assumption that the same rate of interest applies to both borrowing and lending. To take an example, 1980, the federal rate on interest of households was 0.275, and the combined federal and state rate was 32.5 percent. With the adjustment for banks, $m$ is 0.284, as shown in the table. In 1981 it became 25.8 percent and, under the TRA, 22.4 percent. The third row in the table shows that the combined statutory rate for dividends in 1980

12. The Treasury provided estimates of the household rates for all years. However, for comparability with King and Fullerton we want to use the TAXSIM rate for 1980. We therefore use the Treasury estimates to indicate how the 1980 TAXSIM rate would change over the period. That is, later years' Treasury numbers were multiplied by the ratio of the TAXSIM rate for 1980 to the Treasury rate for 1980.

13. Feldstein and Frisch (1977); Feenberg and Rosen (1983).

14. Two other alternative adjustments have been suggested but are not used here. The first takes explicit account of the interest ceiling on time deposits. The other was put forth by Feldstein and Summers (1979). Both of these are described in detail in King and Fullerton (1984).

is 47.5 percent, decreased significantly in 1981, and decreased again in 1986.

The statutory capital gains rate from the TAXSIM model for 1980 is 28 percent, but King and Fullerton use a 14 percent rate to account for step-up of basis at death and the selective realization of losses and gains. Also, capital gains are taxed only upon realization and thus offer a deferral advantage that depends on the average length of the holding period. As explained by King and Fullerton, the 14 percent rate is approximately halved because of this advantage.[15]

The corresponding personal rates for noncorporate income ($\tau_{nc}$) and for housing deductions ($\tau_n$) in table 10-4 reflect the average brackets for those activities. The changes in these rates in 1981 and 1986 reflect the statutory decreases for all personal rates.

The marginal effective tax rate on nonprofit institutions is assumed to be zero. The reason is that contributions to retirement accounts are not taxable at personal rates. Since savings and interest earnings are taxed when retirement income is paid out, the treatment is equivalent to a consumption tax, provided the individual remains in the same bracket. Contributions to nonqualified accounts are relatively small, and the taxation of interest income can be postponed until retirement. In this case the present value of those tax payments is very small.

The taxation of income received through insurance companies follows some complicated procedures described in King and Fullerton.[16] For our purposes, the tax rates for the years 1980 through 1983 are shown in table 10-5 to be 6.9 percent for dividends, 28 percent statutory rate for retained earnings, and $0.149 + 3.88\pi$ for debt, where $\pi$ is the inflation rate. In 1984 the complicated procedures were replaced by a simple 20 percent exclusion, so the effective rate on interest income is 80 percent of the

Table 10-5.  *Personal Marginal Tax Rates for Insurance Companies, 1980–90*[a]

| Item | 1980–83 | 1984–85 | 1986–90 |
|---|---|---|---|
| Interest | $0.149 + 3.88\pi$ | 0.368 | 0.340 |
| Dividends | 0.069 | 0.069 | 0.068 |
| Realized capital gains | 0.280 | 0.280 | 0.340 |

Source: King and Fullerton (1984). See also text.
a. Combined federal and state marginal tax rates.

15. King and Fullerton (1984, pp. 23–24, 222).
16. King and Fullerton (1984, pp. 227–34).

statutory 46 percent tax rate. Thus, it is taxed at 0.368, and the dependence on inflation is eliminated. The following year that rate remained the same, and in 1986 the 20 percent exclusion was repealed when the statutory rate was lowered for all corporations to 34 percent. Intercorporate dividends receive an 80 percent deduction from the corporate rate in 1986, and are thus taxed at 6.8 percent. The special rate for capital gains was repealed.

### Investment Tax Credits

All qualifying equipment and public utility structures received a statutory investment tax credit (ITC) of 10 percent in 1980. Two-thirds of that credit was allowed for equipment with a five- or six-year life, and one-third was allowed for equipment with a three- or four-year life. As shown in table 10-6, under ERTA the rate for automobiles increased from 0.033 to 0.06, while all other equipment received the full 10 percent ITC. The Tax Reform Act of 1986 repealed the ITC altogether. We assume that the companies under consideration have enough taxable profits to enable them to use those credits, although in fact many companies do not.[17] Since the whole investment outlay qualifies for tax credit, the parameter $f_3$ is set to one.

### Inventory Accounting

U.S. corporations are allowed to use any number of consistent accounting methods including last in, first out (LIFO) and first in, first out (FIFO), but they are obligated to use the same method for profits reported to shareholders as they use for profits reported to the taxing authorities. In an environment with no inflation, the two methods yield identical figures, and the choice between them should leave the firm indifferent. With inflation, however, FIFO profits appear to be higher than LIFO profits. Therefore, although firm managers might like to report FIFO profits to shareholders, taxes can be reduced by reporting LIFO profits to the Internal Revenue Service. Of the possible values that exist for our parameter, $v$, we set it equal to zero, assuming that firms act so as to minimize their tax liability. This assumption is consistent with the use of minimum lifetimes and maximum acceleration in the depreciation of assets, discussed below.

17. See, for example, Jorgenson and Sullivan (1981). For the effects of imperfect loss offsets, see Auerbach (1986) or Mayer (1986).

Table 10-6.  *Investment Tax Credit, by Asset Class, 1980–90*

| Asset class | 1980 | 1981–85 | 1986–90 |
|---|---|---|---|
| 1. Furniture and fixtures | 0.100 | 0.10 | 0.0 |
| 2. Fabricated metal products | 0.100 | 0.10 | 0.0 |
| 3. Engines and turbines | 0.100 | 0.10 | 0.0 |
| 4. Tractors | 0.067 | 0.10 | 0.0 |
| 5. Agricultural machinery | 0.100 | 0.10 | 0.0 |
| 6. Construction machinery | 0.100 | 0.10 | 0.0 |
| 7. Mining and oilfield machinery | 0.100 | 0.10 | 0.0 |
| 8. Metalworking machinery | 0.100 | 0.10 | 0.0 |
| 9. Special industry machinery | 0.100 | 0.10 | 0.0 |
| 10. General industrial machinery | 0.100 | 0.10 | 0.0 |
| 11. Office and computing machinery | 0.100 | 0.10 | 0.0 |
| 12. Service industry machinery | 0.100 | 0.10 | 0.0 |
| 13. Electrical equipment | 0.100 | 0.10 | 0.0 |
| 14. Trucks, buses, and trailers | 0.067 | 0.10 | 0.0 |
| 15. Automobiles | 0.033 | 0.06 | 0.0 |
| 16. Aircraft | 0.100 | 0.10 | 0.0 |
| 17. Ships and boats | 0.100 | 0.10 | 0.0 |
| 18. Railroad equipment | 0.100 | 0.10 | 0.0 |
| 19. Instruments | 0.100 | 0.10 | 0.0 |
| 20. Other equipment | 0.100 | 0.10 | 0.0 |
| 21. Industrial buildings | 0.0 | 0.0 | 0.0 |
| 22. Commercial buildings | 0.0 | 0.0 | 0.0 |
| 23. Religious buildings | 0.0 | 0.0 | 0.0 |
| 24. Educational buildings | 0.0 | 0.0 | 0.0 |
| 25. Hospitals | 0.0 | 0.0 | 0.0 |
| 26. Other nonfarm buildings | 0.0 | 0.0 | 0.0 |
| 27. Railroads | 0.100 | 0.10 | 0.0 |
| 28. Telephone and telegraph | 0.100 | 0.10 | 0.0 |
| 29. Electric light and power | 0.100 | 0.10 | 0.0 |
| 30. Gas | 0.100 | 0.10 | 0.0 |
| 31. Other public utilities | 0.100 | 0.10 | 0.0 |
| 32. Farm structures | 0.0 | 0.0 | 0.0 |
| 33. Mining, shafts, and wells | 0.0 | 0.0 | 0.0 |
| 34. Other nonresidential structures | 0.0 | 0.0 | 0.0 |

Source: Fullerton and Henderson (1984), as described in the text.

### Depreciation Allowances

Estimates of the actual economic depreciation of the different assets are provided by Charles R. Hulten and Frank C. Wykoff and are shown in table 10-7.[18] These are carefully distinguished from the tax lifetimes that

18. Hulten and Wykoff (1981).

Table 10-7. *Depreciation and Tax Lifetimes, by Asset Class, 1980–90*

| Asset Class | Hulten-Wykoff depreciation rates | Lifetimes | | | | |
| --- | --- | --- | --- | --- | --- | --- |
| | | 1980 | 1981–83 | 1984 | 1985 | 1986–90 |
| 1. Furniture and fixtures | 0.1100 | 8.00 | 5.0 | 5.0 | 5.0 | 7.0 |
| 2. Fabricated metal products | 0.0917 | 10.00 | 5.0 | 5.0 | 5.0 | 7.0 |
| 3. Engines and turbines | 0.0786 | 12.48 | 5.0 | 5.0 | 5.0 | 7.0 |
| 4. Tractors | 0.1633 | 5.00 | 5.0 | 5.0 | 5.0 | 5.0 |
| 5. Agricultural machinery | 0.0971 | 8.00 | 5.0 | 5.0 | 5.0 | 7.0 |
| 6. Construction machinery | 0.1722 | 7.92 | 5.0 | 5.0 | 5.0 | 5.0 |
| 7. Mining and oilfield machinery | 0.1650 | 7.68 | 5.0 | 5.0 | 5.0 | 5.0 |
| 8. Metalworking machinery | 0.1225 | 10.16 | 5.0 | 5.0 | 5.0 | 7.0 |
| 9. Special industry machinery | 0.1031 | 10.16 | 5.0 | 5.0 | 5.0 | 7.0 |
| 10. General industrial machinery | 0.1225 | 9.84 | 5.0 | 5.0 | 5.0 | 7.0 |
| 11. Office and computing machinery | 0.2729 | 8.00 | 5.0 | 5.0 | 5.0 | 7.0 |
| 12. Service industry machinery | 0.1650 | 8.24 | 5.0 | 5.0 | 5.0 | 7.0 |
| 13. Electrical equipment | 0.1179 | 9.92 | 5.0 | 5.0 | 5.0 | 7.0 |
| 14. Trucks, buses, and trailers | 0.2537 | 5.00 | 5.0 | 5.0 | 5.0 | 5.0 |
| 15. Automobiles | 0.3333 | 3.00 | 3.0 | 3.0 | 3.0 | 5.0 |
| 16. Aircraft | 0.1833 | 7.00 | 5.0 | 5.0 | 5.0 | 5.0 |
| 17. Ships and boats | 0.0750 | 14.40 | 5.0 | 5.0 | 5.0 | 10.0 |
| 18. Railroad equipment | 0.0660 | 12.00 | 5.0 | 5.0 | 5.0 | 5.0 |
| 19. Instruments | 0.1473 | 8.48 | 5.0 | 5.0 | 5.0 | 5.0 |
| 20. Other equipment | 0.1473 | 8.16 | 5.0 | 5.0 | 5.0 | 5.0 |
| 21. Industrial buildings | 0.0361 | 28.80 | 15.0 | 18.0 | 19.0 | 31.5 |
| 22. Commercial buildings | 0.0247 | 47.60 | 15.0 | 18.0 | 19.0 | 31.5 |
| 23. Religious buildings | 0.0188 | 48.00 | 15.0 | 18.0 | 19.0 | 31.5 |
| 24. Educational buildings | 0.0188 | 48.00 | 15.0 | 18.0 | 19.0 | 31.5 |
| 25. Hospitals | 0.0233 | 48.00 | 15.0 | 18.0 | 19.0 | 31.5 |
| 26. Other nonfarm buildings | 0.0454 | 30.90 | 15.0 | 18.0 | 19.0 | 31.5 |
| 27. Railroads | 0.0176 | 24.00 | 15.0 | 15.0 | 15.0 | 20.0 |
| 28. Telephone and telegraph | 0.0333 | 21.60 | 15.0 | 15.0 | 15.0 | 20.0 |
| 29. Electric light and power | 0.0300 | 21.60 | 15.0 | 15.0 | 15.0 | 20.0 |
| 30. Gas | 0.0300 | 19.20 | 10.0 | 10.0 | 10.0 | 15.0 |
| 31. Other public utilities | 0.0450 | 17.60 | 10.0 | 10.0 | 10.0 | 15.0 |
| 32. Farm structures | 0.0237 | 25.00 | 15.0 | 18.0 | 19.0 | 20.0 |
| 33. Mining, shafts, and wells | 0.0563 | 6.80 | 5.0 | 5.0 | 5.0 | 5.0 |
| 34. Other nonresidential structures | 0.0290 | 28.20 | 15.0 | 18.0 | 19.0 | 31.5 |

Sources: Depreciation rates are from Hulten and Wykoff (1981). For public utility structures (assets 27–31), Jorgenson and Sullivan (1981) provide estimates based on the Hulten-Wykoff methodology. Lifetimes are from Fullerton and Henderson (1984), and are described in the text.

are also shown for each year in table 10-7. The first twenty assets will be aggregated to form our machinery category, while the next fourteen assets will form our buildings category. Inventories are not shown in this table because they do not depreciate.

The lifetimes reported for 1980 stem from the estimates of the mid-points of the asset depreciation range (ADR) in Jorgenson and Sullivan.[19] More specifically, the ADR system allowed 20 percent longer or shorter lives for equipment (assets 1–20) and public utility structures (assets 27–31). Because of our assumption of optimizing tax practice, these assets are assigned lives that are 80 percent of ADR midpoints except where the use of a longer lifetime would reduce effective taxes through eligibility for a higher investment tax credit. Hence, these lifetimes are consistent with the ITC vector, shown for 1980 in table 10-6, column two, in that the three- and five-year assets get one-third and two-thirds of the full ITC, respectively.

Under the 1980 law, also, equipment and public utility structures were allowed double declining balance (DDB) with a switch to sum-of-the-years'-digits (SYD).[20] Other structures (assets 21–26 and 32–34) received 150 percent declining balance with a switch to straight line. Since capital consumption allowances are based on historical cost, we use the nominal after-tax discount rate, $\rho$, to calculate their present value, $A_z$. This calculation accounts for the half-year convention, annual allowances, and continuous discounting.[21]

The Economic Recovery Tax Act of 1981 introduced the accelerated cost recovery system (ACRS) under which any depreciable asset fell into one of four classes and was given a tax life of three, five, ten, or fifteen years. These lifetimes, shown in table 10-7, column three, assigned a three-year life to automobiles, a five-year life to other equipment, a ten-year life to some gas and other public-utility structures, and a fifteen-year life to railroads, telephone and telegraph, electric light and power, and all other structures. Machinery and public utilities were to receive DDB switching to SYD, as before, but depreciation was moved up from the last half year. As a result, the three-year class depreciated in only 2.5 years, the five-year class in 4.5 years, and so on. Other structures received 175 percent declining balance till switching to straight line.

For 1981 we analyze only the ultimate version of the law, after a planned phase-in period of several years. That transition was never allowed to occur. In 1982, allowances for machinery and public utilities

19. Jorgenson and Sullivan (1981).
20. This combination is used here as tax-minimizing practice because it can be shown to provide the earliest possible depreciation deductions. See Shoven and Bulow (1975).
21. See King and Fullerton (1984, pp. 210–11).

were cut back to 150 percent declining balance, switching to straight line rather than SYD. Further, the 1982 act decreased the depreciation basis by half of the investment tax credit. Other changes in 1984 and 1985 lengthened lifetimes for structures and are shown in the tables.

In 1986 automobiles were moved from 3 to 5 years, and some other assets were moved from 5 years to 7 or 10 years, but the depreciation method was accelerated to DDB. Some long-lived assets such as public-utility structures received 15 or 20 years with 150 percent declining balance, while nonresidential structures got 31.5 years straight line.

All these changes in the tax laws are captured in the respective $A_z$ parameters for each of the thirty-four assets. These values are then weighted appropriately to obtain the aggregate depreciation allowances for each of our three categories.[22] As explained earlier, each $A_z$ is multiplied by the statutory corporate tax rate, $\tau$, to provide the tax savings $A_d$. Finally, the parameter $f_1$ is set to one, indicating that all equipment and structures depreciate for tax purposes as described above, and $f_2$ is set to zero to indicate no immediate free depreciation of investment.

## The Results

This section includes discussion of results under standard assumptions and alternative assumptions.

### Standard Assumptions

Our primary findings for each year concern the fixed-$p$ calculations for the standard inflation rate of 6.77 percent. For 1980 the overall weighted marginal effective tax rate on corporate capital income in the United States is 37.3 percent. As anticipated, this figure matches exactly the one found in King and Fullerton. The interpretation is that if all assets started with a gross return of 10 percent, and if all capital of all owners were increased by one dollar, the present value of the expected tax would be 37.3 percent of the additional return. It is noteworthy that this effective rate is less than the 46 percent statutory corporate tax rate, because the effective rate incorporates many factors that tend to offset or increase overall taxes.

22. Appendix D of King and Fullerton (1984) describes how the thirty-four values of $A_z$ are weighted to the three categories.

Table 10-8.  *Marginal Effective Tax Rates under Different Inflation Rates, Fixed-*p, *1980*

Percent

| Item | Inflation rate (percent) | | | |
|---|---|---|---|---|
| | *0* | *5* | *6.77*[a] | *10* |
| Asset | | | | |
| Machinery | 3.8 | 14.1 | 17.5 | 22.8 |
| Buildings | 35.6 | 40.5 | 41.2 | 41.9 |
| Inventories | 50.9 | 48.0 | 47.0 | 45.5 |
| Industry | | | | |
| Manufacturing | 44.4 | 51.2 | 52.8 | 55.1 |
| Other industry | 10.0 | 13.7 | 14.6 | 15.8 |
| Commerce | 38.0 | 38.5 | 38.2 | 37.5 |
| Source of Finance | | | | |
| Debt | −1.8 | −12.6 | −16.2 | −22.2 |
| New share issues | 61.1 | 83.7 | 91.2 | 104.6 |
| Retained earnings | 48.5 | 59.5 | 62.4 | 66.6 |
| Owner | | | | |
| Households | 44.2 | 54.7 | 57.6 | 61.9 |
| Tax-exempt institutions | 4.1 | −13.7 | −21.5 | −37.2 |
| Insurance companies | 4.2 | 15.4 | 23.4 | 44.4 |
| Overall corporate sector | 32.1 | 36.3 | 37.3 | 38.5 |
| Noncorporate sector | 16.7 | 17.4 | 17.3 | 16.7 |
| Owner-occupied housing | 13.7 | 12.8 | 12.6 | 12.0 |

Source: Tables 10-8 through 10-16 are authors' calculations.
a. Actual.

Table 10-8 shows the breakdown of this effective tax rate by asset, industry, source of finances, and ownership category for the four inflation rates. The "overall corporate" row near the bottom of the table shows that the effective rate increases somewhat with inflation, from 32.1 percent with zero inflation to 38.5 percent with 10 percent inflation. To help explain this relationship, look at the rates that correspond to the source of finance categories. The effective rates for new shares and retained earnings increase steeply with inflation, since the returns are taxed in nominal terms, but debt-financed investment is subsidized at rates that also increase with inflation. This subsidy arises because corporations can deduct nominal interest at a 49.5 percent rate (the federal plus state statutory rate), while recipients include it at a much lower rate, 23.6 percent (averaged over the three owners). The overall corporate rate near the bottom of the table weighs the rates for the three sources of finance according to the proportions described earlier, so the two effects of inflation offset each other.

The table also shows that the overall rate in the noncorporate sector is much lower and less affected by inflation, ranging from 16.7 to 17.4 percent. This includes personal taxes and property taxes only, where the noncorporate entrepreneur deducts interest costs at a personal rate very similar to the rate of tax on the ultimate interest recipient. The final row is for owner-occupied housing, where the 13.7 percent rate at zero inflation falls to 12.0 percent at high inflation. This rate primarily reflects the property tax, which is levied at a higher rate on homes than it is on business property. The equity-financed portion of homes faces no personal tax, but the debt-financed portion receives a small subsidy that increases with inflation because the homeowner's personal rate for interest deductions (0.329 in 1980) is higher than the rate for household interest recipients (0.284 in 1980).

Under the fully phased-in 1981 law, in the first column of table 10-9, the overall corporate rate for actual inflation falls from 37.3 percent to 22.2 percent. This reduction is attributed primarily to two sources. First, an across-the-board reduction in personal tax rates was instituted by ERTA in an effort to stimulate the economy. Second, there was a considerable reduction in the depreciation lifetimes. As a result of these two factors plus the use of double-declining balance and the ITC, equipment receives a subsidy of 10.2 percent. In addition, structures were previously taxed at 41.2 percent but under 1981 law are taxed at only 26.4 percent. A less significant decline to 43.6 percent occurred for inventories. As pointed out by Fullerton and Henderson, the Economic Recovery Tax Act of 1981 implied substantially disparate tax treatments for depreciable assets on the one hand, and for land and inventories on the other.[23]

In 1982 the method of depreciation was cut back to 150 percent of declining balance for equipment and public utility structures, as reflected in the higher effective tax rates for machinery and structures shown in the next column of table 10-9. Equipment moved from a 10 percent subsidy to a 7 percent tax, and structures increased to a 30 percent tax. Inventories, which do not depreciate, were unaffected. As expected, then, the rates for all the different category breakdowns are higher. In particular, the "other industry" group moves from a small subsidy in 1981 to a 7.4 percent tax in 1982 because it includes public utilities. Thus the overall rate increased to 28 percent in 1982. Since there were no further changes the next year, the same rates are also applicable to 1983.

23. Fullerton and Henderson (1984).

Table 10-9. *Marginal Effective Tax Rates under Actual Inflation (6.77 Percent), Fixed-p, 1981, 1982–83, 1984*

Percent

| Item | 1981 | 1982–83 | 1984 |
|---|---|---|---|
| Asset | | | |
| Machinery | −10.2 | 6.7 | 4.6 |
| Buildings | 26.4 | 29.5 | 30.9 |
| Inventories | 43.6 | 43.6 | 45.1 |
| Industry | | | |
| Manufacturing | 39.7 | 42.7 | 42.8 |
| Other industry | −3.5 | 7.4 | 7.6 |
| Commerce | 23.7 | 26.8 | 28.8 |
| Source of finance | | | |
| Debt | −36.0 | −27.5 | −21.6 |
| New share issues | 77.3 | 80.4 | 74.4 |
| Retained earnings | 49.9 | 53.9 | 52.1 |
| Owner | | | |
| Households | 40.4 | 45.2 | 44.0 |
| Tax-exempt institutions | −31.7 | −24.2 | −16.1 |
| Insurance companies | 14.1 | 20.1 | 15.7 |
| Overall corporate sector | 22.2 | 27.7 | 28.3 |
| Noncorporate sector | 9.6 | 12.0 | 12.5 |
| Owner-occupied housing | 11.4 | 11.4 | 11.4 |

Multiple changes in 1984 had offsetting effects. On the one hand, with no inflation, effective rates would increase from the previous year for two reasons. First, the tax lifetimes for most structures were increased from fifteen to eighteen years, thus reducing the present value of depreciation allowances for these assets. Second, the tax rate on interest income earned by insurance companies rose from 14.9 to 36.8 percent (see table 10-5). Results for the case with zero inflation (not shown) confirm that effective tax rates are higher in 1984 for these two reasons. However, the 1984 law eliminated the way in which the previous insurance company rate depended on inflation. As a consequence, under actual (6.77 percent) inflation in the last column of table 10-9, both the rate for insurance companies and the overall rate fell from the previous year, to 15.7 percent and 28.3 percent, respectively.

The results for 1985 are very similar to those in 1984, but slightly higher, as shown in table 10-10. The reason is that the lifetimes of all structures besides public utilities were extended from eighteen to nineteen years. Consequently, the effective tax rates for machinery and inventories remained the same, whereas the rate for structures rose from 30.9 to 31.4

Table 10-10. *Marginal Effective Tax Rates under Different Inflation Rates, Fixed*-p, *1985*

Percent

| Item | Inflation rate (percent) | | | |
| --- | --- | --- | --- | --- |
| | 0 | 5 | 6.77[a] | 10 |
| Asset | | | | |
| Machinery | −1.6 | 4.6 | 6.4 | 8.9 |
| Buildings | 28.5 | 31.4 | 31.4 | 30.5 |
| Inventories | 49.9 | 45.1 | 43.3 | 40.0 |
| Industry | | | | |
| Manufacturing | 38.2 | 43.2 | 44.3 | 45.8 |
| Other industry | 7.6 | 7.6 | 6.9 | 4.6 |
| Commerce | 30.5 | 29.2 | 28.0 | 25.4 |
| Source of finance | | | | |
| Debt | −5.2 | −21.3 | −27.7 | −40.6 |
| New share issues | 54.7 | 74.6 | 81.2 | 93.0 |
| Retained earnings | 42.1 | 52.4 | 55.4 | 60.3 |
| Owner | | | | |
| Households | 36.2 | 44.2 | 46.4 | 49.9 |
| Tax-exempt institutions | 0.0 | −15.8 | −22.2 | −35.1 |
| Insurance companies | 18.6 | 16.0 | 14.4 | 10.6 |
| Overall corporate sector | 26.8 | 28.6 | 28.6 | 27.9 |
| Noncorporate sector | 12.1 | 12.7 | 12.6 | 12.3 |
| Owner-occupied housing | 12.8 | 11.8 | 11.4 | 10.8 |

a. Actual.

percent. This change pushed the overall corporate rate from 28.3 to 28.6 percent.

Noncorporate rates in these tables generally reflect the personal rate reduction and accelerated allowances enacted in 1981, and the subsequent depreciation cutbacks through 1985. Housing rates reflect personal rate changes in 1981, with no subsequent effects through 1985.

The Tax Reform Act of 1986 reduced the difference in the tax treatment of the various assets. In that spirit, the investment tax credit was repealed. The statutory corporate rate was decreased to 34 percent, and the lifetimes for most assets were lengthened. In the fixed-$p$ case of table 10-11, these changes translate into much higher effective tax rates for machinery, a smaller dispersion among the rates of the three asset classes, and an overall corporate rate of 42.1 percent. For the first time in the decade we examine, the overall effective corporate rate is higher than the statutory corporate rate. Largely because of ITC repeal, the combi-

Table 10-11. *Marginal Effective Tax Rates under Different Inflation Rates, Fixed-*p, *1986–90*
Percent

| Item | Inflation rate (percent) | | | |
|---|---|---|---|---|
| | 0 | 5 | 6.77[a] | 10 |
| Asset | | | | |
| Machinery | 29.6 | 36.9 | 38.9 | 41.9 |
| Buildings | 38.2 | 42.5 | 43.1 | 43.3 |
| Inventories | 44.2 | 43.3 | 42.8 | 41.7 |
| Industry | | | | |
| Manufacturing | 43.9 | 49.8 | 51.1 | 53.1 |
| Other industry | 28.8 | 31.2 | 31.3 | 30.9 |
| Commerce | 37.9 | 39.6 | 39.5 | 38.8 |
| Source of finance | | | | |
| Debt | 17.4 | 9.1 | 5.5 | −1.7 |
| New share issues | 53.3 | 69.4 | 74.7 | 84.0 |
| Retained earnings | 47.6 | 57.0 | 59.6 | 63.7 |
| Owner | | | | |
| Households | 43.9 | 52.1 | 54.4 | 58.0 |
| Tax-exempt institutions | 19.5 | 9.9 | 5.5 | −3.1 |
| Insurance companies | 34.2 | 36.2 | 36.3 | 35.9 |
| Overall corporate sector | 37.7 | 41.4 | 42.1 | 42.6 |
| Noncorporate sector | 21.2 | 21.7 | 21.6 | 21.2 |
| Owner-occupied housing | 12.3 | 11.2 | 10.8 | 10.1 |

a. Actual.

nation of corporate, personal, and property taxes is now greater than the corporate rate by itself.

As seen in table 10-11, the returns to debt-financed investments are now taxed rather than subsidized, at low inflation rates, because corporations deduct interest at a much a lower statutory tax rate. This effect is partly offset by the smaller reduction in the personal rates on interest income. The effective rates for new share issues fell a little because of the lower statutory rates on dividends of households and insurance companies, while capital gains face a higher effective rate than before.

Personal-rate reduction caused the noncorporate rate to fall from about 17 percent in 1980 to about 12 percent in 1985, but additional personal-rate reduction in 1986 is more than offset by ITC and depreciation changes that raise the noncorporate rate to 21 percent for 1986–90. These depreciation changes do not affect owner-housing tax rates, which fall slightly but uniformly throughout the decade.

Figure 10-1.    *Proportion of Investment Taxed at Each Rate, Fixed-p, 1985*

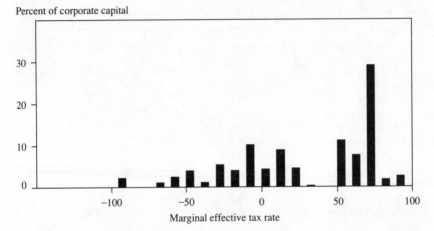

Percent of corporate capital

Marginal effective tax rate

## Histograms and the Effects of Inflation

An interesting and important aspect of this study is not demonstrated in the calculations presented thus far. The overall corporate effective tax rates conceal the distribution of individual tax rates within each year. To illustrate these differences, we present histograms for the fixed-*p* case and the actual inflation rate for 1985 and 1986–90. Figure 10-1 shows the histogram for 1985, where the height of each bar is the sum of the capital stock weights for any individual combinations that are taxed at effective rates falling in each 10 percent interval between −120 and 100 percent.[24] The figure shows that 22.6 percent of the capital stock is subsidized, and 32.0 percent of the capital stock is taxed at rates 80 percent or higher. The highest subsidy in 1985 is 114.7 percent, received by investment projects in assets in the "other industry" category, financed by debt sold to tax-exempt institutions.

The histogram for 1986–90 is shown in figure 10-2. An important point is that the dispersion is much smaller after 1986. This result suggests a considerable reduction in the distortions introduced by the tax system. Also, in 1985 the largest fraction of capital income, 28.6 percent, was taxed at rates that fell between 70 and 80 percent. In 1986, despite the

24. The histogram for 1985 is fairly representative of all the preceding years as well. A histogram for 1980 is presented in King and Fullerton (1984).

Figure 10-2. *Proportion of Investment Taxed at Each Rate, Fixed-*p, *1986-90*

Percent of corporate capital

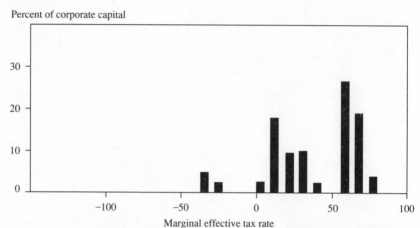

Marginal effective tax rate

increase in the overall mean effective tax rates, the largest fraction of capital, 26.7 percent, is now taxed at rates that fall between 60 and 70 percent. In other words, the increase in the overall average comes from reducing subsidies on some capital rather than from increasing the tax on most capital.

Finally, for the standard assumptions, we look at the effects of inflation on the effective tax rates. Figure 10-3 shows how the overall rate changes as the rate of inflation varies from zero to 10 percent in 1980, 1985, and

Figure 10-3. *Overall Marginal Effective Tax Rates as Inflation Varies, 1980, 1985, 1986*

Marginal effective tax rate

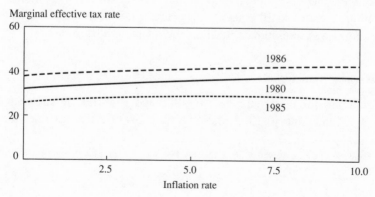

Inflation rate

Figure 10-4.   *Marginal Effective Tax Rates for Assets as Inflation Varies,*
*1985*

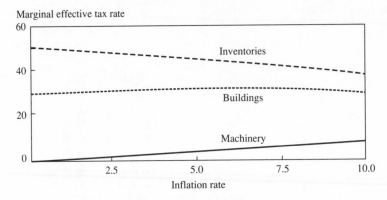

1986–90. The rates for 1980 and 1986–90 lie everywhere above the rate for 1985 and exhibit a moderate tendency to rise with inflation. The schedule for 1985 is almost flat.

However, these schedules are weighted averages of the various categories and thus suppress the considerable variation of rates among categories. To illustrate, we present figures to show the sensitivity of the rates for each of the three assets with respect to inflation. Figure 10-4 shows that in 1985 the difference among the rates for the three assets is very big at low rates of inflation. This difference decreases with inflation. The rate for machinery rises, the rate for buildings remains the same, and the rate for inventories falls slightly.

The Tax Reform Act of 1986 brought the rates for the three assets very close together. As seen in figure 10-5, these rates differ much less than in 1985 when there is no inflation, and they tend to converge as the rate of inflation increases to 10 percent. Once again, it is seen that the effect of the reform was to eliminate much of the interasset distortion.

### Alternative Assumptions

Calculations for the fixed-$r$ case in 1985 and 1986–90 are shown in tables 10-12 and table 10-13.[25] These results show effective tax rates for

---

25. These results are comparable to those found in Fullerton (1987) for the individual arbitrage case.

Figure 10-5.  *Marginal Effective Tax Rates for Assets as Inflation Varies, 1986*

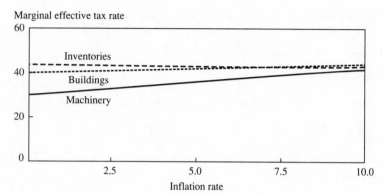

Table 10-12.  *Marginal Effective Tax Rates under Different Inflation Rates, Fixed-r, 1985*

Percent

| Item | Inflation rate (percent) | | | |
|---|---|---|---|---|
| | 0 | 5 | 6.77[a] | 10 |
| Asset | | | | |
| Machinery | −28.6 | 6.1 | 12.9 | 21.7 |
| Buildings | 35.7 | 44.0 | 45.2 | 46.2 |
| Inventories | 53.9 | 51.8 | 50.8 | 48.7 |
| Industry | | | | |
| Manufacturing | 43.9 | 52.3 | 54.1 | 56.6 |
| Other industry | 9.9 | 16.2 | 16.4 | 14.8 |
| Commerce | 37.7 | 39.4 | 39.0 | 37.3 |
| Source of finance | | | | |
| Debt | −2.3 | −71.8 | −129.3 | −491.5 |
| New share issues | 56.1 | 72.6 | 75.9 | 80.5 |
| Retained earnings | 44.5 | 57.0 | 59.9 | 64.0 |
| Owner | | | | |
| Households | 43.3 | 59.0 | 63.1 | 69.7 |
| Tax-exempt institutions | 9.4 | −12.9 | −21.9 | −40.0 |
| Insurance companies | 22.5 | 16.2 | 11.6 | −0.7 |
| Overall corporate sector | 34.4 | 40.9 | 41.9 | 42.8 |
| Noncorporate sector | 15.4 | 15.5 | 15.1 | 14.0 |
| Owner-occupied housing | 27.1 | 25.8 | 25.3 | 24.3 |

a. Actual.

Table 10-13. *Marginal Effective Tax Rates under Different Inflation Rates, Fixed-r, 1986–90*

Percent

| | Inflation rate (percent) | | | |
|---|---|---|---|---|
| Item | 0 | 5 | 6.77[a] | 10 |
| Asset | | | | |
| Machinery | 35.4 | 46.1 | 48.5 | 51.7 |
| Buildings | 43.3 | 50.2 | 51.2 | 52.1 |
| Inventories | 48.1 | 48.9 | 48.9 | 48.6 |
| Industry | | | | |
| Manufacturing | 47.6 | 54.9 | 56.4 | 58.4 |
| Other industry | 35.1 | 40.4 | 41.0 | 41.4 |
| Commerce | 42.9 | 46.9 | 47.3 | 47.4 |
| Source of finance | | | | |
| Debt | 23.0 | 6.8 | −2.3 | −25.9 |
| New share issues | 54.1 | 67.3 | 70.3 | 74.5 |
| Retained earnings | 49.6 | 59.0 | 61.1 | 63.9 |
| Owner | | | | |
| Households | 48.7 | 60.3 | 63.2 | 67.7 |
| Tax-exempt institutions | 26.0 | 14.4 | 9.3 | −0.7 |
| Insurance companies | 38.1 | 41.6 | 41.8 | 41.3 |
| Overall corporate sector | 43.0 | 49.0 | 50.1 | 51.2 |
| Noncorporate sector | 25.3 | 25.9 | 25.7 | 24.9 |
| Owner-occupied housing | 27.3 | 25.7 | 25.2 | 24.1 |

a. Actual.

an equilibrium in which investors have been allowed to adjust their behavior in response to the various incentives. As such, these rates become more relevant in assessing the welfare loss due to the taxation of capital income. The rates for 1985 in table 10-13 are higher than in the fixed-*p* case for almost every breakdown, but the same pattern persists. Debt is still subsidized at rates that grow rapidly with inflation, and machinery is still taxed at lower rates than the other assets. Effects of the 1986 law are also similar to those in the fixed-*p* case. The overall rate of 50.1 percent for 1986–90, compared with the 41.9 percent rate for 1985 implies an additional intertemporal distortion that has to be weighed against the welfare gains arising from the more nearly equal treatment of the different assets.[26]

26. One could calculate Harberger (1966) triangles and measure the welfare loss due to the distortion in the allocation of resources between the corporate and the noncorporate sector, or between machinery and buildings. Examples include Gravelle (1982), Shoven (1976), and Fullerton, Shoven, and Whalley (1983).

A different way to change assumptions involves the proportional sources of financing in the corporate sector. Returning to the fixed-$p$ case, we consider the standard assumption that marginal investment is financed in the same proportions as existing investment. All industries obtain most financing from retained earnings and only about 5 percent from new share issues. The consequence is that very little weight is placed on new shares, for which personal taxes on dividends matter, and great weight is placed on retained earnings, for which capital gains taxes matter. This case resembles the new view of dividend taxes.[27]

An alternative is the old view, which holds that taxes on dividends represent significant investment disincentives, typically modeled with a 50 percent payout rate and therefore equal weights for dividend taxes and capital gains taxes. We do not need to model a signaling role or any other justification for the existence of dividends, because we can achieve the same effect simply by changing the financing shares. We split equity in each industry evenly between new shares and retained earnings, with the effect that dividend taxes and capital gains taxes received equal weight. One could say that a large portion of retained earnings are exhausted on intramarginal investment, such that equity for marginal investments must rely more heavily on new share issues.

Results for the alternative old view appear in table 10-14 for the actual inflation rate (6.77 percent). Since dividend taxes exceed capital gains taxes in 1980, the increase in the weight on new shares raises the overall corporate rate from 37.3 percent under the new view to 45.3 percent under the old view. The breakdown of rates is unchanged for each of the three sources of finance (relative to the new view in table 10-8), but it is higher for every category of asset, industry, and owner. The overall corporate effective rate of 45.3 percent under the old view still falls in 1985, to 35.8 percent, and rises in 1986–90, to 46.2 percent.

Finally, returning again to the fixed-$p$ case under the new view, we perform alternative calculations where the personal statutory tax rates on households are set to zero for interest, dividends, and capital gains. Results in table 10-15 show the portion of the tax wedge attributable to the corporate taxes and property taxes that remain. The difference between these rates and the total effective tax rates in earlier tables indicate the portion of the tax wedge attributable to personal taxes. Table 10-15 shows

---

27. Auerbach (1979); Bradford (1981); King (1977).

Table 10-14.  *Marginal Effective Tax Rates, Old View, Fixed-p, 1980, 1985, 1986–90*[a]

Percent

| Item | 1980 | 1985 | 1986–90 |
|---|---|---|---|
| Asset | | | |
| Machinery | 26.5 | 14.5 | 42.8 |
| Buildings | 48.8 | 38.3 | 47.2 |
| Inventories | 55.4 | 50.5 | 47.4 |
| Industry | | | |
| Manufacturing | 62.3 | 52.9 | 56.2 |
| Other industry | 21.4 | 12.9 | 34.5 |
| Commerce | 45.3 | 34.5 | 43.4 |
| Source of finance | | | |
| Debt | −16.3 | −27.8 | 5.4 |
| New share issues | 91.2 | 81.2 | 74.6 |
| Retained earnings | 62.4 | 55.4 | 59.5 |
| Owner | | | |
| Households | 64.6 | 53.1 | 58.4 |
| Tax-exempt institutions | −9.3 | −12.3 | 10.9 |
| Insurance companies | 29.5 | 19.3 | 39.0 |
| Overall tax rate | 45.3 | 35.8 | 46.2 |

a. $\pi = 0.0677$; equal weights on new shares and retained earnings.

Table 10-15.  *Marginal Effective Tax Rates with No Personal Taxes, New View, Fixed-p, 1980, 1985, 1986–90*[a]

Percent

| Item | 1980 | 1985 | 1986–90 |
|---|---|---|---|
| Asset | | | |
| Machinery | −11.4 | −19.3 | 18.4 |
| Buildings | 16.7 | 9.6 | 23.5 |
| Inventories | 24.3 | 24.1 | 23.5 |
| Industry | | | |
| Manufacturing | 32.1 | 26.4 | 33.4 |
| Other industry | −16.3 | −20.5 | 9.4 |
| Commerce | 12.8 | 5.2 | 19.3 |
| Source of finance | | | |
| Debt | −58.0 | −66.9 | −21.9 |
| New share issues | 49.3 | 45.0 | 45.5 |
| Retained earnings | 47.9 | 43.8 | 44.9 |
| Owner | | | |
| Households | 12.0 | 6.9 | 21.9 |
| Tax-exempt institutions | 4.2 | −1.2 | 16.9 |
| Insurance companies | 36.3 | 24.9 | 42.0 |
| Overall corporate sector | 12.2 | 6.5 | 22.4 |

a. $\pi = 0.0677$.

that the 1980 effective rate on households falls from 57.6 to 12.0 percent, and the overall rate falls from 37.3 to 12.2 percent. Over the decade, this business tax portion of the total tax wedge fell from 12.2 to 6.5 percent in 1985 and then rose to 22.4 percent in 1986–90.

## Conclusion

We examined the tax laws that affected capital income in three sectors of the U.S. economy from 1980 to 1990. We estimated marginal effective tax rates for hypothetical investment projects during that period in order to quantify the incentive effects of the tax system. With the plethora of numbers presented thus far, one can easily lose sight of the important questions that we have been able to answer. We therefore summarize the major findings of this study.

Focusing on the overall effective rates under actual inflation in the fixed-$p$ case, we saw that they started at about 37.3 percent in 1980, remained almost 10 percentage points lower until 1986, and then rose back to 42.1 percent. It would appear that in 1981, when the rates were lowest, the tax system created a more favorable environment for investment and caused fewer intertemporal distortions than in any other year. However, the histograms provided in figures 10-1 and 10-2 suggest that the distribution of rates needs to be evaluated as well.

When a substantial proportion of the capital stock is being subsidized at different rates, as it was in 1985, there may be considerable misallocation of resources and biased economic growth. This misallocation could imply substantial welfare losses. In 1986 the tax rates were distributed more uniformly and hence may have removed a welfare loss.

In addition, we found that equipment constantly received a more favorable tax treatment than the other assets because of the investment tax credit, until 1986. Debt financing was subsidized because of the deductibility of interest payments by corporations. Repeal of the ITC and reduction of the corporate tax rate in 1986 helped reverse both these differences.

Capital income accruing to insurance companies was taxed at rates that increased steeply with inflation. That effect was eliminated in 1984. In general, the overall effective tax rates do not show much sensitivity to the rate of inflation. However, this insensitivity is still the result of offsetting effects. Without indexation of depreciation or interest income, inflation still serves to raise the effective tax rate on assets depreciated

Table 10-16. *Summary of Different Effective Tax Rates, Fixed*-p, *1980–90*

Percent

| | Inflation rate (percent) | | | |
|---|---|---|---|---|
| Item | 0 | 5 | 6.77 | 10 |
| **Overall corporate sector** | | | | |
| New view (standard case) | | | | |
| 1980 | 32.1 | 36.3 | 37.3 | 38.5 |
| 1981 | 19.2 | 21.7 | 22.2 | 22.9 |
| 1982–83 | 24.6 | 27.2 | 27.7 | 28.4 |
| 1984 | 26.5 | 28.3 | 28.3 | 27.6 |
| 1985 | 26.8 | 28.6 | 28.6 | 27.9 |
| 1986–90 | 37.7 | 41.4 | 42.1 | 42.6 |
| Old view (NSI-RE) | | | | |
| 1980 | 35.7 | 43.1 | 45.3 | 49.1 |
| 1981 | 22.8 | 28.3 | 30.0 | 33.0 |
| 1982–83 | 28.0 | 33.5 | 35.2 | 38.1 |
| 1984 | 30.1 | 34.6 | 35.6 | 36.8 |
| 1985 | 30.3 | 34.9 | 35.8 | 37.0 |
| 1986–90 | 39.3 | 44.9 | 46.2 | 48.2 |
| New View[a] | | | | |
| 1980 | 18.6 | 14.4 | 12.2 | 7.8 |
| 1981 | 6.0 | 1.2 | −0.8 | −4.8 |
| 1982–83 | 12.2 | 7.6 | 5.5 | 1.5 |
| 1984 | 14.3 | 8.8 | 6.2 | 0.6 |
| 1985 | 14.6 | 9.2 | 6.5 | 0.9 |
| 1986–90 | 26.8 | 24.0 | 22.4 | 18.8 |
| **Overall noncorporate sector** | | | | |
| 1980 | 16.7 | 17.4 | 17.3 | 16.7 |
| 1981 | 9.2 | 9.6 | 9.6 | 9.3 |
| 1982–83 | 11.5 | 12.0 | 12.0 | 11.7 |
| 1984 | 12.0 | 12.6 | 12.5 | 12.2 |
| 1985 | 12.1 | 12.7 | 12.6 | 12.3 |
| 1986–90 | 21.2 | 21.7 | 21.6 | 21.2 |
| **Owner-occupied housing** | | | | |
| 1980 | 13.7 | 12.8 | 12.6 | 12.0 |
| 1981 | 12.8 | 11.8 | 11.4 | 10.8 |
| 1982–83 | 12.8 | 11.8 | 11.4 | 10.8 |
| 1984 | 12.8 | 11.8 | 11.4 | 10.8 |
| 1985 | 12.8 | 11.8 | 11.4 | 10.8 |
| 1986–90 | 12.3 | 11.2 | 10.8 | 10.1 |

a. Personal rates zero.

on a historical-cost basis and to lower the effective tax rate on assets financed by issuing debt.

Overall rates for different assumptions are summarized in table 10-16. Because the new view puts little weight on dividend taxes, the reduction of personal taxes on dividends is not important enough to offset the loss of ITC and allowances. Overall rates rise from 1980 to 1990. Because the old view puts more weight on personal dividend tax reductions, the overall corporate rate only rises from 45.3 to 46.2 percent from 1980 to 1990. At 10 percent inflation, the overall corporate rate actually falls over the decade, from 49.1 to 48.2 percent.

Business taxes are summarized by setting personal tax rates to zero. Because high corporate taxes on equity-financed investments are offset by the deduction of nominal interest payments on debt-financed investments, the remaining business tax is only 12.0 percent in 1980 at actual inflation. It falls to −0.8 percent for 1981 because the corporate tax and property tax are more than completely offset by the investment tax credit, the accelerated cost recovery system, and nominal interest deductions. The Tax Reform Act of 1986 reestablished the corporate tax system. Table 10-16 shows that the overall tax rate in the corporate sector remains twice the rate in the noncorporate sector, which, in turn, is twice the rate for owner-occupied housing.

## References

Auerbach, Alan J. 1979. "Wealth Maximization and the Cost of Capital." *Quarterly Journal of Economics* 93 (August): 433–46.

———. 1986. "The Dynamic Effects of Tax Law Asymmetries." *Review of Economic Studies* 53 (April): 205–25.

Auerbach, Alan J., and Mervyn A. King. 1983. "Taxation, Portfolio Choice, and Debt-Equity Ratios: A General Equilibrium Model." *Quarterly Journal of Economics* 98 (November): 587–609.

Bradford, David F. 1981. "The Incidence and Allocation Effects of a Tax on Corporate Distributions." *Journal of Public Economics* 15 (February): 1–23.

Bradford, David F., and Don Fullerton. 1981. "Pitfalls in the Construction and Use of Effective Tax Rates." In *Depreciation, Inflation, and the Taxation of Income From Capital*, edited by Charles R. Hulten, 251–78. Washington: Urban Institute Press.

Feenberg, Daniel R., and Harvey S. Rosen. 1983. "Alternative Tax Treatment of the Family: Simulations, Methodology, and Results." In *Behavioral Simulation Methods in Tax Policy Analysis*, edited by Martin S. Feldstein, 7–41. University of Chicago Press.

Feldstein, Martin S., and Daniel J. Frisch. 1977. "Corporate Tax Integration: The Estimated Effects on Capital Accumulation and Tax Distribution of Two Integration Proposals." *National Tax Journal* 30 (March): 37–52.

Feldstein, Martin, and Lawrence H. Summers. 1979. "Inflation and the Taxation of Capital Income in the Corporate Sector." *National Tax Journal* 32 (December): 445-70.

Fraumeni, Barbara M., and Dale W. Jorgenson. 1980. "The Role of Capital in U.S. Economic Growth, 1948–76." In *Capital, Efficiency, and Growth*, edited by George M. von Furstenberg, 9–250. Ballinger.

Fullerton, Don. 1984. "Which Effective Tax Rate?" *National Tax Journal* 37 (March): 23–41.

——. 1987. "The Indexation of Interest, Depreciation, and Capital Gains and Tax Reform in the United States." *Journal of Public Economics* 32 (February): 25–51.

Fullerton, Don, and Yolanda Kodrzycki Henderson. 1984. "Incentive Effects of Taxes on Income from Capital: Alternative Policies in the 1980's." In *The Legacy of Reaganomics: Prospects for Long-Term Growth*, edited by Charles R. Hulten and Isabel V. Sawhill, 45–89. Washington: Urban Institute Press.

Fullerton, Don, John B. Shoven, and John Whalley. 1983. "Replacing the U.S. Income Tax with a Progressive Consumption Tax: A Sequenced General Equilibrium Approach." *Journal of Public Economics* 20 (February): 3–23.

Gordon, Roger H., and Burton G. Malkiel. 1981. "Corporation Finance." In *How Taxes Affect Economic Behavior*, edited by Henry J. Aaron and Joseph A. Pechman, 131–92. Brookings.

Gravelle, Jane G. 1982. "Effects of the 1981 Depreciation Revisions on the Taxation of Income from Business Capital." *National Tax Journal* 35 (March): 1–20.

Hall, Robert, and Dale W. Jorgenson. 1967. "Tax Policy and Investment Behavior." *American Economic Review* 57 (June): 391–414.

Harberger, Arnold C. 1966. "Efficiency Effects of Taxes on Income from Capital." In *Effects of Corporation Income Tax*, edited by Marian Krzyzaniak, 107–17. Wayne State University Press.

Hulten, Charles R., and Frank C. Wykoff. 1981. "The Measurement of Economic Depreciation." In *Depreciation, Inflation, and the Taxation of Income from Capital*, edited by Charles R. Hulten, 81–125. Washington: Urban Institute Press.

Jorgenson, Dale W., and Martin A. Sullivan. 1981. "Inflation and Corporate Capital Recovery." In *Depreciation, Inflation, and the Taxation of Income from Capital*, edited by Charles R. Hulten, 171–238, 311–13. Washington: Urban Institute Press.

King, Mervyn A. 1977. *Public Policy and the Corporation*. London: Chapman and Hall.

King, Mervyn A., and Don Fullerton, eds. 1984. *The Taxation of Income from Capital: A Comparative Study of the United States, United Kingdom, Sweden and West Germany*. University of Chicago Press.

Mayer, Colin. 1986. "Corporation Tax, Finance and the Cost of Capital." *Review of Economic Studies* 53 (January): 93–112.

Miller, Merton H. 1977. "Dept and Taxes." *Journal of Finance* 32 (May): 261–75.

Shoven, John B. 1976. "The Incidence and Efficiency Effects of Taxes on Income from Capital." *Journal of Political Economy* 84 (December): 1261–83.

Shoven, John B., and Jeremy I. Bulow. 1975. "Inflation Accounting and Nonfinancial Corporation Profits: Physical Assets." *Brookings Papers on Economic Activity* 3:557–611.

Summers, Lawrence H. 1987. "Should Tax Reform Level the Playing Field?" *Proceedings of the National Tax Association–Tax Institute of America* (meetings of November 1986), 119–25.

U.S. Board of Governors of the Federal Reserve System. 1980. *Flow of Funds Accounts: Assets and Liabilities Outstanding*. Washington.

———. 1980. *Flow of Funds Accounts: Sector Statements of Saving and Investment*. Washington.

# Appendix

Table A-1. Specific Tax and Inventory Parameters, Nine Countries, 1980, 1985, 1990

| Item | Australia | Canada | France | Germany | Italy | Japan | Sweden | United Kingdom | United States |
|---|---|---|---|---|---|---|---|---|---|
| *1980* | | | | | | | | | |
| Corporate tax rate | 0.4600 | a | 0.5000 | 0.6220 | 0.3625 | 0.5261 | 0.3960 | 0.5200 | 0.4950 |
| Dividend discrimination | 1.0 | 1.5000 | 1.5000 | 2.2700 | 1.3300 | 1.1170 | 1.0 | 1.4290 | 1.0 |
| Inventory indexation | 1.0 | 1.0 | 1.0 | 0.5000 | 0.0 | 0.1000 | 0.5200 | 0.0 | 0.0 |
| Wealth tax rate | | | | | | | | | |
| Machinery | 0.0 | 0.0 | 0.0298 | 0.0099 | 0.0 | 0.0059 | 0.0 | 0.0 | 0.0077 |
| Buildings | 0.0018 | 0.0218 | 0.0191 | 0.0048 | 0.0 | 0.0032 | 0.0 | 0.0270 | 0.0113 |
| Inventories | 0.0 | 0.0 | 0.0298 | 0.0099 | 0.0 | 0.0 | 0.0 | 0.0 | 0.0077 |
| *1985* | | | | | | | | | |
| Corporate tax rate | 0.4600 | a | 0.5000 | 0.6280 | 0.4637 | 0.5606 | 0.3850 | 0.4000 | 0.4950 |
| Dividend discrimination | 1.0 | 1.5000 | 1.5000 | 2.2700 | 1.5625 | 1.1170 | 1.0 | 1.4290 | 1.0 |
| Inventory indexation | 1.0 | 1.0 | 1.0 | 0.5000 | 0.0 | 0.1000 | 0.5900 | 1.0 | 0.0 |
| Wealth tax rate | | | | | | | | | |
| Machinery | 0.0 | 0.0 | 0.0306 | 0.0091 | 0.0 | 0.0068 | 0.0 | 0.0 | 0.0077 |
| Buildings | 0.0018 | 0.0233 | 0.0208 | 0.0033 | 0.0 | 0.0028 | 0.0 | 0.0350 | 0.0113 |
| Inventories | 0.0 | 0.0 | 0.0306 | 0.0091 | 0.0 | 0.0 | 0.0 | 0.0 | 0.0077 |
| *1990* | | | | | | | | | |
| Corporate tax rate | 0.3900 | a | 0.3700 | 0.5810 | 0.4637 | 0.5470 | 0.3000 | 0.3400 | 0.3830 |
| Dividend discrimination | 1.6400 | 1.2500 | 1.3810 | 2.0000 | 1.5625 | 1.0 | 1.0 | 1.3330 | 1.0000 |
| Inventory indexation | 1.0 | 1.0 | 1.0 | 0.0 | 0.0 | 0.1000 | 1.0 | 1.0 | 0.0 |
| Wealth tax rate | | | | | | | | | |
| Machinery | 0.0 | 0.0 | 0.0262 | 0.0091 | 0.0 | 0.0068 | 0.0 | 0.0 | 0.0077 |
| Buildings | 0.0018 | 0.0233 | 0.0195 | 0.0033 | 0.0 | 0.0028 | 0.0 | 0.0350 | 0.0113 |
| Inventories | 0.0 | 0.0 | 0.0262 | 0.0091 | 0.0 | 0.0 | 0.0 | 0.0 | 0.0077 |

a. See appendix to chapter 3.

Table A-2. Part One: Tax Parameters, by Source of Finance, Nine Countries, 1980

| Item | Australia | | | Canada | | | France | | |
|---|---|---|---|---|---|---|---|---|---|
| | Debt | New shares | Retained earnings | Debt | New shares | Retained earnings | Debt | New shares | Retained earnings |
| Personal wealth tax rates | | | | | | | | | |
| Households | 0.0 | 0.0 | 0.0 | 0.0 | 0.0 | 0.0 | 0.0 | 0.0 | 0.0 |
| Tax-exempt institutions | 0.0 | 0.0 | 0.0 | 0.0 | 0.0 | 0.0 | 0.0 | 0.0 | 0.0 |
| Insurance companies | 0.0 | 0.0 | 0.0 | 0.0 | 0.0 | 0.0 | 0.0 | 0.0 | 0.0 |
| Tax rates on interest | | | | | | | | | |
| Households | 0.23 | 0.38 | 0.38 | 0.291 | 0.423 | 0.423 | 0.2800 | 0.5030 | 0.5030 |
| Tax-exempt institutions | a | a | a | 0.0 | 0.0 | 0.0 | 0.2800 | 0.3300 | 0.3300 |
| Insurance companies | 0.37 | 0.02 | 0.02 | 0.0 | 0.0 | 0.0 | 0.0598 | 0.0598 | 0.0598 |
| Tax rate on capital gains | | | | | | | | | |
| Households | 0.0 | 0.0 | 0.0 | 0.211 | 0.211 | 0.211 | 0.0 | 0.0 | 0.0 |
| Tax-exempt institutions | a | a | a | 0.0 | 0.0 | 0.0 | 0.0 | 0.0 | 0.0 |
| Insurance companies | 0.37 | 0.37 | 0.37 | 0.248 | 0.248 | 0.248 | 0.15 | 0.15 | 0.15 |

a. See appendix to chapter 2.

Table A-2  (1980, continued)

| Item | Germany | | | Italy | | | Japan | | |
|---|---|---|---|---|---|---|---|---|---|
| | Debt | New shares | Retained earnings | Debt | New shares | Retained earnings | Debt | New shares | Retained earnings |
| Personal wealth tax rates | | | | | | | | | |
| Households | 0.005 | 0.005 | 0.005 | 0.0 | 0.0 | 0.0 | 0.0 | 0.0 | 0.0 |
| Tax-exempt institutions | 0.0 | 0.0 | 0.0 | 0.0 | 0.0 | 0.0 | 0.0 | 0.0 | 0.0 |
| Insurance companies | 0.007 | 0.007 | 0.007 | 0.0 | 0.0 | 0.0 | 0.0 | 0.0 | 0.0 |
| Tax rates on interest | | | | | | | | | |
| Households | 0.32 | 0.46 | 0.46 | 0.1968 | 0.4362 | 0.4362 | 0.1144 | 0.2731 | 0.2731 |
| Tax-exempt institutions | 0.0 | 0.40 | 0.40 | 0.0 | 0.0 | 0.0 | 0.0117 | 0.0117 | 0.0470 |
| Insurance companies | 0.09 | 0.09 | 0.09 | -0.4351 | -0.3401 | -0.3401 | 0.0973 | 0.0973 | 0.0973 |
| Tax rate on capital gains | | | | | | | | | |
| Households | 0.0 | 0.0 | 0.0 | 0.0 | 0.0 | 0.0 | 0.204 | 0.204 | 0.204 |
| Tax-exempt institutions | 0.0 | 0.0 | 0.0 | 0.0 | 0.0 | 0.0 | 0.0 | 0.0 | 0.0 |
| Insurance companies | 0.0 | 0.0 | 0.0 | 0.0 | 0.0 | 0.0 | 0.0 | 0.0 | 0.0 |

Table A-2  (1980, concluded)

| Item | Sweden | | | United Kingdom | | | United States | | |
|---|---|---|---|---|---|---|---|---|---|
| | Debt | New shares | Retained earnings | Debt | New shares | Retained earnings | Debt | New shares | Retained earnings |
| Personal wealth tax rates | | | | | | | | | |
| Households | 0.006 | 0.017 | 0.017 | 0.0 | 0.0 | 0.0 | 0.0 | 0.0 | 0.0 |
| Tax-exempt institutions | 0.0 | 0.0 | 0.0 | 0.0 | 0.0 | 0.0 | 0.0 | 0.0 | 0.0 |
| Insurance companies | 0.0 | 0.0 | 0.0 | 0.0 | 0.0 | 0.0 | 0.0 | 0.0 | 0.0 |
| Tax rates on interest | | | | | | | | | |
| Households | 0.490 | 0.640 | 0.640 | 0.425 | 0.443 | 0.443 | 0.284 | 0.475 | 0.475 |
| Tax-exempt institutions | 0.0 | 0.0 | 0.0 | 0.0 | 0.0 | 0.0 | 0.0 | 0.0 | 0.0 |
| Insurance companies | $(0.105+1.94\pi)$ | $(0.106+1.36\pi)$ | $(0.106+1.36\pi)$ | 0.265 | 0.177 | 0.177 | $(0.149+3.88\pi)$ | 0.069 | 0.069 |
| Tax rate on capital gains | | | | | | | | | |
| Households | ... | 0.26 | 0.26 | 0.2770 | 0.2770 | 0.2770 | 0.14 | 0.14 | 0.14 |
| Tax-exempt institutions | ... | 0.0 | 0.0 | 0.0 | 0.0 | 0.0 | 0.0 | 0.0 | 0.0 |
| Insurance companies | ... | $(0.05+1.5\pi)$ | $(0.05+1.5\pi)$ | 0.1765 | 0.1765 | 0.1765 | 0.28 | 0.28 | 0.28 |

Table A-2. Part Two: Tax Parameters, by Source of Finance, Nine Countries, 1985

| Item | Australia | | | Canada | | | France | | |
|---|---|---|---|---|---|---|---|---|---|
| | Debt | New shares | Retained earnings | Debt | New shares | Retained earnings | Debt | New shares | Retained earnings |
| Personal wealth tax rates | | | | | | | | | |
| Households | 0.0 | 0.0 | 0.0 | 0.0 | 0.0 | 0.0 | 0.005 | 0.005 | 0.005 |
| Tax-exempt institutions | 0.0 | 0.0 | 0.0 | 0.0 | 0.0 | 0.0 | 0.005 | 0.005 | 0.005 |
| Insurance companies | 0.0 | 0.0 | 0.0 | 0.0 | 0.0 | 0.0 | 0.005 | 0.005 | 0.005 |
| Tax rates on interest | | | | | | | | | |
| Households | 0.24 | 0.41 | 0.41 | 0.318 | 0.423 | 0.423 | 0.2600 | 0.5030 | 0.5030 |
| Tax-exempt institutions | a | a | a | 0.0 | 0.0 | 0.0 | 0.2600 | 0.3300 | 0.3300 |
| Insurance companies | 0.37 | 0.02 | 0.02 | 0.0 | 0.0 | 0.0 | −0.0684 | −0.0684 | −0.0684 |
| Tax rate on capital gains | | | | | | | | | |
| Households | 0.0 | 0.0 | 0.0 | 0.211 | 0.211 | 0.211 | 0.0 | 0.0 | 0.0 |
| Tax-exempt institutions | a | a | a | 0.0 | 0.0 | 0.0 | 0.0 | 0.0 | 0.0 |
| Insurance companies | 0.37 | 0.37 | 0.37 | 0.249 | 0.249 | 0.249 | 0.15 | 0.15 | 0.15 |

a. See appendix to chapter 2.

Table A-2  (1985, continued)

| Item | Germany | | | Italy | | | Japan | | |
|---|---|---|---|---|---|---|---|---|---|
| | Debt | New shares | Retained earnings | Debt | New shares | Retained earnings | Debt | New shares | Retained earnings |
| Personal wealth tax rates | | | | | | | | | |
| Households | 0.005 | 0.005 | 0.005 | 0.0 | 0.0 | 0.0 | 0.0 | 0.0 | 0.0 |
| Tax-exempt institutions | 0.0 | 0.0 | 0.0 | 0.0025 | 0.0010 | 0.0010 | 0.0 | 0.0 | 0.0 |
| Insurance companies | 0.006 | 0.006 | 0.006 | 0.0 | 0.0 | 0.0 | 0.0 | 0.0 | 0.0 |
| Tax rates on interest | | | | | | | | | |
| Households | 0.30 | 0.44 | 0.44 | 0.2249 | 0.4916 | 0.4916 | 0.1141 | 0.2662 | 0.2662 |
| Tax-exempt institutions | 0.0 | 0.40 | 0.40 | 0.1259 | 0.4240 | 0.4240 | 0.0117 | 0.0117 | 0.0117 |
| Insurance companies | 0.09 | 0.09 | 0.09 | 0.0603 | -0.1214 | -0.1214 | 0.0973 | 0.0973 | 0.0973 |
| Tax rate on capital gains | | | | | | | | | |
| Households | 0.0 | 0.0 | 0.0 | 0.0 | 0.0 | 0.0 | 0.1466 | 0.1466 | 0.1466 |
| Tax-exempt institutions | 0.0 | 0.0 | 0.0 | 0.0 | 0.0 | 0.0 | 0.0 | 0.0 | 0.0 |
| Insurance companies | 0.0 | 0.0 | 0.0 | 0.0 | 0.0 | 0.0 | 0.0 | 0.0 | 0.0 |

Table A-2  (1985, concluded)

| Item | Sweden | | | United Kingdom | | | United States | | |
|---|---|---|---|---|---|---|---|---|---|
| | Debt | New shares | Retained earnings | Debt | New shares | Retained earnings | Debt | New shares | Retained earnings |
| **Personal wealth tax rates** | | | | | | | | | |
| Households | 0.007 | 0.021 | 0.021 | 0.0 | 0.0 | 0.0 | 0.0 | 0.0 | 0.0 |
| Tax-exempt institutions | 0.0 | 0.0 | 0.0 | 0.0 | 0.0 | 0.0 | 0.0 | 0.0 | 0.0 |
| Insurance companies | 0.0 | 0.0 | 0.0 | 0.0 | 0.0 | 0.0 | 0.0 | 0.0 | 0.0 |
| **Tax rates on interest** | | | | | | | | | |
| Households | 0.440 | 0.590 | 0.590 | 0.393 | 0.412 | 0.412 | 0.258 | 0.396 | 0.396 |
| Tax-exempt institutions | 0.0 | 0.0 | 0.0 | 0.0 | 0.0 | 0.0 | 0.0 | 0.0 | 0.0 |
| Insurance companies | $(0.103+2.05\pi)$ | $(0.103+1.5\pi)$ | $(0.103+1.5\pi)$ | 0.375 | 0.300 | 0.300 | 0.368 | 0.069 | 0.069 |
| **Tax rate on capital gains** | | | | | | | | | |
| Households | ... | 0.25 | 0.25 | 0.264 | 0.264 | 0.264 | 0.118 | 0.118 | 0.118 |
| Tax-exempt institutions | ... | 0.01 | 0.01 | 0.0 | 0.0 | 0.0 | 0.0 | 0.0 | 0.0 |
| Insurance companies | ... | $(0.06+1.5\pi)$ | $(0.06+1.5\pi)$ | 0.300 | 0.300 | 0.300 | 0.280 | 0.280 | 0.280 |

Table A-2.  Part Three: Tax Parameters, by Source of Finance, Nine Countries, 1990

| | Australia | | | Canada | | | France | | |
| --- | --- | --- | --- | --- | --- | --- | --- | --- | --- |
| Item | Debt | New shares | Retained earnings | Debt | New shares | Retained earnings | Debt | New shares | Retained earnings |
| Personal wealth tax rates | | | | | | | | | |
| Households | 0.0 | 0.0 | 0.0 | 0.0 | 0.0 | 0.0 | 0.0025 | 0.0025 | 0.0025 |
| Tax-exempt institutions | 0.0 | 0.0 | 0.0 | 0.0 | 0.0 | 0.0 | 0.0025 | 0.0025 | 0.0025 |
| Insurance companies | 0.0 | 0.0 | 0.0 | 0.0 | 0.0 | 0.0 | 0.0025 | 0.0025 | 0.0025 |
| Tax rates on interest | | | | | | | | | |
| Households | 0.23 | 0.40 | 0.40 | 0.326 | 0.437 | 0.437 | 0.1700 | 0.4000 | 0.4000 |
| Tax-exempt institutions | a | a | a | 0.0 | 0.0 | 0.0 | 0.0 | 0.3300 | 0.3300 |
| Insurance companies | 0.39 | 0.39 | 0.39 | 0.0 | 0.0 | 0.0 | −0.1365 | −0.1365 | −0.1365 |
| Tax rate on capital gains | | | | | | | | | |
| Households | 0.40 | 0.40 | 0.40 | 0.108 | 0.108 | 0.108 | 0.0 | 0.0 | 0.0 |
| Tax-exempt institutions | a | a | a | 0.0 | 0.0 | 0.0 | 0.0 | 0.0 | 0.0 |
| Insurance companies | 0.39 | 0.39 | 0.39 | 0.337 | 0.337 | 0.337 | 0.15 | 0.15 | 0.15 |

a. See appendix to chapter 2.

377

Table A-2  (1990, continued)

| Item | Germany | | | Italy | | | Japan | | |
|---|---|---|---|---|---|---|---|---|---|
| | Debt | New shares | Retained earnings | Debt | New shares | Retained earnings | Debt | New shares | Retained earnings |
| Personal wealth tax rates | | | | | | | | | |
| Households | 0.005 | 0.005 | 0.005 | 0.0 | 0.0 | 0.0 | 0.0 | 0.0 | 0.0 |
| Tax-exempt institutions | 0.0 | 0.0 | 0.0 | 0.0025 | 0.0025 | 0.0010 | 0.0 | 0.0 | 0.0 |
| Insurance companies | 0.006 | 0.006 | 0.006 | 0.0 | 0.0 | 0.0 | 0.0 | 0.0 | 0.0 |
| Tax rates on interest | | | | | | | | | |
| Households | 0.27 | 0.39 | 0.39 | 0.1667 | 0.4610 | 0.4610 | 0.1141 | 0.2662 | 0.2662 |
| Tax-exempt institutions | 0.0 | 0.40 | 0.40 | 0.1259 | 0.4240 | 0.4240 | 0.0117 | 0.0117 | 0.0117 |
| Insurance companies | 0.09 | 0.09 | 0.09 | 0.0536 | -0.1293 | -0.1293 | 0.0973 | 0.0973 | 0.0973 |
| Tax rate on capital gains | | | | | | | | | |
| Households | 0.0 | 0.0 | 0.0 | 0.0 | 0.0 | 0.0 | 0.1466 | 0.1466 | 0.1466 |
| Tax-exempt institutions | 0.0 | 0.0 | 0.0 | 0.0 | 0.0 | 0.0 | 0.0 | 0.0 | 0.0 |
| Insurance companies | 0.0 | 0.0 | 0.0 | 0.0 | 0.0 | 0.0 | 0.0 | 0.0 | 0.0 |

Table A-2  (1990, concluded)

| Item | Sweden | | | United Kingdom | | | United States | | |
|---|---|---|---|---|---|---|---|---|---|
| | Debt | New shares | Retained earnings | Debt | New shares | Retained earnings | Debt | New shares | Retained earnings |
| Personal wealth tax rates | | | | | | | | | |
| Households | 0.0050 | 0.0018 | 0.0018 | 0.0 | 0.0 | 0.0 | 0.0 | 0.0 | 0.0 |
| Tax-exempt institutions | 0.0 | 0.0 | 0.0 | 0.0 | 0.0 | 0.0 | 0.0 | 0.0 | 0.0 |
| Insurance companies | 0.0 | 0.0 | 0.0 | 0.0 | 0.0 | 0.0 | 0.0 | 0.0 | 0.0 |
| Tax rates on interest | | | | | | | | | |
| Households | 0.300 | 0.300 | 0.300 | 0.319 | 0.333 | 0.333 | 0.224 | 0.320 | 0.320 |
| Tax-exempt institutions | 0.094 | 0.036 | 0.036 | 0.0 | 0.0 | 0.0 | 0.0 | 0.0 | 0.0 |
| Insurance companies | 0.230 | 0.230 | 0.230 | 0.250 | 0.250 | 0.250 | 0.343 | 0.068 | 0.068 |
| Tax rate on capital gains | | | | | | | | | |
| Households | . . . | 0.300 | 0.300 | 0.35 | 0.35 | 0.35 | 0.234 | 0.234 | 0.234 |
| Tax-exempt institutions | . . . | 0.036 | 0.036 | 0.0 | 0.0 | 0.0 | 0.0 | 0.0 | 0.0 |
| Insurance companies | . . . | 0.230 | 0.230 | 0.25 | 0.25 | 0.25 | 0.343 | 0.343 | 0.343 |

Table A-3. Part One: Parameters for Each Asset, by Industry, Nine Countries, 1980

| | Australia | | | Canada | | | France | | |
| --- | --- | --- | --- | --- | --- | --- | --- | --- | --- |
| Item | Manu-facturing | Other industry | Com-merce | Manu-facturing | Other industry | Com-merce | Manu-facturing | Other industry | Com-merce |
| Depreciation rate | | | | | | | | | |
| Machinery | 0.1053 | 0.1429 | 0.1429 | 0.0851 | 0.0922 | 0.1242 | 0.1739 | 0.1709 | 0.1700 |
| Buildings | 0.0444 | 0.0426 | 0.0333 | 0.0445 | 0.0383 | 0.0398 | 0.0541 | 0.0667 | 0.0541 |
| Inventories | 0.0 | 0.0 | 0.0 | 0.0 | 0.0 | 0.0 | 0.0 | 0.0 | 0.0 |
| Proportion with immediate depreciation | | | | | | | | | |
| Machinery | 0.109 | 0.087 | 0.062 | 0.0409 | 0.0060 | 0.0113 | 0.0 | 0.0 | 0.0 |
| Buildings | 0.0 | 0.0 | 0.0 | 0.0 | 0.0 | 0.0 | 0.0 | 0.0 | 0.0 |
| Inventories | 0.0 | 0.0 | 0.0 | 0.0 | 0.0 | 0.0 | 0.0 | 0.0 | 0.0 |
| Proportion with later depreciation | | | | | | | | | |
| Machinery | 1.0 | 1.0 | 1.0 | 0.9591 | 0.9940 | 0.9887 | 1.0 | 1.0 | 1.0 |
| Buildings | 1.0 | 1.0 | 1.0 | 1.0 | 1.0 | 1.0 | 1.0 | 1.0 | 1.0 |
| Inventories | 1.0 | 1.0 | 1.0 | 1.0 | 1.0 | 1.0 | 0.0 | 0.0 | 0.0 |
| Lifetimes | | | | | | | | | |
| Machinery | 0.0 | 0.0 | 0.0 | 0.0 | 0.0 | 0.0 | 8.0 | 8.0 | 8.0 |
| Buildings | 100.0 | 100.0 | 100.0 | 0.0 | 0.0 | 0.0 | 20.0 | 20.0 | 20.0 |
| Inventories | 0.0 | 0.0 | 0.0 | 0.0 | 0.0 | 0.0 | 0.0 | 0.0 | 0.0 |

| | | | | | | | | | |
|---|---|---|---|---|---|---|---|---|---|
| **Type of depreciation[a]** | | | | | | | | | |
| Machinery | 0 | 0 | 0 | 0 | 0 | 0 | 2 | 2 | 2 |
| Buildings | 1 | 1 | 1 | 0 | 0 | 0 | 1 | 1 | 1 |
| Inventories | 0 | 0 | 0 | 0 | 0 | 0 | ⋯ | ⋯ | ⋯ |
| **Exponential tax depreciation rate** | | | | | | | | | |
| Machinery | 0.1365 | 0.2010 | 0.1920 | 0.0 | 0.0 | 0.0 | 0.25 | 0.25 | 0.25 |
| Buildings | 0.0 | 0.0 | 0.0 | 0.0 | 0.0 | 0.0 | 0.0 | 0.0 | 0.0 |
| Inventories | 0.0 | 0.0 | 0.0 | 0.0 | 0.0 | 0.0 | 0.0 | 0.0 | 0.0 |
| **Proportion with investment grant** | | | | | | | | | |
| Machinery | 0.0 | 0.0 | 0.0 | 1.0 | 1.0 | 1.0 | 0.0 | 0.0 | 0.0 |
| Buildings | 0.0 | 0.0 | 0.0 | 1.0 | 1.0 | 1.0 | 0.0 | 0.0 | 0.0 |
| Inventories | 0.0 | 0.0 | 0.0 | 1.0 | 1.0 | 1.0 | 0.0 | 0.0 | 0.0 |
| **Rate of investment grant** | | | | | | | | | |
| Machinery | 0.0 | 0.0 | 0.0 | 0.0467 | 0.0199 | 0.0140 | 0.0 | 0.0 | 0.0 |
| Buildings | 0.0 | 0.0 | 0.0 | 0.0523 | 0.0009 | 0.0061 | 0.0 | 0.0 | 0.0 |
| Inventories | 0.0 | 0.0 | 0.0 | 0.0 | 0.0 | 0.0 | 0.0 | 0.0 | 0.0 |

a. 0 = exponential; 1 = straight line; 2 = declinging balance/straight line.

Table A-3 *(1980, continued)*

| Item | Germany | | | Italy | | | Japan | | |
|---|---|---|---|---|---|---|---|---|---|
| | Manu-facturing | Other industry | Com-merce | Manu-facturing | Other industry | Com-merce | Manu-facturing | Other industry | Com-merce |
| **Depreciation rate** | | | | | | | | | |
| Machinery | 0.174 | 0.230 | 0.238 | 0.119 | 0.119 | 0.119 | 0.0666 | 0.0900 | 0.0910 |
| Buildings | 0.037 | 0.030 | 0.022 | 0.065 | 0.065 | 0.057 | 0.02200 | 0.0248 | 0.0248 |
| Inventories | 0.0 | 0.0 | 0.0 | 0.0 | 0.0 | 0.0 | 0.0 | 0.0 | 0.0 |
| **Proportion with imme-diate depreciation** | | | | | | | | | |
| Machinery | 0.0 | 0.0 | 0.0 | 0.0 | 0.0 | 0.0 | 0.1260 | 0.1315 | 0.0630 |
| Buildings | 0.0 | 0.0 | 0.0 | 0.0 | 0.0 | 0.0 | 0.0 | 0.0 | 0.0 |
| Inventories | 0.0 | 0.0 | 0.0 | 0.0 | 0.0 | 0.0 | 0.0 | 0.0 | 0.0 |
| **Proportion with later depreciation** | | | | | | | | | |
| Machinery | 1.0 | 1.0 | 1.0 | 1.0 | 1.0 | 1.0 | 0.8740 | 0.8685 | 0.9370 |
| Buildings | 1.0 | 1.0 | 1.0 | 1.0 | 1.0 | 1.0 | 1.0 | 1.0 | 1.0 |
| Inventories | 0.0 | 0.0 | 0.0 | 0.0 | 0.0 | 0.0 | 0.0 | 0.0 | 0.0 |
| **Lifetimes** | | | | | | | | | |
| Machinery | 6.0 | 6.0 | 6.0 | 6.5 | 6.5 | 8.3 | 9.53 | 11.29 | 6.62 |
| Buildings | 46.4 | 48.0 | 50.0 | 25.0 | 15.0 | 33.0 | 32.60 | 37.16 | 33.44 |
| Inventories | 0.0 | 0.0 | 0.0 | 0.0 | 0.0 | 0.0 | 0.0 | 0.0 | 0.0 |

| | | | | | | | | | |
|---|---|---|---|---|---|---|---|---|---|
| **Type of depreciation**[a] | | | | | | | | | |
| Machinery | 2 | 2 | 2 | b | b | b | 0 | 0 | 0 |
| Buildings | 1 | 1 | 1 | b | b | b | 0 | 0 | 0 |
| Inventories | ... | ... | ... | b | b | b | 0 | 0 | 0 |
| **Exponential tax depreciation rate** | | | | | | | | | |
| Machinery | 0.250 | 0.250 | 0.250 | 0.119 | 0.119 | 0.119 | 0.2146 | 0.1845 | 0.2938 |
| Buildings | 0.022 | 0.021 | 0.020 | 0.065 | 0.065 | 0.057 | 0.0682 | 0.0601 | 0.0665 |
| Inventories | 0.0 | 0.0 | 0.0 | 0.0 | 0.0 | 0.0 | 0.0 | 0.0 | 0.0 |
| **Proportion with investment grant** | | | | | | | | | |
| Machinery | 0.0 | 0.0 | 0.0 | 0.0 | 0.0 | 0.0 | 0.0288 | 0.0186 | 0.0189 |
| Buildings | 0.0 | 0.0 | 0.0 | 0.0 | 0.0 | 0.0 | 0.0288 | 0.0186 | 0.0189 |
| Inventories | 0.0 | 0.0 | 0.0 | 0.0 | 0.0 | 0.0 | 0.0288 | 0.0186 | 0.0189 |
| **Rate of investment grant** | | | | | | | | | |
| Machinery | 0.0 | 0.0 | 0.0 | 0.0 | 0.0 | 0.0 | 0.0 | 0.0 | 0.0 |
| Buildings | 0.0 | 0.0 | 0.0 | 0.0 | 0.0 | 0.0 | 0.0 | 0.0 | 0.0 |
| Inventories | 0.0 | 0.0 | 0.0 | 0.0 | 0.0 | 0.0 | 0.0 | 0.0 | 0.0 |

a. 0 = exponential; 1 = straight line; 2 = declining balance/straight line.
b. See text of chapter 6.

Table A-3  (1980, concluded)

| Item | Sweden | | | United Kingdom | | | United States | | |
|---|---|---|---|---|---|---|---|---|---|
| | Manu-facturing | Other industry | Com-merce | Manu-facturing | Other industry | Com-merce | Manu-facturing | Other industry | Com-merce |
| Depreciation rate | | | | | | | | | |
| Machinery | 0.077 | 0.197 | 0.182 | 0.0819 | 0.1535 | 0.0831 | 0.1331 | 0.1302 | 0.1710 |
| Buildings | 0.026 | 0.023 | 0.018 | 0.0250 | 0.0250 | 0.0250 | 0.0343 | 0.0304 | 0.0247 |
| Inventories | 0.0 | 0.0 | 0.0 | 0.0 | 0.0 | 0.0 | 0.0 | 0.0 | 0.0 |
| Proportion with imme-diate depreciation | | | | | | | | | |
| Machinery | 0.3 | 0.3 | 0.3 | 1.0 | 1.0 | 1.0 | 0.0 | 0.0 | 0.0 |
| Buildings | 0.0 | 0.0 | 0.0 | 0.540 | 0.540 | 0.012 | 0.0 | 0.0 | 0.0 |
| Inventories | 0.6 | 0.193 | 0.6 | 1.0 | 1.0 | 1.0 | 0.0 | 0.0 | 0.0 |
| Proportion with later depreciation | | | | | | | | | |
| Machinery | 0.7 | 0.7 | 0.7 | 0.0 | 0.0 | 0.0 | 1.0 | 1.0 | 1.0 |
| Buildings | 1.0 | 1.0 | 1.0 | 0.460 | 0.460 | 0.038 | 1.0 | 1.0 | 1.0 |
| Inventories | 0.0 | 0.0 | 0.0 | 0.0 | 0.0 | 0.0 | 1.0 | 1.0 | 1.0 |
| Lifetimes | | | | | | | | | |
| Machinery | ... | ... | ... | 0.0 | 0.0 | 0.0 | a | a | a |
| Buildings | 28.0 | 33.0 | 36.0 | 12.0 | 12.0 | 20.0 | a | a | a |
| Inventories | ... | ... | ... | 0.0 | 0.0 | 0.0 | a | a | a |

| Type of depreciation[b] | | | | | | | | |
|---|---|---|---|---|---|---|---|---|
| Machinery | 0 | 0 | 0 | 0 | 0 | 0 | 0 | 0 |
| Buildings | 3 | 3 | 3 | 1 | 1 | .. | 0 | 0 |
| Inventories | .. | .. | .. | .. | .. | .. | .. | .. |
| Exponential tax depreciation rate | | | | | | | | |
| Machinery | 0.3 | 0.3 | 0.3 | .. | .. | .. | .. | .. |
| Buildings | 0.0 | 0.0 | 0.0 | .. | .. | .. | .. | .. |
| Inventories | 0.0 | 0.0 | 0.0 | .. | .. | .. | .. | .. |
| Proportion with investment grant | | | | | | | | |
| Machinery | 1.0 | 1.0 | 1.0 | 0.459 | 0.002 | 1.0 | 1.0 | 1.0 |
| Buildings | 1.0 | 1.0 | 1.0 | 0.788 | 0.002 | 1.0 | 1.0 | 1.0 |
| Inventories | 1.0 | 1.0 | 1.0 | .. | .. | 1.0 | 1.0 | 1.0 |
| Rate of investment grant | | | | | | | | |
| Machinery | 0.114 | 0.114 | 0.114 | 0.196 | 0.196 | 0.0959 | 0.0902 | 0.0857 |
| Buildings | 0.057 | 0.057 | 0.057 | 0.197 | 0.197 | 0.0 | 0.0978 | 0.0 |
| Inventories | 0.0 | 0.0 | 0.0 | 0.0 | 0.0 | 0.0 | 0.0 | 0.0 |

a. See table 10-7. Data available only on a disaggregated basis.
b. 0 = exponential; 1 = straight line; 3 = straight line with extra 2 percent for five years.

385

Table A-3. Part Two: Parameters for Each Asset, by Industry, Nine Countries, 1985

| Item | Australia | | | Canada | | | France | | |
|---|---|---|---|---|---|---|---|---|---|
| | Manu-facturing | Other industry | Com-merce | Manu-facturing | Other industry | Com-merce | Manu-facturing | Other industry | Com-merce |
| **Depreciation rate** | | | | | | | | | |
| Machinery | 0.1453 | 0.1429 | 0.1429 | 0.0851 | 0.0922 | 0.1242 | 0.1739 | 0.1709 | 0.1700 |
| Buildings | 0.0444 | 0.0426 | 0.0333 | 0.0445 | 0.0383 | 0.0398 | 0.0541 | 0.0667 | 0.0541 |
| Inventories | 0.0 | 0.0 | 0.0 | 0.0 | 0.0 | 0.0 | 0.0 | 0.0 | 0.0 |
| **Proportion with immediate depreciation** | | | | | | | | | |
| Machinery | 0.131 | 0.129 | 0.062 | 0.0348 | 0.0053 | 0.0099 | 0.4 | 0.4 | 0.4 |
| Buildings | 0.0 | 0.0 | 0.0 | 0.0 | 0.0 | 0.0 | 0.0 | 0.0 | 0.0 |
| Inventories | 0.0 | 0.0 | 0.0 | 0.0 | 0.0 | 0.0 | 0.0 | 0.0 | 0.0 |
| **Proportion with later depreciation** | | | | | | | | | |
| Machinery | 1.0 | 1.0 | 1.0 | 0.9652 | 0.9947 | 0.9901 | 0.6 | 0.6 | 0.6 |
| Buildings | 1.0 | 1.0 | 1.0 | 1.0 | 1.0 | 1.0 | 1.0 | 1.0 | 1.0 |
| Inventories | 0.0 | 0.0 | 0.0 | 0.0 | 0.0 | 0.0 | 0.0 | 0.0 | 0.0 |
| **Lifetimes** | | | | | | | | | |
| Machinery | 4.35 | 4.0 | 4.17 | 0.0 | 0.0 | 0.0 | 8.0 | 8.0 | 8.0 |
| Buildings | 25.0 | 3.0 | 25.0 | 0.0 | 0.0 | 0.0 | 20.0 | 20.0 | 20.0 |
| Inventories | 0.0 | 0.0 | 0.0 | 0.0 | 0.0 | 0.0 | 0.0 | 0.0 | 0.0 |

| | | | | | | | | |
|---|---|---|---|---|---|---|---|---|
| **Type of depreciation**[a] | | | | | | | | |
| Machinery | 1 | 1 | 0 | 0 | 0 | 2 | 2 | 2 |
| Buildings | 1 | 1 | 0 | 0 | 0 | 1 | 1 | 1 |
| Inventories | 0 | 0 | 0 | 0 | 0 | ... | ... | ... |
| **Exponential tax depreciation rate** | | | | | | | | |
| Machinery | 0.0 | 0.0 | 0.0 | 0.0 | 0.0 | 0.25 | 0.25 | 0.25 |
| Buildings | 0.0 | 0.0 | 0.0 | 0.0 | 0.0 | 0.0 | 0.0 | 0.0 |
| Inventories | 0.0 | 0.0 | 0.0 | 0.0 | 0.0 | 0.0 | 0.0 | 0.0 |
| **Proportion with investment grant** | | | | | | | | |
| Machinery | 0.0 | 0.0 | 1.0 | 1.0 | 1.0 | 0.0 | 0.0 | 0.0 |
| Buildings | 0.0 | 0.0 | 1.0 | 1.0 | 1.0 | 0.0 | 0.0 | 0.0 |
| Inventories | 0.0 | 0.0 | 1.0 | 1.0 | 1.0 | 0.0 | 0.0 | 0.0 |
| **Rate of investment grant** | | | | | | | | |
| Machinery | 0.0 | 0.0 | 0.0572 | 0.0123 | 0.0071 | 0.0 | 0.0 | 0.0 |
| Buildings | 0.0 | 0.0 | 0.0447 | 0.0256 | 0.0050 | 0.0 | 0.0 | 0.0 |
| Inventories | 0.0 | 0.0 | 0.0 | 0.0 | 0.0 | 0.0 | 0.0 | 0.0 |

a. 0 = exponential; 1 = straight line; 2 = declining balance/straight line.

Table A-3  (1985, continued)

| Item | Germany | | | Italy | | | Japan | | |
|---|---|---|---|---|---|---|---|---|---|
| | Manu-facturing | Other industry | Com-merce | Manu-facturing | Other industry | Com-merce | Manu-facturing | Other industry | Com-merce |
| **Depreciation rate** | | | | | | | | | |
| Machinery | 0.179 | 0.235 | 0.250 | 0.1260 | 0.1260 | 0.1260 | 0.0666 | 0.0900 | 0.0910 |
| Buildings | 0.037 | 0.030 | 0.022 | 0.0650 | 0.0650 | 0.0570 | 0.0222 | 0.0248 | 0.0248 |
| Inventories | 0.0 | 0.0 | 0.0 | 0.0 | 0.0 | 0.0 | 0.0 | 0.0 | 0.0 |
| **Proportion with imme-diate depreciation** | | | | | | | | | |
| Machinery | 0.0 | 0.0 | 0.0 | 0.0 | 0.0 | 0.0 | 0.0525 | 0.0408 | 0.0084 |
| Buildings | 0.0 | 0.0 | 0.0 | 0.0 | 0.0 | 0.0 | 0.0 | 0.0 | 0.0 |
| Inventories | 0.0 | 0.0 | 0.0 | 0.0 | 0.0 | 0.0 | 0.0 | 0.0 | 0.0 |
| **Proportion with later depreciation** | | | | | | | | | |
| Machinery | 1.0 | 1.0 | 1.0 | 1.0 | 1.0 | 1.0 | 0.9425 | 0.9592 | 0.9916 |
| Buildings | 1.0 | 1.0 | 1.0 | 1.0 | 1.0 | 1.0 | 1.0 | 1.0 | 1.0 |
| Inventories | 0.0 | 0.0 | 0.0 | 0.0 | 0.0 | 0.0 | 0.0 | 0.0 | 0.0 |
| **Lifetimes** | | | | | | | | | |
| Machinery | 6.0 | 6.0 | 6.0 | 6.5 | 6.5 | 8.3 | 9.53 | 11.29 | 6.62 |
| Buildings | 25.0 | 25.0 | 25.0 | 25.0 | 15.0 | 33.0 | 32.60 | 37.16 | 33.44 |
| Inventories | 0.0 | 0.0 | 0.0 | 0.0 | 0.0 | 0.0 | 0.0 | 0.0 | 0.0 |

| | | | | | | | | | | |
|---|---|---|---|---|---|---|---|---|---|---|
| **Type of depreciation**[a] | | | | | | | | | | |
| Machinery | 2 | 2 | ... | 2 | b | b | b | 0 | 0 | 0 |
| Buildings | 1 | 1 | ... | 1 | b | b | b | 0 | 0 | 0 |
| Inventories | ... | ... | ... | ... | b | b | b | 0 | 0 | 0 |
| **Exponential tax depreciation rate** | | | | | | | | | | |
| Machinery | 0.30 | 0.30 | ... | 0.30 | 0.126 | 0.126 | 0.126 | 0.2146 | 0.1845 | 0.2938 |
| Buildings | 0.04 | 0.04 | ... | 0.04 | 0.065 | 0.065 | 0.057 | 0.0682 | 0.0601 | 0.0665 |
| Inventories | 0.0 | 0.0 | ... | 0.0 | 0.0 | 0.0 | 0.0 | 0.0 | 0.0 | 0.0 |
| **Proportion with investment grant** | | | | | | | | | | |
| Machinery | 0.0 | 0.0 | ... | 0.0 | 0.3 | 0.3 | 0.3 | 0.0307 | 0.0087 | 0.0048 |
| Buildings | 0.0 | 0.0 | ... | 0.0 | 0.0 | 0.0 | 0.0 | 0.0307 | 0.0087 | 0.0048 |
| Inventories | 0.0 | 0.0 | ... | 0.0 | 0.0 | 0.0 | 0.0 | 0.0307 | 0.0087 | 0.0048 |
| **Rate of investment grant** | | | | | | | | | | |
| Machinery | 0.0 | 0.0 | ... | 0.0 | 0.06 | 0.06 | 0.06 | 0.0 | 0.0 | 0.0 |
| Buildings | 0.0 | 0.0 | ... | 0.0 | 0.06 | 0.0 | 0.0 | 0.0 | 0.0 | 0.0 |
| Inventories | 0.0 | 0.0 | ... | 0.0 | 0.06 | 0.0 | 0.0 | 0.0 | 0.0 | 0.0 |

a. 0 = exponential; 1 = straight line; 2 = declining balance/straight line.
b. See text of chapter 6.

389

Table A-3 (1985, concluded)

| Item | Sweden | | | United Kingdom | | | United States | | |
| --- | --- | --- | --- | --- | --- | --- | --- | --- | --- |
| | Manufacturing | Other industry | Commerce | Manufacturing | Other industry | Commerce | Manufacturing | Other industry | Commerce |
| Depreciation rate | | | | | | | | | |
| Machinery | 0.077 | 0.197 | 0.182 | 0.0819 | 0.1535 | 0.0831 | 0.1331 | 0.1302 | 0.1710 |
| Buildings | 0.026 | 0.023 | 0.018 | 0.0250 | 0.0250 | 0.0250 | 0.0343 | 0.0304 | 0.0247 |
| Inventories | 0.0 | 0.0 | 0.0 | 0.0 | 0.0 | 0.0 | 0.0 | 0.0 | 0.0 |
| Proportion with immediate depreciation | | | | | | | | | |
| Machinery | 0.3 | 0.3 | 0.3 | 0.5 | 0.5 | 0.5 | 0.0 | 0.0 | 0.0 |
| Buildings | 0.0 | 0.0 | 0.0 | 0.29 | 0.29 | 0.012 | 0.0 | 0.0 | 0.0 |
| Inventories | 0.5 | 0.184 | 0.5 | 0.0 | 0.0 | 0.0 | 0.0 | 0.0 | 0.0 |
| Proportion with later depreciation | | | | | | | | | |
| Machinery | 0.7 | 0.7 | 0.7 | 0.5 | 0.5 | 0.5 | 1.0 | 1.0 | 1.0 |
| Buildings | 1.0 | 1.0 | 1.0 | 0.71 | 0.71 | 0.038 | 1.0 | 1.0 | 1.0 |
| Inventories | 0.0 | 0.0 | 0.0 | 0.0 | 0.0 | 0.0 | 1.0 | 1.0 | 1.0 |
| Lifetimes | | | | | | | | | |
| Machinery | ... | ... | ... | 0.0 | 0.0 | 0.0 | a | a | a |
| Buildings | 28.0 | 33.0 | 36.0 | 18.0 | 18.0 | 20.0 | a | a | a |
| Inventories | ... | ... | ... | 0.0 | 0.0 | 0.0 | a | a | a |

| | | | | | | | | |
|---|---|---|---|---|---|---|---|---|
| Type of depreciation[b] | | | | | | | | |
| Machinery | 0 | 0 | 0 | 0 | 0 | 0 | 0 | 0 |
| Buildings | 3 | 3 | 1 | 1 | 1 | 0 | 0 | 0 |
| Inventories | ... | ... | ... | ... | ... | 0 | 0 | 0 |
| Exponential tax depreciation rate | | | | | | | | |
| Machinery | 0.3 | 0.3 | 0.25 | 0.25 | 0.25 | ... | ... | ... |
| Buildings | 0.0 | 0.0 | ... | ... | ... | ... | ... | ... |
| Inventories | 0.0 | 0.0 | ... | ... | ... | ... | ... | ... |
| Proportion with investment grant | | | | | | | | |
| Machinery | 1.0 | 1.0 | 0.179 | 0.002 | 0.0 | 1.0 | 1.0 | 1.0 |
| Buildings | 1.0 | 1.0 | 0.247 | 0.002 | 0.0 | 1.0 | 1.0 | 1.0 |
| Inventories | 1.0 | 1.0 | ... | ... | ... | 1.0 | 1.0 | 1.0 |
| Rate of investment grant | | | | | | | | |
| Machinery | 0.0 | 0.0 | 0.202 | 0.202 | 0.0 | 0.0959 | 0.0902 | 0.0857 |
| Buildings | 0.0 | 0.0 | 0.200 | 0.200 | 0.0 | 0.0 | 0.9780 | 0.0 |
| Inventories | 0.0 | 0.0 | 0.0 | 0.0 | 0.0 | 0.0 | 0.0 | 0.0 |

a. See table 10-7. Data available only on a disaggregated basis.
b. 0 = exponential; 1 = straight line; 3 = straight line with extra 2 percent for five years.

Table A-3. *Part Three: Parameters for Each Asset, by Industry, Nine Countries, 1990*

| | Australia | | | Canada | | | France | | |
|---|---|---|---|---|---|---|---|---|---|
| *Item* | *Manu-facturing* | *Other industry* | *Com-merce* | *Manu-facturing* | *Other industry* | *Com-merce* | *Manu-facturing* | *Other industry* | *Com-merce* |
| Depreciation rate | | | | | | | | | |
| Machinery | 0.1053 | 0.1429 | 0.1429 | 0.0851 | 0.0922 | 0.1242 | 0.1739 | 0.1709 | 0.1700 |
| Buildings | 0.0444 | 0.0426 | 0.0333 | 0.0445 | 0.0383 | 0.0398 | 0.0541 | 0.0667 | 0.0541 |
| Inventories | 0.0 | 0.0 | 0.0 | 0.0 | 0.0 | 0.0 | 0.0 | 0.0 | 0.0 |
| Proportion with immediate depreciation | | | | | | | | | |
| Machinery | 0.0 | 0.0 | 0.0 | 0.0348 | 0.0053 | 0.0099 | | 0.0 | 0.0 |
| Buildings | 0.0 | 0.0 | 0.0 | 0.0 | 0.0 | 0.0 | 0.0 | 0.0 | 0.0 |
| Inventories | 0.0 | 0.0 | 0.0 | 0.0 | 0.0 | 0.0 | 0.0 | 0.0 | 0.0 |
| Proportion with later depreciation | | | | | | | | | |
| Machinery | 1.0 | 1.0 | 1.0 | 0.9652 | 0.9947 | 0.9901 | 1.0 | 1.0 | 1.0 |
| Buildings | 1.0 | 1.0 | 1.0 | 1.0 | 1.0 | 1.0 | 1.0 | 1.0 | 1.0 |
| Inventories | 1.0 | 1.0 | 1.0 | 1.0 | 1.0 | 1.0 | 0.0 | 0.0 | 0.0 |
| Lifetimes | | | | | | | | | |
| Machinery | 0.0 | 0.0 | 0.0 | 0.0 | 0.0 | 0.0 | 7.0 | 7.0 | 7.0 |
| Buildings | 40.0 | 40.0 | 40.0 | 0.0 | 0.0 | 0.0 | 18.0 | 18.0 | 18.0 |
| Inventories | 0.0 | 0.0 | 0.0 | 0.0 | 0.0 | 0.0 | 0.0 | 0.0 | 0.0 |

| | | | | | | | | | |
|---|---|---|---|---|---|---|---|---|---|
| Type of depreciation[a] | | | | | | | | | |
| Machinery | 0 | 0 | 0 | 0 | 0 | 0 | 2 | 2 | 2 |
| Buildings | 1 | 1 | 1 | 0 | 0 | 0 | 1 | 1 | 1 |
| Inventories | 0 | 0 | 0 | 0 | 0 | 0 | ⋮ | ⋮ | ⋮ |
| Exponential tax depreciation rate | | | | | | | | | |
| Machinery | 0.1365 | 0.2010 | 0.1920 | 0.0 | 0.0 | 0.0 | 0.25 | 0.25 | 0.25 |
| Buildings | 0.0 | 0.0 | 0.0 | 0.0 | 0.0 | 0.0 | 0.0 | 0.0 | 0.0 |
| Inventories | 0.0 | 0.0 | 0.0 | 0.0 | 0.0 | 0.0 | 0.0 | 0.0 | 0.0 |
| Proportion with investment grant | | | | | | | | | |
| Machinery | 0.0 | 0.0 | 0.0 | 1.0 | 1.0 | 1.0 | 0.0 | 0.0 | 0.0 |
| Buildings | 0.0 | 0.0 | 0.0 | 1.0 | 1.0 | 1.0 | 0.0 | 0.0 | 0.0 |
| Inventories | 0.0 | 0.0 | 0.0 | 1.0 | 1.0 | 1.0 | 0.0 | 0.0 | 0.0 |
| Rate of investment grant | | | | | | | | | |
| Machinery | 0.0 | 0.0 | 0.0 | 0.0 | 0.0 | 0.0 | 0.0 | 0.0 | 0.0 |
| Buildings | 0.0 | 0.0 | 0.0 | 0.0 | 0.0 | 0.0 | 0.0 | 0.0 | 0.0 |
| Inventories | 0.0 | 0.0 | 0.0 | 0.0 | 0.0 | 0.0 | 0.0 | 0.0 | 0.0 |

a. 0 = exponential; 1 = straight line; 2 = declining balance/straight line.

Table A-3 (1990, continued)

| Item | Germany | | | Italy | | | Japan | | |
|---|---|---|---|---|---|---|---|---|---|
| | Manu-facturing | Other industry | Com-merce | Manu-facturing | Other industry | Com-merce | Manu-facturing | Other industry | Com-merce |
| Depreciation rate | | | | | | | | | |
| Machinery | 0.182 | 0.238 | 0.260 | 0.1260 | 0.1260 | 0.1260 | 0.0660 | 0.0900 | 0.0910 |
| Buildings | 0.037 | 0.030 | 0.022 | 0.0650 | 0.0650 | 0.0570 | 0.0222 | 0.0248 | 0.0248 |
| Inventories | 0.0 | 0.0 | 0.0 | 0.0 | 0.0 | 0.0 | 0.0 | 0.0 | 0.0 |
| Proportion with imme-diate depreciation | | | | | | | | | |
| Machinery | 0.0 | 0.0 | 0.0 | 0.0 | 0.0 | 0.0 | 0.0525 | 0.0408 | 0.0084 |
| Buildings | 0.0 | 0.0 | 0.0 | 0.0 | 0.0 | 0.0 | 0.0 | 0.0 | 0.0 |
| Inventories | 0.0 | 0.0 | 0.0 | 0.0 | 0.0 | 0.0 | 0.0 | 0.0 | 0.0 |
| Proportion with later depreciation | | | | | | | | | |
| Machinery | 1.0 | 1.0 | 1.0 | 1.0 | 1.0 | 1.0 | 0.9475 | 0.9592 | 0.9916 |
| Buildings | 1.0 | 1.0 | 1.0 | 1.0 | 1.0 | 1.0 | 1.0 | 1.0 | 1.0 |
| Inventories | 0.0 | 0.0 | 0.0 | 0.0 | 0.0 | 0.0 | 0.0 | 0.0 | 0.0 |
| Lifetimes | | | | | | | | | |
| Machinery | 6.0 | 6.0 | 6.0 | 6.5 | 6.5 | 8.3 | 9.53 | 11.29 | 6.62 |
| Buildings | 25.0 | 25.0 | 25.0 | 25.0 | 15.0 | 33.0 | 32.60 | 37.16 | 33.44 |
| Inventories | 0.0 | 0.0 | 0.0 | 0.0 | 0.0 | 0.0 | 0.0 | 0.0 | 0.0 |

| Type of depreciation[a] | | | | | | | | |
|---|---|---|---|---|---|---|---|---|
| Machinery | 2 | 2 | 2 | b | b | b | 0 | 0 | 0 |
| Buildings | 1 | 1 | 1 | b | b | b | 0 | 0 | 0 |
| Inventories | ... | ... | ... | b | b | b | 0 | 0 | 0 |
| Exponential tax depreciation rate | | | | | | | | |
| Machinery | 0.3 | 0.3 | 0.3 | 0.1260 | 0.1260 | 0.0126 | 0.2146 | 0.1845 | 0.2938 |
| Buildings | 0.04 | 0.04 | 0.04 | 0.0650 | 0.0650 | 0.0570 | 0.0682 | 0.0601 | 0.0665 |
| Inventories | 0.0 | 0.0 | 0.0 | 0.0 | 0.0 | 0.0 | 0.0 | 0.0 | 0.0 |
| Proportion with investment grant | | | | | | | | |
| Machinery | 0.0 | 0.0 | 0.0 | 0.0 | 0.0 | 0.0 | 0.0307 | 0.0087 | 0.0048 |
| Buildings | 0.0 | 0.0 | 0.0 | 0.0 | 0.0 | 0.0 | 0.0307 | 0.0087 | 0.0048 |
| Inventories | 0.0 | 0.0 | 0.0 | 0.0 | 0.0 | 0.0 | 0.0307 | 0.0087 | 0.0048 |
| Rate of investment grant | | | | | | | | |
| Machinery | 0.0 | 0.0 | 0.0 | 0.0 | 0.0 | 0.0 | 0.0 | 0.0 | 0.0 |
| Buildings | 0.0 | 0.0 | 0.0 | 0.0 | 0.0 | 0.0 | 0.0 | 0.0 | 0.0 |
| Inventories | 0.0 | 0.0 | 0.0 | 0.0 | 0.0 | 0.0 | 0.0 | 0.0 | 0.0 |

a. 0 = exponential; 1 = straight line; 2 = declining balance/straight line.
b. See text of chapter 6.

## Table A-3 (1990, concluded)

| Item | Sweden | | | United Kingdom | | | United States | | |
|---|---|---|---|---|---|---|---|---|---|
| | Manufacturing | Other industry | Commerce | Manufacturing | Other industry | Commerce | Manufacturing | Other industry | Commerce |
| **Depreciation rate** | | | | | | | | | |
| Machinery | 0.077 | 0.197 | 0.182 | 0.0819 | 0.1535 | 0.0831 | 0.1331 | 0.1302 | 0.1710 |
| Buildings | 0.026 | 0.023 | 0.018 | 0.0250 | 0.0250 | 0.0250 | 0.0343 | 0.0304 | 0.0247 |
| Inventories | 0.0 | 0.0 | 0.0 | 0.0 | 0.0 | 0.0 | 0.0 | 0.0 | 0.0 |
| **Proportion with immediate depreciation** | | | | | | | | | |
| Machinery | 0.3 | 0.3 | 0.3 | 0.250 | 0.250 | 0.250 | 0.0 | 0.0 | 0.0 |
| Buildings | 0.0 | 0.0 | 0.0 | 0.040 | 0.040 | 0.002 | 0.0 | 0.0 | 0.0 |
| Inventories | 0.0 | 0.0 | 0.0 | 0.0 | 0.0 | 0.0 | 0.0 | 0.0 | 0.0 |
| **Proportion with later depreciation** | | | | | | | | | |
| Machinery | 0.7 | 0.7 | 0.7 | 0.750 | 0.750 | 0.750 | 1.0 | 1.0 | 1.0 |
| Buildings | 1.0 | 1.0 | 1.0 | 0.960 | 0.960 | 0.048 | 1.0 | 1.0 | 1.0 |
| Inventories | 0.0 | 0.0 | 0.0 | 0.0 | 0.0 | 0.0 | 1.0 | 1.0 | 1.0 |
| **Lifetimes** | | | | | | | | | |
| Machinery | ... | ... | ... | 0.0 | 0.0 | 0.0 | a | a | a |
| Buildings | 28.0 | 33.0 | 36.0 | 25.0 | 25.0 | 25.0 | a | a | a |
| Inventories | ... | ... | ... | 0.0 | 0.0 | 0.0 | a | a | a |

| | | | | | | | | | |
|---|---|---|---|---|---|---|---|---|---|
| **Type of depreciation**[b] | | | | | | | | | |
| Machinery | 0 | 0 | 0 | 0 | 0 | 0 | 0 | 0 | 0 |
| Buildings | 1 | 1 | 1 | 1 | 1 | 1 | 0 | 0 | 0 |
| Inventories | ... | ... | ... | ... | ... | ... | 0 | 0 | 0 |
| **Exponential tax depreciation rate** | | | | | | | | | |
| Machinery | 0.3 | 0.3 | 0.3 | 0.25 | 0.25 | 0.25 | ... | ... | ... |
| Buildings | 0.0 | 0.0 | 0.0 | ... | ... | ... | ... | ... | ... |
| Inventories | 0.0 | 0.0 | 0.0 | ... | ... | ... | ... | ... | ... |
| **Proportion with investment grant** | | | | | | | | | |
| Machinery | 1.0 | 1.0 | 1.0 | ... | ... | ... | 1.0 | 1.0 | 1.0 |
| Buildings | 1.0 | 1.0 | 1.0 | ... | ... | ... | 1.0 | 1.0 | 1.0 |
| Inventories | 1.0 | 1.0 | 1.0 | ... | ... | ... | 1.0 | 1.0 | 1.0 |
| **Rate of investment grant** | | | | | | | | | |
| Machinery | 0.0 | 0.0 | 0.0 | 0.0 | 0.0 | 0.0 | 0.0959 | 0.0902 | 0.0857 |
| Buildings | 0.0 | 0.0 | 0.0 | 0.0 | 0.0 | 0.0 | 0.0 | 0.0978 | 0.0 |
| Inventories | 0.0 | 0.0 | 0.0 | 0.0 | 0.0 | 0.0 | 0.0 | 0.0 | 0.0 |

a. See table 10-7. Data available only on disaggregated basis.
b. 0 = exponential; 1 = straight line.

Table A-4.  Part One: Weights, Nine Countries, 1980

| | Australia | | | Canada | | | France | | |
|---|---|---|---|---|---|---|---|---|---|
| Item | Manu-facturing | Other industry | Com-merce | Manu-facturing | Other industry | Com-merce | Manu-facturing | Other industry | Com-merce |
| *Proportion of* | | | | | | | | | |
| *capital stock* | | | | | | | | | |
| Machinery | 0.241 | 0.054 | 0.115 | 0.2289 | 0.1118 | 0.0966 | 0.2036 | 0.0984 | 0.0755 |
| Buildings | 0.137 | 0.019 | 0.126 | 0.1272 | 0.1564 | 0.0704 | 0.0982 | 0.0861 | 0.0756 |
| Inventories | 0.168 | 0.004 | 0.137 | 0.0970 | 0.0060 | 0.1047 | 0.1577 | 0.1815 | 0.0234 |
| *Proportion by source* | | | | | | | | | |
| *of finance* | | | | | | | | | |
| Debt | 0.192 | 0.199 | 0.193 | 0.3473 | 0.3740 | 0.5091 | 0.440 | 0.440 | 0.438 |
| New share issues | 0.282 | 0.280 | 0.282 | 0.0877 | 0.0811 | 0.0660 | 0.040 | 0.0 | 0.062 |
| Retained earnings | 0.526 | 0.521 | 0.522 | 0.5650 | 0.5419 | 0.4249 | 0.520 | 0.560 | 0.500 |
| *Ownership shares* | | | | | | | | | |
| Debt | | | | | | | | | |
| Households | 0.848 | 0.848 | 0.848 | 0.728 | 0.728 | 0.728 | 0.9630 | 0.963 | 0.963 |
| Tax-exempt institutions | 0.123 | 0.123 | 0.123 | 0.212 | 0.212 | 0.212 | 0.022 | 0.022 | 0.022 |
| Insurance companies | 0.029 | 0.029 | 0.029 | 0.060 | 0.060 | 0.060 | 0.015 | 0.015 | 0.015 |
| New shares | | | | | | | | | |
| Households | 0.599 | 0.599 | 0.599 | 0.838 | 0.838 | 0.838 | 0.7966 | 0.7966 | 0.7966 |
| Tax-exempt institutions | 0.274 | 0.274 | 0.274 | 0.148 | 0.148 | 0.148 | 0.0589 | 0.0589 | 0.0589 |
| Insurance companies | 0.127 | 0.127 | 0.127 | 0.014 | 0.014 | 0.014 | 0.1445 | 0.1445 | 0.1445 |
| Retained earnings | | | | | | | | | |
| Households | 0.599 | 0.599 | 0.599 | 0.838 | 0.838 | 0.838 | 0.7966 | 0.7966 | 0.7966 |
| Tax-exempt institutions | 0.274 | 0.274 | 0.274 | 0.148 | 0.148 | 0.148 | 0.0589 | 0.0589 | 0.0589 |
| Insurance companies | 0.127 | 0.127 | 0.127 | 0.014 | 0.014 | 0.014 | 0.1445 | 0.1445 | 0.1445 |

Table A-4  (1980, continued)

| | Germany | | | Italy | | | Japan | | |
|---|---|---|---|---|---|---|---|---|---|
| Item | Manu-facturing | Other industry | Com-merce | Manu-facturing | Other industry | Com-merce | Manu-facturing | Other industry | Com-merce |
| *Proportion of capital stock* | | | | | | | | | |
| Machinery | 0.2894 | 0.0244 | 0.0359 | 0.2055 | 0.0177 | 0.1649 | 0.2345 | 0.1188 | 0.0376 |
| Buildings | 0.2594 | 0.0256 | 0.0976 | 0.1571 | 0.0059 | 0.1748 | 0.1544 | 0.0789 | 0.0518 |
| Inventories | 0.2130 | 0.0048 | 0.0499 | 0.1806 | 0.0278 | 0.0658 | 0.1185 | 0.0751 | 0.1304 |
| *Proportion by source of finance* | | | | | | | | | |
| Debt | 0.504 | 0.420 | 0.546 | 0.4188 | 0.4188 | 0.4188 | 0.3983 | 0.5983 | 0.4368 |
| New share issues | 0.076 | 0.076 | 0.076 | 0.0010 | 0.0010 | 0.0010 | 0.0492 | 0.0329 | 0.0461 |
| Retained earnings | 0.420 | 0.504 | 0.378 | 0.5802 | 0.5802 | 0.5802 | 0.5525 | 0.3688 | 0.5171 |
| *Ownership shares* | | | | | | | | | |
| Debt | | | | | | | | | |
| Households | 0.73 | 0.73 | 0.73 | 0.9827 | 0.9827 | 0.9827 | 0.8586 | 0.8586 | 0.8586 |
| Tax-exempt institutions | 0.20 | 0.20 | 0.20 | 0.0 | 0.0 | 0.0 | 0.0196 | 0.0196 | 0.0196 |
| Insurance companies | 0.07 | 0.07 | 0.07 | 0.0173 | 0.0173 | 0.0173 | 0.1216 | 0.1216 | 0.1216 |
| New shares | | | | | | | | | |
| Households | 0.758 | 0.617 | 0.751 | 1.0 | 1.0 | 1.0 | 0.7615 | 0.7615 | 0.7615 |
| Tax-exempt institutions | 0.186 | 0.298 | 0.085 | 0.0 | 0.0 | 0.0 | 0.0333 | 0.0333 | 0.0333 |
| Insurance companies | 0.056 | 0.085 | 0.060 | 0.0 | 0.0 | 0.0 | 0.2051 | 0.2051 | 0.2051 |
| Retained earnings | | | | | | | | | |
| Households | 0.0 | 0.0 | 0.0 | 1.0 | 1.0 | 1.0 | 0.7615 | 0.7615 | 0.7615 |
| Tax-exempt institutions | 0.0 | 0.0 | 0.0 | 0.0 | 0.0 | 0.0 | 0.0333 | 0.0333 | 0.0333 |
| Insurance companies | 0.0 | 0.0 | 0.0 | 0.0 | 0.0 | 0.0 | 0.2051 | 0.2051 | 0.2051 |

## Table A-4  (1980, concluded)

| Item | Sweden Manu-facturing | Sweden Other industry | Sweden Com-merce | United Kingdom Manu-facturing | United Kingdom Other industry | United Kingdom Com-merce | United States Manu-facturing | United States Other industry | United States Com-merce |
|---|---|---|---|---|---|---|---|---|---|
| *Proportion of capital stock* | | | | | | | | | |
| Machinery | 0.2635 | 0.0253 | 0.0345 | 0.298 | 0.090 | 0.080 | 0.0867 | 0.0965 | 0.0415 |
| Buildings | 0.2127 | 0.0662 | 0.062 | 0.171 | 0.022 | 0.139 | 0.2167 | 0.1970 | 0.1248 |
| Inventories | 0.1496 | 0.0957 | 0.0905 | 0.135 | 0.005 | 0.060 | 0.1350 | 0.0176 | 0.0842 |
| *Proportion by source of finance* | | | | | | | | | |
| Debt | 0.405 | 0.812 | 0.625 | 0.193 | 0.193 | 0.193 | 0.1981 | 0.4847 | 0.3995 |
| New share issues | 0.024 | 0.009 | 0.018 | 0.044 | 0.044 | 0.044 | 0.0592 | 0.0381 | 0.0443 |
| Retained earnings | 0.571 | 0.179 | 0.357 | 0.763 | 0.763 | 0.763 | 0.7427 | 0.4772 | 0.5562 |
| *Ownership shares* | | | | | | | | | |
| Debt | | | | | | | | | |
| Households | 0.252 | 0.750 | 0.482 | 0.718 | 0.718 | 0.718 | 0.6094 | 0.6094 | 0.6094 |
| Tax-exempt institutions | 0.672 | 0.199 | 0.476 | 0.137 | 0.137 | 0.137 | 0.2371 | 0.2371 | 0.2371 |
| Insurance companies | 0.076 | 0.051 | 0.042 | 0.145 | 0.145 | 0.145 | 0.1534 | 0.1534 | 0.1534 |
| New shares | | | | | | | | | |
| Households | 0.604 | 0.604 | 0.604 | 0.435 | 0.435 | 0.435 | 0.7433 | 0.7433 | 0.7433 |
| Tax-exempt institutions | 0.302 | 0.302 | 0.302 | 0.407 | 0.407 | 0.407 | 0.2154 | 0.2154 | 0.2154 |
| Insurance companies | 0.094 | 0.094 | 0.094 | 0.157 | 0.157 | 0.157 | 0.0412 | 0.0412 | 0.0412 |
| Retained earnings | | | | | | | | | |
| Households | 0.604 | 0.604 | 0.604 | 0.435 | 0.435 | 0.435 | 0.7433 | 0.7433 | 0.7433 |
| Tax-exempt institutions | 0.302 | 0.302 | 0.302 | 0.407 | 0.407 | 0.407 | 0.2154 | 0.2154 | 0.2154 |
| Insurance companies | 0.094 | 0.094 | 0.094 | 0.157 | 0.157 | 0.157 | 0.0412 | 0.0412 | 0.0412 |

Table A-4. Part Two: Weights, Nine Countries, 1985

| Item | Australia | | | Canada | | | France | | |
|---|---|---|---|---|---|---|---|---|---|
| | Manu-facturing | Other industry | Com-merce | Manu-facturing | Other industry | Com-merce | Manu-facturing | Other industry | Com-merce |
| *Proportion of capital stock* | | | | | | | | | |
| Machinery | 0.253 | 0.059 | 0.135 | 0.2289 | 0.1118 | 0.0966 | 0.2036 | 0.0984 | 0.0755 |
| Buildings | 0.129 | 0.022 | 0.135 | 0.1272 | 0.1564 | 0.0704 | 0.0982 | 0.0861 | 0.0756 |
| Inventories | 0.132 | 0.003 | 0.133 | 0.0970 | 0.0060 | 0.1042 | 0.1577 | 0.1815 | 0.0234 |
| *Proportion by source of finance* | | | | | | | | | |
| Debt | 0.247 | 0.309 | 0.294 | 0.3473 | 0.3740 | 0.5091 | 0.440 | 0.440 | 0.438 |
| New share issues | 0.217 | 0.199 | 0.203 | 0.0877 | 0.0811 | 0.0660 | 0.040 | 0.0 | 0.062 |
| Retained earnings | 0.536 | 0.492 | 0.503 | 0.5650 | 0.5419 | 0.4249 | 0.520 | 0.560 | 0.500 |
| *Ownership shares* | | | | | | | | | |
| Debt | | | | | | | | | |
| Households | 0.860 | 0.860 | 0.860 | 0.728 | 0.728 | 0.728 | 0.963 | 0.963 | 0.963 |
| Tax-exempt institutions | 0.115 | 0.115 | 0.115 | 0.212 | 0.212 | 0.212 | 0.022 | 0.022 | 0.022 |
| Insurance companies | 0.025 | 0.025 | 0.025 | 0.060 | 0.060 | 0.060 | 0.015 | 0.015 | 0.015 |
| New shares | | | | | | | | | |
| Households | 0.462 | 0.462 | 0.462 | 0.838 | 0.838 | 0.838 | 0.7958 | 0.7958 | 0.7958 |
| Tax-exempt institutions | 0.383 | 0.383 | 0.383 | 0.148 | 0.148 | 0.148 | 0.0995 | 0.0995 | 0.0995 |
| Insurance companies | 0.155 | 0.155 | 0.155 | 0.014 | 0.014 | 0.014 | 0.1049 | 0.1049 | 0.1049 |
| Retained earnings | | | | | | | | | |
| Households | 0.462 | 0.462 | 0.462 | 0.838 | 0.838 | 0.838 | 0.7958 | 0.7958 | 0.7958 |
| Tax-exempt institutions | 0.383 | 0.383 | 0.383 | 0.148 | 0.148 | 0.148 | 0.0995 | 0.0995 | 0.0995 |
| Insurance companies | 0.155 | 0.155 | 0.155 | 0.014 | 0.014 | 0.014 | 0.1049 | 0.1049 | 0.1049 |

Table A-4  (1985, continued)

| Item | Germany | | | Italy | | | Japan | | |
|---|---|---|---|---|---|---|---|---|---|
| | Manu-facturing | Other industry | Com-merce | Manu-facturing | Other industry | Com-merce | Manu-facturing | Other industry | Com-merce |
| *Proportion of capital stock* | | | | | | | | | |
| Machinery | 0.2894 | 0.0244 | 0.0359 | 0.2055 | 0.0177 | 0.1649 | 0.2861 | 0.0738 | 0.0791 |
| Buildings | 0.2594 | 0.0256 | 0.0976 | 0.1571 | 0.0059 | 0.1748 | 0.1884 | 0.0490 | 0.1090 |
| Inventories | 0.2130 | 0.0048 | 0.0499 | 0.1806 | 0.0278 | 0.0658 | 0.1004 | 0.0436 | 0.0705 |
| *Proportion by source of finance* | | | | | | | | | |
| Debt | 0.504 | 0.420 | 0.546 | 0.3607 | 0.3607 | 0.3607 | 0.4389 | 0.5275 | 0.4864 |
| New share issues | 0.076 | 0.076 | 0.076 | 0.0010 | 0.0010 | 0.0010 | 0.0293 | 0.0246 | 0.0268 |
| Retained earnings | 0.420 | 0.504 | 0.378 | 0.6383 | 0.6383 | 0.6383 | 0.5318 | 0.4429 | 0.4868 |
| *Ownership shares* | | | | | | | | | |
| Debt | | | | | | | | | |
| Households | 0.73 | 0.73 | 0.73 | 0.9480 | 0.9480 | 0.9480 | 0.8781 | 0.8781 | 0.8781 |
| Tax-exempt institutions | 0.20 | 0.20 | 0.20 | 0.0143 | 0.0143 | 0.0143 | 0.0323 | 0.0323 | 0.0323 |
| Insurance Companies | 0.07 | 0.07 | 0.07 | 0.0369 | 0.0369 | 0.0369 | 0.0896 | 0.0896 | 0.0896 |
| New shares | | | | | | | | | |
| Households | 0.758 | 0.617 | 0.751 | 0.8469 | 0.8469 | 0.8469 | 0.8182 | 0.8182 | 0.8182 |
| Tax-exempt institutions | 0.186 | 0.298 | 0.085 | 0.0615 | 0.0615 | 0.0615 | 0.0457 | 0.0457 | 0.0457 |
| Insurance companies | 0.056 | 0.085 | 0.060 | 0.0916 | 0.0916 | 0.0916 | 0.2360 | 0.2360 | 0.2360 |
| Retained earnings | | | | | | | | | |
| Households | 0.0 | 0.0 | 0.0 | 0.8469 | 0.8469 | 0.8469 | 0.7182 | 0.7182 | 0.7182 |
| Tax-exempt institutions | 0.0 | 0.0 | 0.0 | 0.0615 | 0.0615 | 0.0615 | 0.0457 | 0.0457 | 0.0457 |
| Insurance companies | 0.0 | 0.0 | 0.0 | 0.0916 | 0.0916 | 0.0916 | 0.2360 | 0.2360 | 0.2360 |

Table A-4 (1985, concluded)

| | Sweden | | | United Kingdom | | | United States | | |
|---|---|---|---|---|---|---|---|---|---|
| Item | Manu-facturing | Other industry | Com-merce | Manu-facturing | Other industry | Com-merce | Manu-facturing | Other industry | Com-merce |
| *Proportion of capital stock* | | | | | | | | | |
| Machinery | 0.2635 | 0.0253 | 0.0345 | 0.298 | 0.090 | 0.080 | 0.0867 | 0.0965 | 0.0415 |
| Buildings | 0.2127 | 0.0662 | 0.0620 | 0.171 | 0.022 | 0.139 | 0.2167 | 0.1970 | 0.1248 |
| Inventories | 0.1496 | 0.0957 | 0.0905 | 0.135 | 0.005 | 0.060 | 0.1350 | 0.0176 | 0.0842 |
| *Proportion by source of finance* | | | | | | | | | |
| Debt | 0.405 | 0.812 | 0.625 | 0.193 | 0.193 | 0.193 | 0.1981 | 0.4847 | 0.3995 |
| New share issues | 0.024 | 0.009 | 0.018 | 0.044 | 0.044 | 0.044 | 0.0592 | 0.0381 | 0.0443 |
| Retained earnings | 0.571 | 0.129 | 0.357 | 0.763 | 0.763 | 0.763 | 0.7427 | 0.4772 | 0.5562 |
| *Ownership shares* | | | | | | | | | |
| Debt | | | | | | | | | |
| Households | 0.252 | 0.750 | 0.482 | 0.718 | 0.718 | 0.718 | 0.6094 | 0.6094 | 0.6094 |
| Tax-exempt institutions | 0.672 | 0.199 | 0.476 | 0.137 | 0.137 | 0.137 | 0.2371 | 0.2371 | 0.2371 |
| Insurance companies | 0.076 | 0.051 | 0.042 | 0.145 | 0.145 | 0.145 | 0.1534 | 0.1534 | 0.1534 |
| New shares | | | | | | | | | |
| Households | 0.604 | 0.604 | 0.604 | 0.435 | 0.435 | 0.435 | 0.7433 | 0.7433 | 0.7433 |
| Tax-exempt institutions | 0.302 | 0.302 | 0.302 | 0.407 | 0.407 | 0.407 | 0.2154 | 0.2154 | 0.2154 |
| Insurance companies | 0.094 | 0.094 | 0.094 | 0.157 | 0.157 | 0.157 | 0.0412 | 0.0412 | 0.0412 |
| Retained earnings | | | | | | | | | |
| Households | 0.604 | 0.604 | 0.604 | 0.435 | 0.435 | 0.435 | 0.7433 | 0.7433 | 0.7433 |
| Tax-exempt institutions | 0.302 | 0.302 | 0.302 | 0.407 | 0.407 | 0.407 | 0.2154 | 0.2154 | 0.2154 |
| Insurance companies | 0.094 | 0.094 | 0.094 | 0.157 | 0.157 | 0.157 | 0.0412 | 0.0412 | 0.0412 |

Table A-4. *Part Three: Weights, Nine Countries, 1990*

| Item | Australia | | | Canada | | | France | | |
|---|---|---|---|---|---|---|---|---|---|
| | Manu-facturing | Other industry | Com-merce | Manu-facturing | Other industry | Com-merce | Manu-facturing | Other industry | Com-merce |
| *Proportion of capital stock* | | | | | | | | | |
| Machinery | 0.243 | 0.070 | 0.137 | 0.2289 | 0.1118 | 0.0966 | 0.2036 | 0.0984 | 0.0755 |
| Buildings | 0.122 | 0.028 | 0.142 | 0.1272 | 0.1564 | 0.0704 | 0.0982 | 0.0861 | 0.0756 |
| Inventories | 0.125 | 0.004 | 0.130 | 0.0970 | 0.0060 | 0.1047 | 0.1577 | 0.1815 | 0.2340 |
| *Proportion by source of finance* | | | | | | | | | |
| Debt | 0.324 | 0.328 | 0.358 | 0.3473 | 0.3740 | 0.5091 | 0.440 | 0.440 | 0.438 |
| New share issues | 0.195 | 0.194 | 0.185 | 0.0877 | 0.0811 | 0.0660 | 0.040 | 0.0 | 0.062 |
| Retained earnings | 0.481 | 0.478 | 0.547 | 0.5650 | 0.5419 | 0.4249 | 0.520 | 0.560 | 0.500 |
| *Ownership shares* | | | | | | | | | |
| Debt | | | | | | | | | |
| Households | 0.857 | 0.857 | 0.857 | 0.728 | 0.728 | 0.728 | 0.963 | 0.963 | 0.963 |
| Tax-exempt institutions | 0.113 | 0.113 | 0.113 | 0.212 | 0.212 | 0.212 | 0.022 | 0.022 | 0.022 |
| Insurance companies | 0.030 | 0.030 | 0.030 | 0.060 | 0.060 | 0.060 | 0.015 | 0.015 | 0.015 |
| New shares | | | | | | | | | |
| Households | 0.313 | 0.313 | 0.313 | 0.838 | 0.838 | 0.838 | 0.8254 | 0.8254 | 0.8254 |
| Tax-exempt institutions | 0.460 | 0.460 | 0.460 | 0.148 | 0.148 | 0.148 | 0.0857 | 0.0857 | 0.0857 |
| Insurance companies | 0.227 | 0.227 | 0.227 | 0.014 | 0.014 | 0.014 | 0.0889 | 0.0889 | 0.0889 |
| Retained earnings | | | | | | | | | |
| Households | 0.313 | 0.313 | 0.313 | 0.838 | 0.838 | 0.838 | 0.8254 | 0.8254 | 0.8254 |
| Tax-exempt institutions | 0.460 | 0.460 | 0.460 | 0.148 | 0.148 | 0.148 | 0.0857 | 0.0857 | 0.0857 |
| Insurance companies | 0.227 | 0.227 | 0.227 | 0.014 | 0.014 | 0.014 | 0.0889 | 0.0889 | 0.0889 |

Table A-4  (1990, continued)

| Item | Germany Manu-facturing | Germany Other industry | Germany Com-merce | Italy Manu-facturing | Italy Other industry | Italy Com-merce | Japan Manu-facturing | Japan Other industry | Japan Com-merce |
|---|---|---|---|---|---|---|---|---|---|
| *Proportion of capital stock* | | | | | | | | | |
| Machinery | 0.2894 | 0.0244 | 0.0359 | 0.2055 | 0.0177 | 0.1649 | 0.2861 | 0.0738 | 0.0791 |
| Buildings | 0.2594 | 0.0256 | 0.0976 | 0.1571 | 0.0059 | 0.1748 | 0.1884 | 0.0490 | 0.1090 |
| Inventories | 0.2130 | 0.0048 | 0.0499 | 0.1806 | 0.0278 | 0.0658 | 0.1004 | 0.0436 | 0.0705 |
| *Proportion by source of finance* | | | | | | | | | |
| Debt | 0.504 | 0.420 | 0.546 | 0.3607 | 0.3607 | 0.3607 | 0.4389 | 0.5275 | 0.4864 |
| New share issues | 0.076 | 0.076 | 0.076 | 0.0010 | 0.0010 | 0.0010 | 0.0293 | 0.0246 | 0.0268 |
| Retained earnings | 0.420 | 0.504 | 0.378 | 0.6383 | 0.6383 | 0.6383 | 0.5318 | 0.4479 | 0.4868 |
| *Ownership shares* | | | | | | | | | |
| Debt | | | | | | | | | |
| Households | 0.73 | 0.73 | 0.73 | 0.8947 | 0.8947 | 0.8947 | 0.8781 | 0.8781 | 0.8781 |
| Tax-exempt institutions | 0.20 | 0.20 | 0.20 | 0.0273 | 0.0273 | 0.0273 | 0.0323 | 0.0323 | 0.0323 |
| Insurance companies | 0.07 | 0.07 | 0.07 | 0.0780 | 0.0780 | 0.0780 | 0.0896 | 0.0896 | 0.0896 |
| New shares | | | | | | | | | |
| Households | 0.758 | 0.617 | 0.751 | 0.8021 | 0.8021 | 0.8021 | 0.8182 | 0.8182 | 0.8182 |
| Tax-exempt institutions | 0.186 | 0.298 | 0.085 | 0.0982 | 0.0982 | 0.0982 | 0.0457 | 0.0457 | 0.0457 |
| Insurance companies | 0.056 | 0.085 | 0.060 | 0.0997 | 0.0997 | 0.0997 | 0.2360 | 0.2360 | 0.2360 |
| Retained earnings | | | | | | | | | |
| Households | 0.0 | 0.0 | 0.0 | 0.8021 | 0.8021 | 0.8021 | 0.7182 | 0.7182 | 0.7182 |
| Tax-exempt institutions | 0.0 | 0.0 | 0.0 | 0.0982 | 0.0982 | 0.0982 | 0.0457 | 0.0457 | 0.0457 |
| Insurance companies | 0.0 | 0.0 | 0.0 | 0.0997 | 0.0997 | 0.0997 | 0.2360 | 0.2360 | 0.2360 |

Table A-4  (1990, concluded)

| Item | Sweden | | | United Kingdom | | | United States | | |
|---|---|---|---|---|---|---|---|---|---|
| | Manu-facturing | Other industry | Com-merce | Manu-facturing | Other industry | Com-merce | Manu-facturing | Other industry | Com-merce |
| *Proportion of capital stock* | | | | | | | | | |
| Machinery | 0.2635 | 0.0253 | 0.0345 | 0.298 | 0.090 | 0.080 | 0.0867 | 0.0965 | 0.0415 |
| Buildings | 0.2127 | 0.0662 | 0.0620 | 0.171 | 0.022 | 0.139 | 0.2167 | 0.1970 | 0.1248 |
| Inventories | 0.1496 | 0.0957 | 0.0905 | 0.135 | 0.005 | 0.060 | 0.1350 | 0.0176 | 0.0842 |
| *Proportion by source of finance* | | | | | | | | | |
| Debt | 0.405 | 0.812 | 0.625 | 0.193 | 0.193 | 0.193 | 0.1981 | 0.4847 | 0.3995 |
| New share issues | 0.024 | 0.009 | 0.018 | 0.044 | 0.044 | 0.044 | 0.0592 | 0.0381 | 0.0443 |
| Retained earnings | 0.571 | 0.129 | 0.357 | 0.763 | 0.763 | 0.763 | 0.7427 | 0.4772 | 0.5562 |
| *Ownership shares* | | | | | | | | | |
| Debt | | | | | | | | | |
| Households | 0.252 | 0.750 | 0.482 | 0.718 | 0.718 | 0.718 | 0.6094 | 0.6094 | 0.6094 |
| Tax-exempt institutions | 0.672 | 0.199 | 0.476 | 0.137 | 0.137 | 0.137 | 0.2371 | 0.2371 | 0.2371 |
| Insurance companies | 0.076 | 0.051 | 0.042 | 0.145 | 0.145 | 0.145 | 0.1534 | 0.1534 | 0.1534 |
| New shares | | | | | | | | | |
| Households | 0.604 | 0.604 | 0.604 | 0.435 | 0.435 | 0.435 | 0.7433 | 0.7433 | 0.7433 |
| Tax-exempt institutions | 0.302 | 0.302 | 0.302 | 0.407 | 0.407 | 0.407 | 0.2154 | 0.2154 | 0.2154 |
| Insurance companies | 0.094 | 0.094 | 0.094 | 0.157 | 0.157 | 0.157 | 0.0412 | 0.0412 | 0.0412 |
| Retained earnings | | | | | | | | | |
| Households | 0.604 | 0.604 | 0.604 | 0.435 | 0.435 | 0.435 | 0.7433 | 0.7433 | 0.7433 |
| Tax-exempt institutions | 0.302 | 0.302 | 0.302 | 0.407 | 0.407 | 0.407 | 0.2154 | 0.2154 | 0.2154 |
| Insurance companies | 0.094 | 0.094 | 0.094 | 0.157 | 0.157 | 0.157 | 0.0412 | 0.0412 | 0.0412 |

# Index